SOCIAL MEDIA, FUNDAMENTAL RIGHTS AND COURTS

This volume examines European and national higher-court decisions on social media from the perspective of fundamental rights and judicial dialogue.

While the challenges social media poses for public policy and regulation have been widely discussed, the role of courts in this evolving legal area, especially from a fundamental-rights standpoint, has hitherto remained largely underexplored. This volume probes the contribution of national and European judiciaries to the protection of fundamental rights in a social media setting and delves into patterns of dialogue and interaction between domestic courts, the Court of Justice of the EU (CJEU) and the European Court of Human Rights (ECtHR), and between the CJEU and the ECtHR. The book specifically examines the extent and ways in which national and European judges incorporate fundamental rights reasoning in their social media rulings. It also investigates the nature and breadth of the use of European supranational case law in domestic judicial assessment and analyses the engagement of the CJEU and the ECtHR with the other's case law. In doing so, the book instils jurisprudential dynamics into the study of social media law and regulation, exploring in particular the effects of European constitutionalism on the shaping and enforcement of fundamental rights in a social media context.

Written by emerging and established experts in the field, this book will be essential reading for scholars of comparative, European and constitutional law, as well as those with a particular interest in digital technologies and social media.

Federica Casarosa is Research Affiliate at Sant'Anna School of Advanced Studies (SSSA), Italy and Professor at the Centre for Judicial Cooperation, European University Institute (EUI), Italy.

Evangelia Psychogiopoulou is Assistant Professor at the Department of Political Science and International Relations, University of Peloponnese and Senior Research Fellow at the Hellenic Foundation for European and Foreign Policy, Greece.

Routledge Research in Human Rights Law

Civilian Drones, Visual Privacy and EU Human Rights Law
Girish Agarwal

International Human Rights Law and Destitution
An Economic, Social and Cultural Rights Perspective
Luke D. Graham

The European Convention of Human Rights Regime
Reform of Immigration and Minority Policies from Afar
Dia Anagnostou

Decisional Privacy and the Rights of the Child
Georgina Dimopoulos

The Rohingya Crisis
Humanitarian and Legal Approaches
Edited by Manzoor Hasan, Syed Mansoob Murshed and Priya Pillai

Sports Investigations Law and the ECHR
Collection, Use and Exchange of Intelligence
Björn Hessert

The Right of the Child to Play
From Conception to Implementation
Naomi Lott

Social Media, Fundamental Rights and Courts
A European Perspective
Edited by Federica Casarosa and Evangelia Psychogiopoulou

For more information about this series, please visit: www.routledge.com/Routledge-Research-in-Human-Rights-Law/book-series/HUMRIGHTSLAW

Social Media, Fundamental Rights and Courts

A European Perspective

Edited by Federica Casarosa and Evangelia Psychogiopoulou

Routledge
Taylor & Francis Group
LONDON AND NEW YORK

First published 2023
by Routledge
4 Park Square, Milton Park, Abingdon, Oxon OX14 4RN

and by Routledge
605 Third Avenue, New York, NY 10158

Routledge is an imprint of the Taylor & Francis Group, an informa business

British Library Cataloguing-in-Publication Data
A catalogue record for this book is available from the British Library

ISBN: 978-1-032-07466-5 (hbk)
ISBN: 978-1-032-07469-6 (pbk)
ISBN: 978-1-003-20708-5 (ebk)

DOI: 10.4324/9781003207085

Typeset in Galliard
by Apex CoVantage, LLC

Federica Casarosa A mia madre.

Evangelia Psychogiopoulou Στη Σοφία και στον Αλέξανδρο με αγάπη.

Contents

Contributors

Constance Bonzé, Researcher in Private International Law, British Institute of International and Comparative Law

Federica Casarosa, Research Affiliate at the Sant'Anna School of Advanced Studies (SSSA), Italy; Professor at the Centre for Judicial Cooperation, European University Institute; Visiting Fellow, Masaryk University

Maria Concetta Causarano, Research Fellow, Interdepartmental Centre for Law and Technologies (DETECT), University of Pisa

Giovanni De Gregorio, PLMJ Chair in Law and Technology, Católica Global School of Law

Zsuzsa Detrekoi, Fellow, Centre for Media, Data and Society, Central European University

Elizabeth Farries, Co-Director and Assistant Professor, UCD Centre for Digital Policy, University College Dublin

Eveliina Ignatius, Doctoral Researcher, University of Helsinki

Meeli Kaur, Judge, Tallinn Court of Appeals

Tanja Kerševan, Assistant Professor of Journalism, University of Ljubljana

Matthias C. Kettemann, Professor of Innovation, Theory and Philosophy of Law; Head of the Department for Theory and Future of Law, University of Innsbruck

Polina Kulish, Researcher of International Law and PhD student, Friedrich Schiller University Jena

Marta Maroni, Postdoctoral Researcher, Legal Tech Lab and The Erik Castrén Institute, University of Helsinki

Sara Migliorini, Assistant Professor of Global Legal Studies, University of Macau

Joan Solanes Mullor, Tenure Track Professor of Constitutional Law, Universitat Pompeu Fabra

Tuomas Ojanen, Professor of Constitutional Law, University of Helsinki

Oreste Pollicino, Professor of Constitutional Law and Internet Law, Bocconi University

Evangelia Psychogiopoulou, Assistant Professor of EU Policies and Institutions, University of Peloponnese; Senior Research Fellow, Hellenic Foundation for European and Foreign Policy (ELIAMEP)

Martha Routen, Legal Researcher, Freiburg/Breisgau

Rachael Craufurd Smith, Reader in Media Law, Edinburgh Law School

Lorna Woods, Professor of Internet Law OBE, University of Essex

Acknowledgements

We wish to express our gratitude to the scholars and the legal practitioners who contributed to this volume. As a collective effort, this book is the result of smooth and exemplary collaboration with the authors who wrote the chapters in it. Their willingness to share their knowledge on the ongoing evolution of the social media jurisprudence at the national and European levels has made this book possible. Warm thanks go to all the contributors for their responsiveness and patience in addressing our suggestions during the book's preparation.

Federica Casarosa and Evangelia Psychogiopoulou

1 Social media before domestic and European courts

Fundamental rights and judicial dialogue

Evangelia Psychogiopoulou and Federica Casarosa

1. Introduction

Using social media sites and networks has become a prevalent online activity. In 2020, more than half (57 percent) of the people in the European Union (EU) reported participating in social networks (from 36 percent in 2011), with penetration levels reaching 87 percent for younger groups.[1] In 2021, 59 percent of EU enterprises used at least one type of social media, an increase of 22 percent compared to 2015.[2] The average user spends more than an hour a day on social media[3] and does so for a variety of reasons: to connect and communicate with others, to find and share information, to pass spare time, etc. Facebook remains the social network most used for news in Europe, and it is followed by YouTube.[4] Enterprises resort to social networks mostly to enhance their presence online, improve their marketing strategies, interact with partners and customers and create communities of interest around their products and services.[5]

Structural shifts towards a more digital and platform-dominated environment, also driven by the coronavirus pandemic, have intensified the impact of social media on online behaviour and life in general. A 2019 global online user survey revealed that, for a significant proportion of respondents, social media platforms facilitate access to information, ease of communication and freedom of expression.[6] The respondents also considered that social media platforms undermine privacy and intensify everyday distractions and polarisation in politics.[7] Clearly, social media come with both gains and problems. Regarding gains, social networks have expanded the possibilities for individuals to exercise free speech and to seek, receive and impart information. They have also proven useful tools for responding to human rights concerns, communicating injustice, advocating change and enhancing participation in political, social and cultural life. Surely, then, any interference with the right to free speech and the right to seek, receive and impart information through social networks should be carefully circumscribed. This is all the more so given that freedom of expression is also an "enabler" of other rights[8] such as civil, political, economic, social and cultural ones.[9]

DOI: 10.4324/9781003207085-1

The benefits social media platforms provide stem from key characteristics of the internet – in particular its speed and reach – and their own key characteristics – e.g. connectivity, interactivity, participation, etc. However, these same characteristics that enable individuals to disseminate information and share critical views instantaneously also bring important challenges: social media have facilitated the dissemination of illegal content, they have spread hate speech and disinformation, they have exposed children and other vulnerable groups to harmful content and they have created unprecedented risks for privacy and data protection.

The challenges and opportunities social media platforms bring have triggered reflection on regulatory standards in Europe – a daunting task, given the complexity surrounding their services, the quasi-public functions some of these platforms perform and fragmented responsibility between supranational bodies, state institutions, operators and users for respect for public values and the public interest in the digital environment.[10] Emerging platform regulation models relying on a mix of regulatory, self-regulatory and co-regulatory processes have shown promise in addressing underlying problems while preserving innovation, successful business models and the many perceived benefits social platforms generate. In such a context, considerable attention has been given to supranational institutions and the role of the state in platform governance, the policy objectives that should underpin regulatory action and the specific policy issues to attend to – an attempt, among other issues, to correct deficiencies in self-regulation, especially in terms of the transparency, accountability and oversight of platforms. Regulatory efforts have also sought to address anew the relationship between public bodies, private companies and citizens in order to guarantee a fundamental rights-compliant digital space and the operation and use of social networks in accordance with fundamental rights standards. At the EU level, for instance, implementing fundamental rights through rulemaking to cope with the challenges of digitalisation has been a central concern in the regulatory process, with emphasis on freedom of expression and information, privacy, data protection and the principle of non-discrimination. EU institutions have sought to ingrain fundamental rights in the development of EU law and policies on platform governance, devising rules that comply with and enhance the fundamental rights enshrined in the Treaties and the EU Charter of Fundamental Rights (CFR).[11] The fundamental rights implications of national attempts at platform regulation have also sparked debate,[12] whereas platform operators have been invited to re-evaluate their content standards and develop content moderation and transparency practices that comply with and ensure respect for fundamental rights.[13]

Against this background, less consideration has been given to the role of courts – national and European courts alike – in protecting and enforcing fundamental rights in this evolving legal area. In recent years, national courts in Europe, the Court of Justice of the EU (CJEU) and the European Court of Human Rights (ECtHR) have increasingly ruled on social media disputes. Significantly, they have done so while mostly operating in a non-social-media-specific legal context. As laws and regulations tend to lag behind technology and the way that technology companies operate, applicable laws have for the most part rarely targeted social media and their fundamental rights repercussions. Seen in this light, the aim of this book is to study the fundamental rights dimension of the social media jurisprudence of national courts in a selected set of EU Member States and the UK – given its recent departure from the EU – alongside the social media jurisprudence of the CJEU and the ECtHR. The book identifies and analyses relevant case law and investigates the incorporation of fundamental rights in judicial reasoning. It also explores the influence that CJEU and ECtHR decisions have reciprocally had and their influence on the reasoning of national courts as instances of judicial dialogue. Thus, while the book seeks to identify and capture the effects of fundamental rights analysis in judicial output, it also delves into the ways in which the CJEU and the ECtHR interact and examines how national courts make use of European case law to tackle the fundamental rights implications of social media.

The concept of "social media" employed in this study requires some clarification, as it has guided the identification of the court rulings reviewed. Concerning social media platforms, for instance, due to the "platformisation" of the internet,[14] it is not easy to draw clear boundaries among the different types of platforms operated by internet players that could be considered to be "social media". In fact, several companies providing online services related to matters as diverse as accommodation (AirBnB), transport (Uber), the sale of goods (eBay), etc., provide internal fora for communication and exchanges among users. However, these exchanges are rather ancillary activity closely associated with the provision of the platform's services; for example, for user support or evaluation purposes. In this book, "social media" is understood as meaning digital communication platforms[15] that focus their main business activity on the creation of online fora where users can express their thoughts, views and ideas via text, images, videos, etc. The underlying premise is that such platform operators offer services that display common characteristics; in particular, connective communication/participation and creative expression.

Social media platforms have fundamentally transformed our means of communication, bringing with them notions of self-expression that are firmly based on a sense of participation. As Natalie Fenton pertinently observed, "[a]s we post our photographs on Flickr, discuss the latest film on Facebook, alert people to a nugget of information on Twitter, we have a sense that we are participating in something that is going on out there; that rather than being told what to do or what to think through the linear provision of information, we can join in the telling through a pulsating network of digital social communication".[16] Participation in the communicative act can take place for several purposes (personal, public, social, political, cultural, economic, etc.) and it can coincide with information needs. However, connecting and relating with others appear to be the primary motivations for using social networks. Such connective communication goes hand in hand with creative expression and content generation.[17] Content on social networks is mainly published by users. Social networks publish limited content of their own and mostly mediate between content producer users and audience users.[18]

This book investigates the case law on social networks like Facebook, LinkedIn, Xing and others. Given that they share the same features of connective communication/participation and creative expression, it also explores court rulings involving blogs and micro-blogs like Twitter; content-sharing sites such as YouTube, Instagram, Flickr, etc.; wiki-based knowledge-sharing tools like Wikipedia; chat rooms; and messaging applications. Cases involving search engines are not included in the analysis, as they do not provide a means of communication. Cases concerned with legacy media that have shifted their activity to the online world and cases involving digital, native news media are similarly not covered. They are only discussed if the dispute adjudicated is connected to the publication of user-generated content or it informs on the legal qualification of social media (for instance, due to legal distinctions made by the deciding judge). Therefore, to give an example, the book's case sample contains cases on allegedly defamatory posts in the "readers' comments" section of an online newspaper with reference to published articles, but it does not include cases on allegedly defamatory news articles as such.

2. Regulating social media in Europe

Due to the rapid development characterising the evolution of information and communication technologies and the ongoing process of platformisation, the regulatory framework applicable to social media in Europe is still work in progress. Regulatory efforts span from less interventionist approaches covering the adoption of technology-neutral provisions that guarantee a level of flexibility over potential technological change to sector-specific interventions that address the role of social media regarding, for instance, misinformation or copyright protection. Crucially, the regulatory model is not uniform but largely depends on the type and degree of engagement of the private sector that the legislator aims at, ranging from hard law to co-regulation that requires the cooperation of social media.[19] Several regulatory mechanisms and processes must therefore be taken into account in order to frame a clear picture of the rules that govern the behaviour of social media, their operation and their use. This is primarily due to the broad array of actors that are involved in standard-setting on a wide range of topics, from illegal content and illegal activity online to personal data protection, the protection of minors, consumer protection and the ever-increasing role of algorithmic curation of content provision by recommender systems.[20]

EU institutions play a crucial role in the development of rules addressing different facets of social media conduct and use, with the significance of co-regulatory initiatives as a response to failings in self-regulation being increasingly acknowledged.[21] To start with, provisions that are relevant to social media were contained in EU legislation on electronic commerce (the e-Commerce Directive), the foundation of the EU's digital economy and its principal framework on issues of liability for hosting illegal content online.[22] The e-Commerce Directive, which dates back to 2000, at the time of its adoption opted for a market-strengthening strategy which excluded liability from the shoulders of digital intermediaries, including hosting providers, insofar as they do not actively take part in the process of information exchanging through their services so as to have knowledge or control over the information that is transmitted or stored.[23] However, other pieces of EU law gradually overlapped with these rules and took steps to impose obligations on social media or created liabilities. For instance, in the revised Audiovisual Media Services Directive,[24] social media may fall into the category of video-sharing platforms[25] if the provision of programmes and user-generated videos constitutes an "essential functionality" of these services.[26] Video-sharing platforms are obliged to adopt appropriate measures in order to protect minors from harmful content and all users from content containing incitement to violence or hatred and from content the dissemination of which constitutes an activity which is a criminal offence under Union law, along with obligations regarding audio-visual commercial communications.[27] According to Directive 2019/790 on copyright and related rights in the digital single market,[28] social media coming under the definition of so-called online content-sharing service providers (OCSSPs)[29] perform acts of communication to the public when they give access to copyright-protected works or other protected subject matter uploaded by their users and are therefore directly liable for copyright infringement by these uploads.[30] The directive's liability exemption mechanism then rests on a series of cumulative "best efforts" obligations to a) obtain authorisation; b) ensure the non-availability of specific, protected content for which relevant and necessary information has been provided by the rightholders; and c) put in place notice and "stay down" mechanisms, in addition to acting expeditiously to disable access to or remove protected content on receipt of a sufficiently substantiated notice.[31]

Other EU rules seek to respond to the challenge of illegal online content where it can be qualified as hate speech, incitement to terrorism or pornography. Relevant legislative acts include the Directive to combat the sexual abuse and sexual exploitation of children and child pornography,[32] the Terrorism Directive,[33] the Regulation on the dissemination of terrorist content online[34] and Council Framework Decision 2008/913/JHA on combating certain forms and expressions of racism and xenophobia by means of criminal law.[35] The latter deploys efforts to curb hate speech as illegal speech by means of a criminal law approach to racism and xenophobia. Among other issues, the framework decision requires the Member States to criminalise public "incit[ement] to violence or hatred directed against a group of persons or a member of such a group defined by reference to race, colour, religion, descent or national or ethnic origin"[36] and to punish acts of publicly condoning, denying or grossly trivialising certain crimes such as genocide.[37]

More recently, increasing concern over the effects of illegal and harmful content online[38] and the ability of platforms to gather user information and data and consequently retain significant power over individual choices[39] has triggered a more structured, interventionist approach culminating in the Digital Services Act (DSA),[40] the Digital Markets Act,[41] and the set of proposals for a Regulation on Artificial Intelligence[42] and a Media Freedom Act.[43] The DSA, in particular, aspires to modernise the legal framework provided in the e-Commerce Directive by following an all-encompassing approach vis-à-vis digital intermediaries and puts forward an updated definition of hosting providers covering and distinguishing between online platforms and very large ones. Although the liability exemption of the e-Commerce Directive persists, the DSA increases the number of obligations incumbent on operators. It also provides safeguards for users' rights, including the right to defence through internal complaint-handling mechanisms provided by online platforms and out-of-court dispute settlement procedures to contest decisions taken in response to allegedly illegal content or content that is incompatible with the online platform's terms and conditions. Acknowledging that digital hate speech can deter people from expressing their views and participating in online debates, the European Commission has also presented an initiative, based on Article 17(1) TEU,[44] for a Council decision extending the list of areas of crime in Article 83(1) TFEU[45] to hate speech, including online hate speech and hate crime.[46]

These recent initiatives may serve to remedy the fragmentation of the legal framework emerging from the increasing number of national laws that have sprung up across Europe. Legislators at the national level have also pondered social media regulation[47] – a process that has encountered significant difficulties, given the global nature of the internet, rapid technological change and constantly evolving practices of communication and access to news, content and information. Germany's Network Enforcement Act, which was passed in 2017, stands prominently among these national attempts at regulation.[48] It forces platforms to remove "manifestly unlawful content" within 24 hours and also requires complaint procedures for decisions targeting unlawful content to be set up. In France, the so-called *Loi Avia* requiring digital intermediaries to remove "manifestly illegal" content on notice with a strict deadline with the risk of incurring harsh fines was adopted but then partially overturned after the Constitutional Council affirmed a set of violations of the proportionality test.[49]

The Council of Europe (CoE) has also been active in standard-setting, particularly with a view to ensuring respect for human rights in the digital environment. The ensuing recommendations and declarations are of a non-binding nature, and some of them directly address social media.[50] The 2012 Recommendation of the CoE's Committee of Ministers (CoM) on the protection of human rights with regard to social networking services stresses the role of social networks as human rights enablers.[51] It also acknowledges that human rights can be threatened on social networks. It therefore recommends that party members in consultation with the private sector and civil society develop coherent strategies to protect and promote respect for human rights.[52] Similar calls are made in a 2018 CoM Recommendation on the roles and responsibilities of internet intermediaries.[53] This Recommendation concentrates on "a wide, diverse and rapidly evolving range of players", which "facilitate interactions on the internet" encompassing social networking sites.[54] It invites party members to take all necessary measures to ensure, among other things, that internet intermediaries fulfil their responsibilities to respect human rights.

Social networking platforms have also developed self-regulatory rules, usually in the form of codes of conduct or terms of service, on issues such as content removal policies and data processing practices.[55] For instance, they have voluntarily committed to content moderation with a focus on illegal content and content that breaches community standards, and they have also implemented changes to regularly publish transparency reports. To ensure "fair decision-making based on standards and values", Facebook's Oversight Board was established to "oversee important matters of expression" via "principled, independent decisions" and "policy advisory opinions on Facebook's content policies".[56] However, the burden of decision-making on what to take down and what to leave up has led social platforms to openly acquiesce with efforts at regulation – a move towards relinquishing some responsibility for moderation to legislators.[57]

3. Fundamental rights in social media case law

In the light of ongoing efforts by a plurality of actors to regulate digital intermediaries – including social media – and address the fundamental rights challenges that digitalisation brings through rulemaking, the contribution of European and national courts to the protection and enforcement of fundamental rights in the social media setting has not been sufficiently studied. In the past few years, European courts have been increasingly confronted with social media disputes with important fundamental rights implications, particularly on the right to freedom of expression and its corollary – the right to information, the right to respect for private and family life, the right to protection of personal data and the right to intellectual property, among others. Whereas the ECtHR is a specialised human rights court ruling on individual and state applications alleging violation of the rights set out in the European Convention on Human Rights (ECHR), the constitutional value of the CFR has had a marked bearing on the EU judiciary, whose role as guardians of fundamental rights through reliance on the CFR was bolstered.[58] The social media jurisprudence of the two European courts has gradually blossomed, touching on a range of fields affected by digital innovation from intellectual property, personal data protection and the responsibilities of digital intermediaries to hate speech, offensive content and anonymity online. National courts in Europe have similarly ruled on disputes concerning social media, but the relevant case law has been under-researched from a comparative perspective and in conjunction with the burgeoning European jurisprudence. This book seeks to fill this gap and examines whether fundamental rights are interpreted by European and domestic courts in social media cases, and if so, how. The book embraces two main themes in particular. First, it identifies main issues and trends in judicial reasoning on fundamental rights in national social media jurisprudence and the jurisprudence of the CJEU and the ECtHR; and second, it studies the nature and extent of judicial dialogue between national and European courts, and between the CJEU and the ECtHR in social media cases.

Therefore, on the one hand, the book sheds light on the fundamental rights dimension of national and European social media case law. Considering the importance of social media for the exercise of the right to freedom of expression and the right to seek, receive and impart information but also the challenges social media bring to the enjoyment of fundamental rights, the analysis explores the contribution by national and European judiciaries to the protection of freedom of expression and information, and the limits posed and balancing performed whenever the protection of other rights and interests is at stake. The book examines more specifically the incorporation of fundamental rights reasoning in social media case law and its input to adjudication. The analysis provides useful elements and criteria for verifying whether, and if so how, judges delve into the fundamental rights repercussions of social media. The book aspires to grasp variation in the fundamental rights considerations that impact judicial decision-making and also attests to the complexity that sometimes characterises fundamental rights standards. This may be due to the fact that different sources offer protection of fundamental rights. Consideration is therefore given, among other things, to the influence of the CFR and the ECHR on national social media case law. Complexity may also stem from the need to reconcile competing rights to resolve the dispute at hand and the fact that distinct rights are often approached interchangeably without the judiciary clearly defining their nature and scope. This is particularly true of freedom of expression, freedom of opinion and freedom to receive and impart information but also privacy and the right to protection of personal data in some instances. Other elements of complexity revolve around questions concerning the horizontal application of fundamental rights to private parties. Fundamental rights have a vertical application and are therefore enforceable against the state. From an EU perspective, individuals can invoke the application of the CFR against EU institutions, other EU bodies and Member State authorities when they implement EU law.[59] However, there have been cases in which courts, including the CJEU,[60] have recognised the application of fundamental rights in horizontal relationships. Growing private power may have a role to play in this regard[61] but the conditions under which private bodies, including powerful social platforms, are bound by fundamental rights duties and the breadth of such duties remain unclear.

Concerning judicial dialogue, on the other hand, the book explores the interaction of national judges with the CJEU and the ECtHR and examines the contribution of the jurisprudence of European courts to national judicial reasoning. The book also investigates judicial interaction between the CJEU and the ECtHR, probing the impact of ECtHR jurisprudence on CJEU assessments and vice versa. Judicial dialogue is commonly understood to denote engagement with the case law of other courts[62] and can take many forms – formal and informal. From the different taxonomies to be found in the literature, in the light of the analysis to be conducted, attention is drawn to vertical and horizontal judicial dialogue. Vertical judicial dialogue usually refers to jurisprudential interaction between courts within the context of a formal hierarchical system or between international/regional courts and domestic courts. Horizontal judicial dialogue commonly takes place between courts that operate at the same level or between international/regional courts.

One clear example of vertical dialogue is the preliminary ruling procedure, whereby, according to Article 267 of the Treaty on the Functioning of the European Union (TFEU), any court or tribunal in the EU Member States may (and a final court must) refer a question on the interpretation of EU law or on the validity of EU legislation that is raised in a case pending before it to the CJEU for a preliminary ruling. Once the CJEU has given its answer, the referring court must apply the CJEU ruling and decide the case using it. A step forward in this context is the application of the same CJEU judgment by a court from a different Member State. In this case, the national court has to disentangle the CJEU decision from the specificities of the legal system of the Member State the court of which made the referral and identify the general dictum of the CJEU decision and the national rules subject to it.[63] Dialogue between national courts and the ECtHR is similarly understood as vertical dialogue, whereas dialogue between the CJEU and the ECtHR for the purposes of this volume amounts to horizontal dialogue.

The preliminary ruling procedure, a "formal mechanism" of judicial dialogue between the CJEU and the referring court,[64] differs substantially from instances of judicial dialogue in which courts voluntarily draw on decisions by other courts. Voluntary reference to the jurisprudence of other courts may serve distinct purposes: to acknowledge the rulings of peers, to corroborate the analysis of the deciding judge, to juxtapose the judge's reasoning to the reasoning of others and sometimes even to express disapproval of judicial stances and approaches to similar legal issues elsewhere. Concerning dialogue between the CJEU and the ECtHR, it is worthwhile noting that, pursuant to Article 52(3) of the CFR, the CFR rights which correspond to rights guaranteed in the ECHR shall have the same meaning and scope as the corresponding ECHR rights, although the EU may choose to grant more extensive protection than the ECHR. The Explanations of the Charter stipulate that the scope and meaning of the ECHR-corresponding rights of the CFR are determined *inter alia* by the case law of the ECtHR.[65] The non-regression clause of Article 53 CFR further proclaims that the CFR is not to "be interpreted as restricting or adversely affecting human rights and fundamental freedoms as recognised . . . by international agreements to which the Union or all the Member States are party", including the ECHR. Although the entry into force of the CFR, the EU's own binding list of fundamental rights, has undoubtedly encouraged CFR-centrism on the part of the CJEU,[66] Articles 52(3) and 53 CFR may have a concrete role to play in CJEU interaction with ECtHR case law.

To study the patterns of judicial interaction of national courts with European courts, this book approaches judicial dialogue through case law references. The analysis explores national courts' references to CJEU and ECtHR jurisprudence and their effects on judicial reasoning. The emphasis is naturally on fundamental rights issues, although judicial dialogue with the CJEU may refer to a broader range of issues. As will be shown, in most instances, national courts refer to CJEU/ECtHR case law to show either consistent reasoning (and consistent interpretation of domestic norms with EU law/the ECHR) or comparative reasoning in which the deciding judge uses European "comparative" jurisprudence mostly to strengthen domestic judicial reasoning or find inspiration to resolve the dispute at issue. The study of judicial dialogue between the CJEU and the ECtHR is similarly based on case law references made; the book examines the incorporation of references to ECtHR case law in CJEU rulings and vice versa.

4. The structure of the book

The book is divided in two parts: one dedicated to the jurisprudence of European courts and one to the jurisprudence of national courts. In the first part, two chapters respectively discuss the social media jurisprudence of the CJEU and the ECtHR, which is expanding. The analysis attests to the various types of social media cases that reach European courts and the distinct ways in which the CJEU and the ECtHR engage with fundamental rights. It also identifies main trends in horizontal interaction between the two European courts, with the CJEU being clearly more active in the field.

Evangelia Psychogiopoulou explores the fundamental rights dimension of the social media jurisprudence of the CJEU. The analysis sheds light on the CJEU's balancing of distinct fundamental rights such as the freedom of digital intermediaries to conduct their business, rightholders' right to intellectual property, users' freedom of expression and information and their right to protection of personal data. It also shows that, in certain instances, the interpretative steps taken by the CJEU result in enhanced standards of protection. However, fundamental rights are not always a component of the rulings reviewed. *Glawischnig-Piesczek* stands as a striking example in this respect, given that the CJEU did not engage with the fundamental rights implications of the uptake of automated filtering mechanisms by digital intermediaries. The chapter also discusses occasional dialogue with the ECtHR and concludes that many tensions remain to be resolved. This is due to both the regulation of online platforms amounting to a legal area that is still developing and the need for clearer answers from the CJEU on some points.

In her chapter, Lorna Woods stresses that the ECtHR has recognised the impact of the internet as a communication and information tool and draws on existing principles in its jurisprudence on freedom of expression and the right to respect for private life with a view to ensuring that relevant rights are protected online as offline. The chapter then considers how the existing case law, which is relatively rich, can be adapted to the specific social media context and concludes that the ECtHR jurisprudence is not particularly mature in certain areas. Whereas questions concerning conflicts between users' rights to free speech and privacy are more or less familiar and therefore mostly resolved by applying existing standards, ECtHR case law on social media platforms as internet intermediaries has not developed sufficiently. A broad range of issues in this area and the analytical tools to address them will soon require more attention from the ECtHR.

The second part of the book is devoted to national case law. It consists of ten chapters on the social media jurisprudence of higher courts and judicial dialogue with European courts in ten European countries: Estonia, Finland, France, Germany, Hungary, Ireland, Italy, Slovenia, Spain and the UK. Our country selection combines the study of western European countries with the study of states in central and eastern Europe and reflects the variety of constitutional traditions (i.e. countries with constitutional protection offered to human rights and countries with no written constitution such as the UK) and judicial structures in Europe. For instance, not all the countries studied rely on a constitutional court to uphold constitutional provisions.

Each country chapter follows a similar structure to facilitate consistency in analysis while enabling flexibility to accommodate specificities emerging from national jurisprudence and practice. Following an introductory section on the domestic legal framework of relevance to social media, sources of fundamental rights protection and domestic judicial structures, the first part of each chapter provides a succinct overview of the social media jurisprudence of supreme and (where available) constitutional courts in the countries under study over the past decade or so. The chapters signal the increasing number of social media cases ruled on by domestic courts, and in some country cases it clearly emerges from the analysis that the social media jurisprudence of higher courts is still quite limited with lower courts dealing with the bulk of social media cases.[67] Each contribution aims to verify whether, and if so how, incorporation of a fundamental rights dimension in judicial reasoning impacts domestic courts' decision-making and combines the study of the application of domestic fundamental rights norms with the study of the input offered by the CFR and the ECHR. The next part of each chapter delves into judicial dialogue with European courts and identifies cases in which the national courts refer to and draw on the jurisprudence of the CJEU and the ECtHR. The analysis seeks to differentiate between cases in which CJEU/ECtHR case law is merely "quoted" and cases in which reference to European case law is substantive, with additional analysis, for instance, on how European court rulings support domestic judicial reasoning or in what ways domestic judges distance themselves from application of the guidelines enshrined in them.

Meeli Kaur focuses on social media jurisprudence in Estonia. She reflects on the role of domestic courts in developing legal standards for social media and acknowledges that the lack of social media-specific rules often translates into judges correcting legislative inadequacies through interpretation. The analysis shows that social media cases in Estonia tend to be framed as fundamental rights cases, mostly because they deal with conflicts between the protection of honour and a good name, the right to private and family life and freedom of expression online. Following the ECtHR landmark *Delfi v Estonia* case,[68] Estonian courts have, for balancing purposes, drawn on criteria laid down in ECtHR jurisprudence and extended their scope of application to internet portals and blogs. Clearer standards still need to be developed as those provided by the ECtHR do not appear to be sufficiently detailed.

Marta Maroni, Tuomas Ojanen and Eveliina Ignatius explore Finnish case law in the field of social media and fundamental rights. Finnish social media case law is still developing and the number of cases remains low. Still, certain broad trends can be discerned. On the one hand, courts tend to take a rights-based approach in their assessments and systematically address fundamental rights – in particular, freedom of expression, the right to privacy and the right to protection of personal data. On the other hand, the Finnish judiciary heavily emphasises the importance of the ECHR as interpreted by ECtHR jurisprudence. The ECtHR jurisprudence not only seems to be preferred over CJEU jurisprudence, but it also reduces the significance of domestic constitutional provisions on fundamental rights and other human rights treaties binding on Finland to establish the level of protection afforded.

Sara Migliorini and Constance Bonzé examine social media jurisprudence in France, looking, in particular, at the attitude of the French judiciary to judicial dialogue on issues of fundamental rights. Domestic factors, such as the traditional concise adjudication style of French courts and fragmentation in the judicial task of scrutinising the compatibility of laws with higher-ranking sources of fundamental rights protection, exert a significant influence on patterns of judicial interaction with the European courts. The impact of ECtHR reasoning on the jurisprudence of the Constitutional Court, for instance, is remarkable, even if ECtHR case law is not always expressly mentioned. The Council of State often mentions the ECHR and EU law and incorporates the reasoning of the European courts in its decisions. The Court of Cassation has further to go to make fundamental rights reasoning apparent in its decisions but appears to be open to direct judicial dialogue with the CJEU through the preliminary reference procedure, as is also the Council of State.

Matthias C. Kettemann, Polina Kulish and Martha Routen investigate social media case law in Germany. Most of the cases reviewed mirror the ongoing tension between content regulation by social media platforms through their terms and conditions and users' fundamental rights – in particular, freedom of expression. The difficult balancing exercise involved is mainly performed by civil courts and for the most part lacks coordination: considerable differences can be noted in the jurisprudential treatment of whether and the extent to which a social network should be held to respect the same standards of fundamental rights protection as a state entity due to its influence on public life. The Federal Constitutional Court has not yet openly pronounced on this issue to offer clear guidelines for domestic courts. As for judicial dialogue with European courts, this has yet to develop in the specific area of social media.

Zsuzsa Detrekoi studies Hungarian social media jurisprudence. This is limited and overall reveals the reluctance of national courts to distinguish the approach followed in social media cases from that in traditional media cases. The jurisprudence of the Hungarian Constitutional Court generally demonstrates a common trend of limited protection of the reputation and honour of public figures vis-à-vis freedom of expression in cases involving comments posted on social media. The seminal *MTE* case,[69] which gathered much attention as it also reached the ECtHR, focused on the liability of social media for comments made by their users. The decision of the ECtHR in *MTE v Hungary*[70] appears to have harmonised the standards applicable and impacted interpretation by national courts. This contrasts with the limited influence that ECtHR jurisprudence has generally had on judicial decision-making, despite the occasional reference to some ECtHR ruling to reinforce domestic reasoning.

Irish social media jurisprudence is at the heart of the chapter authored by Elizabeth Farries. The Irish courts seem able to grasp the specificities of social networks and accordingly adapt their interpretation of the domestic legal framework to the ongoing development of social media activity. The social media and fundamental rights jurisprudence in the higher courts in Ireland has so far mostly focused on defamation cases, with implications mainly for privacy, freedom of expression, data protection and anonymity. The analysis makes it clear that, unlike several other countries, there is a preference for judicial dialogue with the CJEU rather than the ECtHR. The Irish courts have referred to and built on CJEU case law on several occasions when ruling on social media cases. They have also made use of the preliminary ruling procedure, with CJEU rulings such as *Schrems I*[71] and *Schrems II*[72] having had profound impacts on national case law.

Federica Casarosa and Maria Concetta Causarano consider social media court rulings in Italy. The body of case law studied is one of the most voluminous in this book. From a fundamental rights perspective, it mostly relates to freedom of expression and the boundaries applicable in the online context, and addresses different types of speakers, including politicians and judges. Both the Court of Cassation and the Constitutional Court have engaged in a process of interpretative adaptation with a view to taking into account the specific features of social media platforms. Such evolutionary hermeneutic efforts do not fail to consider developments in European jurisprudence. However, judicial dialogue preferably leans towards the ECtHR and it is somewhat limited to supporting the reasoning underlying national judicial decisions rather than proactively seeking authentic guidance for assessments to be carried out.

Tanja Kerševan analyses Slovenian social media jurisprudence. The Slovenian judiciary appears to still be getting acquainted with social media cases. Social media case law, which has developed in the absence of legislation specifically targeting social media and other communication services, is limited, especially at the level of the two highest courts in the country: the Supreme Court and the Constitutional Court. The approach of the Slovenian judiciary is overall quite cautious: judges pay attention to the specific circumstances surrounding a case and they show sensitivity to the protection of free speech online and safeguarding personal rights when this is justified. The absence of a sufficient body of domestic social media case law and the need to balance competing fundamental rights in order to resolve cases are considered to be factors that facilitate engagement with the CJEU and ECtHR jurisprudence.

Judicial adjudication in social media cases in Spain is the focus of the chapter by Joan Solanes Mullor. Spanish courts have been particularly active in the context of social media. The Constitutional Court has decided issues as diverse as the right to one's image vis-à-vis consent on Facebook, freedom of expression cases confronting terrorism, the dissemination of images of police officers on social platforms and the collection of personal data by political parties. The Supreme Court and the National High Court have similarly addressed various social media-related issues, from conflicts between freedom of expression and privacy to cases concerning an employer's access to employees' social media data. Spanish courts, which have only seldomly examined the specificities of the digital sphere – for instance, when applying the proportionality test – have engaged with the jurisprudence of European courts in different ways. The analysis indicates strong judicial dialogue on issues concerning the protection of personal data, in which EU law holds a prominent position, and soft judicial dialogue aimed at reinforcing and legitimising the position of the deciding judge by overcoming difficulties such as the novelty or complexity of a case and disagreement between domestic courts.

The last country chapter, by Rachael Craufurd Smith, refers to both the ECHR and EU law as having been influential in terms of the rights and protections relevant for the communications sector in the UK. The chapter invites the reader to reflect on the interaction between two apex courts in the UK, the UK Supreme Court and the Scottish High Court of Justiciary, and European courts, with a focus, post-Brexit, on the ECtHR. The analysis attests to the relatively few social media cases that have found their way to the two apex courts, but points to a variety of legal issues raised, ranging from privacy, entrapment and defamation to contempt of court, personal data protection and intermediary liability. The "bridge" created between the ECtHR and domestic courts by section 2 of the Human Rights Act 1998 has allowed the ECtHR to exert a significant influence on domestic jurisprudence. At the same time, there have been cases in which the UK courts, rather than following blindly the ECtHR jurisprudence, have sought genuine dialogue, advancing interpretations that do not necessarily match or endorse the interpretations of the Strasbourg Court. The fact that ECtHR case law is voluminous, with many potentially relevant cases, has also influenced the ways in which ECtHR jurisprudence is relied upon, eliciting variation in domestic judicial reasoning.

The concluding chapter by Giovanni De Gregorio and Oreste Pollicino reflects on the European jurisprudence highlighting how courts have relied on the use of metaphorical thought to re-contextualise already-existing legal regimes to the digital world. The authors acknowledge that this approach was justified both on the need to adapt the existing legal framework (as a form of legal imagination) but also as a means to compensate the lack of legislative intervention. As a consequence, judicial actors have played a critical role in protecting fundamental rights in the digital realm and they have also provided for guidelines to the legislative powers to intervene.

Notes

1 Eurostat, 'Do You Participate in Social Networks?' <https://ec.europa.eu/eurostat/web/products-eurostat-news/-/edn-20210630-1> accessed 7 September 2022.

2 Eurostat, 'Social Media – Statistics on the Use by Enterprises' <https://ec.europa.eu/eurostat/statistics-explained/index.php?title=Social_media_-_statistics_on_the_use_by_enterprises#Social_media.2C_a_business_paradigm_shift> accessed 7 September 2022.

3 BroadbandSearch.Net reports that the average daily time spent on social media in Europe according to 2022 data is 1 hour and 15 minutes. See <www.broadbandsearch.net/blog/average-daily-time-on-social-media> accessed 7 September 2022.

4 Nic Newman, Richard Fletcher, Craig T Robertson, Kirsten Eddy and Rasmus Kleis Nielsen, 'Digital News Report 2022 (Reuters Institute 2022)' <https://reutersinstitute.politics.ox.ac.uk/sites/default/files/2022-06/Digital_News-Report_2022.pdf> accessed 7 September 2022.

5 See Eurostat (n 2).

6 Statista, 'Share of Internet Users Worldwide Who Believe that Social Media Platforms Have Had an Impact on Selected Aspects of Daily Life as of February 2019' <www.statista.com/statistics/1015131/impact-of-social-media-on-daily-life-worldwide/> accessed 7 September 2022.

7 Ibid.

8 United Nations, Report of the Special Rapporteur on the Promotion and Protection of the Right to Freedom of Opinion and Expression, Frank La Rue, A/HRC/17/27, 16 May 2011, <https://www2.ohchr.org/english/bodies/hrcouncil/docs/17session/a.hrc.17.27_en.pdf> accessed 7 September 2022, para 22.

9 E.g. freedom to conduct a business, the right to education, the right to take part in cultural life, the right to enjoy the benefits of scientific progress and its applications, etc.

10 See indicatively Tarleton Gillespie, 'Governance of and by Platforms', in Jean Burgess, Alice Marwick and Thomas Poell (eds), *The Sage Handbook of Social Media* (Sage 2017) 254; Orla Lynskey, 'Regulation by Platforms: The Impact on Fundamental Rights', in Luca Belli and Nicolo Zingales (eds), *Platform Regulations: How Platforms Are Regulated and How They Regulate Us* (FGV Direito Rio 2017); Natali Helberger, Jo Pierson and Thomas Poell, 'Governing Online Platforms: From Contested to Cooperative Responsibility' (2018) 34(1) *The Information Society* 1; Robert Gorwa, 'What is Platform Governance?' (2019) 22(6) *Information, Communication & Society* 854; Tim Wu, *The Curse of Bigness: How Corporate Giants Came to Rule the World* (Atlantic Books 2020); Daniela Stockmann, 'Tech Companies and the Public Interest: The Role of the State in Governing Social Media Platforms' (2022) *Information, Communication & Society* 1 <www.tandfonline.com/doi/epub/10.1080/1369118X.2022.2032796?needAccess=true> accessed 7 September 2022.

11 On the fundamental rights discussion accompanying the legislative process on the Digital Services Act for instance, see Proposal for a Regulation of the European Parliament and of the Council on a Single Market For Digital Services (Digital Services Act) and amending Directive 2000/31/EC COM/2020/825, 15 December 2020; and European Parliament resolution of 20 October 2020 on the Digital Services Act and fundamental rights issues posed (2020/2022(INI)) <www.europarl.europa.eu/doceo/document/TA-9-2020-0274_EN.html> accessed 7 September 2022. See also Ilaria Buri and Joris van Hoboken, 'The Digital Services Act (DSA) Proposal: A Critical Overview' (DSA Observatory 2020), 28 October 2021 <https://dsa-observatory.eu/wp-content/uploads/2021/11/Buri-Van-Hoboken-DSA-discussion-paper-Version-28_10_21.pdf> accessed 7 September 2022; Joan Barata, 'The Digital Services Act and Social Media Power to Regulate Speech: Obligations, Liabilities and Safeguards', in M Cappello (ed), *Unravelling the Digital Services Act Package*, IRIS Special (European Audiovisual Observatory 2021) 7 <https://rm.coe.int/iris-special-2021-01en-dsa-package/1680a43e45> accessed 7 September 2022; Giancarlo Frosio and Christophe Geiger, 'Taking Fundamental Rights Seriously in the Digital Services Act's Platform Liability Regime' *European Law Journal*, forthcoming, <https://ssrn.com/abstract=3747756>.

12 See indicatively UN Human Rights Committee, 'Concluding Observations on the Seventh Periodic Report of Germany', CCPR/C/DEU/CO/7, 11 November 2021 <https://tbinternet.ohchr.org/Treaties/CCPR/Shared%20Documents/DEU/CCPR_C_DEU_CO_7_47161_E.pdf> accessed 7 September 2022, 10; and Matthias C. Kettemann, 'Follow-up to the Comparative Study on Blocking, Filtering and Takedown of Illegal Internet Content', May 2019 <https://rm.coe.int/dgi-2019-update-chapter-germany-study-on-blocking-and-filtering/168097ac51> accessed 7 September 2021. See also, among others, the project "Network Enforcement Act and Human Rights", hosted by the Max Planck Institute for the Study of Crime, Security and Law, which focuses on the effects on fundamental rights of the Act to Improve Enforcement of the Law in Social Networks (Network Enforcement Act, NetzDG) and related amendments <https://csl.mpg.de/en/projects/netzdg-and-human-rights> accessed 7 September 2022.

13 See for instance David Kaye, Report of the Special Rapporteur on the Promotion and Protection of the Right to Freedom of Opinion and Expression, A/HRC/38/35, 2 April 2018 <https://freedex.org/wp-content/blogs.dir/2015/files/2018/05/G1809672.pdf> accessed 7 September 2022; and Recommendation CM/Rec(2018)2 of the Committee of Ministers to Member States on the roles and responsibilities of internet intermediaries.

14 See Anne Helmond, 'The Platformization of the Web: Making Web Data Platform Ready' (2015) 1(2) *Social Media + Society* 1; and Terry Flew, 'The Platformized Internet: Issues for Internet Law and Policy' (2019) 22(11) *Journal of Internet Law* 4.

15 Terry Flew and Fiona R Martin, 'Introduction', in Terry Flew and Fiona R Martin (eds), *Digital Platform Regulation: Global Perspectives on Internet Governance* (Palgrave Macmillan 2022) 1, 5.

16 Natalie Fenton, 'The Internet and Social Networking', in James Curran, Natalie Fenton and Des Freedman (eds), *Misunderstanding the Internet* (Routledge 2012) 123, at 126.

17 Ibid.

18 Gillespie (n 10).

19 Ian Brown and Christopher Marsden, *Regulating Code: Good Governance and Better Regulation in the Information Age* (MIT Press 2013); Monroe E Price and Stefaan G Verhulst, *Self-Regulation and the Internet* (Kluwer 2004).

20 Concerning the latter, see Sarah Eskens, Natali Helberger and Judith Moeller, 'Challenged by News Personalisation: Five Perspectives on the Right to Receive Information' (2017) 9(2) *Journal of Media Law* 259; Natali Helberger, 'On the Democratic Role of News Recommenders' (2019) 7(8) *Digital Journalism* 993; and Mira Burri, 'Cultural Diversity Policy in the Age of Artificial Intelligence', in Maja Cappello (ed), *Artificial Intelligence in the Audiovisual Sector*, IRIS Special (European Audiovisual Observatory 2020) 69.

21 See, for instance, the 2016 Code of Conduct on Countering Illegal Hate Speech Online <https://ec.europa.eu/info/policies/justice-and-fundamental-rights/combatting-discrimination/racism-and-xenophobia/eu-code-conduct-countering-illegal-hate-speech-online_en#theeucodeofconduct> accessed 7 September 2022. See also the 2022 Strengthened Code of Practice on Disinformation which aspires to respond to the co-regulatory framework envisaged in the Digital Services Act for "very large online platforms" <https://digital-strategy.ec.europa.eu/en/library/2022-strengthened-code-practice-disinformation> accessed 7 September 2022.

22 Directive 2000/31/EC of the European Parliament and of the Council of 8 June 2000 on certain legal aspects of information society services, in particular electronic commerce, in the Internal Market [2000] OJ L 178/1.

23 Art 14 of the e-Commerce Directive stated that intermediaries benefit from a liability exemption as long as they have no knowledge of illegal activities and act promptly on notification. Art 15 of the directive provided that intermediaries have no obligation to monitor user-generated content.

24 See Directive 2018/1808/EU of the European Parliament and of the Council of 14 November 2018 amending Directive 2010/13/EU on the coordination of certain provisions laid down by law, regulation or administrative action in Member States concerning the provision of audiovisual media services (Audiovisual Media Services Directive) in view of changing market realities [2018] OJ L 303/69.

25 According to Art 1(a)(aa) of the Audiovisual Media Services Directive, a video-sharing platform service is a service the principal purpose of which, a dissociable section thereof or an essential functionality of which is devoted to providing programmes, user-generated videos or both to the general public, for which the provider does not have editorial responsibility in order to inform, entertain or educate by means of electronic communication networks and the organisation of which is determined by the provider, including by automatic means or algorithms – in particular, by displaying, tagging and sequencing.

26 See Communication from the Commission, Guidelines on the practical application of the essential functionality criterion of the definition of a "video-sharing platform service" under the Audiovisual Media Services Directive (2020/C 223/02) [2020] OJ C 223/3.

27 See Art 28b of the Audiovisual Media Services Directive.

28 See Directive 2019/790/EU of the European Parliament and of the Council of 17 April 2019 on copyright and related rights in the Digital Single Market and amending Directives 96/9/EC and 2001/29/EC [2019] OJ L 130/92.

29 According to Art 2(6) of Directive 2019/790, an "online content-sharing service provider" is a provider of an information society service the main or one of the main purposes of which is to store and give the public access to a large amount of copyright-protected works or other protected subject matter uploaded by its users, which it organises and promotes for profit-making purposes. Providers of services, such as not-for-profit online encyclopaedias, not-for-profit educational and scientific repositories, open-source software-developing and -sharing platforms, providers of electronic communications services, online marketplaces, business-to-business

cloud services and cloud services that allow users to upload content for their own use do not come under this definition.

30 See Art 17(1) of Directive 2019/790.

31 Ibid, Art 17(4).

32 Directive 2011/93/EU of the European Parliament and of the Council of 13 December 2011 on combating the sexual abuse and sexual exploitation of children and child pornography, and replacing Council Framework Decision 2004/68/JHA [2011] OJ L 335/1.

33 Directive 2017/541/EU of the European Parliament and of the Council of 15 March 2017 on combating terrorism and replacing Council Framework Decision 2002/475/JHA and amending Council Decision 2005/671/JHA [2017] OJ L 88/6.

34 Regulation (EU) 2021/784 of the European Parliament and of the Council of 29 April 2021 on addressing the dissemination of terrorist content online [2021] OJ L 172/79.

35 Council Framework Decision 2008/913/JHA of 28 November 2008 on combating certain forms and expressions of racism and xenophobia by means of criminal law [2008] OJ L 328/55.

36 Ibid, Art 1(1)(a).

37 Ibid, Art 1(1)(c)-(d).

38 See, among others, Communication from the Commission to the European Parliament, the Council, the European Economic and Social Committee and the Committee of the Regions, Tackling Illegal Content Online, Towards an enhanced responsibility of online platforms COM(2017) 555; Commission Recommendation (EU) 2018/334 of 1 March 2018 on measures to effectively tackle illegal content online C/2018/1177 [2018] OJ L 63/50; High Level Group on Fake News and Online Disinformation, A Multi-Dimensional Approach to Disinformation 2018 <https://cadmus.eui.eu/bitstream/handle/1814/70297/DeCockB_2018?sequence=1&isAllowed=y> accessed 7 September 2022; and European Parliamentary Research Service (Scientific Foresight Unit, STOA), Polarisation and the Use of Technology in Political Campaigns and Communication, March 2019 <www.europarl.europa.eu/RegData/etudes/STUD/2019/634414/EPRS_STU(2019)634414_EN.pdf> accessed 7 September 2022.

39 Shoshana Zuboff, *The Age of Surveillance Capitalism: The Fight for a Human Future at the New Frontier of Power* (PublicAffairs 2019); Erik Longo, 'The Risks of Social Media Platforms for Democracy: A Call for a New Regulation', in Bart Custers and Eduard Fosch-Villaronga (eds), *Law and Artificial Intelligence – Regulating AI and Applying AI in Legal Practice* (Springer 2022).

40 Regulation 2022/2065 of the European Parliament and of the Council of 19 October 2022 on a Single Market For Digital Services and amending Directive 2000/31/EC (Digital Services Act) [2022] OJ L 277/1.

41 Regulation (EU) 2022/1925 of the European Parliament and of the Council of 14 September 2022 on contestable and fair markets in the digital sector and amending Directives (EU) 2019/1937 and (EU) 2020/1828 (Digital Markets Act) [2022] OJ L 265/1.

42 Proposal for a Regulation of the European Parliament and of the Council laying down harmonised rules on artificial intelligence (Artificial Intelligence Act) and amending certain Union legislative acts COM/2021/206 final.

43 Proposal for a Regulation of the European Parliament and of the Council establishing a common framework for media services in the internal market (European Media Freedom Act) and amending Directive 2010/13/EU COM(2022) 457 final. See also Commission Recommendation of 16 September 2022 on internal safeguards for editorial independence and ownership transparency in the media sector C(2022) 6536 final.

44 Article 17 TFEU provides inter alia that "[t]he Commission shall promote the general interest of the Union and take appropriate initiatives to that end".
45 Article 83(1) TFEU lays down an exhaustive list of areas of "particularly serious crime with a cross-border dimension", from terrorism and trafficking in human beings to computer crime and organised crime, where the European Parliament and the Council may, by means of directives, establish minimum rules concerning the definition of criminal offences and sanctions applicable in all Member States. Pursuant to Article 83(1) TFEU, on the basis of "developments in crime", the Council, after obtaining the consent of the European Parliament, may adopt a decision identifying additional areas of such particularly serious crime, enabling subsequent adoption of secondary legislation on common standards.
46 See Commission Communication, A more inclusive and protective Europe: Extending the list of EU crimes to hate speech and hate crime COM(2021) 777.
47 On this see Secretary of State for Digital, Culture, Media & Sport and Secretary of State for the Home Department, *Online Harms White Paper*, April 2019 <https://assets.publishing.service.gov.uk/government/uploads/system/uploads/attachment_data/file/793360/Online_Harms_White_Paper.pdf> accessed 7 September 2022; and French Republic, 'Creating a French Framework to Make Social Media Platforms More Accountable: Acting in France with a European vision. Mission Report, "Regulation of social networks – Facebook experiment"', May 2019 <www.numerique.gouv.fr/uploads/Regulation-of-social-networks_Mission-report_ENG.pdf> accessed 7 September 2022.
48 *Netzwerkdurchsetzungsgesetz* (Network Enforcement Act) <www.bmjv.de/SharedDocs/Gesetzgebungsverfahren/Dokumente/NetzDG_engl.pdf?__blob=publicationFile&v=2> accessed 7 September 2022. See also chapter 7 by Matthias C. Kettemann, Polina Kulish and Martha Routen in this volume.
49 *Loi n° 2020–766 du 24 juin 2020 visant à lutter contre les contenus haineux sur internet* <www.legifrance.gouv.fr/jorf/id/JORFTEXT000042031970> accessed 7 September 2022; and Constitutional Council, Decision 2020–801 DC, 18 June 2020 <www.legifrance.gouv.fr/jorf/id/JORFTEXT000042031998/> accessed 7 September 2022. See also chapter 6 by Sara Migliorini and Constance Bonzé in this volume.
50 See Recommendation CM/Rec(2012)4 of the Committee of Ministers to member states on the protection of human rights with regard to social networking services (Adopted by the Committee of Ministers on 4 April 2012 at the 1139th meeting of the Ministers' Deputies); Recommendation CM/Rec(2018)2 of the Committee of Ministers to member states on the roles and responsibilities of internet intermediaries (n 13); Declaration Decl(13/02/2019)1 by the Committee of Ministers on the manipulative capabilities of algorithmic processes (Adopted by the Committee of Ministers on 13 February 2019 at the 1337th meeting of the Ministers' Deputies); and Recommendation CM/Rec(2020)1 of the Committee of Ministers to member states on the human rights impacts of algorithmic systems (Adopted by the Committee of Ministers on 8 April 2020 at the 1373rd meeting of the Ministers' Deputies).
51 See Recommendation CM/Rec(2012)4 (n 50).
52 The Recommendation suggests providing an environment for users that enables the exercise of fundamental rights, raising users' awareness about the fundamental rights implications of using social networking services, protecting users from harm without limiting freedom of expression and access to information, enhancing transparency about data processing and refraining from illegitimate processing of personal data, ensuring the accessibility of social networking services to people with disabilities and resorting to self- and co-regulation where appropriate.
53 See Recommendation CM/Rec(2018)2 (n 13).
54 Ibid, para 4.

55 Jonathan A Obar and Steven S Wildman, 'Social Media Definition and the Governance Challenge: An Introduction to the Special Issue' (2015) 39(3) *Telecommunications Policy* 745; and Gillespie (n 10).
56 Oversight Board Charter <www.oversightboard.com/governance/> accessed 7 September 2022.
57 See Stockmann (n 10).
58 Gráinne de Búrca, 'After the EU Charter of Fundamental Rights: The Court of Justice as a Human Rights Adjudicator?' (2013) 20(2) *Maastricht Journal of European and Comparative Law* 168.
59 See Art 51(1) CFR.
60 Elise Muir, 'The Horizontal Effects of Charter Rights Given Expression to in EU Legislation, from Mangold to Bauer' (2019) 12(2) *Review of European Administrative Law* 185; Eleni Frantziou, 'The Horizontal Effect of the Charter: Towards an Understanding of Horizontality as a Structural Constitutional Principle?' (2020) 22 *Cambridge Yearbook of European Legal Studies* 208; Sacha Prechal, 'Horizontal Direct Effect of the Charter of Fundamental Rights of the EU' (2020) 66 *Revista de Derecho Comunitario Europeo* 66, 407.
61 See Oreste Pollicino, *Judicial Protection of Fundamental Rights on the Internet: A Road Towards Digital Constitutionalism?* (Bloomsbury Publishing 2021).
62 See indicatively Laurence R Helfer and Anne-Marie Slaughter, 'Toward a Theory of Effective Supranational Adjudication' (1997) 107(2) *Yale Law Journal* 273; Allan Rosas, 'The European Court of Justice in Context: Forms and Patterns of Judicial Dialogue' (2007) 1(2) *European Journal of Legal Studies* 1; Aida Torres Pérez, *Conflicts of Rights in the European Union: A Theory of Supranational Adjudication* (OUP 2009) 97; Anthony Arnull, 'Judicial Dialogue in the European Union', in Julie Dickson and Pavlos Eleftheriadis (eds), *Philosophical Foundations of European Union Law* (OUP 2012) 109; Monica Claes, Maartje de Visser, Patricia Popelier and Catherine Van de Heyning (eds), *Constitutional Conversations in Europe* (Intersentia 2012); Antoine Hol, 'Highest Courts and Transnational Interaction – Introductory and Concluding Remarks' (2012) 8(2) *Utrecht Law Review* 1; Michal Bobek, *Comparative Reasoning in European Supreme Courts* (OUP 2013); Bruno de Witte, 'The Preliminary Ruling Dialogue: Three Types of Questions Posed by National Courts', in Bruno de Witte, Juan A Mayoral, Urszula Jaremba, Marlene Wind and Karolina Podstawa (eds), *National Courts and EU Law: New Issues, Theories and Methods* (Edward Elgar Publishing 2016) 15; Amrei Müller (ed) in collaboration with Hege Elizabeth Kjos, *Judicial Dialogue and Human Rights* (Cambridge University Press 2017); Jasper Krommendijk, *National Courts and Preliminary References to the Court of Justice* (Edward Elgar Publishing 2021); Evangelia Psychogiopoulou, 'Judicial Dialogue in Social Media Cases in Europe: Exploring the Role of Peers in Judicial Adjudication' (2021) 22(6) *German Law Journal* 915; Federica Casarosa and Madalina Moraru (eds), *The Practice of Judicial Interaction in the Field of Fundamental Rights. The Added Value of the Charter of Fundamental Rights of the EU* (Edward Elgar Publishing 2022).
63 See Federica Casarosa, 'The Impact of Judicial Interactions Among European and National Courts and Regulators on EU Media Law', in Elda Brogi and Pier Luigi Parcu (eds), *Handbook on EU Media Law and Policy* (Edward Elgar Publishing 2021) 153; and ACTIONES Handbook on the Techniques of Judicial Interactions in the Application of the EU Charter, deliverable of the DG Justice supported project ACTIONES <https://cjc.eui.eu/projects/actiones/actiones-platform/> accessed 7 September 2022, in particular Module 2 on Judicial Interaction Techniques Available to National Judges in the Field of European Fundamental Rights.
64 Monica Claes, 'The Validity and Primacy of EU Law and the "Cooperative Relationship" between National Constitutional Courts and the Court of Justice of the

European Union' (2016) 23(1) *Maastricht Journal of European and Comparative Law* 151.

65 Explanations relating to the CFR [2007] OJ C 303/17. Note that pursuant to Article 52(7) CFR the Explanations "shall be given due regard by the courts of the Union and of the Member States".

66 De Búrca (n 58).

67 See, for instance, chapter 11 by Tanja Kerševan in this volume on Slovenia.

68 *Delfi AS v Estonia* App no 64569/09 (ECtHR, 16 June 2015).

69 Kúria judgment no. Pfv.IV.20.217/2012/5.szám of 13 June 2012.

70 *Magyar Tartalomszolgáltatók Egyesülete and Index.hu Zrt v Hungary* App No 22947/13 (ECtHR, 2 February 2016).

71 Case C-362/14 *Schrems* [2015] ECLI:EU:C:2015:650 (*Schrems I*).

72 Case C-311/18 *Facebook Ireland and Schrems* [2020] ECLI:EU:C:2020:559 (*Schrems II*).

Part 1

The European perspective

2 The CJEU as a fundamental rights adjudicator in social media cases

Evangelia Psychogiopoulou

1. Introduction

In recent years, there has been a sharp increase in preliminary ruling proceedings in social media cases before the Court of Justice of the European Union (CJEU). Relevant CJEU decisions touch on various areas of EU law, from protection of personal data and rules concerning jurisdiction in civil matters to intellectual property and liability rules for digital intermediaries. In many of these cases, the CJEU has engaged in fundamental rights reasoning. This shows that the CJEU is cognisant of and attentive to the fundamental rights repercussions of social media operation and use. Social media and their fundamental rights implications have received much attention from scholars and the international community.[1] On the one hand, social networks have been praised as fundamental rights enablers because they promote the exercise of a broad range of freedoms – in particular, freedom of expression and information, freedom of the arts and freedom of assembly and association. On the other hand, they offer a space that may threaten the exercise of fundamental rights, especially the right to respect for private and family life, the right to protection of personal data and the right to intellectual property, and they have been deplored for spurring the spread of illegal and harmful content, which creates substantial challenges for public order and national security, crime prevention, stability in democratic processes and the protection of the rights of others, including children's rights.

CJEU social media case law has so far mostly focused on issues regarding the right to freedom of expression and information, the right to respect for private life, the right to protection of personal data, freedom to conduct a business and the right to intellectual property. This chapter seeks to shed light on the place of fundamental rights in CJEU decision-making in social media disputes. Section 2 examines CJEU case law in social media cases with a fundamental rights component. Section 3 discusses CJEU social media case law without a fundamental rights component, delving into the implications (if any) of this lack for the protection of fundamental rights. Section 4 explores CJEU interaction with the jurisprudence of the European Court of Human Rights (ECtHR) in cases where the CJEU engages in fundamental rights

DOI: 10.4324/9781003207085-3

analysis. The aim here is to probe the input of ECtHR case law in CJEU judicial output, taking into account that, according to the Charter of Fundamental Rights (CFR) of the EU, the European Convention on Human Rights (ECHR) is the *minimum* standard of fundamental rights protection in the EU for the CFR rights that correspond to the rights safeguarded by the ECHR.[2] The focus is on cases addressing social media and cases concerning behaviour in a social media setting, although, as will be shown, the term "social media" is rarely employed by the CJEU.

2. Fundamental rights in CJEU social media jurisprudence

Fundamental rights are increasingly integrated in CJEU assessment of social media disputes. So far, fundamental rights reasoning has been developed mostly in cases concerning the liability of digital intermediaries, social media publications and the protection of personal data, platform data processing practices and the interaction of consumer protection law with data protection rules in the social media environment.

2.1 *The liability of digital intermediaries*

The liability of digital intermediaries was for years governed by Directive 2000/31/EC, the e-Commerce Directive,[3] which the Digital Services Directive sought to modernise.[4] The e-Commerce Directive provided certain intermediaries with a limited exemption from secondary liability resulting from illegal behaviour by users.[5] Under Articles 13 and 14 of the e-Commerce Directive in particular, digital intermediaries offering access to a communication network or hosting information provided by a recipient of their services were exempted from liability, so long as two conditions were met. First, they needed to transmit or store information in a merely "technical, automatic and passive" manner, which implied that they had "neither knowledge of nor control over the information which is transmitted or stored".[6] Second, they had to take expeditious action after they obtained knowledge of infringements or became aware of them. According to the directive, this did not preclude requiring intermediaries to terminate or prevent infringement through injunctions.[7] However, Article 15(1) of the e-Commerce Directive provided that Member States shall not impose a general obligation on digital intermediaries to monitor the information they transmit or store or to actively seek facts or circumstances that may indicate illegal activity. Relevant provisions were preserved and integrated in the Digital Services Act.[8] Most CJEU rulings concerning the liability of digital intermediaries that have a fundamental rights component have so far involved cases concerning alleged copyright infringements. These are explored in the discussion that follows.

2.1.1 *Injunctions to prevent infringement of intellectual property rights*

The prohibition of imposing a general duty on digital intermediaries to monitor content and actively look for instances of infringement has a clear free speech rationale. Although Article 15(1) of the e-Commerce Directive was originally linked to arguments about digital innovation, market liberalism and taking steps to promote the development of digital platforms without entrusting them with burdensome duties, the policy discourse was subsequently reframed. In the 2010s, the CJEU established that a general obligation to monitor content transmitted or stored online using tools that "might not distinguish adequately between unlawful content and lawful content" may undermine freedom of expression and freedom of information, which are protected under Article 11 CFR.[9] For instance, in *SABAM* the CJEU held that, pursuant to Article 15 of the e-Commerce Directive interpreted in the light of the CFR, an online social networking platform could not be ordered to filter content indiscriminately in order to prevent infringement of intellectual property rights. An injunction requiring an online platform to introduce a filtering system enabling active monitoring of users' data would evidently seek to protect the right to intellectual property enshrined in Article 17(2) CFR.[10] However, such an injunction could lead to the blocking of lawful content and therefore fell short of guaranteeing a fair balance between the right to intellectual property and users' freedom to receive and impart information.[11] Moreover, conscious of the digital market-building dimension, the CJEU unsurprisingly found that by mandating a "complicated, costly [and] permanent" screening system "at [the operator's] own expense", the injunction would also result in a violation of the online platform's freedom to conduct its business, which is protected under Article 16 CFR.[12] In addition, the CJEU held that the injunction could violate users' right to the protection of their personal data enshrined in Article 8 CFR, as installation of the contested filtering system would involve "the identification, systematic analysis and processing of information connected with the profiles created on the social network by its users".[13]

In *Telekabel Wien*, the CJEU declared that fundamental rights do not preclude a court injunction that prohibits intermediaries (i.e. internet access providers) from allowing users to access protected works online without authorisation.[14] While the CJEU confirmed that an injunction requiring the adoption of complex technical solutions and costly measures restricts the operator's freedom to conduct a business,[15] in this case it placed emphasis on the fact that the intermediaries would remain free to determine the measures to adopt[16] and that they would escape liability if they showed that reasonable measures had been taken.[17] However, the CJEU also held that the measures taken should comply with the right to information[18] by not "affecting internet users who are using the provider's services in order to lawfully access information".[19] They should also be sufficiently effective to protect the right to intellectual property by preventing unauthorised access to protected content[20] or by discouraging such access and rendering it more difficult.[21]

YouTube and Cyando derived from a domestic dispute concerning infringement of intellectual property rights by YouTube users and users of "Uploaded", a file-hosting and sharing platform operated by Cyando.[22] In this case, the

CJEU ruled that domestic rules requiring an online platform to be notified of alleged copyright infringement through use of its services before being served an injunction was compatible with EU law.[23] Through a combined reading of the e-Commerce Directive and Article 8(3) of Directive 2001/29/EC (the Copyright Directive),[24] which requires Member States to enable injunctions against intermediaries whose services are used for copyright infringements, the CJEU held that national legislation averted a situation in which an intermediary is exposed to an injunction without having been offered the opportunity to remedy the infringement and prevent it from recurring. By default, the CJEU observed, the intermediary would need to engage in active monitoring of the content uploaded by its users to avoid infringement and thus an injunction.[25] Not only would this be incongruent with Article 15 of the e-Commerce Directive[26] and the logic of the liability rules set out in the directive,[27] but it would also be incompatible with striking a fair balance between the right to intellectual property, the intermediary's freedom to conduct a business and users' right to freedom of expression and information.[28] Effectiveness in protecting the right to intellectual property yet called for caution. Application of the national legal framework, the CJEU added, should not delay the cessation of copyright infringement in such a way as to cause disproportionate damage to the rightholders.[29] The CJEU did not clarify what would amount to such disproportionate damage.[30]

2.1.2 *Secondary vs. primary (or direct) liability for infringement of intellectual property rights by users*

In *YouTube and Cyando*, the CJEU clarified that, for an online platform to be excluded from the scope of the liability exemption provided in Article 14 of the e-Commerce Directive, knowledge or awareness of specific illegal acts committed by its users was required.[31] This interpretation, the CJEU held, not only reflected the wording of the directive, which required actual knowledge of illegality or awareness of apparent illegality for loss of the liability exemption,[32] but was also in line with the balance that Article 14 of the directive sought to achieve between distinct rights and interests, including freedom of expression.[33] Pursuant to this Article, digital intermediaries were to act expeditiously to remove or disable access to content as soon as they gained knowledge or awareness of illegality.[34] Such an obligation, the CJEU ruled, could be fulfilled in line with free speech requirements only in relation to *specific* content.[35]

Directive 2019/790 on copyright and related rights in the digital single market (the CDSM Directive) deviated, in its Article 17, from the liability framework in the e-Commerce Directive now incorporated in the Digital Services Act.[36] Online content-sharing service providers (OCSSPs),[37] a sub-set of hosting service providers, are made *directly* liable for copyright infringement by their users. The basic rule set forth is that OCSSPs perform an act of communication to the public[38] when they offer access to protected content uploaded by their users, and they are therefore required to obtain authorisation from the rightholders.[39] To escape liability if no authorisation is granted,[40] OCSSPs are mandated to demonstrate that they have made their *best efforts* on various fronts, besides acting expeditiously to disable access to or remove protected content from their websites on receipt of a sufficiently substantiated notice.[41] In particular, they need to show that they have made their best efforts to obtain an authorisation; to ensure, in accordance with high industry standards of professional diligence, the "unavailability of specific protected content" for which they have received "relevant and necessary information" from the rightholders; and to prevent future uploads of the protected content that has been the subject of a sufficiently substantiated notice.[42]

In *Poland v Parliament and Council*,[43] the last two features of this specific liability scheme were challenged from a fundamental rights perspective. Poland argued that relevant provisions translated into requirements for operators to engage in preventive monitoring of users' content by means of automatic filtering tools.[44] This, Poland claimed, was a serious limitation of users' right to freedom of expression and information: it was a form of prior restraint determined by automation and it did not preclude the risk of lawful content being blocked.[45]

The CJEU agreed that the EU legislator introduced a limitation on freedom of expression and information by *de facto* requiring "service providers to carry out a prior review of the content that users wish to upload" once rightholders have provided them with "the relevant and necessary information".[46] It also accepted that in the absence of alternatives and depending on the volume and characteristics of the prior review task to be performed,[47] this implied use of automated filtering tools.[48] However, in proceeding to examine whether the limitation on freedom of expression and information could be justified in accordance with Article 52(1) CFR,[49] the CJEU replied in the affirmative, emphasising the free speech rationale of the safeguards built into the OCSSPs' liability scheme[50] while making clear that automatic filtering is permissible only when lawful content remains unaffected.

As a point of departure, the CJEU noted that the limitation of freedom of expression and information was prescribed by law. While it was true that the CDSM Directive did not define the actual measures OCSSPs had to adopt, it provided that best efforts should be made in accordance with high industry standards of professional diligence. This, the CJEU held, allowed adaptation to both OCSSPs' specificities and "the development of industry practices and available technologies".[51] Echoing *Telekabel Wien*, the CJEU took the view that leaving the choice of measures to operators themselves could facilitate compliance with requirements for a fair balance to be struck between OCSSPs' freedom to conduct a business and users' freedom of expression and information.[52]

Article 17(7) of the CDSM Directive was then juxtaposed to the best-efforts requirements. Article 17(7) of the directive stipulates that cooperation between OCSSPs and rightholders shall not result in preventing the lawful availability of protected content uploaded by users, including content covered by a copyright exception or limitation. It also renders mandatory users' exercise of certain optional copyright exceptions, established in the Copyright Directive, for quotation, criticism and review and also caricature, parody and pastiche. The CJEU held that the relevant provisions laid down an ***obligation of result***; namely, keeping legal content online, with normative hierarchy vis-à-vis the lower-level, best-effort obligations.[53] The CJEU also pointed to the fact that, according to Article 17(9) of the CDSM Directive, the directive should "in no way affect legitimate uses, such as uses under exceptions or limitations provided for in Union law".[54] On this basis, it ruled that the essence of freedom of expression and information was preserved.

As for proportionality, having noted that the limitation reviewed was appropriate and necessary to protect rightholders' right to intellectual property,[55] the CJEU drew attention to the numerous limits imposed by the CDSM Directive with a clear free speech mindset – in particular, the exclusion of any *ex ante* measures filtering and blocking lawful content[56] and the mandatory copyright exceptions laid down.[57] The CJEU also stressed that liability should only be incurred on condition that the rightholders provide OCSSPs with "the relevant and necessary information" concerning the content that should be made unavailable.[58] Moreover, application of the directive, as Article 17(8) states, should not result in a general monitoring obligation,[59] and OCSSPs should not be required to make "an independent [content] assessment" in the light of information received and the exceptions applicable.[60] For the CJEU, all these elements were safeguards of freedom of expression and information.

Ex post safeguards in the CDSM Directive coming into play once OCSSPs unjustifiably block lawful content also received consideration.[61] Requirements for effective and expeditious complaint and redress mechanisms for users went hand in hand with requirements for human review of complaints challenging decisions disabling access to or removing uploaded content,[62] access to impartial out-of-court redress mechanisms and efficient judicial remedies for asserting use of copyright exceptions.[63] Furthermore, the directive made provision for stakeholder dialogues to discuss best practice and advise on the application of the provisions enacted, with consideration given, among other things, to the use of copyright exceptions, users' access to information concerning OCSSPs' implementation practices and the balancing of fundamental rights.[64] Against this backdrop, the CJEU concluded that the specific liability regime for OCSSPs was compatible with users' freedom of expression and information and fairly balanced the right to intellectual property.

2.1.3 Direct liability for communication to the public

In *YouTube and Cyando*, the CJEU also clarified, by means of reliance on fundamental rights, the conditions under which an online platform the users of which illegally make copyright-protected content available to the public *itself* carries out an "act of communication" within the meaning of Article 3(1) of the Copyright Directive on the right of communication to the public and is therefore *directly* liable for copyright infringement. Drawing on earlier case law, the CJEU affirmed that the concept of communication to the public must be interpreted in the light of the fair balance that the Copyright Directive seeks to achieve between the interests of rightholders in protecting their right to intellectual property and the fundamental rights of users of protected content – in particular, freedom of expression and information.[65] Against this inherent fundamental rights background to the Copyright Directive, the CJEU held that due consideration should be given, in particular, to the "importance of the internet to freedom of expression and information"[66] and the criteria progressively developed in its case law concerning interpretation of the concept of communication to the public.[67] These included "the indispensable role" of the operator and the "deliberate nature of its intervention".[68]

Concerning the first criterion, the CJEU stated that a platform operator should be seen as playing such an indispensable role if, without it, it would be impossible or at least more complex for users to freely share illegal content on the internet.[69] Concerning deliberate conduct, the CJEU mentioned several factors for the referring court to consider: refraining from adopting appropriate technological measures that can be reasonably expected from a diligent operator to effectively counter copyright infringements; participating in selecting protected content illegally communicated to the public; providing tools for illegal sharing of content; knowingly promoting the latter – for instance, with a financial model that encourages the illegal sharing of content; and abstaining from expeditiously taking measures to disable access to protected content once the platform operator is informed of the infringement.[70] The various elements singled out by the CJEU in order to establish direct liability of a platform operator for copyright infringement, alongside its users' liability for illegal uploads,[71] show that the liability regime assessed differs substantially from the direct liability scheme in Article 17 of the CDSM Directive. Whether an online platform qualifies as an OCSSP or not thus becomes crucial in deciding the rules applicable.

2.2 *Social media publications and the processing of personal data*

In other instances, the CJEU has delved into the implications of EU data-protection legislation for content published by third parties on social media. *Buivids*, for instance, focused on a YouTube publication and the processing of personal data in this context without permission.[72] The case derived from proceedings concerning the posting of a video recording made by an individual in a Latvian police station, allegedly in order to inform of police malpractice. Asked to clarify whether the video recording and publication at issue came within the scope of Directive 95/46/EC[73] (the Data Protection Directive, repealed by Regulation 2016/679[74]), the CJEU confirmed that both constituted processing of personal data,[75] ruling out the application of certain exceptions contained in the directive.[76] As these exceptions departed from the directive's objective to ensure the protection of the fundamental rights of natural persons with regard to the processing of personal data – i.e. the right to respect for private and family life enshrined in Article 7 CFR and the right to protection of personal data enshrined in Article 8 CFR – they should be interpreted strictly. For example, the CJEU found that publication of the video on YouTube, by enabling "access to personal data by an indefinite number of people", could not come within the scope of the exception in the directive for purely personal or household activities.[77]

The CJEU subsequently examined whether the processing of the personal data at hand was "processing of personal data carried out solely for journalistic purposes" within the meaning of Article 9 of the Data Protection Directive. This required Member States to provide certain exemptions or derogations for such processing, provided that such exemptions or derogations were "necessary to reconcile the right to privacy with the rules governing freedom of expression".[78] The journalistic derogation,[79] the CJEU stated, applied to "every person engaged in journalism",[80] understood as encompassing all activities the purpose of which is to disclose to the public information, opinions or ideas.[81] Given the importance of free speech in democratic societies, journalism should be interpreted broadly,[82] regardless of the medium used and taking into account that methods for disseminating information had evolved and proliferated.[83] At the same time, only activity the sole purpose of which was to disclose to the public information, opinions or ideas should be treated as "journalistic activity" – a matter for the national court to establish.[84] Should the journalism definition be met, the journalistic derogation, the CJEU held, should apply only in so far as was *strictly necessary* to reconcile the rights involved.[85] This was also left to the national court to determine, with guidance given on the basis of ECtHR jurisprudence, as is discussed on the following pages.

2.3 *Processing of personal data by social media platforms*

Ground-breaking CJEU decisions like *Schrems I*[86] and *Schrems II*[87] in the field of personal data protection have stemmed from disputes involving social media platforms, but they were not about the specificities of these platforms or behaviour in the social media setting. Instead, these rulings focused on the competences and tasks of Member States' data protection authorities, duly recognising the fact that the establishment of these authorities forms an essential component of protection of the fundamental rights of individuals regarding the processing of personal data.

Other CJEU rulings have addressed the data processing practices of social media platforms. *Facebook Ireland and others*, for instance, focused on interpretation of the General Data Protection Regulation (GDPR) in the light of the CFR, in the context of injunction proceedings seeking to bring an end to Facebook processing the personal data of internet users using technologies such as cookies, plug-ins and pixels enabling the collection of browsing behaviour data.[88] While most of the questions referred to the CJEU also focused on the allocation of competences among Member States' supervisory authorities,[89] the CJEU also clarified issues germane to the territorial scope of the GDPR. It held, in particular, that effective protection of the right to protection of privacy and the protection of personal data – the objective of the GDPR – should work against a restrictive interpretation of the requirement laid down in Article 3(1) of the GDPR on its territorial scope for the processing of personal data to be carried out "in the context of the activities of an establishment of a controller" (or a processor) in the EU.[90] In the case at hand, domestic proceedings had been brought against Facebook Belgium, which was responsible for the advertising and marketing of the Facebook group in Belgium, but the disputed processing of personal data was carried out by Facebook Ireland,[91] which assumed full responsibility for all data processing operations in the EU as the sole controller.[92] According to the CJEU, the processing of personal data by Facebook Ireland (i.e. the collection of data on users' browsing behaviour) should be regarded as being conducted "in the context of the activities" of Facebook Belgium. This was because the purpose of such processing was to enable an efficient Facebook advertising strategy.[93]

2.4 *Joint controllers with social media platforms*

In *Wirtschaftsakademie Schleswig-Holstein*,[94] the CJEU was asked to pronounce on the interpretation of the Data Protection Directive in the context of proceedings concerning the lawfulness of an order adopted by the Independent Data Protection Centre for the German Land of Schleswig-Holstein. This required a private legal education company, Wirtschaftsakademie, to deactivate its Facebook fan page because it had failed to inform the page visitors that Facebook collected and processed their personal data by means of cookies. The issue for the referring court was whether Wirtschaftsakademie, as the administrator of the relevant Facebook fan page, could be held liable for a breach of data protection rules as a "controller" of personal data. The crux of the analysis was as follows. As the aim of the directive was to ensure a high level of protection of the fundamental rights and freedoms of natural persons – in particular, their right to privacy with respect to the processing of personal data[95] – the concept of "controller" was broadly defined in Article 2(d) of the directive as the "natural or legal person . . . which alone or jointly with others determines the purposes and means of the processing of personal data".[96] This broad definition sought to ensure "effective and complete protection of the persons concerned".[97] Therefore, the concept of controller was not tied to a single entity but could encompass several actors taking part in the processing of personal data.[98]

The CJEU found that, while Facebook Inc. and, for the EU, Facebook Ireland, determined the purposes and means of processing the personal data of Facebook's users and fan page visitors,[99] jointly with them Wirtschaftsakademie determined the purposes and means of the processing of the personal data of the visitors to its own fan page. It did so first by enabling Facebook, through the creation of the Wirtschaftsakademie fan page, to place cookies on the devices of the fan page visitors,[100] and second, by requesting specific Facebook statistics, thus concretely influencing the processing of personal data required for their production.[101] Crucial in establishing that Wirtschaftsakademie was a joint controller was the CJEU's focus on individual data processing operations rather than data processing by the social network in general.[102] Wirtschaftsakademie made possible and contributed to specific processing operations conducted by Facebook and therefore played a part in determining the purposes and means of the processing of personal data taking place.

Fashion ID originated in a request for a preliminary ruling made in proceedings between an online clothing retailer, Fashion ID, which had embedded Facebook's "Like" plugin on its website, and a consumer protection association, which argued that, through the plugin, Fashion ID transmitted the personal data of its website visitors to Facebook without their consent and in violation of its duty to inform them.[103] The principal question raised with the CJEU was whether Fashion ID should be deemed a "controller". Here again, the CJEU accepted that joint responsibility was not excluded.[104] This was in accordance with the aim pursued by the Data Protection Directive; that is, "ensur[ing] a high level of protection of the fundamental rights and freedoms of natural persons"[105] entailing "effective and complete protection of data subjects".[106] The CJEU reiterated that, for a natural or legal person to be considered a "controller" jointly with others, the person should partake in the determination of the purposes and means of processing, with liability being limited to the processing operation(s) for which that person actually determines the purposes and means.[107] Joint liability should not necessarily imply equal engagement in the processing of personal data, in the same stages of the processing, with the same degree[108] and access of all the persons involved to the personal data.[109]

2.5 *The intersection of consumer protection and data privacy*

In *Fashion ID*, the CJEU found that the Data Protection Directive did not preclude Member States from allowing consumer protection associations to bring or defend legal proceedings against persons allegedly responsible for infringements of personal data protection.[110] The recognition that an association could commence or represent a data subject in legal proceedings was seen as contributing to comprehensive protection. As the underlying objective of the directive was to ensure "effective and complete protection of . . . [the] right to privacy, with respect to the processing of personal data",[111] the national legislation at issue did not undermine but instead contributed to the realisation of the objective pursued.[112]

In *Meta Platforms Ireland*,[113] authorising a consumer protection association to bring an action protecting the interests of consumers as data subjects was found to be in compliance with the GDPR objective of ensuring effective protection of the right to protection of personal data.[114] The ruling originated in proceedings brought by the German Federal Union of Consumer

Organisations and Associations concerning the App Centre service of Meta Platforms Ireland (formerly Facebook Ireland) for failure to obtain informed consent to the processing of personal data occurring when use was made of a free games application. Legislation in Germany adopted to transpose Directive 2009/22 on injunctions for the protection of consumers' interests[115] already allowed legal proceedings by consumer protection associations against a person allegedly responsible for an infringement of data protection laws[116] by using rules to protect consumers and combat unfair commercial practices,[117] independently of a specific infringement of a data subject's right to data protection and without a mandate. The issue for the referring court was whether Article 80(2) GDPR, which enables Member States to introduce a representative action mechanism against infringement of data protection laws subject to certain conditions and independently of a data subject's mandate, henceforth precluded the existence of standing to bring representative proceedings on the basis of rules other than data protection rules. Resorting to fundamental rights, the CJEU quashed a restrictive interpretation of Article 80(2) GDPR. For an entity to enjoy standing under Article 80(2) GDPR, it was sufficient, the CJEU held, to claim that the impugned data processing was liable to affect the rights which identified or identifiable natural persons derive from the GDPR without having to prove actual harm suffered in a given situation as a result of a specific infringement of data protection rights.[118] This interpretation was considered to be consistent with the requirements of Article 8 CFR, Article 16 TFEU,[119] a provision similar to Article 8 CFR, and the objectives of the GDPR; namely, to ensure effective protection of fundamental rights and, in particular, "a high level of protection of the right of every person to the protection of personal data".[120] As infringement of data protection rules could concurrently give rise to a violation of rules in other legal areas,[121] the domestic legislation was found to strengthen the rights of data subjects, contributing to a high level of protection.[122]

3. Social media cases without fundamental rights analysis: A missing element?

Certain influential CJEU rulings dealing with social platforms have been issued with the CJEU resorting to customary interpretation of EU secondary legislation without engaging in fundamental rights analysis. In *Schrems*,[123] for instance, the CJEU accepted that the use of Facebook by Max Schrems as a private Facebook account user for activities such as publishing, lecturing, operating websites, fundraising and being assigned consumer claims for enforcement did not preclude reliance on the consumer forum provisions in Council Regulation No 44/2001 on jurisdiction and the recognition and enforcement of judgments in civil and commercial matters[124] in order to bring actions for alleged privacy violations. Taking note of the special jurisdiction rules laid down to protect "consumers",[125] which enabled proceedings in the courts of the Member State where the consumer was domiciled, the CJEU held that interpreting the notion of "consumer" in a restrictive way, thus excluding the previously mentioned activities for their alleged professional nature, would prevent effective defence of consumers' rights, including data protection rights. Jurisdiction over the protection of personality rights was the focus of *Bolagsupplysningen and Ilsjan*.[126] This case stemmed from domestic proceedings concerning the rectification of allegedly incorrect information published online about an Estonian company which had its main business activities in Sweden, the deletion of related negative comments on a discussion forum and the compensation sought. According to Article 7(2) of Regulation No 1215/2012 on jurisdiction and the recognition and enforcement of judgments in civil and commercial matters,[127] in matters relating to tort, delict or quasi-delict, a person domiciled in a Member State can be sued in another Member State in the courts of "the place where the harmful event occurred or may occur". In *eDate Advertising and Others*, the CJEU interpreted this special jurisdiction rule as covering both the place of the event giving rise to the damage and the place where the damage occurred.[128] The CJEU found that a natural person can bring an action for damages in respect of all the harm caused before the courts of the Member State where the damage caused by the online publication occurred most significantly; that is, where reputation is enjoyed the most. In *Bolagsupplysningen and Ilsjan*, the CJEU accepted that this "centre of interests" jurisdictional basis can also be invoked by legal persons,[129] clarifying that it should then reflect the place where commercial reputation is most firmly established and, accordingly, be determined by reference to the place where the legal person carries out the main part of its economic activities.[130] Given the ubiquitous nature of the internet, the CJEU also held that an action for the rectification and removal of the disputed content should be a single and indivisible application lodged with the courts enjoying jurisdiction to rule on an application for compensation for damage in its entirety.[131]

The lack of fundamental rights analysis in the cases reviewed does not appear to have had a significant bearing on their jurisprudential outcome. After all, the EU rules governing jurisdiction in civil and commercial matters are closely associated with objectives about access to justice and fundamental rights, such as the right to an effective remedy and to a fair trial, guaranteed by Article 47 CFR.[132] Particularly regarding the consumer protection special jurisdiction rules laid down, these can also be seen as being inherently linked to the EU objective of ensuring a high level of consumer protection set forth in the TFEU[133] and Article 38 CFR, which proclaims that "Union policies shall ensure a high level of consumer protection". However, there have also been cases on interpretation of EU secondary legislation that reflects fundamental rights safeguards where the absence of fundamental rights analysis by the CJEU is disconcerting. This is the case of *Glawischnig-Piesczek*,[134] in which the CJEU refrained from examining the closely related fundamental rights aspects of the questions raised in the context of proceedings concerning the publication of an insulting and defamatory comment about a politician on a Facebook user's page.[135] The CJEU was asked to clarify, among other issues, whether domestic courts could order digital intermediaries to remove or block access to content that is "identical" and "equivalent" to content previously found to be illegal, in the light of the prohibition of general monitoring laid down in Article 15 of the e-Commerce Directive. Underlining that the e-Commerce Directive allows monitoring "in a specific case",[136] the CJEU took the view that injunctions targeting "identical" content amounted to "specific" monitoring[137] and were therefore allowed. Concerning injunctions on "equivalent" content – namely, content that conveys the same message with a slightly different wording – the CJEU ruled that these were also permissible if limited to specific elements properly identified by the competent court and on condition that the digital intermediary is not required to engage in an "independent assessment" of the content to be removed or blocked, "since the latter has recourse to automated search tools and technologies".[138]

Glawischnig-Piesczek cleared the way for court injunctions mandating monitoring of content "identical" and "equivalent" to content formerly declared to be illegal, with the CJEU putting forward a relaxed interpretation of the prohibition on general monitoring. Article 15 of the e-Commerce Directive was interpreted in the past as precluding an operator from being ordered to monitor all the data of all its users to prevent infringement.[139] In *YouTube and Cyando*, the CJEU accepted that exposure to injunctions without prior notification of alleged copyright infringement would, in practice, result in a general monitoring obligation vis-à-vis all the content uploaded by users in violation of Article 15 of the e-Commerce Directive.[140] With *Glawischnig-Piesczek*, injunctions covering the data of all users became permissible, provided that the monitoring pertains to specific content (the same content already found to be illegal) and equivalent, *as specified*, content, although the CJEU admittedly abstained from providing substantive guidance on how specification of such equivalent content is to take place.[141] The CJEU's understanding that monitoring all users for specific and specified content escapes the prohibition in Article 15 of the e-Commerce Directive went hand in hand with emphasising technical solutions for automated content moderation considered to preclude an independent review. However, automated detection mechanisms are notorious for being context-blind.[142] Reliance on a combination of human review and automation could assuage the risk of unjustified removals of legitimate expression, but the CJEU openly declared that intermediaries should not be required to engage in an independent assessment of the content in question. Given the important fundamental rights repercussions of the issues brought to the attention of the CJEU, especially from a free speech perspective, one would have expected a fundamental rights-oriented assessment, despite the fact that the national court's referral did not formulate any fundamental rights questions.

4. Judicial dialogue with the ECtHR

The CJEU has made use of ECtHR case law in a limited number of the cases reviewed, yet with important jurisprudential results. The CJEU has mostly drawn on ECtHR rulings to give flesh to the rights enshrined in the CFR, clarify legitimate limitations on their exercise, guide assessment of whether these limitations can be justified and assist in balancing distinct rights and freedoms.

In *Buivids*, for instance, the CJEU resorted to ECtHR case law to support the referring court in its balancing of the right to freedom of expression and the right to privacy when applying Article 9 of the Data Protection Directive. Having affirmed that the exemptions and derogations set forth in Article 9 of the directive to facilitate journalism should apply so long as they were necessary[143] – an issue for the national court to examine – the CJEU drew attention to Article 52(3) CFR,[144] according to which the CFR rights which correspond to ECHR rights shall have the same meaning and scope as the latter, although the EU may opt to grant more extensive protection. Holding that Articles 7 and 11 CFR respectively enshrine rights corresponding to those guaranteed in Article 8 ECHR on the right to respect for private life and Article 10 ECHR on freedom of expression,[145] the CJEU pointed to a number of criteria developed by the ECtHR for national courts to consider: "contribution to a debate of public interest; the degree of notoriety of the person affected; the subject of the news report; the prior conduct of the person concerned; the content, form and consequences of the publication; and the manner and circumstances in which the information was obtained and its veracity".[146]

In *Poland v Parliament and Council*, reliance on ECtHR jurisprudence, again with mention of Article 52(3) CFR,[147] contributed to clarifying the scope of protection in Article 11 CFR and the nature of limitations on the exercise of freedom of expression and information. The CJEU built on ECtHR case law to exemplify the point that "sharing of information on the internet via online content-sharing platforms" falls within the scope of freedom of expression.[148] The CJEU referred, in particular, to ECtHR case law, according to which freedom of expression and information applies not only to the content of information but also to the means of dissemination.[149] The CJEU also recalled ECtHR case law recognising that the internet constitutes "one of the principal means by which individuals exercise their right to freedom of expression and information",[150] highlighting that, for the ECtHR, "in light of their accessibility and capacity to store and communicate vast amounts of information", internet sites, especially online content-sharing platforms, "play an important role in enhancing the public's access to news and facilitating the dissemination of information".[151] The fact that "user-generated expressive activity on the internet provid[es] an unprecedented platform for the exercise of freedom of expression" was also noted.[152] Against this background, the CJEU held that the prior review requirements deriving from Article 17 of the CDSM Directive for OCSSPs in relation to the content that their users wish to upload[153] and the ensuing use of automation and filtering tools[154] were liable to restrict "an important means of disseminating online content".[155] They were therefore a limitation of freedom of expression and information.

The CJEU then examined whether the limitation at issue could be justified. Here, use of ECtHR case law was made to elucidate the way in which limitations on the exercise of fundamental rights should be assessed, particularly regarding legality. Observing that legislation entailing a limitation on the exercise of fundamental rights should lay down "clear and precise rules governing the scope and application of the measure in question" with "minimum safeguards" providing sufficient and effective guarantees against the risk of abuse,[156] the CJEU referred to ECtHR case law to shed light on the legal requirements at issue. Following ECtHR case law, the CJEU stated, prior restraints on a means of dissemination, although not prohibited by Article 10 ECHR per se, posed a risk to compliance with freedom of expression and information and therefore necessitated "a particularly tight legal framework".[157] In *Ahmet Yildirim v Turkey*, the CJEU noted, the ECtHR found a violation of Article 10 ECHR due to a decision of the Turkish courts to block access to the entire Google Sites service as a means to block access to a particular website on Google Sites that was deemed to be offensive, deploring the fact that the applicable legislation did not require the judiciary to examine whether the measure, which severely affected the rights of internet users, was necessary.[158] For the ECtHR, the Turkish legislation did not satisfy the ECHR "foreseeability" requirement; namely, that restrictive laws must be formulated with sufficient precision to enable any individual – if need be, with appropriate advice – to regulate their own conduct. At the same time, the ECtHR also found in cases like *Delfi v Estonia*[159] that the ECHR did not preclude restrictive legislation from being formulated in sufficiently open terms to keep pace with changing circumstances.[160] On the basis of such considerations, the CJEU held that the principle of legality had been ensured: the best effort provisions in Article 17 of the CDSM Directive, while not defining the actual measures for OCSSPs to adopt, had been formulated in a way that allowed adaptation to "the particular circumstances of the various . . . service providers [involved] and also to the development of industry practices and of available technologies".[161]

5. Conclusion

In the past few years, references from national courts to the CJEU for preliminary rulings in social media cases have been on the rise, with the CJEU acquiring a prominent role in relevant disputes. The preceding analysis has shown that social media platforms have triggered reflection on a range of legal issues in EU law. Many of the social media-related cases adjudicated by the CJEU have involved analysis of fundamental rights. The emphasis in these cases has mostly been on interpreting EU secondary legislation, covering social media, in ways that reflect the specificities of online intermediaries while complying with fundamental rights and requirements to balance them and effectively protect them. In cases like *SABAM* and *YouTube and Cyando*, for instance, the CJEU interpreted EU rules on copyright protection and on the prohibition of general monitoring duties imposed on digital intermediaries with a view to striking a balance between the freedom of digital intermediaries to conduct their business, rightholders' right to intellectual property, users' freedom of expression and information and their right to protection of personal data, where applicable. In *YouTube and Cyando*, when determining the scope of the liability exemption set out in the e-Commerce Directive for digital intermediaries and when defining the concept of communication to the public within the meaning of the Copyright Directive, the CJEU openly acknowledged that the interpretations advanced were in line with the balance that EU secondary legislation *itself* sought to achieve between distinct rights and interests. In a similar vein, in *Buivids*, the CJEU restrictively interpreted the exceptions in the Data Protection Directive which rendered the system of protection established inapplicable, with the argument that these exceptions digressed from the fundamental rights standards defined in relevant EU legislation *itself* and should therefore be narrowly interpreted.

Fundamental rights have also contributed to interpretations of EU law increasing the protection offered. In *Buivids*, for example, in the light of the importance of freedom of expression in a democratic society, the journalistic derogation set out in EU data protection legislation was interpreted broadly, irrespective of the medium used and embracing citizen journalism on social media.[162] In other instances, the CJEU's emphasis on effectiveness in the protection of fundamental rights has resulted in enhanced standards. In *Facebook Ireland and Others*, after having underlined that the objective of the GDPR is to ensure effective protection of the right to protection of personal data, the CJEU expanded its applicability by broadly interpreting one of the criteria for the territorial scope of the GDPR; namely, that the processing of personal data takes place "in the context of the activities of an establishment of a controller" in the EU. In *Wirtschaftsakademie Schleswig-Holstein* and *Fashion ID*, ensuring effective protection of fundamental rights led to an expansive interpretation of the concept of controller, broadening the applicability of data protection rules to more actors. In *Meta Platforms Ireland*, fundamental rights assisted in an interpretation of the GDPR enabling national legislation on personal data protection-related representative actions based on claims in legal areas other than data protection to persist. The CJEU ruled out a restrictive interpretation of Article 80(2) of the GDPR as linking permissible representative actions to a specific infringement of data protection rights, taking the view that this would undermine the effective protection of the right to protection of personal data.

In some cases, the CJEU has not engaged with fundamental rights. This lack of engagement has been striking in certain instances. In *Glawischnig-Piesczek*, for example, the CJEU relaxed the prohibition of general monitoring requirements contained in Article 15 of the e-Commerce Directive and linked this evolutionary interpretation of Article 15 to the uptake of automated filtering mechanisms by digital intermediaries.[163] However, the CJEU did not discuss automation from a fundamental rights perspective despite its undisputed fundamental rights implications. In other instances, CJEU reasoning has been genuinely based on fundamental rights. In *Poland v Parliament and Council*, the CJEU upheld the specific liability regime of the CDSM Directive for OCSSPs by carrying out a thorough assessment of the free speech safeguards built into it. Of course, the attention given to fundamental rights in this ruling is inextricably linked to the fact that Poland sought annulment of the relevant provisions precisely on free speech grounds.

When engaging with fundamental rights, the CJEU has occasionally drawn on ECtHR case law. In *Buivids*, for instance, ECtHR case law was used to support the referring court in balancing the fundamental rights at stake, with attention channelled to ECtHR criteria developed for this purpose. In *Poland v Parliament and Council*, ECtHR case law helped clarify the scope of the protection afforded to freedom of expression and information, what may constitute a limitation to its exercise and the considerations to take into account when assessing whether a limitation can be justified, particularly regarding compliance with the principle of legality. Clearly, CJEU case law on social media does not develop in a vacuum.

The analysis has also made it clear that CJEU case law on social media is naturally fact-specific. CJEU adjudication takes place on a case-by-case basis, which inevitably suggests a disjointed approach to the legal challenges raised by social media. In fact, in the cases to date, discerning definite answers in the CJEU's reasoning regarding the fundamental rights implications of social media is not easy or straightforward. Many tensions remain to be resolved. *Poland v Parliament and Council* is telling in this respect. The CJEU's assessment of the specific liability regime for OCSSPs regarding compliance with fundamental rights came with a caveat: the evaluation carried out should not prejudge any subsequent examination in relation to Member States' measures to transpose the CDSM Directive or OCSSPs' measures to comply with it. Online platform regulation is a legal area that is still developing,[164] and therefore, more references for preliminary rulings are expected to reach the CJEU. Clearer answers will also be required. Cases like *Glawischnig-Piesczek* reopen important questions for social networks (for instance, what general monitoring is) that the CJEU will eventually have to address.

Notes

1 See, for instance, Rebecca MacKinnon, Elonnai Hickok, Allon Bar and Hae-in Lim, *Fostering Freedom Online: The Role of Internet Intermediaries* (United Nations Educational, Scientific and Cultural Organization 2014); Rikke Frank Jørgensen (ed), *Human Rights in the Age of Platforms* (The MIT Press 2019); Giovanni de Gregorio, *Digital Constitutionalism in Europe. Reframing Rights and Powers in the Algorithmic Society* (Cambridge University Press 2022). See also Council of Europe, Recommendation CM/Rec(2012)4 of the Committee of Ministers to member states on the protection of human rights with regard to social networking services (4 April 2012); Recommendation CM/Rec(2018)2 of the Committee of Ministers to member states on the roles and responsibilities of internet intermediaries (7 March 2018); United Nations, Report of the Special Rapporteur David Kaye on the promotion and protection of the right to freedom of opinion and expression, A/HRC/38/35, 6 April 2018 <https://freedex.org/wp-content/blogs.dir/2015/files/2018/05/G1809672.pdf> accessed 17/5/2022.

2 On this, see Art 52(3) CFR, which reads: "In so far as this Charter contains rights which correspond to rights guaranteed by the Convention for the Protection of

Human Rights and Fundamental Freedoms, the meaning and scope of those rights shall be the same as those laid down by the said Convention. This provision shall not prevent Union law providing more extensive protection". For details, see Steve Peers and Sacha Prechal, 'Article 52', in Steve Peers, Tamara Hervey, Jeff Kenner and Angela Ward (eds), *The EU Charter of Fundamental Rights: A Commentary* (Hart Publishing 2021) 1611.

3 Directive 2000/31/EC of the European Parliament and of the Council of 8 June 2000 on certain legal aspects of information society services – in particular, electronic commerce, in the Internal Market ('Directive on electronic commerce') [2000] OJ L 178/1. For details, see Giancarlo Frosio (ed), *Oxford Handbook of Online Intermediary Liability* (OUP 2020).

4 See Regulation (EU) 2022/2065 of the European Parliament and of the Council of 19 October 2022 on a Single Market For Digital Services and amending Directive 2000/31/EC (Digital Services Act) [2022] OJ L 277/1.

5 See Giovanni Sartor, *Providers Liability: From the eCommerce Directive to the Future, In-Depth Analysis for the IMCO Committee* (European Parliament 2017) <www.europarl.europa.eu/RegData/etudes/IDAN/2017/614179/IPOL_IDA(2017)614179_EN.pdf> accessed 17/5/2022.

6 See recital 42 of the e-Commerce Directive. In *L'Oréal and others* (Case C-324/09 [2011] ECLI:EU:C:2011:474), the CJEU held that an operator is liable where it "plays an active role of such a kind as to give it knowledge of, or control" over the hosted content (see paras 113 and 116).

7 See Art 14(3) and recital 45 of the e-Commerce Directive.

8 Articles 13, 14 and 15 of the e-Commerce Directive correspond to Articles 5, 6 and 8 of the Digital Services Act.

9 See Case C-70/10 *Scarlet Extended* [2011] ECLI:EU:C:2011:771, para 52 and Case C-360/10 *SABAM* [2012] ECLI:EU:C:2012:85, para 50.

10 See *SABAM* (n 8), paras 38 and 40–41.

11 Ibid, paras 48 and 51.

12 Ibid, para 46.

13 Ibid, paras 48–49.

14 Case C-314/12 *UPC Telekabel Wien* [2014] ECLI:EU:C:2014:192.

15 Ibid, paras 48–50.

16 Ibid, para 52.

17 Ibid, paras 53–54.

18 Ibid, para 55.

19 Ibid, para 56.

20 Ibid, para 62.

21 Ibid. The CJEU noted that putting a complete end to intellectual property infringements may not be feasible due to the lack of adequate means or circumvention of protective measures taken (see para 60).

22 Joined Cases C-682/18 and C-683/18 *YouTube and Cyando* [2021] ECLI:EU:C:2021:503.

23 Ibid, paras 129 and 137.

24 Directive 2001/29/EC of the European Parliament and of the Council of 22 May 2001 on the harmonisation of certain aspects of copyright and related rights in the information society [2001] OJ L 167/10.

25 *YouTube and Cyando* (n 21), para 136.

26 Ibid, para 137.

27 Ibid, para 129.

28 Ibid, paras 138–139.

29 Ibid, para 141.

30 João Pedro Quintais and Christina Angelopoulos, 'YouTube and Cyando Joined Cases C-682/18 and C-683/18 (22 June 2021) ECLI:EU:C:2021 (Case Comment)' (2022) 1(1) *Auteursrecht* 46.
31 *YouTube and Cyando* (n 21), para 118.
32 See Art 14(1)(a) of the e-Commerce Directive.
33 *YouTube and Cyando* (n 21), para 113, referring to recitals 41 and 46 of the e-Commerce directive.
34 Ibid.
35 Ibid.
36 Directive (EU) 2019/790 of the European Parliament and of the Council of 17 April 2019 on copyright and related rights in the Digital Single Market and amending Directives 96/9/EC and 2001/29/EC [2019] OJ L 130/92.
37 An OCSSP, as defined in Art 2(6) of the CDSM Directive, is a provider of "an information society service of which the main or one of the main purposes is to store and give the public access to a large amount of copyright-protected works or other protected subject-matter uploaded by its users, which it organises and promotes for profit-making purposes". Certain operators (i.e. not-for-profit online encyclopaedias and educational and scientific repositories, open source software-developing and sharing platforms, providers of electronic communications services, online marketplaces, business-to-business cloud services and cloud services that allow users to upload content for their own use) do not come within the scope of this definition.
38 See Art 3 of the Copyright Directive.
39 See Art 17(1) of the CDSM Directive.
40 Ibid, Art. 17(4).
41 This mirrors the obligation incumbent on operators in accordance with Article 14(1) of the e-Commerce Directive and now Article 6(1) of the Digital Services Act. According to Article 17(3) of the CDSM Directive, the limitation of liability established in Article 14(1) of the e-Commerce Directive is inapplicable in this context. This should henceforth be construed as a reference to Article 6(1) of the Digital Services Act.
42 The CDSM Directive qualifies the liability scheme introduced for certain operators in line with the principle of proportionality. See Art 17(6) of the CDSM Directive.
43 Case C-401/19 *Poland v Parliament and Council* [2022] ECLI:EU:C:2022:297.
44 Ibid, paras 24 and 39–40.
45 Ibid, para 41.
46 Ibid, para 53.
47 The CJEU referred to the number of files uploaded, the type of protected subject matter and Article 17(5) of the CDSM Directive, which determines the elements to take into account when examining compliance with service providers' obligations in accordance with the principle of proportionality (e.g. the type, the audience and the size of the service, the type of works or other subject matter uploaded by the users of the service, the availability of suitable and effective means and their cost for service providers).
48 *Poland v Parliament and Council* (n 42), para 54.
49 Pursuant to Article 52(1) CFR, a limitation must be provided by law, respect the essence of the rights and freedoms involved and subject to the principle of proportionality, be necessary and genuinely meet objectives of general interest recognised by the Union or the need to protect the rights and freedoms of others.
50 João Pedro Quintais, 'Article 17 Survives, But Freedom of Expression Safeguards Are Key: C-401/19 – Poland v Parliament and Council' <http://copyrightblog.kluweriplaw.com/2022/04/26/article-17-survives-but-freedom-of-expression-safeguards-are-key-c-401–19-poland-v-parliament-and-council/> accessed 17 May 2022.

51 *Poland v Parliament and Council* (n 42), paras 72–73.
52 Ibid, para 77.
53 Ibid, paras 77–78.
54 Ibid, para 79.
55 Ibid, paras 82–83. The CJEU noted that combining requirements for best efforts to obtain an authorisation with requirements to act expeditiously, on receiving a sufficiently substantiated notice, to disable access to or remove the notified content, as suggested by Poland, would be a less restrictive measure but not as effective for protecting intellectual property rights.
56 Ibid, para 85.
57 Ibid, para 87. The CJEU also noted that, pursuant to the CDSM Directive, OCSSPs are required to inform users, in their terms and conditions, that use of protected content under copyright exceptions provided for by EU law is allowed. See Ibid, para 88.
58 Ibid, para 89.
59 Ibid, para 90.
60 Ibid.
61 Ibid, para 93.
62 Ibid, para 94.
63 Ibid, para 95.
64 Ibid, paras 96–97.
65 *YouTube and Cyando* (n 21), paras 64–65. On the fundamental rights-based approach followed by the CJEU in its interpretation of Art 3(1) of the Copyright Directive, see Felix Reda and Joschka Selinger, 'YouTube/Cyando – An Important Ruling for Platform Liability – Part 1' <http://copyrightblog.kluweriplaw.com/2021/07/01/youtube-cyando-an-important-ruling-for-platform-liability-part-1/> accessed 17 May 2022.
66 Ibid, para 65.
67 On these, see Pedro Quintais and Angelopoulos (n 29).
68 *YouTube and Cyando* (n 21), para 68. See also para 82 and *Stichting Brein* (Case C-610/15 [2017] ECLI:EU:C:2017:456), a case focusing on whether making available and managing an online sharing platform enabling users, by means of metadata indexation and a search engine, to locate and share copyright protected content via a peer-to-peer network came within the scope of the concept of "communication to the public" under Article 3(1) of the Copyright Directive.
69 *YouTube and Cyando* (n 21), para 77.
70 Ibid, paras 84–85.
71 Ibid, paras 71–72 and 75–76.
72 Case C-345/17 *Buivids* [2019] ECLI:EU:C:2019:122.
73 Directive 95/46/EC of the European Parliament and of the Council of 24 October 1995 on the protection of individuals with regard to the processing of personal data and on the free movement of such data [1995] OJ L 281/31.
74 Regulation (EU) 2016/679 of the European Parliament and of the Council of 27 April 2016 on the protection of natural persons with regard to the processing of personal data and on the free movement of such data, and repealing Directive 95/46/EC (General Data Protection Regulation, GDPR) [2016] OJ L 119/1.
75 *Buivids* (n 71), paras 35 and 39.
76 See Art 3(2) of the Data Protection Directive.
77 *Buivids* (n 71), para 43.
78 See Art 9 of the Data Protection Directive.
79 This is now to be found in a similar provision in the GDPR: Art 85.
80 *Buivids* (n 71), paras 52 and 55.
81 Ibid, paras 51 and 53.

82 Ibid, para 53.
83 Ibid, para 59.
84 Ibid, paras 58–60.
85 Ibid, paras 63 and 68.
86 Case C-362/14 [2015] *Schrems* ECLI:EU:C:2015:650 (*Schrems I*).
87 Case C-311/18 *Facebook Ireland and Schrems* [2020] ECLI:EU:C:2020:559 (*Schrems II*).
88 Case C-645/19 *Facebook Ireland and Others* [2021] ECLI:EU:C:2021:483.
89 Lorna Woods, 'Who Has Jurisdiction Over Facebook Ireland? The CJEU Rules on the GDPR 'One Stop Shop' <https://infolawcentre.blogs.sas.ac.uk/2021/07/13/who-has-jurisdiction-over-facebook-ireland-the-cjeu-rules-on-the-gdpr-one-stop-shop/> accessed 17 May 2022.
90 *Facebook Ireland and Others* (n 87), para 91.
91 Ibid, para 93.
92 Ibid, para 86.
93 Ibid, para 93.
94 Case C-210/16 *Wirtschaftsakademie Schleswig-Holstein* [2018] ECLI:EU:C:2018:388.
95 Ibid, para 26.
96 Ibid, para 27.
97 Ibid, para 28.
98 Ibid, para 29.
99 Ibid, para 30.
100 Ibid, para 35.
101 Ibid, para 36. Wirtschaftsakademie could request audience statistics on matters such as visitors' age, sex, relationship and occupation, their lifestyle, online purchasing habits, etc. Ibid, para 38.
102 René Mahieu, Joris van Hoboken and Hadi Asghari, 'Responsibility for Data Protection in a Networked World: On the Question of the Controller, "Effective and Complete Protection" and its Application to Data Access Rights in Europe' (2019) 10(1) *JIPITEC* 85.
103 Case C-40/17 *Fashion ID* [2019] ECLI:EU:C:2019:629.
104 Ibid, para 67.
105 Ibid, para 65.
106 Ibid, para 66.
107 Ibid, paras 74 and 85.
108 Ibid, para 70.
109 Ibid, paras 69 and 82.
110 Ibid, para 63.
111 Ibid, para 50.
112 Ibid, para 51.
113 Case C-319/20 *Meta Platforms Ireland* [2022] ECLI:EU:C:2022:322.
114 Ibid, para 73.
115 Directive 2009/22/EC of the European Parliament and of the Council of 23 April 2009 on injunctions for the protection of consumers' interests [2009] OJ L 110/30.
116 *Meta Platforms Ireland* (n 112), para 61.
117 Ibid, para 77.
118 Ibid, para 72.
119 Ibid, para 73.
120 Ibid.
121 Ibid, para 78.
122 Ibid, para 74.

123 Case C-498/16 *Schrems* [2018] ECLI:EU:C:2018:37.
124 Council Regulation (EC) No 44/2001 of 22 December 2000 on jurisdiction and the recognition and enforcement of judgments in civil and commercial matters [2001] OJ L 12/1.
125 *Schrems* (n 122), para 30.
126 C-194/16 *Bolagsupplysningen and Ilsjan* [2017] ECLI:EU:C:2017:766.
127 Regulation (EU) No 1215/2012 of the European Parliament and of the Council of 12 December 2012 on jurisdiction and the recognition and enforcement of judgments in civil and commercial matters [2012] OJ L 351/1.
128 Joined Cases C-509/09 and C-161/10 *eDate Advertising and Others* [2011] ECLI:EU:C:2011:685.
129 *Bolagsupplysningen and Ilsjan* (n 125), para 38.
130 Ibid, para 41.
131 Ibid, para 48. These can be the courts of the publisher's Member State of establishment or the courts of the Member State where the centre of interests of the person concerned are based.
132 See indicatively recitals 1, 3 and 38 of Regulation 1215/2012.
133 See inter alia Art 169(1) TFEU.
134 C-18/18 *Glawischnig-Piesczek* [2019] ECLI:EU:C:2019:821.
135 On this, see Daphne Keller, 'Facebook Filters, Fundamental Rights, and the CJEU's *Glawischnig-Piesczek* Ruling' (2020) 69(6) *GRUR International* 616; Aleksandra Kuczerawy and Clara Rauchegger, 'Injunctions to Remove Illegal Online Content under the eCommerce Directive: Glawischnig-Piesczek' (2020) 57(5) *CMLR* 1495; and Valentina Golunova, 'In Tech We Trust? Fixing the Evolutionary Interpretation by the Court of Justice of the Prohibition of General Monitoring in the Era of Automated Content Moderation', in Evangelia Psychogiopoulou and Susana de la Sierra (eds), *Digital Media Governance and Supranational Courts: Selected Issues and Insights from the European Judiciary* (Edward Elgar Publishing 2022) 53.
136 See recital 47 of the e-Commerce Directive.
137 *Glawischnig-Piesczek* (n 133), paras 34–35.
138 Ibid, paras 45–47.
139 See *L'Oréal and Others* (n 6), para 139. See also *Scarlet Extended* (n 8), para 36.
140 *YouTube and Cyando* (n 21), paras 136–137.
141 *Glawischnig-Piesczek* (n 133), para 45.
142 See Committee of Experts on Internet Intermediaries, *Algorithms and Human Rights. Study on the Human Rights Dimensions of Automated Data Processing Techniques and Possible Regulatory Implications* (Council of Europe 2017); Robert Gorwa, Reuben Binns and Christian Katzenbach, 'Algorithmic Content Moderation: Technical and Political Challenges in the Automation of Platform Governance' (2020) 7(1) *Big Data & Society* 1; Emma Llansó, Joris van Hoboken, Paddy Leerssen and Jaron Harambam, *Artificial Intelligence, Content Moderation, and Freedom of Expression* (Transatlantic Working Group 2020) <www.ivir.nl/publicaties/download/AI-Llanso-Van-Hoboken-Feb-2020.pdf> accessed 17 May 2022; and Paul Keller, 'Article 17 Stakeholder Dialogue: What We Have Learned so Far – Part 1' <http://copyrightblog.kluweriplaw.com/2020/01/13/article-17-stakeholder-dialogue-what-we-have-learned-so-far-part-1/> accessed 17 May 2022.
143 See *Buivids* (n 71), para 63.
144 Ibid, para 65.
145 Ibid.
146 Ibid, para 66. The CJEU referred specifically to the ECtHR ruling in *Satakunnan Markkinapörssi Oy and Satamedia Oy v Finland* App No 931/13 (27 June 2017).
147 *Poland v Parliament and Council* (n 42), para 44.

148 Ibid, para 45.
149 Ibid, para 46.
150 Ibid.
151 Ibid. The CJEU referred to the ECtHR rulings in *Cengiz and Others v Turkey* App Nos 48226/10; 14027/11 (1 December 2015) and *Vladimir Kharitonov v Russia* App No 10795/14 (23 June 2020).
152 *Poland v Parliament and Council* (n 42), para 46.
153 Ibid, para 53.
154 Ibid, para 54.
155 Ibid, para 55.
156 Ibid, para 67.
157 Ibid, para 68.
158 Ibid, paras 66–67.
159 *Delfi v Estonia* App. No. 64569/09 (ECtHR, 16 June 2015), para 121.
160 *Poland v Parliament and Council* (n 42), para 74.
161 Ibid, para 73.
162 Dirk Voorhoof, 'Court of Justice of the European Union: *Sergejs Buivids v. Datu Valsts Inspekcija*' (2019) 4(1) *IRIS* 4.
163 On this see Golunova (n 134).
164 For details, see Chapter 1 in this volume by Evangelia Psychogiopoulou and Federica Casarosa.

3 Social media jurisprudence

The European Court of Human Rights

Lorna Woods

1. Introduction

The European Court of Human Rights (ECtHR) has recognised the impact of the Internet as a communication and information tool. Of the many types of service available, social media has become the prevalent – perhaps dominant – form of service, allowing users easily to contribute, share and re-share content, as well as to receive information.[1] The ability for private individuals to engage with disparate audiences means that the Internet, but specifically social media, is potentially uniquely democratic, allowing a platform for alternative and dissenting views. Yet, problems are evident, including: child abuse; hate speech; dis/misinformation.[2] Social media platforms are an important venue for the exercise of rights but also have the potential to undermine democracy, equality and human rights. Consequently, government intervention is increasing, with impacts on human rights too.

While fundamental rights should apply no matter the communications technologies used, the respective affordances of different technologies may give rise to distinct issues. Although social media shares some of the key attributes of the Internet that distinguish it from offline communications systems – scale, reach, speed – differences exist. While the Internet and its management are decentralised,[3] mainstream social media currently provides a locus of activity, hosting content, as well as being an organising entity[4] of content provider by its users. Whether centralised or not, choices about control and organisation have an impact on the content (e.g. its existence and visibility) on the site, influencing users' expression rights, impacting their privacy and constraining their autonomy,[5] and potentially constitute a form of expression in itself. Indeed, there are wider questions about the nature of speech and who is a speaker in digital environments. Nonetheless, the relationship between platforms' or instances' choices about control and organisation and the extent of their consequent awareness of and responsibility for different types of content is, however, one of the key issues in this field. Personalisation – one of the main tools deployed by platforms in selecting content for users' attention – has raised questions about the impact of "surveillance capitalism"[6]

DOI: 10.4324/9781003207085-4

on a marketplace of ideas, as well as the privatisation of control over speech (whether in furtherance of a government agenda or not[7]).

Against this background, this chapter explores the extent to which the principles developed offline by the ECtHR in relation to rights offline may be straightforwardly applied online and highlights issues that are particularly relevant to social media. In considering the jurisprudence, the chapter identifies two broad groups of issues: those dealing with the position of social media platforms and the digital environment itself; and those pertaining to the content on those platforms – notably, hate speech and disinformation. It also notes the extent to which these developments take place within a closed system of ECHR case law and the extent to which developments in other arenas are taken into account.

2. Applicability of Article 10 ECHR to social media

The ECtHR has seen social media through the framework of Article 10 of the European Convention on Human Rights (ECHR).[8] This is unsurprising. It has historically taken a technology-neutral approach to the material scope of the right and has accepted that other types of online service (e.g. peer-to-peer networks[9]) are protected by Article 10 ECHR.[10] Freedom of expression famously protects the offensive, shocking and disturbing in the interests of tolerance and pluralism.[11] Moreover, the Internet is an "unprecedented platform for the exercise of freedom of expression".[12] Article 10 ECHR – whether online or off – is not unlimited,[13] but any interference must be justified in accordance with Article 10(2) ECHR: the restriction should be lawful, for a legitimate purpose (as identified in Article 10(2) ECHR, or the last sentence of Article 10(1) ECHR) and necessary in a democratic society. The nature of any penalties imposed on speech is a significant factor in the finding of or lack of proportionality, and the ECtHR is sensitive to concerns around censorship, as we shall see later. The extent to which the national authorities have considered the impact on fundamental rights will also be a factor; a national rule that is, in principle, unproblematic can still constitute an interference with rights, if badly applied.[14]

The ECtHR has taken a wide view of when expression is involved (including naked hiking[15] or the wearing of symbols[16]), suggesting that communicative shortcuts – e.g. emojis, likes, up/down-votes – should all be protected. In *Melike*, clicking the like button was held to show approval of the content liked and, as such, was a form of exercising freedom of expression online.[17] Uploading material or sharing it – even without comment – also constitutes expression.[18] Interference with the means of dissemination, as well as with the speech itself, constitutes an interference.[19] As a corollary, there has been a broad scope given to the meaning of "victim", including corporate bodies.

One question that is connected to speech on social media is how we treat "bots"[20] or automated speech. If the ECtHR has accepted that rights are not limited to human beings, how do we distinguish between, on the one hand, companies and, on the other, bots and other automated techniques?[21] To suggest that legal personality is key merely rephrases the original question. Historically, software may have been seen as a form of expression, linked to a human's creativity. What, however, if the bot's actions are not under human direction – as in the case of a machine learning chatbot?[22] For the time being, it may be unnecessary to address this question, and we can treat the bot as a tool used for communication and assume that the rights at issue are those of the person deploying the bot. This is similar to the treatment of an app for sharing a photo of a voting slip – though there, the right was that of the provider of the app, not the user.[23]

3. Obligations on non-state actors

The ECHR addresses interference arising from the actions of state parties.[24] Most social media platforms are operated by private actors, however. The actions of a private actor can be imputed to the state, though there is no clear line of jurisprudence identifying when the state exerts sufficient control over a private actor for this imputation to be made. This point is important, given the reliance on so-called voluntary or self-regulatory measures to fulfil policy goals. It seems self-evident that, when a state requires the platforms do something (e.g. use a particular technology) or delegates specific responsibility to a private actor, state responsibility would be engaged.[25] Beyond this, the reasoning of the ECtHR in *Tierfabriken* is instructive – at least in relation to content moderation decisions. The case concerned the decision, by a private company, not to broadcast an advertisement, basing its decision on the state prohibition of political advertising. The ECtHR held that "[d]omestic law . . . therefore made lawful the treatment of which the applicant complained".[26] This suggests that any of the platform's choices that reflect domestic legal provisions have an impact on users' ability to say what they want and would trigger Article 10 ECHR directly.[27] This case also suggests that the model of using private actors as gatekeepers to further governmental policy, which we see being introduced via regulation of social media, is not novel to the social media context.

Where positive obligations arise,[28] the ECtHR has often assessed restrictions taking into account a "fair balance" between the individual claiming the right and the rights of others and the community, subject to the margin of appreciation enjoyed by the state.[29] Relevant factors are: the expression at stake; its capability to contribute to public debate; the nature and scope of restrictions; the availability of alternative venues; and the weight of countervailing rights of others or the public.[30] How social media platforms would be assessed is uncertain; there is not just one platform and they have different features. Moreover, it is unclear the amount of speech or its nature that is relevant to public debate – or whether it is the space for public debate that is important. Cases identifying the value of the Internet have variously identified all three, but also ascribed those aspects to particular platforms.[31] It may depend on the platform's size, though exact matching of reach would be unlikely to be required to show that there was a viable alternative platform. The arguments are different if a user seeks particular types of information – provided that information is not obtainable elsewhere.[32] Issues become more complex when a platform claims the benefit of speech rights against its users. For example, should a social media site run by a religious organisation be entitled to prohibit speech contrary to the relevant religion? In the *Pussy Riot* case, the ECtHR accepted that, even in a quasi-public venue, people seeking to access those venues could be expected to follow rules of behaviour there, or face penalties.[33] More generally, newspaper editors do not have to publish reader letters. Since *Autronic*,[34] the ECtHR has held those who are part of the chain of transmission can benefit from freedom of expression. In that instance, the satellite company had chosen which channel to broadcast, exercising at a very blunt level some form of choice over content. The ECtHR has not directly faced the question of whether a company which has no role in the choice of content also can claim Article 10 ECHR rights, independently of those of the speaker. For example, a traditional telephone operator provides the mechanism across which people may communicate, but it exercises no influence over the content. Does the operator "speak" by providing the network, irrespective of any actual use of that network? If a state were to impose conditions on the provision of that network – for example whether encryption technologies are permitted[35] – would that constitute an interference with the rights of the operator? It seems likely that this is the position.[36] There is, however, a tension here with this approach and net neutrality, which requires carriers not to distinguish between items of content transmitted. Of course, while platforms may benefit from Article 10 ECHR, they "are vicariously subject to the 'duties and responsibilities' which authors take on when they disseminate their opinions to the public"[37] and their rights can be limited according to the conditions of Article 10(2) ECHR – requiring action by the state to hold the balance between platform and user.

This brings us to intermediary immunity, introduced to EU Member States by the e-Commerce Directive[38] but now accepted as part of desirable operating conditions for platforms.[39] Does removal of that immunity constitute a violation of Article 10 ECHR; what are a platform's duties and responsibilities? The leading case is *Delfi*,[40] which concerned a news portal and its liability for the comments of its users posted below the news story. Underpinning the case was a dispute as to how Delfi's role should be understood: as publisher of the defamatory content or as an intermediary imparting third-party content. The Grand Chamber accepted that actors who had different roles in the creation and dissemination of content should be subject to differentiated and graduated responsibilities, already set out in a Council of Europe recommendation.[41] Here, the ECtHR distinguished between a "professionally managed" news portal, run on "a commercial basis" and which encouraged its users to respond to the news articles it published (factors which were also relevant to the proportionality analysis) and a social media platform "where the platform provider does not offer any content and where the content provider may be a private person running the website or blog as a hobby",[42] though this description seems not to fit well with the large social media platforms which effectively push content at users through automated systems (e.g. autoplay default on). Central to its finding in this case was that the news portal was not a neutral intermediary (given the level of control over the comments and the fact that comments responded to the portal's own news stories) and that it operated the site for gain. It found there was no fault with the national court's characterisation of the site as a publisher (which could not claim the benefit of immunity under the e-Commerce Directive). The ECtHR also noted that "the impugned comments . . . mainly constituted hate speech and speech that directly advocated acts of violence";[43] there was no dispute as to their illegality.

Delfi has been followed by several cases, but even taking into account the fact-specific nature of the assessment, it seems that there has been a shift in emphasis in the jurisprudence. *MTE*, a chamber judgment, found a violation of Article 10 ECHR in relation to a news portal which had been held liable for users' comments, applying *Delfi*. The facts were different, arguably justifying the different conclusion.[44] As in *Delfi*, the site maintained a notice and take-down regime, but the comments complained of were "devoid of [their] pivotal elements of hate speech and incitement of violence". Moreover, the applicants included a non-profit actor. In *Phil*,[45] concerning positive obligations under Article 8 ECHR, the relevant remarks were found in an anonymous comment to a blog posted by a not-for-profit association; the blog did not moderate comments. The ECtHR identified four factors to assess the appropriate balance between Articles 8 and 10 ECHR, developing from *Delfi*: the context of the comments; the measures the intermediary applied to prevent or remove defamatory comments; the liability of the authors (as opposed to the platform[46]); and – in line with *MTE* – any consequences for the platform. *Phil* seems to narrow the criteria from *Delfi* slightly; nonetheless, these four factors now appear to be the starting point for analysis. The ECtHR found no violation of Article 8 ECHR. Notably, the comments were (comparatively) mild, were not connected with the topic of the article, and they were removed the day after Mr Phil complained with an apology posted.

The starting point in *Delfi* was the graduation of responsibility for different actors. Linked to this is the distinction between publisher and intermediary, or that between knowledge of content and innocent distribution (which also informs the immunity provisions in the e-Commerce Directive).[47] We might question whether this distinction implies that the graduation of responsibility is similarly binary, or whether there is greater nuance in the attribution of responsibility. Given the lack of attention to this question in media cases, in which the position of editor and publisher as speakers was assumed, it is unlikely that that jurisprudence will be particularly helpful in developing a more nuanced model. Another issue is whether there is a distinction between active and passive intermediaries in terms of what is expected of them. While the ECtHR has emphasised the value of the Internet itself as a forum for discussion, suggesting that there should be no distinction, it has tended to do so in the context of sites operated by media organisations.[48] Might there be a distinction between such sites and at least some social media platforms? In the subsequent *Magyar Jeti*, which concerned liability for a hyperlink, the ECtHR noted that:

> [a]lthough Internet news portals are not publishers of third-party comments in the traditional sense, they can assume responsibility under certain circumstances for user-generated content.[49]

While the question of whether an intermediary is active or neutral might depend to some extent on the control and organisation functions of the platform,[50] including its moderation practices (as recognised in *Delfi*), both *Delfi* and *MTE* had an agenda-setting role for the user comments. This agenda-setting function might distinguish these sorts of platforms from other intermediaries. This is important: linking moderation and take-down regimes to an increased likelihood of being categorised as a publisher could disincentivise platforms from providing these safeguards. Support for this interpretation might be found in *Høiness*,[51] which concerned the posting by anonymous users of gossip on a newspaper-operated forum (rather than a comments section after an article). The action was brought by the subject of the comment under Article 8 ECHR because national law had not provided a remedy; the ECtHR found no violation. Although the site was run by a professional news organisation, the ECtHR recognised that the debate forums were not particularly integrated in the presentation of news and thus could not be taken to be a continuation of the editorial articles.[52] Arguably, this case then did not concern an "active" intermediary. However, *Høiness* is not clear-cut; the content in issue was not hate speech and this could also have influenced the ECtHR's reasoning.

Despite the boundary between active and passive, the nature of the content is increasingly a key consideration. In *MTE*, concerning defamation, the ECtHR contrasted the comments there with the "clearly unlawful" nature of the speech in *Delfi*. In *Høiness* and in *Phil*, the ECtHR noted that the comments did not constitute hate speech, suggesting not only that content remains important but that, in this, the ECtHR is taking a binary approach to the classification of content (hate speech versus everything else). It suggests that platforms will be required to do more (or do it faster) when hate speech is in issue than other claims. On one level, this seems proportionate: speech bad enough to be criminalised is likely worse than those triggering other cases and therefore justifies a requirement of greater action by a platform. It is uncertain, however, whether the approach to hate speech applies to all criminal content. Further, should all civil actions automatically be treated at the same lower level of intensity by the ECtHR? Moreover, the focus on content is unfortunate from the perspective of platforms. They cannot predict what sorts of content will be posted by third parties and so would need to prepare for hateful speech, which might lead to concerns about general monitoring with its implications for privacy, as well as concerns about the chilling effect.[53] Indeed, the ECtHR itself recognised this problem in *Phil.*[54] Surely, questions about the appropriate response should come after a determination of the level of responsibility a platform has.

It is unclear the extent to which the ECtHR envisages the same standards applying to all types and sizes of platforms, despite the distinction it made in *Delfi*. It has recognised that the chilling effect of potential liability for third-party content in comments sections could be particularly problematic for a non-commercial website.[55] Any service making money out of hosting would seem to be open to higher standards than other platforms. The focus on commercial motivation is different from the approach taken in relation to journalism (itself usually profit-motivated) where the emphasis is on the societal function of journalism. Moreover, the extent to which platform size plays a role in that assessment is uncertain; is the importance of size to do with the resources of platform or the size of the likely audience?

In *Sanchez*,[56] a politician did not delete unlawful third-party comments on the public wall of his Facebook account over six weeks and was convicted of incitement to hatred. This might have been an opportunity for the ECtHR to take a more graduated approach to liability. While the ECtHR noted that there was a shared responsibility between the social media platform and the user, Sanchez's choice to make his account public entailed obligations.[57] It also distinguished between the situation where liability arose directly from Sanchez's own expression and when it arose from his failure to act, implying that it would be easier to justify an interference in the latter over the former.[58] Dissenting Judge Mouru-Vikström highlighted that the ECtHR here had taken a different approach from *Delfi*, in which the Grand Chamber distinguished between large and professional sites and social media and sites administered by individuals as a hobby, but not explained why. This case has now been referred to the Grand Chamber. Questions about shared responsibility may also be difficult in decentralised systems, where content from one instance flows across to others in the system.

A further difficult issue relates to whether it is reasonable for a victim to sue the platform or the person posting the problematic content,[59] and anonymity is a factor in this. While the ECtHR weights this as just one factor, the underlying assumption is that it is harder for a user to challenge anonymous comments than when the speaker is identified. This suggests that, where platforms allow anonymity, they put themselves (more) in line for litigation, though they will not always lose.[60] In *KU*, national rules forbad the disclosure of user details by the communications provider so as to support freedom of expression and the right to anonymous expression. This meant that the perpetrator of a criminal offence could not be prosecuted. Even though damages could be obtained from the Internet service provider, according to the ECtHR, the state had failed in its positive obligations under Article 8 ECHR.[61] *KU*, however, concerned an extreme case. An unknown author placed an advert on an Internet dating site in the name of a minor, exposing him to paedophiles and constituted a grave form of interference with an essential aspect of private life.[62] *KU* does not require that states ban anonymity, but identifies cases in which the state cannot require confidentiality. Nonetheless, there are questions about the impact on anonymous speech, especially in relation to journalism.[63]

4. The impact of journalism ethics

The ECtHR has drawn on its approach towards the traditional media as a form of fourth estate,[64] but recognises that the traditional approach to editorial control (where editors control content and take responsibility for it) may need refining, especially where user-generated content[65] is in issue.[66] As noted, the role of editors and even publishers has not been critically analysed, nor their role as gatekeepers as well as speakers much acknowledged. The special position of journalists is subject to the expectation that they operate in good faith and in accordance with the tenets of responsible journalism.[67] Journalists should not be held liable for the comments of others revealed, for example, in interviews. The ECtHR noted this in relation to a news portal in *MTE*,[68] but this has not been applied to platforms more generally.[69] Where (well-known) professional journalists contribute to online discussions, the limits of permissible criticism are broad.[70] The ECtHR has recognised that citizen journalists, including bloggers, can fulfil the public watchdog role;[71] whether this recognition depends on the blogger's acceptance of journalistic of codes of practice or whether it relates to the speaker's actual practice has not yet been determined.[72]

The ECtHR has also recognised that the responsibilities of the journalist may vary depending on the context – that, for example audio-visual media have a much more immediate and powerful effect than the print media.[73] Do social media services that deliver audio-visual content, have a similar such effect? This the ECtHR, albeit in a decade old judgment, rejected:

> "the choices inherent in the use of the Internet and social media mean that the information emerging therefrom does not have the same synchronicity or impact as broadcasted information".[74]

Given the increase in the number of people accessing the news via social media, in live streaming, and the rise of the influencer, this position may change, if it has not already done so. The ECtHR has also suggested that with the increased range and quality of information available to individuals, "monitoring compliance with journalistic ethics takes on added importance".[75] This boundary between ethical journalism and other content is potentially difficult to define, especially when journalists may increasingly be freelance[76] and news reporting crowd-sourced or even automated.

Freedom of expression is important but not more so than any other right. When balancing Article 10 ECHR with the Article 8 rights of the subject of the story in cases involving the media, the ECtHR has developed a list of relevant considerations that reflect the public interest in journalism but has repeatedly emphasised the journalists' responsibilities (and the ethical framework surrounding their work).[77] Nonetheless, states, when faced with competing fundamental rights, will have a wide margin of appreciation.[78] In analysing this balance for speech online, the ECtHR has determined that the risk of harm arising from speech on the Internet is higher than that posed by traditional media,[79] although the ECtHR has not really analysed the mechanics of this impact beyond noting the speed at and extent to which information can spread[80] and the fact that content remains available somewhere on the Internet, seemingly indefinitely.

Social media accounts are, moreover, used by some people as a storage facility. While their own accounts are within their control, this is not so in respect of information on other people's accounts. The so-called right to be forgotten is important in giving some control back to data subjects, but in so doing potentially infringes the free speech rights of the person posting. This tension has not yet been raised before the ECtHR in the context of private individuals, but there is a developing line of cases in relation to legacy media. While the starting point – the factors identified by the ECtHR in *Axel Springer*[81] (noted previously) – may be the same, the emphasis is different, especially in relation to search engines. Building on the reasoning of the CJEU in *Google Spain*,[82] the ECtHR in *ML and WW* argued that, unlike primary publishers, search engine operators' primary interest is not in the publication of the information but in locating information about the subject of a search and building a profile on him/her.[83] Not only does the searchable quality of the Internet sites mean that privacy through obscurity or the elapsing of time is less possible, but the perishable nature of news which influences some of the ECtHR's decisions as regards reporting would no longer be a factor.[84] Two recent cases illustrate the change of emphasis, at least where private individuals (as opposed to public figures) are concerned and confirm that Article 8 ECHR may include a right to be forgotten even when the media as primary publisher are concerned.

In *Hurbain*, the ECtHR found that an order of a domestic court to a newspaper to anonymise on its online archive a 17-year-old story did not constitute an interference with the editor's freedom of expression.[85] The ECtHR underlined the length of time since the publication of the article and that the measures imposed did not require anonymisation of the original print article. It also emphasised, however, that this ruling should not be understood as requiring the media to check their archives in a systematic way and on an ongoing basis. While length of time appears significant in this case, it is not entirely clear how long a period of time would be required to bring this reasoning into play.[86] *Biancardi*,[87] which did not refer to *Hubain*, concerned the fining of a newspaper editor for non-compliance with an order to de-list. The ECtHR, in finding no violation of Article 10 ECHR, again emphasised the fact that the delisting did not imply the erasure of the story.[88] It relied on factors central to *Hurbain*: the period for which the article remained online and the status of the subject of the story as a private individual.[89] The fact that the ECtHR found no violation in *Biancardi*, where the article was kept online for three years after the reported events and the court proceedings were still ongoing, suggests that the period in which journalists' stories retain their newsworthiness sufficient to overturn the Article 8 rights of a private person is short. This finding is in contrast to *ML and WW*, in which the archives were older. The ECtHR characterised *ML and WW* as public figures, however. *Hurbain* has been referred to the Grand Chamber so the question may be revisited. Given that much social media content is likely to be about private actors and concerns information of no great public interest, it would seem likely that the balance would tip more clearly in favour of Article 8 ECHR, though whether this approach would be the same for take-down as well as de-indexing is uncertain. The archive aspect of the media on the Internet does not seem relevant to private persons on social media.

Another issue is the republication of material made publicly available through breach of confidence – this could be a particular problem with regard to social media (e.g. "revenge porn"). The ECtHR has recognised that the publication of such material undermines its confidentiality, but the subject's right is not entirely depleted. In *Ovchinnikov*, the ECtHR held limitations were acceptable "to prevent further airing of the details of an individual's private life which do not come within the scope of any political or public debate on a matter of general importance".[90] The ECtHR has not yet had to consider stay down orders or mechanisms to prevent sharing of content (dynamic blocking[91]), which are now coming before the CJEU.[92] Presumably, the same principles should apply so that, taking the example of revenge porn, the sensitivity of the material, plus the impact on the victim (e.g. not knowing who has seen it in combination with the virality of content on the Internet[93]), the likely manner in which the information was obtained[94] and circumstances of initial disclosure – all of which come from existing jurisprudence – would tip the balance in favour of Article 8 ECHR, provided the other criteria (lawfulness and safeguards against arbitrary exercise of power, and the proportionality of any punishment) were satisfied. With stay-down orders, however, there is a risk of "general monitoring" with implications for the privacy of users. In its jurisprudence on surveillance, however, the ECtHR has stopped short of a total prohibition on mass surveillance.[95] It might be that, when an appropriate case comes before it, the ECtHR would develop a similar distinction to that evolving within the EU; that looking at everything is not permissible (general monitoring); but looking for something in everything is (specific monitoring)?[96]

5. Political speech, hate speech and the impact of social media

Political speech, especially the speech of politicians, is highly protected, whether online or off. It may nonetheless be legitimately restricted under Article 10(2) ECHR; for example, when it constitutes wanton denigration.[97] The ECtHR is concerned to protect public debate, so speech which does not contribute to such debate or follow the rules of debate would not be protected to such a high degree.[98] In *Tierbefrier*, the ECtHR found no violation of Article 10 ECHR in relation to someone penalised for material obtained using covert filming mechanisms and which made assertions of fact that were not backed up by evidence.[99] The ECtHR noted the applicant had "disrespected the 'rules of intellectual battle of ideas' ".[100] An emphasis on the need for speech to contribute to debate might weigh against much speech on some sites, either in terms of the topics discussed or the use of abusive language, pile-ons and the like.

Hate speech, a growing problem on social media, is unlikely to be highly protected by Article 10 ECHR. It may be necessary "to sanction or even prevent all forms of expression which spread, incite, promote or justify hatred based on intolerance",[101] subject to the test of proportionality. Even criminal law measures may be justified and the state enjoys a wider margin of appreciation when violence is threatened.[102] Factors for assessing proportionality include whether the statements were made against a tense political or social background; whether they could be understood as a direct or indirect call for violence or as a justification for violence, hatred or intolerance, especially where they are sweeping attacks on entire ethnic, religious or other groups; the manner in which the statements were made; and their capacity to lead to harmful consequences.[103] Although freedom of expression is of the highest importance, tolerance and respect for the equal dignity of all human beings constitute the foundations of a democratic, pluralistic society. In this, the online case law follows the offline jurisprudence.[104] Diversity of opinion is not entirely content neutral, specifically as regards hate speech, and politicians in particular have obligations in this regard.[105] Moreover, some speech may even fall outside the protection of the ECHR altogether by virtue of Article 17 ECHR.[106] While some commentators[107] have been critical of this case law, any difficulties do not seem specifically related to the characteristics of social media, save to the extent that those platforms give a venue for this sort of speech and contribute to its prevalence.

Most of the cases have concerned circumstances in which the speaker has complained about a penalty imposed for hate speech; what, however, if the state fails to take action against hateful speech? Allowing hate speech to flourish unchecked may silence those in the minority groups on the receiving end.[108] This is also seen in the context of intimidation of or violence towards journalists and, in the online context, particularly women journalists. There is a consistent line of authority concerning states' failure to investigate. In *Ismayilova*, covertly recorded video clips, including video of sexual activity, were uploaded on the Internet. The covert filming in her home, as well as the intimate aspects of Ismayilova's life that were affected, triggered Article 8 ECHR; the failure of the state to investigate constituted a breach of its positive obligations.[109] It was also a violation of the state's positive obligations under Article 10 ECHR.[110] In *Volodina*, the applicant's former boyfriend, as part of a campaign of harassment, shared private photographs on a social network.

Russia was similarly in breach of its obligations here, suggesting that states are under an obligation to take protective measures and to carry out effective investigations – this time under Article 3 ECHR (freedom from torture).[111] This is especially the case where online harassment forms part of a campaign of harassment and violence more generally.

Article 8 ECHR has also been deployed in these contexts to protect the rights of vulnerable groups.[112] The ECtHR has repeatedly held that states may be under an obligation to take action, even in the sphere of the relations of individuals between themselves.[113] Article 8 ECHR is a broad right going beyond privacy and the protection of reputation.[114] The ECtHR has recognised that the state is under an obligation to secure an individual's physical and psychological integrity.[115] Effective deterrence against grave acts involving fundamental values and essential aspects of private life requires efficient criminal law provisions, especially where vulnerable individuals – including children[116] – are concerned. Rape and sexual abuse implicate "essential aspects of private life";[117] this could be applied to online sexual misconduct (e.g. revenge porn). Any national laws introduced to satisfy the state's positive obligations must be adequately enforced. In *Beizaras and Levickas*,[118] the decision by the prosecutor's office not to initiate criminal proceedings against homophobic posts on Facebook, which included calls for violence, constituted a violation of the state's obligations under Article 8 ECHR. Anti-minority demonstrations should be criminalised, affording effective protection against harassment, threats and verbal abuse, including those online.[119] For less serious acts, the state's obligation to maintain and enforce an adequate legal framework could be satisfied by civil remedies or – presumably – a regulatory regime. State obligations have arisen in relation to the verbal harassment of a boy with disabilities[120] and the negative stereotyping of the Roma in state-sponsored schoolbooks.[121] In principle, the failure to take action in relation to school bullying (and, by analogy, cyberbullying) falls within Article 8 ECHR, but there must be some basis on which state authorities should be aware of the risk.[122] More generally, there must be a certain level of seriousness to trigger the application of Article 8 ECHR.[123] Many social media users express themselves in ways that might be regarded as offensive, but such "vulgar abuse" did not reach the threshold[124] in England and Wales to allow service out of the jurisdiction in a defamation claim, meaning the claim failed. This threshold did not constitute a violation of the state's positive obligations.[125] The ECtHR has suggested that the importance of the Internet (and, by implication, social media[126]) will give a state a wide margin of appreciation.[127]

6. Misinformation and disinformation

One distinctive aspect of social media has been the *proliferation*[128] of "fake news": misinformation, disinformation and malinformation.[129] Freedom of expression does not automatically exclude lies and misleading statements from its ambit,[130] and the ECtHR has always emphasised that people cannot be required to prove the truth of an opinion or value judgment.[131] To the contrary, state limitations on such content would need to be carefully considered and comply with the requirements of Article 10(2) ECHR. The jurisprudence of the ECtHR is not, however, indifferent as to whether falsehoods and inaccurate information circulate; reliable information is the basis for criticism and for holding those in power to account.[132] The ECtHR's jurisprudence on the media envisages an orientation towards truth-telling. In *Stoll*, the Grand Chamber emphasised the importance of "an accurate factual basis" to "provide 'reliable and precise' information".[133] Albeit in the specific context of a conflict with Article 8 ECHR, the ECtHR has referred to the obligations in Article 10(2) ECHR to suggest that "no one can be relieved of responsibility for accusations without any factual basis".[134] The extent to which this principle could apply more generally may receive judicial attention. In *Avagyan*,[135] the claimant posted on Instagram saying that there had been no real cases of COVID-19 in her region. She was convicted of spreading untrue information and fined 30,000 roubles. The case has been communicated. It perhaps should be understood against the pandemic which has given rise to "an infodemic",[136] with potentially serious consequences.[137] Minimising the health impacts may be a legitimate aim in itself. Additionally, states may be under positive obligations to protect health[138] or to ensure that relevant information is available, even if there is scientific uncertainty about the precise nature and extent of these risks.[139] This does not, however, necessarily justify criminalising speech.

Specific issues arise from the way many platforms select and promote information (and also people to follow and groups to join): they seem designed to highlight content that elicits strong reactions from users.[140] They do not necessarily promote informed sources. It is also more difficult to rely on the flow of information to counter untruths when information flows are personalised.[141] The Council of Europe has recognised the potential of AI-driven tools (including tools that promote or moderate content) "to identify individual vulnerabilities and exploit accurate predictive knowledge, and to reconfigure social environments in order to meet specific goals and vested interests".[142] Arguably, states could impose content-neutral obligations on platforms (e.g. requiring them to allow users to curate their own feeds or to promote authoritative sources; or controls over how targeted advertising systems are used). The EU Code on Disinformation, which identifies good practice in dealing with disinformation beyond just removal of content, includes such techniques, as does the Digital Services Act in the EU.[143] Insofar as content remains available even if its audience is curtailed, following the logic in *Hurbain* and *Biancardi*, this is a less intrusive measure than take-down, giving some support to the aphorism that freedom of speech does not mean freedom of reach.[144]

While an interference with a user's right to receive inaccurate information could be subjected to a standard analysis under Article 10 ECHR, the question of whether states are under a positive obligation (beyond the specific contexts already noted) to ensure reliable information is much less clear-cut.

This question has not received much attention. The ECtHR seems to envisage a right of the public to be adequately informed,[145] suggesting that the right to receive is not limited to the right to obtain specific pieces of information.[146] Beyond this, it is unclear what the right to be adequately informed looks like. In the context of a Moldovan case on public service broadcasting, the ECtHR reiterated that the state is the ultimate guarantor of pluralism, ensuring access to "impartial and accurate information and a range of opinion and comment".[147] This principle applies whether or not the actors subject to those obligations are private or public actors and, presumably, could extend beyond the broadcasting sector. Certainly, the need "to optimise the quality and reliability of information on the Internet" has been recognised.[148] This, however, is a long way from saying that there is a positive obligation on the states: Moldova already had chosen to provide state broadcasting and the ECtHR's comments operated as a counter to one-sided political reporting. Nonetheless, there remains a recognition of the importance of accuracy, as well as diversity.

7. Proportionality, blocking orders and other responses

State responses to problems must be proportionate. This principle raises distinctive aspects as regards the Internet. A key issue has been that of blocking, particularly when a large social media platform is blocked on the basis of some problematic content. This leads to "collateral censorship"[149] of all other users of the platform. This is not to say that a state can never resort to blocking measures, but that any such order must carefully weigh up all the options available. Any system that allows for blocking orders must provide safeguards against abuse.[150] Orders can be targeted at individual posts. *GRA Stiftung gegen Rassismus und Antisemitismus* concerned a fine and take-down order following a successful defamation action. This, the ECtHR found to be disproportionate, constituting a chilling effect on speech.[151] The implications for take-down orders are uncertain. In its judgment, the ECtHR referred to the earlier case of *Lewandowska-Malec* as authority – a case which makes clear that it was the cumulative effect of a criminal conviction and the aggregation of the penalties that were crucial.[152] It seems unlikely that take down orders would never be permissible; imagine the case of child sexual abuse with the state not permitted to stop the ongoing commission of that crime. It also seems unlikely that take-down orders and fines (or even imprisonment) could never be used in conjunction. That would mean that the state would have to choose between stopping the ongoing commission of the offence or punishing the offender. Again, the point is likely to be fact-sensitive, and it is notable that both *Stiftung gegen Rassismus* and *Lewandowska-Malec* concern defamation actions against public interest actors[153] and are thus cases when Article 10 ECHR concerns are likely to weigh heavily. They may provide little guidance for when serious crimes are in issue. On social media platforms, it may be that there are other options short of take-down of content that can better balance the interests when non-criminal speech is in issue.[154] The UN Special Rapporteur suggested that it:

> may be appropriate to use measures such as downranking, demonetizing, friction, warnings, geoblocking and countermessaging, and the criteria for application of these measures should also be transparently disclosed to allow users to govern their behaviour accordingly and understand when these measures have been applied.[155]

8. Conclusion

This chapter asked whether the existing ECHR jurisprudence could be applied straightforwardly to cases involving social media. In some regards, the answer is “yes”; the ECtHR has relied heavily on its own jurisprudence, rarely engaging with the decisions of other courts. Particularly in cases where the domestic challenge involves the user, long-standing principles about the importance of freedom of speech, concerns around hate speech and the approach to balance with Article 8 ECHR are applied. As with the offline world, the application in a given case will be fact-sensitive, a point that has arisen again and again. In the cases to date, the ECtHR has highlighted two Internet-specific issues: virality (especially when considered Article 8 ECHR) and the democratic potential of the Internet. This latter aspect raises the question of the extent to which those on social media should be treated as akin to journalists, a question for which it seems difficult to identify clear principles for determining the answer. Moreover, there is a linked issue about the extent to which the provision of social media spaces in itself serves a democracy-enhancing function, as a forum for debate and as an archive, given problems around – for example – hate speech and misinformation. Misinformation – an area in which take-down would be unlikely to be proportionate – points to the need to develop new approaches to the management of information that would be more likely to survive an Article 10(2) analysis. If the value of social media is found in the provision of a forum and, to some extent, divorced from the nature of the content carried, the approach to intermediary liability – which, rather than developing a graduated function-based approach to responsibility, seems now to rely heavily on the nature of the content – may need revisiting, especially if decentralised systems become more prevalent. Certainly, the role of platforms (and the impact of the surveillance capitalism model) has not yet been fully analysed and the question of whether social media platforms are themselves speakers, even functioning as editors or publishers, not yet clearly answered. Other issues have not yet been specifically addressed, perhaps the most sensitive of which is the freedom of the platforms to moderate content, though the approaches either to broadcasting regulation or to media editors may still prove useful models at least in part. In this, we might say that the case law surrounding social media intensifies some of the debates already existing around enforcement of rights offline, especially the difficulty of balancing conflicting rights and positive obligations in highly dynamic environments.

Notes

1 *Cengiz and Ors v Turkey* App nos 48226/10 and 14027/11 (ECtHR, 1 December 2015), para 49.
2 Barrie Sander, 'Democratic Disruption in the Age of Social Media: Between Marketized and Structural Conceptions of Human Rights Law' (2021) 32(1) *European Journal of International Law* 159, 164–166.
3 Wolfgang Benedek and Matthias C Ketterman *Freedom of Expression and the Internet* (2nd ed) (Council of Europe 2019) 25. A discussion of the likely impact of Web3 lies outside the scope of this contribution.
4 Increasingly, some users operate across multiple platforms; this does not affect the fact that there are individual platforms which should be considered separately; to a large extent, this may be true of decentralised platforms because the software, which provides the communications framework, constitutes a common theme across instances.
5 Shoshana Zuboff, *The Age of Surveillance Capitalism: The Fight for a Human Future at the New Frontier of Power* (Profile Books 2019) – while there have been some critiques of Zuboff's work the description of the business model remains powerful. See also Jaron Lanier, *Ten Arguments for Deleting Your Social Media Accounts Right Now* (Henry Holt and Co 2018).
6 Zuboff (n 5).
7 Frank Pasquale 'Platform Neutrality: Enhancing Freedom of Expression in Spheres of Private Power' (2016) 17(2) *Theoretical Inquiries in Law* 487–513.
8 *Delfi AS v Estonia* App no 64569/09 (ECtHR, Grand Chamber, 16 June 2015), para 131.
9 *Neij and Sunde Kolmisoppi (The Pirate Bay) v Sweden*, App no 40397/12 (ECtHR, 19 February 2013).
10 Lorna Woods, 'Social Media: It Is Not Just About Article 10', in David Mangan and Lorna E Gillies (eds), *The Legal Challenges of Social Media* (Edward Elgar 2017).
11 E.g. *Handyside v UK*, Series A No. 24, (ECtHR, 7 December 1976); *Fressoz and Roire v France* App no 29183/95 (ECtHR, Grand Chamber, 21 January 1999), para 45; *Perna v Italy* App no 48898/99, (ECtHR 6 May 2003), para 39.
12 *Delfi* (n 8), para 110.
13 Recognised also by the Advocate General in Case C-18/18 *Glawischnig-Piesczek v Facebook Ireland* [2019] ECLI:EU:C:2019:458, para 65; the Court was silent on freedom of expression, [2019] ECLI:EU:C:2019:821.
14 See e.g. *Üçdağ v Turkey* App no 23314/19 (ECtHR, 31 August 2021).
15 *Gough v UK* App no 49327/11 (ECtHR, 28 October 2014).
16 *Vajnai v Hungary* App no 33629/06 (ECtHR, 8 July 2008); *Donaldson v UK* App no. 56975/09 (ECtHR, 25 January 2011).
17 *Melike v Turkey* App no 35786/19 (ECtHR, 15 June 2021).
18 *Kilin v Russia* App no 10271/12 (ECtHR, 11 May 2021).
19 *Autronic AG v Switzerland* Series A no. 178 (ECtHR, 22 May 1990), para 47.
20 A bot – short for robot – is a software program that performs automated, repetitive, pre-defined tasks; these tasks are typically simple and carried out at a much higher rate than human activity. Bots are not limited to text-based, but can include chatbots (and include virtual assistants – e.g. Siri and Cortana). Bots are not necessarily "good" or "bad"; that depends on their function ranging from indexing a search engine to carrying out DdoS attacks. Bots which operate on social media platforms can be used to automatically generate messages, act as a follower of users and to create fake accounts.
21 Some countries' company law could accept autonomous systems as legal persons, but not all: e.g. Shawn Bayern *et al.*, 'Company Law and Autonomous Systems: A Blueprint for Lawyers, Entrepreneurs, and Regulators' (2017) 9 *Hastings Science and Technology Law Journal* 135.

22 E.g. European Parliament Resolution, Recommendations to the Commission on Civil Law Rules on Robotics, 16 February 2017 (A8–0005/2017); Simon Chesterman, 'Artificial Intelligence and the Limits of Legal Personality' (2020) 69 *International and Comparative Law Quarterly* 819; Paulius Cerka *et al.*, 'Is It Possible to Grant Legal Personality to Artificial Intelligence Software Systems?' (2017) 33 *Computer Law and Security Review* 685; cf Migle Laukyte, 'AI as a Legal Person' (2019) *ICAIL '19: Proceedings of the Seventeenth International Conference on Artificial Intelligence and Law* 209.

23 *Magyar Kétfarkú Kutya Párt* v *Hungary* App no 201/17 (ECtHR, Grand Chamber, 20 January 2020).

24 Eg *Norman* v *UK* App no 41387/17 (ECtHR, 6 July 2021), paras 76–77.

25 Eg *Vukota-Bojic v Switzerland* App no. 61838/10 (ECtHR, 18 October 2016) para 47. See discussion: Lorna Woods, *The Carnegie Statutory Duty of Care and Fundamental Freedoms*, December 2019 <https://d1ssu070pg2v9i.cloudfront.net/pex/pex_carnegie2021/2019/12/05125454/The-Carnegie-Statutory-Duty-of-Care-and-Fundamental-Freedoms.pdf> accessed 17 January 2022.

26 *VgT Verein gegen Tierfabriken v Switzerland* App no 24699/94, (ECtHR, 28 June 2001), para 47.

27 Cf reasoning of Advocate General in Case C-401/19 *Poland v Council and Parliament* (CJEU, Opinion, 15 July 2021).

28 See e.g. *Mouvement Raëlien Suisse v Switzerland* App no 16354/06 (ECtHR, Grand Chamber, 13 July 2012), para 62; *Tierfabriken* (n 26), para 46; see also Judge Pinto de Albuquerque's dissenting opinion in *Barbalescu* v *Romania* App no 61496/08 (ECtHR, 12 January 2016) para 23.

29 *Appleby v UK* App no 44306/98 (ECtHR, 6 May 2003); *Iltalehti and Karhuvaara v Finland* App no 6372/06 (ECtHR, 6 April 2010) para 42.

30 *Appleby* (n 29), paras 42–43 and 47–49.

31 *Cengiz* (n 1) paras 49–52.

32 *Kalda v Estonia* App no 64569/09 (ECtHR, 19 January 2016); *Ramazan Demir v Turkey* App no 68550/17 (ECtHR, 9 February 2021); *Jankovsis v Lithuania* App no 21575/08 (ECtHR, 17 January 2017); *Mehmet Reşit Arslan and Orhan Bingöl* App no 47121/06 (ECtHR, 18 June 2019); *Akdeniz v Turkey* App no 20877/10 (ECtHR, 11 February 2014).

33 *Alekhina v Russia* App no 38004/12 (ECtHR, 17 July 2018), though a violation was found in this case because of the disproportionate nature of the penalties.

34 *Autronic* (n 19).

35 *Telegram Messenger v Russia* App no 13232/18, pending, concerned a request for information from the Federal Security Service to facilitate the breaking of Telegram's encryption. Telegram refused to cooperate and was fined. Telegram has brought a case before the ECtHR arguing that this constitutes an infringement of its right to impart information.

36 *Pirate Bay* (n 9); *Cengiz* (n 1), para 53; *Magyar Tartalomszolgáltatók Egyesülete and Index.hu Zrt (MTE) v Hungary* App no 22947/13 (ECtHR, 2 February 2016), paras 60–61, *Magyar Kétfarkú Kutya Párt* (n 23).

37 *Sürek v Turkey (no. 1)* App no 26682/95 (ECtHR, Grand Chamber, 8 July 1999), para 63.

38 Directive 2000/31/EC on certain legal aspects of information society services [2000] OJ L 178/1. Regulation 2022/2065 The Digital Services Act [2022] OJ L277/1 maintains the conditional immunity approach.

39 Declaration on Freedom of Communication on the Internet, 28 May 2003; Recommendation CM/Rec(2011)7 of the Committee of Ministers to member states on a new notion of media (adopted on 21 September 2011). Post-*Delfi*, there is Recommendation CM/Rec(2018)2 on the roles and responsibilities of internet intermediaries.

40 *Delfi* (n 8).
41 Ibid, para 113; CM/Rec(2011)7 (n 39).
42 *Delfi*, (n 8), para 116.
43 Ibid, para 117.
44 Robert Spano, 'Intermediary Liability for Online User Comments under the European Convention on Human Rights' (2017) 17 *Human Rights Law Review* 665; see also *MTE* (n 36).
45 *Phil v Sweden* App no 74742/14 (ECtHR, 7 February 2017).
46 Contrast *KU v Finland* App no 2872/02 (ECtHR, 2 December 2008), discussed later (n 61).
47 This point was noted in *Tamiz v UK* App no 3877/14 (ECtHR, 19 September 2017), para 84.
48 *MTE* (n 36); *Standard Verlagsgesellschaft mbH v Austria (no. 3)* App no 39378/15 (ECtHR, 7 December 2021).
49 *Magyar Jeti ZRT v Hungary* App no 11257/16 (ECtHR, 4 December 2018), para 66.
50 Contrast *Tamiz* (n 47) which might be seen as providing a more technical service.
51 *Høiness v Norway* App no 43624/14 (ECtHR, 19 March 2019).
52 *Høiness* (n 51), para 71; the ECtHR also highlighted the unforeseen nature of the comments in *Phil* (n 45).
53 Sander (n 2) 171.
54 *Phil* (n 45), para 31.
55 Ibid.
56 *Sanchez v France* App no 45581/15 (ECtHR, 2 September 2021).
57 Ibid, para 100.
58 Note the reasoning of the ECtHR in *Delfi* (n 8) on this point, para 153; in their joint concurring opinion, Judges Raimondi, Karakaş, De Gaetano and Kjølbro noted the significance of this point to the outcome, para 5. Cf dissenting opinion Judges Sajó and Tsotsoria, para 34.
59 *Delfi*, (n 8), para 147.
60 See e.g. *Phil* (45).
61 *KU* (n 46), paras 47–48. Note the ECtHR referred to the Data Retention Directive (Directive 2006/24/EC) although that directive was subsequently annulled by the European Court of Justice for inadequate safeguards for privacy rights: Joined Cases C-293/12 and C-594/12 *Digital Rights Ireland v Minister for Communications, Marine and Natural Resources, Minister for Justice, Equality and Law Reform, Commissioner of the Garda Síochána, Ireland, The Attorney General and Kärntner Landesregierung, Michael Seitlinger, Christof Tschohl and others,* (CJEU, 8 April 2014).
62 *KU* (n 46), para 46; this reasoning extends to other vulnerable individuals.
63 *Standard Verlag (no 3)* (n 48).
64 *Times Newspapers Ltd v the United Kingdom (nos. 1 and 2)* App nos 3002/03 and 23676/03 (ECtHR, 10 March 2009), para 27.
65 The meaning of user-generated content is discussed in Lorna Woods, 'User Generated Content: Freedom of Expression and the Role of the Media in a Digital Age', in Merris Amos, Jackie Harrison and Lorna Woods (eds), *Freedom of Expression and the Media* (Martinus Nijhoff Publishers 2012) 142–143.
66 *Delfi* (n 8), para 113.
67 *Observer and Guardian* v *UK*, Series A no. 216 (ECtHR, 26 November 1991); *Stoll* v *Switzerland* App no 69698/01 (ECtHR, Grand Chamber, 10 December 2007), para 104.
68 *MTE* (n 36).
69 Cf *Kilin* (n 18), where prosecution for sharing content without comment was not a violation of Article 10 ECHR.

70 *Niskasaari and Otavamedia Oy v Finland* App no 32297/10 (ECtHR, 23 June 2015), paras 9 and 54–59, in the context of an Internet discussion site; this implies that journalistic ethics apply to journalists here too.
71 *Cengiz* (n 1), para 52; *Falzon v Malta* App no 45791/13 (ECtHR, 20 March 2018), para 57.
72 See generally Ellen Hovlid, 'Finding a Judicial Definition of Journalism: A Challenging Exercise in the Digital Age', in Mart Susi (ed), *Human Rights, Digital Society and the Law: A Research Companion* (Taylor & Francis 2019); Joanna Kulesza, *International Internet Law* (Routledge 2012) 52.
73 *Purcell v Ireland* App no 15404/89 (EComHR, 16 April 1991); *Jersild v Denmark* Series A no 298 (ECtHR, 23 September 1994), para 31, *Delfi* (n 8), para 134; a radio interview is also less impactful than a television interview – *Schweizerische Radio- und Fernsehgesellschaft SRG v Switzerland* App no 34124/06 (ECtHR, 21 June 2012), para 64.
74 *Animal Defenders International v UK* App no 48876/08 (ECtHR, Grand Chamber, 27 January 2011), para 119.
75 *Stoll* (n 67), para 104.
76 In *Arnarson v Iceland* App no 58781/13 (ECtHR 13 June 2017), the ECtHR applied the normal rules for journalists' ethics to a freelance journalist (para 43).
77 *Ovchinnikov v Russia* App no 24061/04 (ECtHR, 16 December 2010), para 42.
78 *Axel Springer AG v Germany* App no 39954/08 (ECtHR, Grand Chamber, 7 February 2012); *Von Hannover v Germany (no 2)* App nos 40660/08 and 60641/08 (ECtHR, Grand Chamber, 7 February 2012).
79 *Delfi* (n 8), para 33; *Węgrzynowski and Smolczewski* v *Poland*, App no 33846/07 (ECtHR,16 July 2013), para 98.
80 *Cicad v Switzerland* App no 17676/09 (ECtHR, 7 June 2016).
81 *Axel Springer* (n 78).
82 C-131/12 *Google Spain SL and Google Inc. v Agencia Española de Protección de Datos (AEPD) and Mario Costeja González* (CJEU, Grand Chamber 13 May 2014).
83 *ML and WW v Germany* App no 60798/10 and 65599/10 (ECtHR, 28 June 2018), para 97.
84 *Times Newspapers* (n 64), para 47.
85 *Hurbain v Belgium* App no 57292/16 (ECtHR, 22 June 21); cf *Węgrzynowski and Smolczewski* (n 79).
86 See e.g. *Éditions Plon v France* App no 58148/00 (ECtHR, 18 May 2004), para 53; *ML and WW* (n 83).
87 *Biancardi v Italy* App no 77419/16 (ECtHR, 25 November 2021).
88 *Biancardi*, (n 87), para 59.
89 Ibid, para 62.
90 *Ovchinnikov* (n 77), para 50.
91 Communication from the Commission to the European Parliament, the Council and the European Economic and Social Committee, Guidance on certain aspects of Directive 2004/48/EC of the European Parliament and of the Council on the enforcement of Intellectual Property Rights COM (2017) 708 final, p 21.
92 See e.g. *Glawischnig-Piesczek* (n 13), though it did not consider the impact of Article 11 EU Charter; Case C-401/19 *Poland v Parliament and Council* [2022] ECLI:EU:C:2022:297
93 *Cicad* (n 80), para 59.
94 *Societe editrice de Mediapait and Ors v France* App nos 281/15 and 34445/15 (ECtHR,14 January 2021).
95 *Big Brother Watch v UK* App nos 58170/13, 62322/14 and 24960/15 (ECtHR, Grand Chamber, 25 May 2021); cf Joined Cases C-511/18 *La Quadrature du Net*, C-512/18 *French Data Network* and C-520/18 *Ordre des barreaux francophones et gemanophone* [2020] ECLI:EU:C:2020:791.

96 Case C-401/19 *Poland v Parliament and Council* (n 92). See also chapter 2 in this volume.
97 *Savva Terentyev v Russia* App no 10692/09 (ECtHR, 28 August 2018); the domestic courts failed to take context into account when coming to its balance leading to the ECtHR finding a violation on that basis.
98 See e.g *Kilin* (n 18); *ZB v France* App no 46883/15 (ECtHR, 2 September 2021).
99 *Tierbefreier v Germany* App no 45192/09 (ECtHR, 16 January 2014); on covert filming see also *Bremner v Turkey* App no 37428/06 (ECtHR, 13 October 2015) under Article 8 ECHR.
100 *Tierbefreier* (n 99) para 56.
101 *Erbakan v Turkey* App no 59405/00 (ECtHR, 6 July 2006), para 56.
102 *Perinçek v Switzerland* App no 27510/08 (ECtHR, Grand Chamber, 15 October 2015), paras 229–241; *Savva Terentyev v Russia* App no 10692/09 (ECtHR, 28 August 2018), para 65.
103 *Perinçek* (n 102), paras 204–208; *Willem v France* App no 10883/05 (ECtHR, 16 July 2009).
104 E.g *Sanchez* (n 56); *Gündüz v Turkey* App no 35071/97 (ECtHR, 4 December 2003).
105 Council of Europe, Committee of Ministers Recommendation on hate speech R (97) 20 (30 October 1997).
106 E.g. *Belkacem v Belgium* App no 34367/14 (ECtHR, 27 June 2017); See generally Giovanni Bonello, 'Freedom of Expression and Incitement to Violence', in Joseph Casadevall *et al.* (eds), *Freedom of Expression: Essays in Honour of Nicolas Bratza* (Wolf Legal Publishing 2012).
107 Jacob Mchangama and Natalie Alkiviadou 'Hate Speech and the European Court of Human Rights: Whatever Happened to the Right to Offend, Shock or Disturb?' (2021) 21(4) *Human Rights Law Review* 1008; Philippe Yves Kuhn, 'Reforming the Approach to Racial and Religious Hate Speech under Article 10 of the European Convention on Human Rights' (2019) 19 *Human Rights Law Review* 119.
108 The UN Special Rapporteur on Freedom of Expression has recently noted what she calls "gendered censorship" in her Report on Promotion and protection of the right to freedom of opinion and expression (A/76/258) 30 July 2021, <https://undocs.org/A/76/258> accessed 4 January 2022, para 12.
109 *Ismayilova v Azerbaijan* App nos 65286/13 and 57270/14 (ECtHR, 10 January 2019).
110 *Ismayilova* (n 109), paras 158–159.
111 *Volodina v Russia* App no 41261/17 (ECtHR, 9 July 2019).
112 *Behar v Bulgaria* App no 29335/13 (ECtHR, 16 February 2021).
113 E.g. *Evans v United Kingdom* App no 6330/05 (ECtHR, Grand Chamber, 10 April 2007), para 75.
114 *Tysiąc v Poland* App no 5410/03 (ECtHR 20 March 2007); *Botta v Italy* App no 21439/93 (ECtHR, 24 February1998).
115 *Glass v UK* App no 61827/00 (ECtHR, 9 March 2004) paras 74–83; *KU* (n 46), para 43.
116 *KU* (n 46), paras 45–49.
117 *MC v Bulgaria* App no 39272/98 (ECtHR, 4 December 2003).
118 *Beizaras and Levickas v Lithuania* Appl no 42188/15 (ECtHR, 14 January 2020).
119 *Király and Dömötör v Hungary* App no 10851/13 (ECtHR, 17 April 2017), para 80.
120 *Đorđević v Croatia* App no 41526/10 (ECtHR, 24 July 2012), paras 87–88.
121 *Aksu v Turkey* App nos 4149/04 and 41029/04 (ECtHR, Grand Chamber, 22 March 2012); on the facts Aksu lost but the principle was recognised.
122 *Đorđević v Croatia* (n 120).

123 *Medžlis Islamske Zajednice Brčko and Others v Bosnia and Herzegovina* App no 17224/11 (ECtHR, Grand Chamber, 27 June 2017), para 76.
124 The threshold related to service out of the jurisdiction which requires that there be a "real and substantial tort" as set down in *Dow Jones & Co Inc v Jameel* [2005] EWCA Civ 75.
125 *Tamiz* (n 47).
126 Note the potential relevance of failure to action arguments in *Sanchez* (n 56).
127 *Tamiz* (n 47) para 90; in *Mosley v UK* App no 48009/08 (ECtHR, 10 May 2011) the ECtHR identified factors for deciding on the breadth a state's margin of appreciation, and in cases where the balancing exercise has been undertaken by the national authorities, the ECtHR will require strong reasons to change their conclusions (para 79).
128 E.g. literature cited by E Seger *et al.*, *Tackling Threats to Informed Decision-making in Democratic Societies: Promoting Epistemic Security in a Technologically Advanced World* (Alan Turing Institute 2021).
129 Carme Colomina *et al.*, *The Impact of Disinformation on Democratic Processes*, 22 April 2021 (EP/EXPO/DROI/FWC/2019–01/LOT6/R/02) list a range of possible definitions for this term: pp 3–5.
130 Ibid, pp 11–12. The issue of state-sponsored propaganda and disinformation as a weapon of war or as a tactic as hybrid warfare lies outside the scope of this contribution.
131 *Lingens v Austria* App no 9815/82 (ECtHR, 8 July 1986), para 46.
132 Bernard Williams, *In the Beginning was the Deed* (Princeton University Press 2005) 74.
133 *Stoll* (n 67), para 103; *Bédat v Switzerland* App no 56925/08 (ECtHR, Grand Chamber, 29 March 2016); note also the reasoning in *Tierbefreier* (n 99) on contribution to debate.
134 *Cicad* (n 80), para 58.
135 *Avagyan v Russia* App no 36911/20 (nyd).
136 This term has been used by e.g. the World Health Organisation, see e.g. <www.who.int/news/item/11-12-2020-call-for-action-managing-the-infodemic> accessed 18 January 2021.
137 Coloma *et al.* (n 129), pp 12, 21.
138 This is limited to where there is a direct connection between the claim and the state inaction: see e.g. *Sentges v the Netherlands* App no 27677/02 (ECtHR, 8 July 2003); *Pentiacova v Moldova* App no 14462/03 (ECtHR, 4 January 2005).
139 *Vilnes & Ors v Norway* App nos 52806/09 and 22703/10 (ECtHR, 5 December 2013), para 235, 239–240; it is unclear when the duty to provide information will be triggered.
140 Claire Wardle and Hossein Derakhshan *Information Disorder: Toward an Interdisciplinary Framework for Research and Policymaking* (Council of Europe, DGI 2017) 9 <https://rm.coe.int/information-disorder-toward-an-interdisciplinary-framework-for-researc/168076277c> accessed 12 August 2021; Kate Jones *Online Disinformation and Political Discourse: Applying a Human Rights Framework*, Chatham House Research Paper, 2019 <www.chathamhouse.org/sites/default/files/2019-11-05-Online-Disinformation-Human-Rights.pdf> accessed 12 August 2021, 6 and 16.
141 Nicholas Negroponte, *Being Digital* (Vintage Books 1995); Eli Pariser, *The Filter Bubble: How the New Personalized Web Is Changing What We Read and How We Think* (Penguin Books 2011); note the existence of "filter bubbles" is contested, see e.g. Wardle and Derakhshan (n 140), pp 52–53.
142 Declaration by the Committee of Ministers on the manipulative capabilities of algorithmic processes (Decl(13/02/2019)1), 13 February 2019, para 9.

143 Digital Services Act (n 38).
144 Renee Diresta, 'Free Speech is Not the Same as Free Reach', *Wired*, 30 August 2018.
145 *Sunday Times (No 1) v UK* App no 6538/74 (ECtHR, 26 April 1979), para 66 – see also e.g. *Sener v Turkey* App no 26680/95 (ECtHR, 18 July 2000), para 46; *Ukrainian Media Group v Ukraine* App no 72713/01 (ECtHR, 29 March 2005), para 38.
146 The ECtHR has recognised a right to specific information in some contexts: e.g. *Társaság a Szabadságjogokért v Hungary*, App no 37374/05 (ECtHR, 14 April 2009); *Youth Initiative for Human Rights v Serbia*, App no 48135/06 (ECtHR, 25 June 2013).
147 *Manole v Moldova* App no 13936/02 (ECtHR, 13 July 2010).
148 Council of Europe, Recommendation on measures to promote the public service value of the Internet (CM Rec (2007) 16), 7 November 2007; the EU Code on Disinformation could be seen as the sort of response that was envisaged, though it now seems that the European Democracy Action Plan is pushing for stronger obligations.
149 *Yildirim v Turkey* App no 3111/10 (ECtHR, 18 December 2012); *Cengiz* (n 1); but cf *Akdeniz* (n 33).
150 E.g. *Kharitonov v Russia* App no 10795/14 (ECtHR, 20 June 2020).
151 *GRA Stiftung gegen Rassismus und Antisemitismus v Switzerland*, App no 18597/13 (ECtHR, 9 January 2018), para 78.
152 *Lewandowska-Malec v Poland* App no 39660/07 (ECtHR, 18 September 2012), para 70.
153 A local councillor and a foundation against racism and antisemitism respectively.
154 Woods (n 25).
155 Irene Khan, Public Comment by UN Special Rapporteur on Freedom of Opinion and Expression on Facebook Oversight Board Case no. 2021–009, 9 September 2021 <www.ohchr.org/Documents/Issues/Opinion/Legislation/Case_2021_009-FB-UA.pdf> accessed 4 January 2022.

Part 2

The national perspective

4 Social media before higher courts in Estonia

Delfi says it all

Meeli Kaur

1. Introduction

The Internet has given people significant benefits in exercising their right to freedom of expression. In this evolving area of law, Estonian courts play a major role in developing legal standards for social media disputes. They carry out multiple "balancing exercises" to strike a fair balance between the distinct, fundamental rights at stake. The Constitution of the Republic of Estonia[1] (Constitution) establishes that justice is administered solely by the courts.[2] The courts are independent in their activity and administer justice in accordance with the Constitution and legislation.[3] The structure of Estonia's court system is one of the simplest in Europe. It consists of three instances.[4] The first instance is comprised of county courts. County courts are general courts which hear civil, criminal and misdemeanour matters. Administrative courts are courts of first instance which hear administrative matters. The second instance consists of courts of appeal, which, following appeals, review judgments by the county and administrative courts. The Supreme Court is the third instance.

The Supreme Court is the highest court in Estonia and reviews court judgments in cassation proceedings. It is composed of a Civil Chamber, a Criminal Chamber, an Administrative Law Chamber and a Constitutional Review Chamber. The Supreme Court verifies the constitutionality of a legislative or regulatory act, omission to adopt such an act and international agreements following substantiated petitions, court judgments or court orders.[5] No pre-trial proceedings are required when appeals are filed with the Constitutional Review Chamber. Appeals may also be heard by Special (*ad hoc*) Panels or by the Supreme Court *en banc*. The Supreme Court *en banc* is comprised of all the justices in the Supreme Court and is the highest body in the Court. It has two kinds of functions: administration of justice and court administration. In the former, the Supreme Court *en banc* verifies the constitutionality of a legislative or regulatory act if the Constitutional Review Chamber deems it necessary for the case to be adjudicated by the Court in this composition.[6]

DOI: 10.4324/9781003207085-6

The key source of fundamental rights and freedoms is the Constitution.[7] It is inspired by the European Convention on Human Rights (ECHR). There are references to the ECHR as a source of inspiration in the transcripts of the sittings of the Constitutional Assembly held in 1991.[8] Article 45 of the Constitution deals with competing rights – personality rights on the internet, on the one hand, and freedom of expression online, on the other. It is relevant because it provides everyone with the right to disseminate any information in any manner (including on social media). It reads as follows:

> *Everyone has the right to freely disseminate ideas, opinions, beliefs and other information by word, print, picture or other means. This right may be restricted by a law to protect public order, morals, or the rights and freedoms, health, honour and good name of others. This right may also be restricted by a law for state and municipal public servants, to protect a state secret or trade secret or information received in confidence, which has become known to them by reason of their office, or the family and private life of others, as well as in the interests of the administration of justice.*
>
> *There shall be no censorship.*

Article 45 of the Constitution guarantees the absence of state censorship: the state is prohibited from creating national institutions to censor freedom of expression or to assess freedom of expression. Decisions by private publishers prohibiting the publication of a particular form of self-expression are not considered state censorship, as they do not amount to an exercise of public authority.[9]

Regarding the protection of personality rights, Article 17 of the Constitution provides that no one's honour or good name shall be defamed. Although the article is formulated without reservations, this does not mean that this fundamental right is absolute. The exercise of any fundamental right is, in fact, restricted by the second paragraph of Article 19 of the Constitution, which provides that everyone, when exercising rights and freedoms and fulfilling duties, must respect and consider the rights and freedoms of others, and must observe the law. However, the practical significance of the restriction in this provision is low, as specific fundamental rights clauses are applied to determine the material constitutionality of a violation of fundamental rights. For example, restrictions on freedom of expression for the protection of private life include the right of inviolability of private and family life, which also concerns the protection of personal data (Article 26 of the Constitution), inviolability of the home (Article 33) and the right of confidentiality of messages (Article 43).

The Penal Code[10] does not criminalise violations of the rights to honour or a good name of others through freedom of expression. Protection is sought in civil proceedings. The Law of Obligations Act[11] provides non-contractual remedies in the event of a violation of personality rights. The relevant provisions are general, they are also applicable to journalists and they are technology-neutral. There are no special rules to address the specificities of social media, which leaves the interpretative task to judges. Under the Law of Obligations Act, the victim can demand rectification of incorrect information (section 1047), termination of unlawful activities (section 1055) and compensation for pecuniary and non-pecuniary damage (sections 131 and 134).

Section 1046(1) of the Law of Obligations Act provides that defamation of a person, *inter alia*, by passing undue value judgments, by unjustified use of the name or image of a person or by breaching the inviolability of the private life or another personality right of a person is unlawful unless otherwise provided by law. Section 1046(2) of the Law of Obligations Act sets out when a violation of a personality right is not unlawful but justified, considering other legal rights protected by law, the rights of third parties and public interest. Therefore, the unlawfulness of an act is established on the basis of a comparative assessment of different legal rights and interests protected by law. Assessment by courts is also required in cases concerning incorrect information. Section 1047(3) of the Law of Obligations Act provides that disclosure of information or facts is not deemed unlawful if the person who discloses the information or facts has a legitimate interest in such disclosure and has checked the information or facts with a thoroughness which corresponds to the gravity of the potential violation.

In Estonia every year, there is a significant increase in the number of internet media cases. For example, in 2010, 16 cases were lodged with the county courts concerning disclosure of incorrect information, and in 2020, the number of cases had increased to 34.[12] Two decisions of the Supreme Court between 1 January 2009 and 31 December 2020 can be linked to social media.[13] Both cases have played significant roles in the development of case law on both social media and traditional news media that operate online news portals. In addition, between 1 January 2009 and 31 December 2020, there were 20 judgments by courts of appeal.[14] However, the judgments of the courts of appeal did not contain as much reasoning as did those of the county courts. This is explained by the fact that, if a court of appeal adheres to the reasoning of the court of first instance, it does not have to substantiate its judgment and can only specify that it agrees with the reasoning of the lower court.[15] The same applies to Supreme Court judgments.[16] The limited number of Supreme Court judgments identified can also be attributed to the strict requirements for acceptance of an appeal in cassation.[17]

In the judgments analysed, there was a judicial dialogue dimension through references to Articles 8 and 10 ECHR and to the case law of the European Court of Human Rights (ECtHR). In general, in these cases, claimants demanded that a person who disclosed incorrect information should refute the information, or in cases of defamation, requests were made to remove the offensive comments and to pay compensation for non-pecuniary damage. If another personality right of a person was violated – for example, by unjustified use of their image – the claimant demanded compensation for non-pecuniary damage.[18] The claims were directed against persons who posted information and also against owners of internet news portals who invited third parties to post comments.

2. Fundamental rights in national jurisprudence

Social media cases tend to be framed as fundamental rights cases because they deal with two competing fundamental rights: protection of one's honour and good name (in some cases also the right to private and family life) and protection of freedom of expression online. Sections 1043 and 1046 of the Law of Obligations Act are designed to ensure freedom of expression and protection of everyone's honour and good name. In conjunction with the general provisions in the Law of Obligations Act, domestic courts also apply the relevant articles of the Constitution to justify interference with freedom of expression. According to Articles 436(7) and 438(1) of the Code of Civil Procedure, the application of the law and the qualification of the claim is the responsibility of the court, and in making a judgment, a court is not bound by the legal allegations made by the parties.

The principle of proportionality is a central criterion for the constitutionality of any interference. It derives from Article 11 of the Constitution, which states that rights and freedoms may be restricted only in accordance with the Constitution. Such restrictions must be necessary in a democratic society and must not distort the essence of the rights and freedoms restricted. This means, in practice, that if a fair balance must be struck in social media cases between distinct fundamental rights at stake, such as those in Articles 17 and 45 of the Constitution, the courts have to carry out a balancing exercise on a case-by-case basis, since the rights involved are not hierarchical and have equal weight. The obligation to carry out balancing stems from sections 1046(2) and 1047(3) of the Law of Obligations Act. It is not apparent from any of the judgments analysed that national jurisprudence has a preference for a particular set of rights over others.

As was mentioned previously in this chapter, there are two decisions by the Supreme Court that are considered cornerstones in social media case law: one concerning the liability of an internet news portal for defamatory or other types of unlawful comments posted by users and another concerning the jurisdiction of the relevant court. The first one – the judgment of the Supreme Court of 10 June 2009 – is important because it reiterated the principle that Estonia does not exclude the liability of internet news portals as new media publishers for defamatory and degrading comments posted on their sites by anonymous third parties. Publishing news and comments on an internet portal is also a journalistic activity, and an owner of an internet news portal is a publisher.[19] In the case at issue, the legal dispute between the parties related to whether the entrepreneur defendant was publisher in the meaning of section 1047 of the Law of Obligations Act,[20] whether what was published (the comments) was unlawful and whether the defendant was liable. According to the facts of the case, the defendant owned one of the largest internet news portals in Estonia.

On its website, readers could anonymously post comments below the articles published. At the time, at the end of the body of the news articles, there were the words "add your comment" and fields for comments. The comments were posted by readers in reaction to the news article. The defendant could not edit or moderate these comments, but it could remove them using an automatic word filtering system or on being alerted by readers.

In 2006, the defendant published an article on its portal that attracted 185 comments. About 20 of them contained personal threats and offensive language directed at a natural person. This person brought a civil suit before a court against the internet news portal and claimed non-pecuniary damage. The Supreme Court upheld the court of appeal's judgment in substance, sharing the lower court's opinion that the activity of the defendant in publishing the comments was not merely of a technical, automatic and passive nature. The Supreme Court pointed out that the aim of the defendant was not merely to provide an intermediary service, but that the defendant had an economic interest in the posting of comments. Moreover, the defendant determined which of the comments were to be published or not. Called on to examine whether the court of appeal had applied Article 45 of the Constitution correctly, the Supreme Court explained that the exercise of any fundamental right was restricted by the second sentence of Article 19 of the Constitution. The Supreme Court went on to explain that the right to freedom of expression, protected by Article 45 of the Constitution, was restricted by the prohibition on defaming a person's honour and good name, which was protected by Article 17 of the Constitution. The Supreme Court interpreted the prohibition as not completely precluding any interference with a person's honour and good name, but only defamation thereof (section 1046 of the Law of Obligations Act). It concluded that interference by an internet portal operator with the freedom of expression of the persons posting comments was, however, justified by the obligation on the portal operator to respect the honour and good name of third parties, as arose from Article 17 of the Constitution and section 1046 of the Law of Obligations Act. The defendant was not exempted from liability.[21] The Supreme Court dismissed the defendant's appeal and upheld the lower court's judgment, which awarded the claimant 5000 EEK (320 EUR) in compensation for non-pecuniary damage.

The defendant lodged an application with the ECtHR against Estonia and alleged that its freedom of expression had been violated in breach of Article 10 ECHR by the fact that it had been held liable for third-party comments posted on its internet news portal. The ECtHR held that there had been no violation of Article 10 ECHR.[22] The ECtHR considered it important for the Supreme Court to recognise the differences between the roles of a publisher of printed media, on the one hand, and of an internet portal operator engaged in media publications for an economic purpose, on the other. It agreed with the Supreme Court's finding that the defendant, by making public the comments on its news articles on the Delfi news portal, was not a passive, purely technical service provider. Furthermore, the ECtHR pointed out that this distinction was in line with international instruments[23] in this field, which manifested a certain development in favour of distinguishing between the legal principles regulating their activities. The impugned comments, as assessed by the Supreme Court, constituted hate speech and speech that directly advocated acts of violence.

Taking account of these findings, the ECtHR confirmed that the case concerned the "duties and responsibilities" of internet news portals under the second paragraph of Article 10 ECHR when they provided a platform for user-generated comments for economic purposes. The ECtHR expressly stated that "the case did not concern other fora on the internet where third-party comments can be disseminated, for example an internet discussion forum or a bulletin board where users can freely set out their ideas on any topic without the discussion being channelled by any input from the forum's manager; or a social media platform where the platform provider does not offer any content and where the content provider may be a private person running the website or blog as a hobby".[24] In order to assess the proportionality of the interference at issue, the ECtHR analysed the following factors: the context of the comments, the measures applied by the applicant company in order to prevent or remove defamatory comments, the liability of the actual authors of the comments as an alternative to the applicant company's liability and the consequences of the domestic proceedings for the applicant company.

The other decision by the Supreme Court which played a significant role in developing case law on social media and on internet news portals dealt with the jurisdiction of the relevant court. In an order of 21 December 2017, the Supreme Court decided on a procedural issue. Due to the cross-border nature of the Internet, the question concerned the jurisdiction of the competent court. To interpret Article 7(2) of Regulation (EU) No 1215/2012 of the European Parliament and of the Council[25] concerning special jurisdiction in matters relating to tort, delict or quasi-delict,[26] the Supreme Court decided to stay proceedings and refer to the Court of Justice of the European Union (CJEU) for a preliminary ruling. In its *Bolagsupplysningen v Ilsjan* judgment,[27] the CJEU ruled that a legal person could bring an action for rectification of incorrect information, removal of comments relating to that person and compensation for all damage sustained before the courts of the Member State in which its centre of interests was located.[28] In connection with an action for rectification of incorrect information and removal of harmful comments, the CJEU ruled that a person who had alleged that his personality rights had been infringed should not bring an action for rectification of that information and removal of those comments relating to him before the courts of each Member State in which the information published on the internet was accessible. The CJEU observed that an application for the rectification of incorrect information and the removal of comments was a single and indivisible application and could, consequently, only be made before a court with jurisdiction to rule on the entirety of an application for compensation for damage pursuant to past case law.[29] Although this order is not directly related to the fundamental rights, it can have far-reaching consequences for the standard of protection of the fundamental rights involved, in the sense that the competent court can also have an effect on the applicable law.[30]

3. Judicial dialogue with the CJEU and the ECtHR

Higher courts in Estonia have not been very eager to refer to or further analyse the judgments of the ECtHR. This is because, when adhering to the reasoning in the judgment of the lower court, the courts of appeal and the Supreme Court do not need to substantiate their judgments; they only specify that they adhere to the reasoning in the judgment of the lower court.[31] Therefore, in order to analyse judicial dialogue between domestic higher courts and European supranational courts, judgments by county courts have also been considered. In at least eight judgments, the county courts and the courts of appeal relied on Article 10 ECHR in combination with the Constitution or the Law of Obligations Act, or both, and assessed whether the requirements for applying Article 10(2) ECHR were met. On the other hand, there have been no references to the Charter of Fundamental Rights of the European Union (CFR). One reason, among others, for favouring the ECHR may be that Commentaries on the Constitution[32] contain several references to judgments by the ECtHR under Article 45 of the Constitution and the courts have referred to this case law. The Commentaries on the Constitution observe that "freedom of expression must be furnished in the light of democratic perceptions and practices recognised in the European cultural and judicial area".[33] The case law of the ECtHR thus clearly complements the interpretation of constitutional rights in Estonia.

The judgments by the ECtHR that have most frequently been referred to are the previously mentioned *Delfi* judgment[34] and *Magyar Tartalomszolgáltatók Egyesülete and Index.hu Zrt v Hungary (MTE)*.[35] Additionally, there have been three or more references to *A. v Norway*[36] in connection with Article 8 ECHR and to *Lingens v Austria*[37] in connection with assessing acceptable criticism. Based on these judgments, the domestic courts referred to the case law of the ECtHR in order to cope with the challenges that modern journalism faces when assessing whether interference with the freedom of expression was necessary in a democratic society and proportionate to the legitimate aim pursued. Since Estonia has not enacted rules specifically concerning online journalism, with the help of ECtHR case law, domestic courts can base their analysis on certain criteria when resolving similar cases. Although the final decision depends largely on the circumstances of the particular case, domestic courts use the case law of the ECtHR to strengthen and corroborate their judicial reasoning in order to strike a balance between competing constitutional rights. This is demonstrated by the fact that some judgments include a reference to the ECHR by quoting the reasons of the ECtHR judgment. As a direct consequence, this form of reasoning ensures consistent interpretation of domestic law with the ECHR.

Examining these judgments in more detail now, in a judgment of 18 June 2019,[38] a county court was called on to assess whether the principles laid down in the *Lingens* judgment were transferable to the case at hand. The defendant quoted paragraph 42 of *Lingens*,[39] arguing that, due to the claimant's status, the limits of acceptable criticism were broader. However, the county court observed that the circumstances of the two cases were different. The reference to *Lingens* was not appropriate because the claimant was not a politician, and the comments written by the defendant on Facebook did not amount to a political debate.

Moreover, four judgments by a county court[40] contain multiple references to ECtHR case law, relying on Articles 8 and 10 ECHR in combination with the provisions of the Law of Obligations Act. The influence of ECtHR case law on judicial reasoning is illustrated by a judgment of 8 May 2018.[41] The circumstances of the case were similar to the *Delfi* case: an article was published on an internet news portal containing the name of the claimant. The article was about an incident in which, during repair work on a house, bird nests under the roof with baby birds were walled in. The article attracted 524 comments. About 28 of them contained personal threats and offensive language directed at the claimant – the natural person who allegedly ordered the repair work. In this case, the county court had to assess whether the publication of such comments was such a severe violation of the claimant's rights that freedom of expression had to be interfered with. The county court referred to Articles 8 and 10(2) ECHR in conjunction with the relevant ECtHR case law: *Pfeifer v Austria*[42] and *A. v Norway*.[43] Additionally, the court quoted paragraph 76 of the *MTE* judgment, according to which the

> offence may fall outside the protection of freedom of expression if it amounts to wanton denigration, for example where the sole intent of the offensive statement is to insult, but the use of vulgar phrases in itself is not decisive in the assessment of an offensive expression.

The county court used the assessment in *MTE* to describe the style of communication on internet portals, pointing out that the expressions used in the comments, albeit belonging to a low stylistic register, are common in communication on many of them. As the circumstances of the case were identical to *Delfi*, the county court followed the same criteria established by the ECtHR in that case and found that interference with freedom of expression was "necessary in a democratic society". In the county court's view, the

> defendant exceeded certain limits, particularly with regard to the claimant's reputation and rights. This was not the traditional task of journalistic practice, that is, to disseminate information and ideas on all matters of public interest in a manner consistent with its duties and responsibilities.[44]

The county court noted that the case was not comparable with the circumstances set out in *Bladet Tromsø and Stensaas v Norway*,[45] in which the articles concerned facts and were not primarily defamatory or intended to accuse certain individuals of cruelty to animals.[46] Regarding the content in the user comments, the county court found that the comments at issue could not be justified, as they were unreasonably offensive and extreme. Furthermore, as in *Delfi*, the county court took into consideration that the comments were posted in reaction to an article published by the defendant company on its professionally managed news portal run on a commercial basis. In conclusion, the Internet news portal was held liable for the third-party comments and was ordered to pay 1500 EUR in compensation for non-pecuniary damage.[47] On 16 January 2019, the Tallinn Court of Appeal upheld the county court's judgment.[48] The court of appeal rejected the defendant's argument that, in assessing the comments, the county court had failed to take into account the reasoning of the ECtHR in *MTE*. In response, the court of appeal noted that the circumstances in *MTE* were not transferable directly to the case at hand, and the county court did consider various rights: the right to freedom of expression and protection of the rights of others.[49]

The same reasoning as in the judgment of the Harju County Court of 8 May 2018 is found in a judgment of the same court of 28 November 2019, in which the county court assessed the main text and the comments posted on a blog.[50] This judgment illustrates that the *Delfi* case law spread to other cases closely related to social media, such as this one, where the content provider was a private person running the blog. In this case, the county court found that interference with the blogger's freedom of expression was justified. It noted that the comments contained incitement to violence and were intended to insult the claimant. Moreover, holding the blogger liable for the main text of the blog and the comments posted by readers, the county court considered that the defendant was a professional blogger who earned income by managing a web environment.

Another judgment by the Harju County Court on 21 December 2015[51] also concerned the treatment of animals. Comments that allegedly contained incorrect information were published on a closed Facebook group called "Cat lovers". In the comments, the defendant, a natural person, criticised the claimant's organisation, a non-profit organisation offering shelter for stray cats. The county court used the ECtHR case law to justify its assessment that value judgments and opinions that accompanied the statements published were appropriate. The county court quoted the fundamental principles established by the ECtHR concerning the question of whether interference with freedom of expression is "necessary in a democratic society" as is summarised in judgments such as *Hertel v Switzerland*,[52] *Steel and Morris v the United Kingdom*,[53] *Mouvement raëlien suisse v Switzerland*[54] and *Animal Defenders International v the United Kingdom*.[55] On the basis of ECtHR case law, the county court noted that freedom of expression constituted one of the essential foundations of a democratic society and that it was applicable not only to "information" or "ideas" that were favourably received or regarded as inoffensive or as a matter of indifference, but also to those that offended, shocked or disturbed. Such were the demands of pluralism, tolerance and broadmindedness, without which there was no "democratic society". The county court found that the contents of the comments did not overstep the acceptable limits of freedom of expression under Article 10 ECHR, taking into account that the information was published in a social network closed group where only members who had registered in the group could communicate through the administrator. Therefore, when justifying that interference with freedom of expression was not necessary, the county court considered the scope of the dissemination of information to be important: the defendant had not disclosed the information to an unspecified number of persons. Moreover, the county court justified its reasoning by analysing the contents of the comments and noted that the defendant's motive was not to harm the claimant. Instead, the defendant wished to share her feelings and thoughts with other members who shared a similar way of thinking and attitude to cats. The county court concluded that "considering the interests of both parties, the defendant's freedom of expression is not subject to restrictions, as the person has the freedom to hold opinions and to receive and impart information and ideas without interference by public authorities".[56]

In a judgment of the Harju County Court on 28 March 2016,[57] the county court used the criteria laid down in *Delfi* and *MTE*. The claimant sued an internet news portal that published two articles about him. At the end of the body of the news articles, third parties could post comments.[58] According to the findings of the county court, the comments were humiliating and defamatory. The county court noted that Article 8 ECHR came into play because the attack on the claimant's reputation had a certain level of seriousness and was made in a manner causing prejudice to personal enjoyment of the right to respect for private life.[59] The county court quoted paragraph 139 of *Delfi* to stress that the rights guaranteed under Articles 8 and 10 ECHR deserved equal respect. For its assessment of proportionality, the county court considered it necessary to analyse the criteria laid down in *Delfi*: the context of the comments, the measures applied by the news portal to prevent or remove defamatory comments and liability of the actual authors of the comments as an alternative to that of the news portal.[60] Additionally, the county court took into account the conduct of the injured party as in the *MTE* case.[61] In *MTE*, the ECtHR observed that the domestic courts did not consider that the injured party never requested the internet portals to remove the comments but opted to seek justice directly before the court. In that case, the comments were removed immediately on the claimant's request. However, using *Perinçek v Switzerland*[62] to furnish the concepts, the county court found that the case at hand was different from *Delfi* because the comments in question did not include hate speech or speech inciting violence.[63] In sum, the county court did not impose objective liability on the news portal for the third-party comments. It considered the comments to be simply offensive and vulgar and found that the notice-and-take-down system was an appropriate tool to balance the rights and interests of all involved. The Tallinn Court of Appeal upheld the county court's judgment.[64] It emphasised that a distinction had to be made between a portal operator and a traditional publisher – in particular, regarding the content of third-party comments. The court of appeal agreed that, to assess whether the defendant could be held liable for the comments posted by third parties, the general criteria for liability set out in *Delfi* had to be taken into account. It also agreed with the county court's finding that the measures taken by the defendant were sufficient and that the defendant could only be held liable for failing to take immediate action to remove clearly unlawful comments because the comments at issue did not contain elements of hate speech or incitement to violence.

Another example to show how domestic courts use ECtHR case law in connection with unjustified use of a person's image is a judgment by the Tallinn Court of Appeal on 13 February 2019.[65] In this case, the defendant, a private, limited liability company, used photos of the claimant without her consent on its Facebook and Instagram pages to advertise jewellery. The court of appeal found a violation of section 6(1) of the Advertising Act[66] in conjunction with section 1045(1)7) of the Law of Obligations Act. Section 6(1) of the Advertising Act provides that a person shall not be referred to or used in advertising in any manner, including by using the voice, images or pictorial representations of the person, unless prior written consent has been obtained from that person. In order to strengthen its reasoning about the state's positive obligations concerning respect for private life, the court of appeal referred to *Von Hannover v Germany (no. 2)*[67] and explained that, by introducing such a measure – written consent – the state had fulfilled its positive obligation to effectively protect a person's privacy, which also includes protection against misuse of a person's image.

4. Conclusion

The courts play a major role in developing legal standards for social media cases. If there are no special rules to address the specificities of social media, leaving the interpretative task to judges, the courts are required to be creative and substitute any legislative inadequacy. To do so, the courts have to carry out multiple "balancing exercises" to strike a fair balance between the distinct, fundamental rights at stake. The speed of technological development and the nature of the Internet with the challenges that modern journalism offers make this task for judges even more complex. The borderless and transnational nature of the Internet requires novel interpretations of the law on a daily basis.

ECtHR case law provides that the rights under Articles 10 and 8 ECHR deserve equal respect and emphasises the fact that a balance must be struck that retains the essence of both rights.[68] The same principle applies in Estonia. Social media cases tend to be framed as fundamental rights cases because they deal with two competing fundamental rights: the protection of honour and good name (in some cases also the right to private and family life), on the one hand, and the protection of freedom of expression online, on the other. Regarding interference with freedom of expression, the Estonian courts acknowledge the fundamental principles concerning whether interference with freedom of expression is "necessary in a democratic society". They make good use of European sources of fundamental rights protection and apply standards which are in conformity with the principles embodied in Article 10 ECHR. This is important because the ECtHR does not take the place of domestic courts.[69] In exercising its supervisory jurisdiction, the ECtHR has to satisfy itself that domestic courts have applied standards which are in conformity with the principles of Article 10 ECHR and, moreover, that they have relied on an acceptable assessment of the relevant facts. This kind of judicial dialogue has ensured interpretation of domestic rules consistent with the ECHR. As a result, Estonian courts have not encountered possible different standards emerging from the ECtHR case law.

It is noteworthy that the *Delfi* case, which laid down the foundation for social media cases in ECtHR case law, is from Estonia. As is demonstrated by Estonian case law, it has not been a difficult task for Estonian courts to undertake the balancing exercise between freedom of expression and the protection of honour and good name using the criteria laid down in the ECtHR jurisprudence. Recent case law in Estonia shows that the principles that were established in the *Delfi* precedent have also been extended to other cases, now including internet portals and blogs. Estonian courts use the criteria laid down in *Delfi* not only to apply the proportionality principle to identify the specific aspects of freedom of expression in cases concerning market players playing an intermediary role on the Internet but also in other cases – for instance, concerning bloggers. In *Delfi*, the ECtHR observed that this was the first case in which it had been called on to examine a complaint of this type in the evolving field of technological innovation and delineated the scope of its inquiry in the light of the facts of the case.[70] Does the judgment say it all? Judges Raimondi, Karakaş, De Gaetano and Kjølbro found the judgment to be too vague, and stated in their joint, concurring opinion that "the Court should have seized the opportunity to state more clearly the principles relevant to assessment of a case such as the present one".[71] This opinion that the ECtHR should have clarified the principles underlying its assessment seems justified. The domestic courts need standards to carry out balancing exercises on a case-by-case basis, on the one hand, and to apply standards which are in conformity with the principles embodied in Article 10 ECHR, on the other. However, despite the previously mentioned opinion, it still seems fair to conclude that *Delfi* says it all.

Notes

1 Constitution of the Republic of Estonia (*Eesti Vabariigi põhiseadus*), RT 1992, 26, 349; RT I, 15/5/2015, 2.

2 Pursuant to the Constitution, other administrative authorities created to carry out the functions of administering justice, such as labour dispute committees formed to settle individual labour disputes and the Industrial Property Committee created to settle intellectual property-related disputes, are not included in the court system.

3 Art 146 of the Constitution.
4 The Courts Act (*Kohtute seadus*), RT I 2002, 64, 390; RT I, 28/1/2021, 3, provides the legal basis for court administration and court services.
5 Constitutional Review Court Procedure Act (*Põhiseaduslikkuse järelevalve kohtumenetluse seadus*), RT I 2002, 29, 174; RT I, 7/3/2019, 4, sections 2(1) and 4. A petition may be filed by the President of the Republic, the Chancellor of Justice, the council of a local authority or the Estonian Parliament (*Riigikogu*).
6 Ibid, section 3(3).
7 The present Constitution was adopted on the basis of Article 1 of the Constitution which entered into force in 1938 and a referendum held on 28 June 1992.
8 Eva Lillemaa, Käti Mägi, Indrek-Ivar Määrits, Liiri Oja, Maria Sults and Ksenia Žurakovskaja-Aru in Ülle Madise and others (eds), *Eesti Vabariigi põhiseadus: Kommenteeritud väljaanne* (5th edn., Sihtasutus Iuridicum 2020) 237. <https://pohiseadus.ee/public/PSkomm2020.pdf> accessed 25 February 2023.
9 Rait Maruste and Karmen Turk, in Ülle Madise and others (eds), *Eesti Vabariigi põhiseadus: Kommenteeritud väljaanne* (5th edn., Sihtasutus Iuridicum 2020) 562.
10 Penal Code (*Karistusseadustik*), RT I 2001, 61, 364; RT I, 21/5/2021, 9. The Criminal Code (*Kriminaalkoodeks*), RT 1992, 20, 288, expired in 2002. The Criminal Code provided criminal liability for defamation and insult, whereas the Penal Code, which is now in force, provides liability for defamation and insult of, for example, a representative of state authority or a court, judge or lay judge in connection with their duties. It also criminalises activities which publicly incite hatred, violence or discrimination, or which threaten to kill or cause damage.
11 Law of Obligations Act (*Võlaõigusseadus*), RT I 2001, 81, 487; RT I, 8/12/2021, 11.
12 This number contains not only social media cases but also other cases concerning traditional news media that operate on the Internet and news portals that have similar features to social media.
13 Judgment of the Supreme Court of the Republic of Estonia no. 3–2–1–43–09 of 10 June 2009; Order of the Supreme Court of the Republic of Estonia no. 2–16–4631 of 21 December 2017. The information was collected from the publicly accessible Estonian case law databases www.riigiteataja.ee and www.riigikohus.ee.
14 The information about relevant domestic case law was collected from xLaw, a knowledge management system for lawyers.
15 Art 654(6) of the Code of Civil Procedure.
16 Ibid, Art 689(5).
17 Ibid, Art 679(3).
18 See, for example the judgment of the Tallinn Court of Appeal of 13 February 2019 in civil case no. 2–17–19184.
19 Following this Supreme Court judgment, the lower courts resolved the issue of liability regarding comments relating to online news articles in a similar manner.
20 According to section 1047(1) of the Law of Obligations Act, violation of personality rights by way of disclosure of incorrect information is unlawful. The Estonian words *avaldama* and *avaldaja* mean "to publish" and "publisher" or "to disclose" and "discloser". To publish means to communicate information to third parties and the publisher is the person who communicates the information to third parties.
21 It should be noted that the Supreme Court found that section 10 of the Information Society Services Act (*Infoühiskonna teenuse seadus*), RT I 2004, 29, 191 did not apply in the present case. Section 10 of this act sets out situations in which the service provider is not liable for the information stored at the request of a recipient of the service.
22 *Delfi v Estonia* App no 64569/09 (ECtHR, 16 June 2015).
23 Council of Europe documents: Declaration on freedom of communication on the Internet (Adopted by the Committee of Ministers on 28 May at the 840th meeting of the Ministers' Deputies; Recommendation CM/Rec(2007)16 of the

Committee of Ministers to member states on measures to promote the public service value of the Internet; Recommendation CM/Rec(2011)7 of the Committee of Ministers to member states on a new notion of media; Recommendation CM/Rec(2014)6 of the Committee of Ministers to member States on a Guide to human rights for Internet users (Adopted by the Committee of Ministers on 16 April 2014 at the 1197th meeting of the Ministers' Deputies).

24 Ibid, para 116.

25 Regulation (EU) No. 1215/2012 of the European Parliament and of the Council of 12 December 2012 on jurisdiction and the recognition and enforcement of judgments in civil and commercial matters (recast) [2012] OJ L 351/1.

26 Art 7(2) of Regulation (EU) No. 1215/2012 provides that a person domiciled in a Member State may be sued in another Member State in matters relating to tort, delict or quasi-delict, that is, in the courts of the place where the harmful event occurred or may have occurred.

27 Case C-194/16 *Bolagsupplysningen v Ilsjan* [2017] ECLI:EU:C:2017:766.

28 For a legal person pursuing an economic activity, the centre of interests of such a person must reflect the place where its commercial reputation is most firmly established and where it carries out the main part of its economic activities. It may coincide with the place of its registered office when it carries out all or the main part of its activities in the Member State in which that office is situated. The location of that office is not, however, in itself, a conclusive criterion.

29 The CJEU referred to its case law: Case C-68/93 *Shevill and Others* [1995] ECLI:EU:C:1995:61, paras 25, 26 and 32; and Joined Cases C-509/09 and C-161/10 *eDate Advertising and Others* [2011] ECLI:EU:C:2011:685, paras 42 and 48. The CJEU ruled in *eDate Advertising and Others* that, in the event of an alleged infringement of personality rights by means of content placed online on an internet website, the person who considers that his rights have been infringed has the option of bringing an action for liability in respect of all the damage caused, either before the courts of the Member State in which the publisher of that content is established or before the courts of the Member State in which the centre of his interests is based. That person may also, instead of an action for liability in respect of all the damage caused, bring his action before the courts of each Member State in the territory of which content placed online is or has been accessible. Those courts have jurisdiction only in respect of the damage caused in the territory of the Member State of the court seized.

30 To clarify, there are European Union regulations on private international law which deal with the question of the applicable law in cross-border cases. However, they do not fully cover issues such as evidence and procedure. See, for example, Article 1(3) of Regulation (EC) No 864/2007 of the European Parliament and of the Council of 11 July 2007 on the law applicable to non-contractual obligations (Rome II) [2007] OJ L 199/40, which states that this regulation shall not apply to evidence and procedure, without prejudice to Articles 21 and 22. Articles 21 and 22 concern formal validity and burden of proof.

31 See Articles 654(6) and 689(5) of the Code of Civil Procedure.

32 Rait Maruste and Karmen Turk, in Ülle Madise et al. (eds), *Eesti Vabariigi põhiseadus: Kommenteeritud väljaanne* (5th edn., Sihtasutus Iuridicum 2020) 542.

33 Ibid.

34 *Delfi v Estonia* (n 22).

35 *Magyar Tartalomszolgáltatók Egyesülete and Index.hu Zrt v Hungary* App no 22947/13 (EctHR, 2 February 2016).

36 *A. v Norway* App no 28070/06 (EctHR, 9 April 2009).

37 *Lingens v Austria* App no 9815/82 (EctHR, 8 July 1986).

38 Judgment of the Tartu County Court of 18 June 2019 in civil case no. 2–18–17361.
39 The ECtHR analysed the protection of politicians under Art 10(2) ECHR, stating that this protection extends to politicians too. However, the limits of acceptable criticism are wider as regards a politician as such than as regards a private individual. The ECtHR explained that a politician inevitably and knowingly lays himself open to close scrutiny of his every word and deed by both journalists and the public at large, and he must consequently display a greater degree of tolerance.
40 Judgment of the Harju County Court of 21 December 2015 in civil case no. 2–15–3860; Judgment of the Harju County Court of 28 March 2016 in civil case no. 2–15–15724; Judgment of the Harju County Court of 8 May 2018 in civil case no. 2–17–11523; Judgment of the Harju County Court of 28 November 2019 in civil case no. 2–17–11524.
41 Judgment of the Harju County Court of 8 May 2018 in civil case no. 2–17–11523.
42 *Pfeifer v Austria* App no 12556/03 (EctHR, 15 November 2007).
43 *A. v Norway* (n 36).
44 Para 19 of the judgment of the Harju County Court of 8 May 2018 in civil case no. 2–17–11523.
45 *Bladet Tromsø and Stensaas v Norway* App no 21980/93 (EctHR, 20 May 1999).
46 In para 63 of the *Bladet Tromsø and Stensaas* judgment, the ECtHR considered it important that the thrust of the impugned articles was not primarily to accuse certain individuals of committing offences or of cruelty to animals. The articles were part of an ongoing debate of evident concern to the local, national and international public in which the views of a wide selection of interested actors were reported.
47 To clarify, the comments had already been removed on the claimant's request.
48 Judgment of the Tallinn Court of Appeal of 16 January 2019 in civil case no. 2–17–11523.
49 In *MTE*, the ECtHR found that Hungarian courts did not perform any balancing at all between the right to freedom of expression and the right to reputation, and therefore concluded that there had been a violation of Art 10 ECHR. In order to differentiate the cases, *Delfi* dealt with clearly unlawful speech amounting to hate speech and incitement to violence, while *MTE* dealt with offensive and vulgar speech.
50 Judgment of the Harju County Court in civil case no. 2–17–11523 (n 40).
51 Judgment of the Harju County Court in civil case no. 2–15–3860 (n 40).
52 *Hertel v Switzerland* App n. 25181/94 (ECtHR, 25 August 1998), para 46.
53 *Steel and Morris v UK* App no 68416/01 (ECtHR, 15 February 2005), para 87.
54 *Mouvement raëlien suisse v Switzerland* App no 16354/06 (ECtHR, 13 July 2012), para 48.
55 *Animal Defenders International v UK* App no 48876/08 (ECtHR, 22 April 2013), para 100.
56 Para 20 of the judgment of the Harju County Court of 21 December 2015 in civil case no. 2–15–3860.
57 Judgment of the Harju County Court in civil case no. 2–15–15724 (n 40).
58 The same business model was used as in the *Delfi* case.
59 Para 64 of *A. v Norway* (n 36).
60 Para 142 of the *Delfi* judgment (n 22).
61 Para 83 of the *MTE* judgment (n 35).
62 *Perinçek v Switzerland* App no 27510/08 (ECtHR, 15 October 2015).
63 Ibid, para 79.
64 Judgment of the Tallinn Court of Appeal of 29 July 2016 in civil case no. 2–15–15724.

65 Judgment of the Tallinn Court of Appeal in civil case no. 2–17–19184 (n 18).
66 Advertising Act (*Reklaamiseadus*), RT I 2008, 15, 108, RT I, 01.07.2020, 13.
67 *Von Hannover v Germany (no. 2)* App Nos 40660/08 and 60641/08 (ECtHR, 7 February 2012), para 98.
68 Para 110 of the *Delfi* judgment (n 22).
69 Ibid, para 127.
70 Ibid, para 111.
71 Ibid, para 9 of the joint, concurring opinion.

5 A rights-based approach to social media under the midnight sun

Social media before courts and other constitutional actors in Finland

Marta Maroni, Tuomas Ojanen and Eveliina Ignatius

1. Introduction

The intersection between social media and fundamental rights is entering into the Finnish scene of constitutionalism in which courts and other constitutional actors in Finland are increasingly ruling on cases involving fundamental rights in social media settings. While freedom of expression, the right to privacy and the right to the protection of personal data tend to be affected most often and most directly, increasing case law indicates that the use of social media also impacts several other fundamental rights, including the right to equality, the right to non-discrimination and freedom of religion.

Finland has a written constitution with a broad and modern catalogue of fundamental rights (Chapter II of the Constitution).[1] The domestic system for the protection of fundamental rights is complemented by international human rights treaties.[2] Finland has ratified and incorporated all regional and international human rights treaties adopted within the framework of the Council of Europe, the United Nations and the International Labour Organization. As Section 22 of the Finnish Constitution obliges public authorities to guarantee the observance of fundamental rights and human rights, the European Convention on Human Rights (ECtHR) and other international human rights treaties binding upon Finland are regarded as enjoying "semi-constitutional status". As a matter of constitutional law, international human rights treaties are understood as providing the minimum standard of rights protection and, accordingly, courts and public authorities are expected to offer higher standards of rights protection under the constitutional system. In practice, the domestic tendency in recent years has been towards the *harmonisation* of constitutional and international protection of rights through the influence of the ECtHR and international human rights treaties, as interpreted by the European Court of Human Rights (ECtHR) and other international treaty bodies.[3] This tendency is also visible in Finnish case law concerning social media, where the protection of fundamental rights is almost invariably based on the standards and reasoning of the ECtHR.

DOI: 10.4324/9781003207085-7

As with the other Nordic countries, there is no constitutional court in Finland, and the Finnish constitutional system is still far from being a fully-fledged judicial review typical of continental constitutional courts and their counterpart in the United States. Instead, the current Finnish system of constitutional review is a peculiar mix of abstract *ex ante* and tangible *ex post* forms of constitutional review. The primary authority of constitutional interpretation and review is *the Constitutional Law Committee of Parliament* whereas judicial review by courts is primarily intended to plug loopholes left in the abstract *ex ante* review of the constitutionality of government bills by the Constitutional Law Committee, since unforeseen constitutional problems may arise when the courts apply the law in particular cases. The limited role of judicial review is codified in Section 106 of the Constitution which obliges courts to give primacy to the provision in the Constitution when the application of an Act of Parliament is in "evident conflict" with the Constitution.[4] Especially the criterion of "evident conflict" is intended to limit the role of courts in reviewing the constitutionality of Acts of Parliament.[5] Judicial review by the courts is limited to individual cases and the courts do not have the right to assess an Act at a general level, nor can they declare an Act unconstitutional and, accordingly, null and void. The requirement of an "evident conflict" also functions to channel the constitutional interpretations and arguments applied at the legislative stage by the Constitutional Law Committee to the concrete legal argumentation of the judiciary. This is because, as a rule, a court should not regard the conflict as evident within the meaning of Section 106 if the Constitutional Law Committee has already considered the relevant Act of Parliament to be in harmony with the Constitution. In practice, courts often tend to avoid the application of Section 106 by trying to interpret the Act in harmony with the Constitution.

This chapter analyses the approach of Finnish courts to fundamental rights in a social media setting: how do courts safeguard fundamental and human rights in the context of social media? In doing so, it also reflects on the role of the courts in safeguarding fundamental rights in social media. While addressing these questions, the chapter also sheds light on judicial dialogue between Finnish actors and European courts in cases involving the interface between fundamental rights and social media. Given that the Constitution still acknowledges a form of *weak judicial review*, the following discussion also considers the Constitutional Law Committee of Parliament, as well as the Parliamentary Ombudsman[6] and some other quasi-judicial actors who have dealt with fundamental rights in a social media context.

The bulk of Finnish case law is still relatively meagre, but it is growing incrementally,[7] especially if social media is understood broadly so as to include blogging sites, webpages and discussion and review networks alongside a range of social networks such as a Twitter, Facebook and TikTok.[8] Social media cases can be found from both main branches of the Finnish court system, i.e. from ordinary courts dealing with civil suits and criminal cases, and from administrative courts reviewing the decisions of executive authorities. However, as the purpose of this chapter is illustrative rather than exhaustive, the following analysis is based on a selection of the most significant cases, mainly from the Supreme Court (KKO) and the Supreme Administrative Court (KHO).[9]

Generally, the structures and patterns of fundamental rights adjudication in the context of social media by Finnish courts and other constitutional actors are still in the process of taking shape. In other words, the reasoning of the Finnish judiciary system is still "unripe" when it comes to elaborating complex social phenomena associated with social media platforms. This having been said, the case law discussed in this chapter demonstrates that, when Finnish courts and other actors deal with harm on social media, they are inclined to adopt a rights-based approach. In doing so, they systematically refer to ECtHR case law, which becomes an integral part of the domestic judicial reasoning up to the point where it is often difficult to separate the two. This strong impact of ECtHR case law on Finnish courts might be considered problematic as a matter of constitutional law, since the ECtHR is only intended to provide a minimum standard of rights protection. However, there is less judicial reference to EU law, including the well-established case law of the Court of Justice of the European Union (CJEU) on social media.[10] The limited references to EU law and CJEU case law practically result in disengaging with questions concerning the liability of social media platforms[11] when it comes to the dissemination of harmful content and the violation of privacy. In other words, social media platforms themselves are never involved in the disputes.

This chapter is divided as follows. The following section (Section 2) provides an overview of Finnish jurisprudence on the interface between fundamental rights and social media. Section 3 examines how Finnish courts and other actors have used case law from the two European courts. Section 4 provides a brief conclusion.

2. Fundamental rights in social media jurisprudence

From the early 1990s onwards, the constitutional tendency has increasingly been towards rights-based judicial review in Finland. One distinct dimension of this tendency is that courts have gradually begun to refer to constitutional provisions on fundamental rights and international human rights treaties binding upon Finland. In particular, the courts carefully engage with the ECtHR, as interpreted by the ECtHR, but other human rights treaties are also cited.

The Supreme Administrative Court has been for a long time at the forefront of this judicial tendency, but in recent years, the Supreme Court and lower courts have also referred to constitutional provisions on fundamental rights and international human rights treaties with the ECtHR at their apex. Primarily, courts have given judicial effect to fundamental rights and human rights indirectly, through interpreting ordinary legislation and other enactments in harmony with fundamental rights and human rights (the rights-oriented interpretation approach). However, there is also case law representing the direct application of fundamental rights and human rights by courts, i.e. judgments in which courts directly invoke these rights in their judicial reasoning in order to decide a case. Moreover, the judicial practice revolving around rights has included a tendency to apply "balancing" and "weighting" in cases which have required courts to strike a balance between various rights. For instance, there are relatively many examples of case law in which courts have balanced the right to privacy and the protection of personal data, on the one hand, and freedom of expression and the right to information, on the other.[12] In the context of social media, some sort of judicial preference for privacy rights at the expense of freedom of expression can be noted earlier, resulting in the ECtHR finding several times a violation of Article 10 ECtHR on freedom of expression by Finland in the 2000s.[13]

Emerging Finnish case law on the interface between fundamental rights and social media can largely, if not exclusively, be seen as a continuum of the previously mentioned judicial tendencies. Case law on social media shows that judicial reasoning in social media cases often includes fundamental rights and human rights. Several cases involve judicial reasoning that aims at striking a balance between various conflicting rights. While freedom of expression and the right to privacy, including the right to the protection of personal data, are the fundamental rights that are most affected in social media cases, there is also case law that involves other rights, such as the right to equality and the right to non-discrimination,[14] freedom of thought, conscience and religion.[15]

In what follows, the analysis focuses on a selected number of cases from the Supreme Court of Finland. The analysis of the cases shows that the Supreme Court places emphasis on the protection of privacy when carrying out its balancing exercise concerning freedom of expression. This might relate to the fact that the use of social media comes with greater risks to privacy because of the possibility of making information widely available and accessible. Domestic courts carefully consider these aspects. Specifically, although the starting point of courts is to acknowledge that the same standard or level of rights protection should be afforded online as much as offline, each case offers different perspectives on how the Finnish Supreme Court relates to the nature of the Internet and the affordances of social media platforms and their use.

This section now moves to discuss some cases revolving around privacy and freedom of expression. The core issue of the first case, the YouTube case (KKO 2018:81), is whether the publication on YouTube of a video that was important for the public debate – namely, the use of force by state authorities – could infringe the right of privacy of two children and their best interest. Although, the Supreme Court recognised the importance of the publication, when balancing various interests, it established that children should enjoy a greater protection of privacy. The video displayed the dramatic moment of two children being taken away by social service personnel who were accompanied by police. The video showed vividly the children´s feelings, and their faces were only partially blurred. Furthermore, the setting (a house courtyard) and the context made them identifiable on the video.

The guardian of the children had recorded the video and sent it to another person, who had made it available for the public at the guardian's request.

They both were prosecuted for dissemination of information violating personal privacy by making available to many persons the children's private life in a way that would cause harm, suffering and contempt for them. The Supreme Court, in deciding the case, recognised that the action and the use of force by the authorities was an issue of social significance and that denouncing its abuse should be a prerequisite for democratic society. As such, the publication of the video served the purpose of making the conduct of the authorities public, and usually, in such cases, freedom of expression enjoys broad protection. The Court also noted, however, that revealing the identity of the children did not add any value to the message that the video wished to convey.

The Supreme Court, in finding that the publication of the video clearly went beyond what is admissible, emphasised both the form of communication (a video) and its form of dissemination (the Internet). The Court noted that images and videos have greater impact than words and remarked that the protection of children's privacy bore more weight than the parent's freedom of expression. Furthermore, the Court found that the fact that the video was made accessible to anyone and published on the Internet aggravated the situation. In the balancing process, the Court considered the risk that it is almost impossible to delete information once published. In addition, the Court reasoned that an online video might re-emerge any time, and this makes the publication even more harmful.[16] Thus, in this case, the degree of protection of privacy became broader precisely because of the impact of social media in making information available.

In the second case (KKO 2018:51) considered for the purpose of this chapter, the Supreme Court had to decide between the protection of privacy of a person convicted of child exploitation and the dissemination of invasive information about them on Facebook. The Supreme Court regarded the Internet as an important means for disseminating information, but the Court also noted the risks for the protection of privacy, which deserves to be protected online as much as offline. The case involved the person sharing the information (the applicant) claiming their freedom of expression against being charged for a violation of privacy. The accused had taken a picture of the person convicted from their Facebook profile, linked it to news reporting the conviction and had also posted it on a Facebook page called "Paedophilia victims". A lively debate followed the publication of the post, and to a certain extent, the applicant had moderated the debate by deleting some of the comments. The Supreme Court, in confirming that a violation had occurred, held that such a publication was liable to cause stigmatisation.

The third case (KKO 2019:81) was a defamation case. Here, the Supreme Court began its reasoning by assessing the nature of online speech and the degree of protection to be afforded to it. The Supreme Court agreed on the suspension of distribution and the destruction of online messages and comments in which the applicant was called a supporter of paedophiles.

In this case, the applicant requested the suspension of distribution and the taking down of four online messages, in which they were called a protector of paedophiles and implied that they were a paedophile themself. Two of these messages contained their name and picture. The Finnish lower courts dismissed the applicant's request by submitting that the content of the messages was vague and could not be considered manifestly unlawful. The courts noted that the messages were inaccurate and that, consequently, they could not have been regarded as true by alert readers. They could therefore not have caused harm or contempt. The lower courts also observed that the content of the messages did not contain any information about the applicant's private life and the Court of Appeal also pointed to the fact that views expressed on the Internet are often sharp and coloured.

The Supreme Court challenged these interpretations. The Court started by recalling the scope of privacy, which, at its core, protects matters of personal identity and the right to live without unwanted attention. The Supreme Court further held that public stigmatisation can affect a person's life, opportunities and interaction in society. Nonetheless, the Supreme Court also highlighted that privacy needs to be balanced against freedom of expression, which enjoys broader protection when it relates to debates of public interest. In order to balance the previously mentioned rights, the Supreme Court put at the centre of its analysis the status of the person, arguing that an individual unknown to the public should enjoy a strong protection of privacy. Overall, the Court considered the online messages threatening, not relevant to matters of general interest, and causing the applicant financial loss and difficulties in obtaining employment and livelihood. However, the Supreme Court also pointed out that the comments section was an integral part of the publication. The Court noted in particular:

> Comments can be read immediately below the posts produced by the publisher. Thus, they have gained a wider distribution than the customary Internet forum. Published texts are not just about sub-style writing or hints that are vague or insignificant in content.[17]

Aside from cases revolving around privacy rights and freedom of expression, several cases in the social media context have also brought about tension concerning the right to non-discrimination in recent years. One of the most significant cases is still the landmark ruling by the Supreme Court in case KKO 2012:58. In this case, a member of the Finnish Parliament had published a blog entry on his website in which he had described Islam as a paedophile religion. He also claimed that stealing and living a parasitic life at the expense of the welfare system constitutes a national and even genetic characteristic of Somalis. The question for the Supreme Court to answer was whether the politician was guilty of a breach of the sanctity of religion and ethnic agitation by his actions. Originally, the legislation on incitement to hatred (ethnic agitation) was enacted in order to implement the obligation under the International Convention on the Elimination of All Forms of Racial Discrimination, as well as the obligation under Article 20(2) of the International Covenant on Civil and Political Rights, according to which "any advocacy of national, racial or religious hatred that constitutes incitement to discrimination, hostility or violence shall be prohibited by law".[18]

The Helsinki District Court and the Court of Appeal had previously acquitted the defendant of the charge of incitement to hatred, but the Court of Appeal convicted him for breach of the sanctity of religion. The Supreme Court convicted the politician for both ethnic agitation – a charge known elsewhere as incitement to racial or ethnic hatred – as well as for the breach of the sanctity of religion.[19] Before the Court, the defendant had invoked freedom of expression and claimed that the intention of his blog entry had been to criticise the Finnish authorities and the press for their uncritical acceptance and treatment of Somalis as an ethnic group.

The Supreme Court noted that the defendant's intention was to provide a critique of the press and authorities. However, the Court then emphasised that such an intention does not justify defaming and insulting. The Court concluded that the defendant had clearly understood the defamatory and insulting nature of his text, although part of it was written in an ironic style. Since the defendant had also been actively involved in politics, the Court took the view that this activity should also be taken into account when assessing the boundaries between freedom of expression and its restrictions. The Supreme Court concluded that the claim made about Somalis as a group was defamatory and insulting and that the statements were also likely to arouse intolerance, contempt and even hatred and that such "hate speech" does not enjoy the protection of freedom of expression.

As a result, the Supreme Court sentenced the politician to a 50-day fine (300 EURO) and ordered him to delete the parts of the blog text that included incitement to hatred/ethnic agitation. As a consequence of the judgment, the politician also had to resign from the chair of the Administration Committee of Parliament.

In recent years, cases involving ethnic agitation and hate speech by local or national politicians have become quite common in social media, and they have often sparked heated debate over the limits of freedom of expression. In 2021, the World Press Freedom Index, compiled by Reporters Without Borders, ranked Finland second in press freedom, but it simultaneously warned that the Finnish media is increasingly under threat by online hate speech. According to the NGO, this was especially the case on social media platforms which "amplify disinformation".[20]

3. Judicial dialogue with the CJEU and the ECtHR

From the outset, one key component of the constitutional tendency towards rights-based judicial review has been the so-called "constitutional dialogue" between domestic courts (as well as other Finnish actors), European courts (the ECtHR and the CJEU) and other international human rights organisations. This section illustrates this judicial dialogue between Finnish courts and European courts through references to case law. As already mentioned,

ECtHR case law sets the standard for the reasoning of Finnish courts in cases involving fundamental and human rights. In the context of social media, too, it is possible to appreciate how the Finnish judiciary mostly enters into dialogue with the ECtHR, whose judgments direct and shape decision-making by the Finnish courts.

The case law of the two European courts has become an important source of law that has increasingly contributed to the Europeanisation of Finnish law since the 1990s.[21] In particular, the two highest Courts – i.e. the Supreme Court and the Supreme Administrative Court – tend to cite individual judgments by the ECtHR at length, but detailed references to ECtHR case law can also be found from lower courts.[22] The same can be said about judicial references by Finnish courts to case law from the CJEU in cases falling within the scope of the application of EU law.[23] Nowadays, the Constitutional Law Committee of Parliament is also accustomed to taking notice of the case law of the two European courts when considering the compatibility of legislative proposals with the Constitution and international human rights treaties.

However, while there is much judicial dialogue between Finnish courts, as well as the Constitutional Law Committee of Parliament and European courts, genuine constitutional dialogue between major domestic constitutional actors is still sporadic. For example, the interpretive practice of the Constitutional Law Committee tends to be based on formal, isolated and monologic opinions with only rare references to case law from domestic courts on fundamental and human rights. Even in cases involving interpretive tensions between the Committee and the courts, the Committee has been prone to disregard judicial interpretations. Similarly, the practice of the Finnish courts leaves much to be desired when they refer to the interpretive practice of the Committee.[24]

3.1 *Judicial dialogue between Finnish courts and European courts in the context of social media*

This section offers insights into the strong judicial dialogue between Finnish domestic courts and the European supranational courts in the context of social media disputes. Finnish courts often reproduce patterns of the ECtHR reasoning, and this trend indicates that the ECtHR is particularly central in developing the Finnish judicial analysis on fundamental rights. The section first returns to the cases introduced in section 2 and then demonstrates, through additional cases, how European supranational courts influence Finnish legislative decision-making, which naturally impacts on the courts' decision.

The previously discussed cases required the Supreme Court to untangle the tensions between freedom of expression and privacy rights. These are very complex rights to balance, especially in the context of social media, which poses new challenges in protecting fundamental rights. Generally, the Supreme Court adopts a broad protection of privacy, thus conforming to the European approach in which privacy is taken very seriously.[25] For example, in the YouTube case (KKO 2018:81), the Supreme Court started its interpretation by considering that the ECtHR and the CJEU had "consistently held that the concept of privacy must not be interpreted narrowly but has a broad meaning which cannot be defined exhaustively at all".[26] Drawing on the ECtHR, the Supreme Court introduced the core dimensions of privacy, such as the right to determine how and in what context a person might appear in public, the protection of personal identity as well as a person's physical and mental integrity and the right to live in peace without being subjected to unwanted attention. The Supreme Court emphasised that children have their own rights and it referred to the ECtHR rulings *K.U. v Finland*, and *Kurier Zeitungsverlag und Druckerei GmbH v Austria* to remark that children's privacy deserves special protection due to their vulnerable position.[27]

Likewise, in the case concerning the sharing of private information about a convicted person on social media (KKO 2018:51), the Supreme Court rooted its reasoning in ECtHR case law on the right to privacy and recalled that privacy relates to the need of a person to define their interaction with others. In order to decide on the case, the Supreme Court highlighted that freedom of expression is a limited right. Here, the Supreme Court reverted to the ECtHR's *Hannover v Germany*[28] and emphasised that the very first criterion for assessing freedom of expression is to evaluate whether the publication at stake contributes to a debate of general interest, which generally encompasses political and criminal issues. Furthermore, the Supreme Court reasoned that it is also important to evaluate for whom the publication is intended – i.e. whether it is meant to satisfy the curiosity of a particular readership. The Supreme Court also considered that a private individual enjoys particularly strong protection of privacy. In this regard, persons convicted or suspected of a crime also enjoy their right to privacy, which is determined on a case-by-case basis. The Supreme Court acknowledged the significance of debating a crime, but found that to reveal the identity of a convicted person is not relevant.

The influence of ECtHR case law is not limited to the framing of rights, but it is also prominent in the endeavour of the Finnish judiciary to conceptualise the Internet, rethinking speech and visibility in the digital environment. For example, in most cases, the Supreme Court refers to key findings of the ECtHR concerning the Internet; for example, that the Internet plays a significant role for the transmission of information and that, at the same time, it poses greater risks for the protection of privacy than traditional media.[29]

Again, the YouTube case (KKO 2018:81) provides an interesting example regarding the use of ECtHR jurisprudence. In this case, the Supreme Court devoted much attention to ECtHR case law when evaluating the way images and people are made public and followed the ECtHR's steps in transferring the criteria traditionally applied to the press to the Internet – i.e. the quality and seriousness of the invasion of privacy; the reach of the dissemination; and whether there was consent.[30] In the defamation case (KKO 2019:81), the Supreme Court engaged with the thorny question of how to consider vulgar speech, which is not necessarily unlawful, though it relates to how people use social media and to issues of credibility concerning online information. These issues were much disputed in the cases of *Delfi v Estonia*[31] and *MTE v Hungary* (2016).[32] However, in the YouTube case, the Supreme Court – as discussed previously – considered comments in which the applicant was called a protector of paedophiles to be threatening and unlawful. The lower court first ruled that Internet users express themselves in ways that can be considered offensive or derogatory, but many comments are likely to be so insignificant that they do not necessarily damage the reputation of others. However, the Supreme Court overruled this finding and noted that a person is not obliged to tolerate allegations of a violent crime that are not substantiated by the facts. This passage crucially informed the reasoning of the Supreme Court, which argued that, although expression must be considered in its context and that online discussions use exaggerated and harsh language, there is a need to discern between comments infringing privacy and insults. The Supreme Court ruled that the publication of the profile picture in this context was a serious intrusion into the person's private life, especially because the picture had been taken secretly and without the person's consent. Furthermore, the Supreme Court considered the publications as a whole and the terms used to address the person – e.g. "online snitch" and "protector of paedophiles" – vulgar and derogatory in style.

Throughout the decision, the Supreme Court referred in detail to ECtHR jurisprudence, while there were fewer references to CJEU case law. Hence, this case demonstrates how ECtHR case law influences domestic judicial reasoning when balancing rights. However, it is also evident that the Finnish judiciary can, on occasion, deploy supranational cases uncritically. In other words, Finnish domestic courts might use passages of supranational cases even when these have been generally perceived as being problematic (e.g. by dissenting opinion and by scholars).[33] This appears in case KKO 2019:81, where the Supreme Court considered the commenting messages on social media to be an integral part of an online publication. With this finding, the Court aligned itself with the ECtHR ruling in *Delfi v Estonia*, where the ECtHR regarded the commenting space under a newspaper article to be a part of the publication. It is important to remind ourselves, however, that the issue of how to understand the commenting space was, at that time, still unresolved. The question was: Is a commenting space an unmonitored space for user-generated content or an edited space in which the publisher can be held liable for third party wrongdoing? Some scholars highlighted that, under the e-Commerce Directive[34] and CJEU reasoning, the commenting space could be understood as a hosting space.[35] However, the proposed Digital Services Act establishes that the comments section in an online newspaper can be considered an ancillary feature to the main service represented by the publication of news under the editorial responsibility of the publisher.[36]

The cases discussed reveal the extent to which ECtHR and, to a lesser extent, CJEU case law is ingrained in the Supreme Court's reasoning. This remaining part shows how the European supranational courts also influence judicial reasoning through Finnish legislation. In 2013, the Parliament amended the Criminal Code of Finland (39/1889) in the light of ECtHR case law. This change included restrictive subsections to provisions for dissemination of information violating personal privacy (Chapter 24, Section 8) and defamation (Chapter 24, Section 9). The restrictive subsections have already been applied several times in social media-related cases concerning speech crimes, such as defamation. Vivid examples are the previously discussed defamation cases decided by the Supreme Court. The Bill emphasises that the courts must pay attention to the latest case law of the ECtHR and content of expression crimes must be compatible with fundamental rights and human rights and align with ECtHR case law.[37]

Case law shows that the courts have adopted this practice; for example, in case KKO 2022:1, the Supreme Court took ECtHR case law widely into account by explicitly referring to several cases concerning social media. In this case, a freelance journalist had called a municipal politician a racist, a Nazi and a Nazi clown in a Facebook post that was published to a limited group of people. Paying close attention to ECtHR case[38] law as well as to national case law, the Court assessed the distinct rights (journalists' freedom of expression and politicians' right to private life, including protection of reputation and honour). The Supreme Court concluded that the wording of the restrictive subsection of the defamation provision (Chapter 24, Section 9 of the Criminal Code) was open about the method and the instrument of the presentation, and thus that the criticism of political activities could be presented on social media.

The nature of the judicial dialogue in social media-related case law suggests that the ECtHR's jurisprudence has a strong influence on domestic judicial argumentation and deliberation. Some cases even display such judicial deference to ECtHR case law in which the courts seem to passively substitute their own reasoning for rulings by the ECtHR. The courts hardly reflect any critical approach in their reasoning, nor do they argue why certain cases are chosen. This kind of judicial minimalism raises concerns, since domestic courts are not supposed to just passively defer to the minimum standard of rights protection illustrated by ECtHR case law. Instead, they are expected to provide a high standard of protection under the domestic system for the protection of fundamental rights.

While judicial dialogue with the ECtHR is already multifaceted, judicial dialogue between domestic courts and the CJEU in social media cases has, to date, remained virtually non-existent. This is striking in the light of the central role of the EU in social media regulation and the fact that the CJEU's case law is systematically and routinely invoked by Finnish courts in other types of cases. The lack of references by Finnish courts to CJEU case law on fundamental rights in the social media setting may be owing to the fact that case law involving EU law and fundamental rights has generally remained very sparse in Finland until now, although this is hardly a comprehensive explanation. However, given the prominent role of the EU in the field of social media regulation, it is most likely only a matter of time until judicial references to EU law, including CJEU case law, will increase in social media cases.

3.2 Judicial dialogue and other domestic constitutional actors

The reasoning of the quasi-judicial actors also contains judicial dialogue with the European courts. The Parliamentary Ombudsman, for example, often refers to ECtHR case law in its decisions. A decision by the Parliamentary Ombudsman on teachers' freedom of expression is illustrative, since it includes comprehensive references to ECtHR case law concerning freedom of expression. In this case, the complainant (a teacher) had received a note from their employer for writing a blog post that the employer considered to be a breach of the employee's loyalty obligation. The Parliamentary Ombudsman concluded that the note entailed interference with the freedom of expression enjoyed by the employee and that there was no acceptable justification for this interference. Thus, the Ombudsman decided that there had been a violation of the complainant's freedom of expression under Section 12 of the Constitution and Article 10 ECtHR.

Similarly, the main domestic authority of constitutional interpretation and review – the Constitutional Law Committee of Parliament – considers ECtHR and EU law, including the EU Charter of Fundamental Rights and the case law of the two European courts. The Constitutional Law Committee usually invokes constitutional provisions, the ECtHR and the EU Charter of Fundamental Rights, including the case law of the European courts, on fundamental and human rights in tandem. This has been the case when the Committee has issued opinions on social media-related legislation as well. However, due to the abstract nature of the Committee's opinions, potential questions related to social media are not invoked in detail or further discussed. Basically, the Committee has repeatedly stated that the freedom of expression must be understood in a broad sense to cover also communication online and as a medium-neutral fundamental right. Communication through information networks, however, can bring about relevant new perspectives to the balancing of fundamental rights and rights-based constitutional review in general by the Committee.

4. Conclusion

This chapter provided an overview of contemporary Finnish case law pertaining to social media and fundamental rights. Although the overall number of cases remains modest, case analysis emphasises two central trends and patterns. The first is the rights-based approach: Finnish courts and other actors systematically consider fundamental and human rights when assessing social media-related cases. In particular, freedom of expression, the right to privacy, and the right to the protection of personal data are the most directly impacted rights by social media. However, other rights, such as freedom of religion and the right to non-discrimination, are also involved in some cases. Another pattern is that Finnish courts take advantage of ECtHR jurisprudence as the main source for establishing the level of rights protection in social media cases. By contrast, judicial dialogue with the CJEU is still rare, and constitutional dialogue between major domestic constitutional actors also remains quite sporadic.

The willingness of the courts to put much emphasis on ECtHR case law might raise some concerns: the use of ECtHR jurisprudence as the main source for establishing the level of rights protection seems to have resulted in marginal significance for both fundamental rights enshrined in the Finnish Constitution and other human rights treaties binding upon Finland. Yet, the constitutional doctrine is that international human rights obligations, including the ECtHR, "only" feature as minimum standards of rights protection and that the domestic constitutional system of rights protection should offer a higher level of protection. These tendencies towards passive and minimalist interpretive approaches by the Finnish courts to social media cases may at least partially originate in traditional constitutional conceptions regarding rights, courts and majoritarian notions of democracy. These conceptions are still strong enough to keep effective judicial protection of fundamental and human rights at a minimum level also in social media cases on the Finnish scene of constitutionalism, unless authoritative reasons, such as legislative enactments or judgments by the European courts, clearly require otherwise.

Overall, the domestic courts are little by little recognising the constitutional relevance of social media in contemporary society, although they have hardly been at the forefront of constitutional developments pertaining to social media. Given also that judiciaries have traditionally had rather marginal legal roles on the Nordic scene of constitutionalism, it is quite unlikely that Finnish courts can ever achieve a principal role in ensuring the protection of fundamental rights in the social media. Instead, the courts are more likely to be still committed to adjudicating from the premise that the legislature has the competence to determine the content of fundamental rights and that judicial powers must then be exercised in this pre-legislated legal framework. Indeed, there is hardly room in traditional constitutional thinking for judicial activism and "law-making" by the Finnish courts. Hence, domestic and supranational legislators should primarily intervene and provide the regulatory framework within which courts then further adjudicate fundamental rights in individual cases involving social media.

Notes

1 The authors would like to thank the editors, Federica Casarosa and Evangelia Psychogiopoulou, for their comments on an early draft. Marta Maroni would like to acknowledge the support received from the Academy of Finland research projects: AlgoT – Potential and Boundaries of Algorithmic Transparency (decision n 324116) and POP – Is this Public or Private? (decision n 321995).

For the Finnish constitutional system for the protection of fundamental and human rights, see e.g. Martin Scheinin, 'Finland', in Martin Scheinin (ed), *International Human Rights Norms in the Nordic and Baltic countries* (Martinus Nijhoff Publishers 1996) 257–280; and Tuomas Ojanen, 'Finland', in Laurence Burgorgue-Larsen (ed), *La Chartre des droits fondamentaux de l'Union européenne saisie par les juges en Europe/The EU Charter of Fundamental Rights as Apprehended by National Judges* (Pedone 2017).

2 The terms "constitutional rights", "fundamental rights" and "basic rights" are often used interchangeably in European and Nordic constitutional discourse to refer to

rights enshrined in the domestic constitutions. The term "human rights", in turn, is typically used in international law to denote rights guaranteed by international human rights treaties, such as the ECtHR or the International Covenant on Civil and Political Rights (ICCPR). In this chapter, the concept of fundamental rights denotes rights enshrined in the Finnish constitution, whereas the notion of human rights refers to rights enshrined in international human rights treaties binding upon Finland.

3 For an overview of the domestic status and effects of international human rights treaties in Finland, see Tuomas Ojanen, 'Human Rights in Nordic Constitutions and the Impact of International Obligations', in Helle Krunke and Björg Thorarensen (eds), *The Nordic Constitutions: A Comparative and Contextual Study* (Hart Publishing 2018) 133.

4 Tuomas Ojanen, 'From Constitutional Periphery toward the Center – Transformations of Judicial Review in Finland' (2009) *Nordisk tidsskrift for menneskerettigheter* 194. See in detail, Juha Lavapuro, Tuomas Ojanen and Martin Scheinin, 'Rights-Based Constitutionalism in Finland and the Development of Pluralist Constitutional Review' (2011) 9 *International Journal of Constitutional Law* 505. See also Juha Lavapuro, Tuomas Ojanen and Martin Scheinin, 'Intermediate Constitutional Review in Finland: Promising in Theory, Problematic in Practice', in John Bell and Marie-Luce Paris (eds), *Rights-Based Constitutional Review: Constitutional Courts in a Changing Landscape* (Edward Elgar Publishing 2016) 218.

5 For background on Section 106, see Tuomas Ojanen, 'From Constitutional Periphery toward the Center – Transformations of Judicial Review in Finland' (2009) 27 *NJHR* 194, 202–206.

6 The Parliamentary Ombudsman oversees and promotes the legality of actions taken by public authorities and the implementation of fundamental and human rights.

7 In 2009–2020, there were 20 cases related to social media in the highest courts of Finland.

8 Cf. Evangelia Psychogiopoulou and Federica Casarosa, 'Social Media before Domestic Courts in Europe: An Analysis of Free Speech Cases' (2020) 27(6) *Maastricht Journal of European and Comparative Law* 791.

9 The selected cases are from the period 2012–2022.

10 Cf. Marta Maroni and Elda Brogi, 'Freedom of Expression and the Rule of Law: The Debate in the Context of Online Platform Regulation', in Elda Brogi and Pier Parcu (eds), *Research Handbook on EU Media Law and Policy* (Edward Elgar Publishing 2021). For an overview of privacy and EU case law, cf. Susanna Lindroos-Hovinheimo, *Private Selves: Legal Personhood in European Privacy Protection* (Cambridge University Press 2021). Otherwise, Finnish courts often invoke CJEU case law in other types of cases. For an overview of Finnish court practice regarding the case law of the ECtHR and the CJEU, see Tuomas Ojanen, 'Eurooppatuomioistuimet ja suomalaiset tuomioistuimet' ('European Courts and Finnish Courts') (2005) 103 *Lakimies* 1210. See also Lavapuro et al. (n 4)

11 Maroni and Brogi (n 10).

12 For these constitutional and judicial tendencies, see Lavapuro et al. (n 4) 233–242.

13 See e.g. ECtHR, *Flinkkilä and Others v Finland* App No 25576/04 (6 April 2010); ECtHR, *Jokitaipale and Others v Finland* App No 43349/05 (6 April 2010), ECtHR, *Iltalehti and Karhuvaara v Finland* App. No. 6372/06 (6 April 2010); and ECtHR, *Tuomela and Others v Finland* App No 25711/04 (6 April 2010). See also ECtHR, *Selistö v. Finland* App No 56767/00 (16 November 2004); ECtHR, *Karhuvaara and Iltalehti v Finland* App No 53678/00 (16 November 2004); and ECtHR, *Nikula v Finland* App No 31611/96 (21 March 2002).

14 The right to equality and the right to non-discrimination have played a role in, for example, the debate over hate speech and criminal cases about ethnic agitation (see e.g. Supreme Court case, 2012:58)

15 Freedom of religion was one of the core issues of a very recent case of the Helsinki District Court case 22/113590 that took place in March 2022. The case has received international media attention, as it concerns the freedom of expression of a well-known Finnish politician who was accused of incitement against a minority group on three counts. Two of the charges concerned publications and statements on social media. See e.g. Reuters, 'Paivi Rasanen: Finnish MP in Bible Hate Speech Trial' (24 January 2022) <www.reuters.com/world/europe/finnish-court-clears-lawmaker-charges-over-homosexuality-comments-2022-03-30/> accessed 14 July 2022.

16 Supreme Court case KKO 2018:81, para 43.

17 Supreme Court case KKO 2019:81, para 26.

18 The legislation criminalises hate speech, hate crimes, the financing of racist activities and prohibits and criminalises membership in organisations that promote and incite racial discrimination. In 2011, legislation on incitement to hatred was amended to implement Council Framework Decision 2008/913/JHA and the Additional Protocol to the Convention on Cybercrime (ETS 189), see Government Bill 317/2010, 12.

19 In its judgment, the Supreme Court took notice of Article 10 of ECtHR case law, in particular ECtHR, *Feret v Belgium* App No 15615/07 (16 July 2009).

20 Reporters Without Borders, Index 2021 <https://rsf.org/en/index?year=2021> accessed 14 July 2022.

21 For more details about the application of EU law by Finnish courts, see Tuomas Ojanen, 'From Constitutional Periphery toward the Center – Transformations of Judicial Review in Finland' (2009) 27(2) *Nordic Journal of Human Rights/ Nordisk Tidsskrift for Menneskerettigheter* 194, 198–201. For an overview of the Finnish court practice regarding the case law of the ECtHR and the CJEU, see Ojanen (n 10) 1210.

22 However, Finnish quasi-judicial organs, such as the Parliamentary Ombudsman, often refer to the ECtHR and the case law of the ECtHR in their reasoning. See e.g. Parliamentary Ombudsman Resolution 1307/2018, titled "*The Municipality Violated the Teacher's Freedom of Expression*", adopted 7 October 2019.

23 See, for example, judgment KHO 2012:55 by the Supreme Administrative Court in which it ruled that a public university was obliged to deliver data on professorial salaries to a newspaper, which had requested the data to be used for editorial purposes, provided that the newspaper granted the university with appropriate commitments and other adequate guarantees concerning the security of the data. The reasoning of the Court discussed at length the impact of the Data Protection Directive, as well as CJEU judgments in Case C-73/07 *Satakunnan Markkinapörssi and Satamedia* [2008] ECLI:EU:C:2008:727, Joined Cases C-465/00, C-138/01, C-139/01 *Österreichischer Rundfunk and others* [2003] ECLI:EU:C:2003:294, and Joined Cases C-92/09 and C-93/09 *Volker and others* [2010] ECLI:EU:C:2010:662. For an overview of Finnish court practice regarding the case law of the ECtHR and the CJEU, see Ojanen (n 10).

24 Even when making references to it, judicial practice appears to be selective, as well as being usually confined to cases only involving the application of section 106 of the Constitution, which provides for the primacy of the Constitution in cases in which the court finds the application of an Act of Parliament to be in *evident* conflict with the Constitution.

25 Bilyana Petkova, 'Privacy as Europe's First Amendment' (2019) 25 *European Law* 149; Tuomas Ojanen, 'Privacy Is More Than Just a Seven-Letter Word: The Court of Justice of the European Union Sets Constitutional Limits on Mass Surveillance: Court of Justice of the European Union, Decision of 8 April 2014 in Joined Cases C- 293/12 and C-594/12, Digital Rights Ireland and Seitlinger and Others' (2014) 10 *European Constitutional Law Review* 528, 529.

26 See KKO 2018:81, para 9. Specifically, the Court refers to two cases: ECtHR, *Amann v. Switzerland*, App no 27798/95 (16 February 2000) para 65; Joined Cases C-92/09 and C-93/09, *Volker und Markus Schecke GbR and Hartmut Eifert* [2010] ECLI:EU:C:2010:662, paras 52 and 59.

27 See KKO 2018:81, para 11.2.

28 ECtHR, *von Hannover v Germany* (no. 2) App no 40660/08 and 60641/08 (07 February 2012).

29 For the benefits, see ECtHR, *Cengiz and Others v Turkey* App no 48226/10 and 14027/11 (1 December 2015) para 49, for the dangers, see ECtHR, *Delfi v Estonia* App no 64569/09 (16 June 2015) 319, para 110.

30 Similarly, in the case KKO 2019:81, when the Court decided on privacy matters, it considered the following criteria: the way the article or image is published and presented; the accuracy and the quality of the information published; whether the person consented to be photographed; and whether the photographs were taken in secret or by other unauthorised means.

31 ECtHR, *Delfi v Estonia* App no 64569/09 (16 June 2015). For an analysis of the cases cf. Marta Maroni, 'The Liability of Internet Intermediaries and the European Court of Human Rights', in Tuomas Ojanen and Bilyana Petkova (eds), *Fundamental Rights Protection Online: The Future Regulation of Intermediaries* (Edward Elgar Publishing 2020) 255.

32 ECtHR, *Magyar Tartalomszolgáltatók Egyesülete and Index.hu Zrt v Hungary* App no 22947/13 (2 February 2016).

33 See e.g. Maroni (n 31).

34 Directive 2000/31/EC of the European Parliament and of the Council of 8 June 2000 on certain legal aspects of information society services, in particular electronic commerce in the internal market (E-Commerce Directive).

35 As a hosting space, it is shielded from liability under certain circumstances. Cf. Lisl Brunner, 'The Liability of an Online Intermediary for Third Party Content: The Watchdog Becomes the Monitor: Intermediary Liability after *Delfi v Estonia*'*Human Rights Law Review* 16(1) 163–174. Dirk Voorhoof offers more sources on the debate in 'Qualification of News Portal as Publisher of Users' Comment May Have Far-Reaching Consequences for Online Freedom of Expression: *Delfi AS v. Estonia*' (*Strasbourg Observers*, 25 October 2013) <https://strasbourgobservers.com/2013/10/25/qualification-of-news-portal-as-publisher-of-users-comment-may-have-far-reaching-consequences-for-online-freedom-of-expression-delfi-as-v-estonia/> accessed 11 January 2018. See also Martin Husovec, 'General Monitoring of Third-Party Content: Compatible with Freedom of Expression?' (2016) 11(1) *JIP&P* 17.

36 See Recital 13, Proposal for a Regulation of the European Parliament and of the Council on a Single Market for Digital Services (Digital Services Act) and amending Directive 2000/31/EC, COM(2020) 825. See also Sara Tommasi, 'The Liability of Internet Service Providers in the Proposed Digital Services Act' (2021) 29 *European Review of Private Law* 925, 938.

37 Government Bill 19/2013, pp. 37–38. See also Constitutional Law Committee Opinion 16/2013.

38 Several ECtHR's cases are referred and in particular the court emphasises that the ECtHR has in it cases ECtHR, *von Hannover v Germany* (no. 2) App. no 40660/08 and 60641/08 (7 February 2012) and ECtHR, *Axel Springer AG v. Germany* App. No 39954/08 (February 2012) specified the principles that must be applied when weighing up the freedom of expression on the one hand and the protection of private life on the other.

6 Judicial dialogue *à la Française*

Social media and fundamental rights in the French higher courts

Sara Migliorini and Constance Bonzé

1. Introduction

This chapter contributes to the understanding of judicial dialogue in the French courts and attempts to convey the unique way in which French higher courts have been approaching it in fundamental rights, digital law and social network matters. As anticipated in our title, French higher courts have engaged and continue to engage in productive judicial dialogue with both the Court of Justice of the European Union (CJEU) and the European Court of Human Rights (ECtHR). Nonetheless, the way that this dialogue happens is not always very apparent to the untrained observer. This uniqueness is due primarily to the traditional, concise adjudication style of French courts and the compartmentalisation among three different courts of the task of overseeing the compatibility of laws with higher-ranking domestic and international sources of fundamental rights.

In this chapter, we review the relevant case law of the three French higher courts on fundamental rights and social media (Section 2) and then advance a critical explanation of how they engage in judicial dialogue (Section 3). In this introduction, we briefly present some legislative provisions related to social media, the roles of each court and their tasks with respect to fundamental rights.

Direct references to social media are scarce in black letter law. The courts predominantly rely on general interpretation principles to adapt existing rules and decide cases involving social media. However, three interesting rules have recently been introduced, which nonetheless have only limited scope. The Education Code requires schools to train students in the responsible use of social media, and the training must include education on "the protection of privacy and respect for intellectual property, free speech and human dignity, and the rules applicable to the processing of personal data".[1] In a different field, the Internal Security Code facilitates access to social media users' shared personal data by the Ministry of Internal Affairs when it carries out administrative enquiries relating to "activities likely to affect public or state security".[2] Finally, the Public Health Code requires companies manufacturing health products to

DOI: 10.4324/9781003207085-8

make public agreements they enter into with social media influencers.[3] Outside these limited rules, social media are not directly regulated by law.

The higher courts have therefore for the most part applied existing laws to cases involving social networks, carefully assessing similarities and differences with offline situations and showing openness to adaptation. Importantly, courts have applied the 29 July 1881 law on freedom of the press to Internet-based platforms. This law sanctions written and oral statements made in a public setting which constitute insults, defamation or incitement to commit crimes and offences.[4]

Fundamental rights are protected in France by the Constitution[5] and supranational sources of law, which, according to Article 55 of the Constitution, rank higher than domestic laws, such as the European Convention on Human Rights (ECHR) and the EU Charter of Fundamental Rights.[6]

There are three higher courts in the French judicial system. The *Conseil Constitutionnel* (CC) is France's Constitutional Court. It oversees the compliance of ordinary laws with the Constitution[7] either when directly asked by a group of MPs regarding a bill yet to be made into law or through a preliminary ruling procedure.[8] The *Conseil d'Etat* (Council of State, CE) has a dual function: it is the highest court in the administrative branch of the judiciary and it also advises the government on the preparation of draft laws and decrees. The *Cour de Cassation* (CCass) is the highest court for civil and criminal matters. It ensures consistent and correct application of the law by lower courts, but it is not competent to review the facts of a case.

These three courts have different relationships with international and supranational sources. The CE and the CCass are empowered to carry out *contrôles de conventionnalité* – i.e. to assess whether domestic laws comply with international conventions, including the ECHR and EU law. In their decisions, they can refer to EU and international sources, and they do so, although not consistently or very extensively. This is arguably due to the traditional adjudication style of French courts, which is very concise, without references to previous cases and only contains mere citations of the rules of law applied with minimal explication of the way these rules are applied.

The CE applies the ECHR in all areas of public authority action. The field of administrative immigration decisions is the area in which review of administrative court actions regarding the ECHR is most frequently exercised.[9] Other fields of administration action in which the ECHR is relevant are administrative sanctions,[10] professional sanctions made by independent administrative authorities[11] and tax matters.[12] The CE also takes into account the ECtHR's interpretation of the ECHR and in its case law refers to qualifications or legal categories derived from ECtHR decisions.[13]

The CCass only formally acknowledged the need to respect ECtHR decisions in 2011.[14] Previously, the ECtHR censored CCass decisions on several occasions.[15] The style in which the CCass drafted its decisions was notoriously complex, and it was often criticised for being obscure, including by the ECtHR.[16] On 1 October 2019, the drafting of CCass decisions underwent a drastic reform: the traditional single sentence was replaced with a more direct style and more developed reasoning. One of the stated aims of the reform, along with enhancing the clarity and legibility of the decisions, was to "demonstrate that they serve the fundamental rights of individuals".[17]

Conversely, the CC cannot directly refer to decisions by other courts and it is not competent to assess the compatibility of domestic laws with the ECHR or EU law.[18] This does not mean that it does not take these sources into consideration. On the contrary, the CC is directly inspired by the ECHR and ECtHR case law. For example, the ECHR and the ECtHR's jurisprudence have contributed to the CC recognising new rights, such as the right to respect for private life,[19] freedom of marriage[20] and the principle of human dignity.[21] ECtHR case law has also enriched the French understanding of certain rights; for example, freedom of expression.[22]

2. Fundamental rights in national jurisprudence

All three French higher courts engage in judicial dialogue with the CJEU and the ECtHR in their unique way, as is demonstrated by recent case law on social media and fundamental rights matters.

2.1 The Constitutional Court (Conseil Constitutionnel)

A few times, the CC has been confronted with the question of how to strike a fair balance between different fundamental rights in the realm of social media. More specifically, in the time frame under consideration (2009–2021), the CC has directly adjudicated on social media issues on three occasions.[23] All three procedures originated from applications by more than 60 MPs regarding the compatibility of draft laws with the Constitution before they entered into force. In all three decisions, the CC was called on to assess whether the draft law was compatible with the fundamental rights enshrined in the Constitution. This assessment required balancing distinct rights and interests, which the CC carried out on a case-by-case basis against the backdrop of its previous relevant decisions.

In all three decisions, freedom of speech was the main fundamental right at stake, and the CC had to assess whether the contested bills struck a fair balance with other rights and interests of constitutional rank. In all three decisions, in line with its traditional case law, the CC recalled its established stance on freedom of speech.[24] Building on ECtHR case law, the CC considered the exercise of freedom of speech as a condition for democracy and one of the guarantees necessary to ensure respect for other rights and freedoms. In addition, the CC considered that freedom of speech is of particular importance in the use of online public communication services – such as social media – given the widespread development of such services and their importance for democratic participation and the expression of ideas and opinions. The CC had previously ruled that the right to free speech and the freedom to communicate implied a need to ensure free access to Internet-based communication services.[25] However, the CC had also recalled that the exercise of freedom of speech is not absolute and that laws may prohibit practices amounting to abuse which may undermine public order. Such legitimate restrictions on the exercise of freedom of speech have to be carefully limited – i.e. they have to be necessary, appropriate and proportionate to the objective pursued.[26] Importantly, the French Constitution authorises the legislator to use criminal liability to sanction abuses of free speech.[27] In such cases, one key aspect of the assessment of the proportionality of restrictions on freedom of speech is certainty or uncertainty regarding the legality of the speech likely to be suppressed: the CC will most likely consider an infringement of freedom of speech to be disproportionate when the legal qualification of the targeted speech is controversial.

In the first case in 2018,[28] the CC was called on to assess some provisions in a new electoral law (the Electoral Code) which prohibited the dissemination of false information in online communication services – including social media – during the three months preceding a general election.[29] Article L. 163–2 of the Electoral Code established a summary procedure[30] for an order to cease disseminating false information via online communication services when the information was "likely to alter the sincerity of the ballot". The CC upheld this provision, subject to a "reservation of interpretation" – i.e. a directive that the judicial and administrative authorities should give a particular meaning to a certain provision in order for its application to be compatible with the Constitution.[31] In its reasoning, the CC examined Art. L. 163–2 of the Electoral Code with regard to, on the one hand, freedom of speech and, on the other hand, the need to ensure a genuine election under Article 3 of the Constitution (*la sincérité du scrutin*). The CC noted that Art. L. 163–2 of the Electoral Code was aimed at preventing deception and manipulation of citizens ahead of a vote by massive dissemination of false information in online public communication services, thus ensuring clarity in the electoral debate. This aim could, in principle, justify a restriction on freedom of speech. In line with its judicial technique, the CC then carefully assessed whether the balance struck by the legislator between these distinct fundamental rights and interests of constitutional rank was appropriate and proportionate. First, the CC looked at the various elements in Article L. 163–2 of the Electoral Code that allowed a good balance. It noted that the summary procedure could only target content published in online public communication services, which lend themselves more easily than other means of communication to massive and coordinated manipulation because of the way they are distributed. The CC also noted that the legislator had strictly delimited the information covered by the provision, both in terms of content and way of dissemination. In particular, regarding content, Article L. 163–2 of the Electoral Code did not cover opinions, parodies, partial inaccuracies or simple exaggerations but only information "for which it is possible to objectively demonstrate falseness".[32] On the other hand, dissemination was only covered if it was "artificial or computerised, deliberate and spread by mass distribution".[33] Finally, the CC directed authorities to interpret the law as meaning that only "manifestly" inaccurate or misleading information could be targeted, when it "manifestly" posed a risk of altering the genuineness of the election. The CC found that, subject to such interpretative reservations, the contested provision in the Electoral Code enacted legitimate restrictions on freedom of speech and therefore it was deemed compatible with the Constitution.

In the same decision, another provision in the Electoral Code, Article 11, was contested. Article 11 required online platform operators to take measures to put in place a system allowing their users to report false information and to successively implement additional measures to enhance the transparency of their algorithms and counteract accounts massively spreading false information. The applicant MPs argued that the provision violated both freedom of speech and freedom to conduct a business as protected by the French Constitution. The CC assessed Article 11 of the Electoral Code against the backdrop of these two constitutional freedoms and found that it did not violate them. As with the previous provision in the Electoral Code, the CC assessed all the elements that allowed it to strike a fair balance among the distinct interests at hand. Regarding freedom of speech, the CC considered that the notion of "false information" was to be understood as only covering a limited number of instances (information "for which it is possible to objectively demonstrate falseness") and thus limited the scope of the provision. In addition, the CC noted that, in the case of a dispute, a court would be called on to assess on a case-by-case basis whether the measures enacted by the social media operator were necessary, appropriate and proportionate to the objective pursued – i.e. to ensure clarity of the electoral debate and respect for the principle of genuineness in the vote. Regarding the freedom to conduct a business, the CC noted that Article 11 of the Electoral Code merely required online platform operators to implement a system for reporting and counteracting false information which must be accessible and visible to users, but according to the means that they deemed appropriate, and to make such measures public in the three months preceding an election. In the CC's view, such a mechanism would not disproportionately interfere with freedom of speech and freedom to conduct a business and was therefore compliant with the Constitution.

Notably, in a subsequent decision,[34] a similar mechanism which would have applied irrespective of elections and with no time limit was judged unconstitutional by the CC. The CC was called on to adjudicate on a law aiming at combating hate content on the Internet (the Law Against Hate Content) by instituting new obligations for online communication service operators – including social media. The relevant provisions created an obligation for online communication service operators to withdraw illegal content on the request of a user. While users were required to provide the reasons why they deemed the content illegal, the Law Against Hate Content required operators to take down all illegal content within an hour of the user's request. In addition, it established criminal liability and a substantial fine for each breach. The CC reviewed the different elements in the mechanism at hand in order to assess whether the restriction on freedom of speech was proportionate. In the CC's view, the provision would prompt online platform operators to systematically take down content reported by users whether it was manifestly illegal or not because of the difficulty in assessing its illegal nature within the one-hour time limit. This systematic take-down would only be encouraged by the consequences attached to any breach; namely, criminal liability, a substantial fine and the absence of any possibility of exoneration from liability. Consequently, the CC found that the contested provisions impaired the exercise of freedom of speech in a way that was not necessary, appropriate and proportionate and were therefore unconstitutional.

The last decision reported here concerns the question of data harvesting from social media by tax law enforcement authorities. In 2019, the CC was called on to review Article 154 of the *Loi de Finance pour 2020* (the Budget Law),[35] which authorised the tax and customs administrations to collect and use data publicly accessible on social networks and marketplaces for the purpose of investigating a limited number of tax and customs offences. In practice, the mechanism allowed the tax administration to collect and store massive amounts of data from social media and process them using an algorithm. If the algorithm identified circumstantial elements suggesting that the subject had committed one of the relevant fiscal offences, the data had to be reviewed by a human officer and assessed without exclusive recourse to artificial intelligence (AI). Article 154 of the Budget Law set a series of different deadlines after which the data collected had to be destroyed, according to their relevance to the investigation and their nature. The Budget Law implemented this mechanism on an experimental basis and for a period of three years.

The applicants argued that Article 154 of the Budget Law set up an online surveillance system which infringed on individuals' constitutional right to private life and to the protection of personal data. In addition, they claimed that it unconstitutionally restricted freedom of speech, since fear of surveillance could lead social media users to self-censor.

The CC reasoned as follows. First, it stated that the issue at hand required careful balancing of three separate constitutional guarantees: the fight against tax fraud and tax evasion; the right to private life, which included protection of personal data; and finally, freedom of speech. The CC continued its reasoning by identifying the interferences created by Article 154 of the Budget Law with the rights to private life and free speech. Regarding the right to private life and protection of personal data, the CC noted that Article 154 of the Budget Law empowered law enforcement authorities to "collect large volumes of data published on [social media], relating to a large number of people, in an undifferentiated manner, and to use such data by aggregating them and making cross-checks and correlations". The CC concluded that the contested provisions infringed the right to respect for private life, including when the data were made public by the person to whom it related.[36] As for interference with the exercise of freedom of speech, the CC stated that the previously mentioned interference with the right to the protection of personal life was "likely to dissuade the use of [social media], or otherwise lead citizens to limit their use".

The CC then reviewed the conditions attached to the mechanism for harvesting and processing personal data in Article 154 of the Budget Law in order to assess whether the previously mentioned interferences with fundamental rights were justified. It concluded that the legislator "combined [the mechanism at hand] with specific guarantees which in fact [ensured] a fair balancing between the right to private life and the constitutional objective of fighting tax fraud and tax evasion".[37] These guarantees were, among others, the limited time for which data could be stored and the limited uses for which it could be processed.[38] Moreover, the CC observed that enforcement authorities could only start a criminal, fiscal or customs procedure against a data subject after having carried out an individual assessment of the person's situation, which could not be based exclusively on the results of automated data processing by an algorithm.[39] The CC therefore for the most part validated Article 154 of the Budget Law.[40]

2.2 *The* Conseil d'Etat

In the time period considered (2009–2020), the CE was called on to adjudicate on issues regarding social media in about 53 cases.[41] This body of decisions encompasses the following six broadly defined areas: a) use of social networks in connection with local and national elections and elected representatives (18 decisions); b) use of information available on social media as evidence supporting administrative decisions protecting public order, especially in the field of anti-terrorism activities (17 decisions); c) protection of personal data available on social networks from intrusion by public authorities (6 decisions); d) review of administrative decisions regarding inappropriate use of social media by civil servants and members of the armed forces (6 decisions); and e) review of decisions by independent authorities regarding regulation of the use of social media (4 decisions) and use of social media to diffuse useful information and contacts regarding pandemic-related administrative measures (2 decisions).[42]

Unlike the CC, the CE can refer to external supranational sources in its reasoning and it did so in almost a third of the decisions considered regarding social networks. The CE referred explicitly to the ECHR in 17 decisions and on one occasion to both the ECHR and the EU Charter of Fundamental Rights. Nonetheless, as is explained later, this relatively low percentage of direct references to European supranational sources is not a sign of a lack of consideration of these sources or a lack of willingness to engage with the European supranational courts. Indeed, the CE has traditionally engaged in productive judicial dialogue with the CJEU.[43] For instance, in recent times, the CE was the originator of a question for a preliminary ruling in the *Google LLC* case on the territorial reach of the right to be forgotten.[44]

A recent decision offers an interesting example of social media litigation before the CE – in particular, regarding free speech and its restrictions. In

Barakacity,[45] the CE was called on to decide on the legitimacy of a Ministerial decree dissolving an association called Barakacity based on Article L. 212–1 of the Internal Security Code (*Code de la securité intérieure*). This provision empowers the government to dissolve any association or *de facto* group of people which poses a threat to national security and, in particular, if the group "either incites discrimination, hatred or violence against a person or a group of people because of their origin or their membership or their non-membership of an ethnic group, nation, race or religion; or propagates ideas or theories tending to justify or encourage such discrimination, hatred or violence; or engages on or from the French territory in activity with a view to provoking acts of terrorism in France or abroad".[46]

Article L.212–2 was introduced in the Internal Security Code with a law of 10 January 1936[47] in response to anti-Semitic ideas promoted by far-right leagues (*les ligues d'extrême droite*) in the 1920s and 1930s in France. In the past, the CE exercised intensive reviews of dissolutions of associations. For example, the dissolution of a neo-Nazi group was annulled twice by the CE, first for violation of the obligation to state reasons[48] and then for violation of the principle of equality of arms.[49] More recently, several dissolutions have been pronounced on two of the grounds provided for in Article L. 212–2 – i.e. incitement of hate and terrorism.[50]

Barakacity was a French association employing 47 people in France and abroad, the main objective of which was "implementation, promotion and development" of humanitarian actions in France and abroad. Following a series of social media posts, the government dissolved the association by decree on the basis of Article 212–1 of the Internal Security Code. Previously, the president of the association had posted messages on social networks in connection with national or international news, either from his personal accounts or from those of the association, both of which had several tens of thousands of subscribers. For several years, these messages had merely reflected critical opinions on issues such as the Israeli-Palestinian conflict, the situation of the Rohingyas in Burma and France's political situation. The CE conceded that such opinions could not, in themselves, be regarded as falling within the scope of the provisions in Article L. 212–1 of the Internal Security Code, although they did not bear any link with the association's objectives. However, between August and September 2020, the social media posts from the association and the president's Facebook accounts had addressed matters such as the trial of the Christchurch attacker and glorified his death as a martyr. These posts had given rise to numerous hateful comments inciting violence and murder. Both the posts and the reactions that they created triggered the government's decision to dissolve Barakacity.

The association tried to argue that it had posted warnings to social media users against hate speech on several occasions, but the CE established that these warnings were too general and distant in time from the 2020 posts and that the association had not, in fact, carried out any specific action aimed at removing the posts or otherwise mitigated or counteracted their effects.

Therefore, the CE upheld the dissolution. Facebook was not a party to the proceedings and, as far as it emerges from the decision, had not taken any action to take down or otherwise address the hateful posts and comments that appeared on the association and president's pages. In any event, the CE did not discuss the need for Facebook to take action, as this was not part of the arguments raised by the parties. The association also argued that the decree ordering its dissolution violated freedom of association. The CE agreed that the dissolution of the association by decree amounted to a restriction of freedom of association but concluded that this interference was justified by the seriousness of the danger to public order and public security resulting from the facts at hand.

2.3 The Cour de Cassation

In the time-period considered (2009–2020), the CCass adjudicated 72 cases regarding social media.[51] While there were no decisions of the plenary of the court, all three civil sections – the commercial section, the employment section and the criminal section – of the CCass adjudicated cases regarding social media. This section focuses on one area where the CCass case law progressively integrated fundamental rights reasoning: protection of private life and free speech at work. All the cases considered were adjudicated by the Employment Section of the CCass (*Chambre Sociale*).

Tension between employers and employees in matters of free speech is far from new. In the past, the CCass upheld dismissal decisions based on employee behaviour that had no link to the company or to the work performed. For instance, in a full-court decision of 1978, the dismissal of a schoolteacher for getting divorced was considered justified.[52] In the 1990s, the CCass adopted a more protective approach to employee free speech outside work vis-à-vis the employer.[53]

The increasing use of new technologies at work has raised new questions concerning the right of employees to free speech outside work. For instance, at the turn of the millennium, French courts were confronted with the issue of free speech in employees' private correspondence exchanged via their work computers. In an early case, *Nikon*, the CCass stated that "the employer cannot, without violating the employee's fundamental right to private life, know of their personal messages sent and received on a computer tool made available to them by the employer".[54] The issues brought before French courts gradually diversified, involving employee use of social media both outside and in the workplace. Faced with cases of dismissal following employee activity on social media, the initial approach of the CCass was to analyse the employee's social media posts in the light of the notion of "gross misconduct" (*faute grave*). In a first line of jurisprudence, the characterisation of gross misconduct justifying dismissal depended on the public or private character of offensive or insulting comments made by the employee against the employer on social media and whether the author intended to limit the recipients to a restricted group of people. In 2018, the CCass ruled that comments posted by an employee on her Facebook account, which was only accessible by a closed pre-approved group of 14 people, was a conversation of a private nature that did not justify dismissal for serious misconduct.[55] Similarly, comments posted on a Facebook account which was only accessible by "a very limited number" of persons approved by the employee did not constitute public insults justifying a dismissal.[56]

In more recent decisions, the CCass has seemingly departed from the notion of gross misconduct and the criterion of the number of recipients of the comment or information at issue, and instead, has considered whether employees' use of social media qualifies as a breach of their contractual obligations. In *PB*,[57] the claimant – an employee of a clothing brand – published a confidential photograph of the brand's new collection on her Facebook account. The company dismissed the employee for breach of her contractual obligation of confidentiality. In an attempt to rely on the previously described line of cases, the employee argued that she had posted the picture on a Facebook account which was only accessible by a limited number of pre-approved persons – i.e. her Facebook "friends". As a consequence, the employee argued, the post was private in nature and could not justify her dismissal.

The CCass did not discuss the private or public nature of the post. It admitted that the employee's Facebook account was private but proceeded to weigh the employer's right to present evidence in court against the employee's right to respect for private life. While the principle of fairness in the administration of evidence meant that the employer could not use a stratagem to gather evidence, the post in question had been spontaneously communicated to the employer by another employee of the company authorised to access the private Facebook account as a "friend". Therefore, the employer did not trick or coerce to access the account in question. The CCass then relied on the rights to a fair trial and to respect for private life under Articles 6 and 8 ECHR, Article 9 of the French Civil Code and Article 9 of the French Code of Civil Procedure.[58] It concluded that the right to evidence justified the production of elements that infringe privacy, provided that such production is indispensable to the exercise of this right and that the infringement is proportionate to the aim pursued.

In another recent case, *Oeuvres hospitalières*,[59] the director of an institution for vulnerable adults had been dismissed for gross misconduct after posting a photograph on his Facebook page showing him naked in a church. The employee contested his dismissal, basing his argument on the lack of breach of his contractual obligations and his freedom of expression. The Court of Appeal ruled that the director had failed to fulfil the obligations inherent in his duties, including ensuring the integrity and safety of the residents of the institution, and that the fact that the photograph was accessible by the general public, including the director's subordinates and the residents of the institution, was an abuse of his freedom of expression that was likely to cause harm to the employer. Relying on Article L. 1121–1 of the French Labour Code, the CCass overturned the decision. It reiterated that a fact drawn from an employee's private life cannot justify a dismissal unless it constitutes a breach of an obligation arising from the employment contract. According to the CCass, this was not the case here. Even though the post was accessible by the public, the CCass did not retain the notion of gross misconduct discussed by the Court of Appeal, and instead solely focused on the lack of a contractual breach. The CCass then turned to assessing whether the post was an abuse of the director's freedom of expression. In line with its jurisprudence regarding offline cases,[60] the CCass found that it was not because it was not offensive, defamatory or excessive.

3. Judicial dialogue *à la française*

Understanding the French higher courts' stance towards judicial dialogue with the CJEU and the ECtHR on social media matters requires familiarity with both the jurisdictions and the different relationships that the courts entertain with supranational sources of law and their specific adjudication styles. The CC is not competent to assess the compatibility of domestic laws with the ECHR or EU law,[61] but, as previously mentioned, it does take into account relevant international and European sources of law without directly referring to them. In particular, the CC's approach to free speech and its restrictions of it, including the proportionality test, is greatly influenced by the ECtHR's case law.[62]

The CE and the CCass are empowered to carry out "*contrôles de conventionnalité*", – i.e. to assess whether domestic laws comply with international conventions, including the ECHR, the EU Charter of Fundamental Rights and EU law in general. Both courts have been actively engaging in direct judicial dialogue with supranational courts.[63] Direct references to the ECHR and EU law can be found in their decisions, but they are nonetheless scarce due to their adjudication styles.

The CE seems to use direct references quite often and generally aligns its jurisprudence with the ECHR and the CJEU. As an example, in *Barakacity*, which was discussed in the previous section, the CE referred explicitly to the ECHR. This reference was a mere "*au visa de*" – i.e. a mere mention of the ECHR with no discussion regarding its provisions and ECtHR case law. However, the decision in *Barakacity* appears to have closely followed and adopted views consistent with the jurisprudence of the ECtHR. Indeed, a parallel can be drawn between the CE's decision in *Barakacity* and the ECtHR's decision in *Beizaras and Levickas v Lithuania*,[64] which was issued a few months previously. In this case, the ECtHR ruled that certain comments on social media regarding the applicants' sexual orientation constituted an incitement to hatred and violence and an undisguised call for attacks on their physical and mental integrity, from which the applicants had to be protected under relevant criminal laws. Therefore, failure on the part of the relevant public authorities to discharge their positive obligation to investigate these comments in an effective manner amounted to a violation of Articles 8 (right to private life) and 14 (non-discrimination) ECHR. In both cases, both the CE and the ECtHR considered comments posted on social media to pose a serious and real danger to the safety of the people or groups targeted. Both decisions clearly highlighted that, while social media belong to the virtual world, their impact on physical reality is far from theoretical and courts and authorities need to act to protect the physical integrity and rights of the victims of hate comments on social media. The dissolution of the association by the government was upheld by the CE in *Barakacity*, while the failure to investigate the hate comments by the Lithuanian authorities was condemned by the ECtHR in *Beizaras and Levickas v Lithuania*. In both cases, the CE and the ECtHR found that the individuals responsible for the social media pages hosting the hate comments had to try to rectify them. This seems to suggest that, for both courts, private parties are under a duty to make an effort to minimise the damage that could possibly result from hate comments on social media. While not citing it directly, the CE does follow and take into account the ECtHR's reasoning in social media cases.

Admittedly, in the CCass case law, the instances of judicial dialogue seem less developed. For example, in the *Oeuvres hospitalières* case discussed previously, the CCass adopted a progressive stance towards free speech on social media outside work, but it only explicitly referred to the French labour code. Nonetheless, the CCass is an important proponent of judicial dialogue with the CJEU.[65] The lack of direct mentions of EU law and international sources of fundamental rights can therefore probably be explained, once again, by the specific adjudication style of the CCass and judicial inertia regarding any change to it. As was mentioned in the introduction, the CCass only formally acknowledged the need to respect the decisions of the ECtHR in 2011.[66]

4. Conclusion

The preceding analysis has shown that French courts engage in judicial dialogue, especially on issues of fundamental rights, but they maintain a certain national attitude towards it. The constraints of adjudication style and jurisdiction boundaries of the three higher courts are important factors shaping how each court takes into account the broader landscape of European case law, the ECHR and the EU Charter.

Social media is certainly an area where French higher courts are receptive and engage in judicial dialogue, which contributes to enhancing judicial dialogue between the French higher courts, the CJEU and the ECtHR overall. So far, in cases involving social media, freedom of speech and the protection of private life have been the fundamental rights most frequently discussed before French higher courts. Both the CC and the CE generally align their jurisprudence with the CJEU and ECtHR's case law, although direct references are not systematic. The CCass, although seemingly reluctant at first, recently made direct references to the ECHR in cases involving the protection of private life.

Going forward, we can expect a growing number of cases in matters of digital law and social media, which will certainly prompt French higher courts to make direct or indirect references to EU law and exchanges with the CJEU and the ECtHR.

Notes

1 Article L312–9 of the Education Code (*Code de l'éducation*).
2 Article R236–2 and Article R236–12 of the Internal Security Code (*Code de la sécurité intérieure*).
3 Article L1453–1 of the Public Health Code (*Code de la santé publique*).
4 Articles 23 to 41–1, Chapter IV of the law of 29 July 1881 on the freedom of the press (*Loi du 29 juillet 1881 sur la liberté de la presse*), as modified by Article 93–3 of the French Criminal Code (instituted by law n° 82–652 of 29 July 1982 on audiovisual communication). See Conseil Constitutionnel, 16 September 2011, no. 2011–164 QPC; Cass. crim., 30 October 2012, no. 10–88825.
5 In France fundamental rights are protected by a legal framework located at the top of the hierarchy of norms: the constitutionality block (*bloc de constitutionnalité*). The constitutionality block serves as a basis for constitutionality review carried out by the *Conseil Constitutionnel* and is composed of the Constitution of 4 October 1958, the Declaration of the Rights of Man and of the Citizen of 1789, the Preamble to the 1946 Constitution and the 2004 Charter of the Environment.
6 The relationship between these sources and the Constitution is, of course, the object of many studies and much discussion, but it is outside of the scope of this chapter.
7 Conseil Constitutionnel, 16 July 1971, no. 71–44 DC.
8 Under Article 61–1 of the Constitution, a priority preliminary ruling (*question prioritaire de constitutionnalité*) is the right of any person who is a party to a trial or proceeding to argue that a legislative provision infringes the rights and freedoms guaranteed by the Constitution. On referral by the *Conseil d'Etat* or the *Cour de Cassation*, the *Conseil Constitutionnel* gives a ruling and, if necessary, repeals the legislative provision.
9 In particular, Article 8 ECHR, since the decisions CE ass. of 19 April 1991, *M. Belgacem*, Rec. p. 152 and CE ass. of 19 April 1991, *Mme Babas*, Rec. p. 162.
10 Such as withdrawals of driving licence points, CE opinion of 27 September 1999, *Rouxel*, Rec. p. 280.
11 CE ass. of 3 December 1999, *Didier*, Rec. p. 399.
12 CE ass. of 12 April 2002, *Société anonyme financière Labeyrie*, Rec. p. 137.
13 For example, its interpretation of the notion of 'property' within the meaning of Article 1 of the First Protocol to the ECHR. See the decisions CE Ass. of 30 November 2001, *Ministre de la défense c/ M. Diop*, Rec. p. 605 and CE Ass. of 6 December 2002, *Draon*, Rec. p. 423.
14 Cass., Assemblée plénière, 15 April 2011, no. 10–17.049.
15 For instance, the *Cour de Cassation* recognised the right of transsexuals to change their civil status following a condemnation by the ECtHR (*B. v France*, App. 13343/87, 25 March 1992). More recently, the ECtHR condemned the *Cour de Cassation* for having convicted activists who had called for a boycott of Israeli products. The ECtHR ruled that the *Cour de Cassation* had violated Article 10 ECHR (freedom of expression). See *Baldassi and others v France*, App. 15271/16 (ECtHR, 11 June 2020).

16 See *Affaire Quilichini v France*, App. 38299/15 (ECtHR, 14 March 2019) para 44: "The Court observes, as in the *Fabris* case, that the Court of Cassation did not respond, at least explicitly, to the Convention plea and thus excluded the possibility of preventing, if necessary, a violation similar to those it had already found. A more detailed statement of reasons would have enabled the Court to take better account of the reasoning of the Court of Cassation".
17 Bertrand Louvel, 'President of the Cour de Cassation in 2019, in a Video Presentation of the Reform' <https://vimeo.com/327671045> accessed 5 March 2022. See also Section 3.
18 Decision no. 74–54 DC of 15 January 1975, collection p. 19.
19 Decision no. 99–416 DC of 23 July 1999, collection p. 100.
20 Decision no. 2003–484 DC of 20 November 2003, collection p. 438.
21 Decision no. 94–343/344 DC of 27 July 1994.
22 Decision no. 2021–948 QPC of 24 November 2021.
23 Referred to in endnotes 28, 34 and 35. A complete account of CC decisions regarding Internet-based services and of decisions that may have an effect on social media in general is outside the scope of this chapter. Where relevant to the purposes of this chapter, we refer to such decisions in endnotes.
24 In the French legal order, freedom of expression is enshrined in Article 11 of the Declaration of the Rights of Man and of the Citizen of 1789 (*La Déclaration des droits de l'homme et du citoyen*): "Free communication of thoughts and opinions is one of the most precious rights of man; every citizen may therefore speak, write and print freely, except for the abuse of this freedom in cases determined by the law".
25 Decision no. 2009–580 DC of 10 June 2009, *Hadopi I.*
26 Ibid, para 15.
27 Art. 34 of the Constitution.
28 Decision 2018–773 DC of 20 December 2018.
29 For clarity, we refer here to the version of the named provision in the Electoral Code as modified by the law referred to the CC for constitutional assessment in the case at hand.
30 The *procedure de référé* is a general summary procedure that is available in cases of urgency. It allows a decision to be made on the basis of summary evidence in a short time. It is an adversarial procedure during which both parties are present to discuss the factual and legal arguments in dispute.
31 The CC uses this tool as a way of "completing" and fine-tuning the legislative process. See, for example, Bertrand Mathieu, 'Le Conseil constitutionnel "législateur positif" ou la question des interventions du juge constitutionnel français dans l'exercice de la fonction législative' (2010) 62(2) *Revue internationale de droit comparé* 507.
32 Decision 2018–773 DC (no. 28) para 21.
33 Ibid.
34 Decision no. 2020–801 DC of 18 June 2020.
35 Decision no. 2019–796 DC of 27 December 2019.
36 Ibid, para 83. It is worth noticing here that the CC did not refer to Article 22 of Regulation (EU) 2016/679 (General Data Protection Regulation) OJ L 119, 04.05.2016 and the use of automated processing. This is probably due to its strict mandate to review laws in light of the Constitution.
37 Ibid, para 93.
38 Ibid, paras 85–88.
39 Ibid, para 90.
40 The *Conseil Constitutionnel* invalidated only a part of the Budget Law which allowed the use of massive data harvesting for one offence for which the enforcement

authorities already had enough information, while it upheld the same mechanism for all the other offences.

41 This research was conducted on the *Legifrance* website, the official repository of France's law and case law, which is available at www.legifrance.gouv.fr. We used the following keywords: "*réseau(x) social(aux)*" and "*opérateurs de plateforme en ligne*", which gave 55 results, two of which were excluded because they were not relevant to the topic at hand (i.e. no social media relevance in the case). The same search was later combined with "*Convention Européenne des Droits de l'Homme*" and "*Charte des Droits*" to extract direct references by the CE to these texts. In addition, it should be mentioned that, as testimony to the increasing importance that issues surrounding social media have acquired in the past two decades, the CE has also carried out a substantial amount of research aimed at understanding the impact of social media on society and its implications for its jurisdictional work, dedicating three of its annual studies to different issues related to social media ('*Le numérique et les droits fondamentaux*,' étude annuelle du Conseil d'Etat 2014; '*Puissance publique et plateformes numériques: accompagner l'"ubérisatio?"*' étude annuelle du Conseil d'Etat 2017). The CE's 2022 annual study will also focus on social networks (Conseil d'Etat, 'Les réseaux sociaux,' nouveau cycle annuel de conférences du Conseil d'État et sujet de l'étude annuelle 2022' (*Le Conseil d'Etat Actualités*, 18 October 2021) <www.conseil-etat.fr/actualites/les-reseaux-sociaux-nouveau-cycle-annuel-de-conferences-du-conseil-d-etat-et-sujet-de-l-etude-annuelle-2022> accessed 5 March 2022.

42 References to all the selected decisions and a classification of them are available from the authors.

43 While the French CE has been found at fault for not submitting a question for a preliminary ruling to the CJEU on one occasion (Case C-416/17 *Commission européenne c/ République française* [2018] EU:C:2018:811), it generally submits references for preliminary rulings to the CJEU.

44 Case C-507/17 *Google LLC* (successor in law to *Google Inc. v Commission nationale de l'informatique et des libertés (CNIL)*) [2019] EU:C:2019:772.

45 CE, 25 November 2020, no. 445774, ECLI:FR:CEORD:2020:445774.20201125. This decision was made using an emergency procedure (*référé*) but it has since been fully confirmed using the ordinary procedure: CE 24 September 2021, Association Barakacity, no. 445979.

46 Article L212–1, 6th and 7[h] paragraphs (translated by the authors).

47 See *La loi du 10 janvier 1936 sur les groupes de combat et milices privées.*

48 CE, *Fédération d'action nationale et européenne (FANE)*, 31 October 1984, no. 28070.

49 CE, *Fédération d'action nationale et européenne (FANE)*, 26 June 1987, no. 67077.

50 CE, *Association des musulmans de Lagny-sur-Marne*, 26 July 2016, no. 401379; CE, *Association des musulmans de Lagny-sur-Marne*, 15 December 2017, no. 401378; CE, *Association Fraternité musulmane Sanâbil (Les Epis)*, 23 December 2016, no. 406012; CE, *Association Fraternité musulmane Sanâbil (Les Epis)*, 26 January 2018, no. 407220; CE, *Association Rahma de Torcy Marne-la-Vallée*, 26 January 2018, no. 421312.

51 Legifrance was used for the case law collection. The keywords used were "réseau(x) social (aux)", "Facebook" and "Twitter". The result was 302 decisions. A manual search allowed relevant results to be selected. Results where mentions of the selected words were merely incidental and did not relate to the substance of the case were excluded. Full references for the selected cases are available from the authors.

52 Cass. ass. plén., 19 May 1978, no. 76–41.211, *aff. Roy.*

53 Cass. soc., 17 April 1991, no. 90–42.636; Cass. soc., 20 November 1991, no. 89–44.605; Cass. soc., 22 January 1992, no. 90–42.517.
54 Cass. soc. 2 October 2001, *Sté Nikon France*, no. 99–42.942, para 6.
55 Cass. soc., 12 September 2018, no. 16–11.690.
56 Cass. civ. 1re, 10 April. 2013, no. 11–19.530.
57 Cass. soc., *PB*, 30 September 2020, no. 19–12.058.
58 Article 9 of the French Civil Code provides that "Everyone has the right to privacy". Article 9 of the French Code of Civil Procedure provides that "It is for each party to prove in accordance with the law the facts necessary for the success of its claim".
59 Cass. soc., 23 June 2021, no. 19–21.651.
60 Cass. soc., 30 October 2002, no. 00–40.868, Cass. soc., 21 March 2018, no. 16–20.516. Cass. soc., 9 January 2002, no. 99–45.875. Cass. soc., 15 January 2020, no. 18–14177.
61 Decision no. 74–54 DC (n 18).
62 See also our discussion in Section 2.1 of this chapter.
63 Refer to the statistics provided in Section 2 of this chapter.
64 ECtHR, *Beizaras and Levickas v. Lithuania* App. 41288/15 (14 January 2020).
65 At the time of writing, there are 24 pending questions for preliminary ruling submitted by the CCass to the CJEU.
66 Cass., no. 10–17.049 (n 14).

7 Social media before German courts

Balancing societal values, platform rules and individual rights

Matthias C. Kettemann, Polina Kulish and Martha Routen

1. Introduction

Increased litigation involving social media companies and their users objecting to deleted content or blocked accounts has led to unusual circumstances in which the perimeters of fundamental rights and, by proxy, the extent of the power and influence of social media platforms are being negotiated on the basis of contractual terms and conditions in civil law cases. While an important judgment handed down by one of the highest German courts has provided important guidelines, the interaction between national law and the terms of service of social media platforms has impacted both the conception of the private and public order of online communication and the roles of platforms, the legislator and courts in ensuring an adequate balance of the rights involved.

Based on an intensive analysis of German case law, this chapter analyses how social media and their rules are treated by German courts and how the German judiciary balances societal values, platform rules, rights and obligations and individual rights. After an introduction to the German legal system (1), we assess the role of fundamental rights in social media jurisprudence (2), appraise the extent to which judicial dialogue with European supranational courts takes place in social media cases (3) and provide conclusions (4).

In Germany, social media are primarily regulated by the *Medienstaatsvertrag* (State Media Treaty)[1] and the *Netzwerkdurchsetzungsgesetz* (NetzDG, Network Enforcement Act).[2] The former came into force in April 2020 and sets transparency and non-discrimination rules for intermediaries (i.e. platforms). The latter came into force in 2017 and contains compliance rules that oblige social media platforms of a certain size to delete illegal content (such as the use of symbols associated with the Nazi regime, hate speech, insults and defamation).[3] There have been two recent amendments. The first was in April 2021. It expanded the reporting obligations on platforms to more efficiently combat right-wing extremism and hate crime. The second was in June 2021 and it strengthened the rights of social media users.[4] Furthermore, platforms are required to implement a procedure in which complainants and

DOI: 10.4324/9781003207085-9

users who object to decisions to delete their content can seek a reassessment.[5] The amending legislation also modified the *Telemediengesetz* (TMG, Telemedia Act)[6] by simplifying and expediting how users affected by illegal content (e.g. insults) can demand specific information about the offender (such as the name of the offender) from the social media platform provider for legal proceedings. The amendment also implemented Directive (EU) 2018/1808, which amended the Audiovisual Media Services Directive and contains new mandatory compliance regulations to protect people against unlawful content on video sharing platforms like YouTube.[7] In addition, the *Jugendschutzgesetz* (Protection of Young Persons Act) has recently been amended to cover Internet-related risks, such as cyber-grooming, scams and online bullying.[8]

Fundamental rights are protected in Articles 1 to 19 of the *Grundgesetz* (GG, German Constitution),[9] while further fundamental rights, such as the right to informational self-determination, have been developed by the *Bundesverfassungsgericht* (BVerfG, Federal Constitutional Court).[10] Protective guarantees are also provided by the European Convention on Human Rights (ECHR) and the EU Charter of Fundamental Rights (CFR). The ECHR has the formal status of a federal statute.[11] However, according to the BVerfG, the fundamental rights in the GG are to be interpreted in the light of the ECHR and the case law of the European Court of Human Rights (ECtHR),[12] thus *de facto* elevating the ECHR to the quasi-constitutional level.[13]

The national court system consists of regional and federal (supreme) courts exercising general or specialised jurisdictions, of which the *Bundesgerichtshof* (BGH) is the highest judicial authority for civil and criminal matters. The *BVerfG* adjudicates on questions of constitutional relevance, predominantly complaints regarding the constitutionality of public authority acts (*Verfassungsbeschwerden*).[14] It does not act as an appellate court but offers extraordinary legal recourse in which it exclusively examines whether fundamental rights have been sufficiently considered by a decision-making body. Most recently, the *BVerfG* entered into a primacy conflict with the Court of Justice of the European Union (CJEU), although not in the area of social media law, in which it implemented and nuanced the right to be forgotten – i.e. the right of an individual to have an organisation erase personal data.[15]

Despite a number of higher regional court judgments concerning social media and dealing with issues such as allegations of hate speech, insults and unwarranted removal of content, the *BVerfG* has issued only one decision regarding social media in the past decade. In 2019, it ordered a preliminary injunction against Facebook, which had blocked a right-wing political party's user account for sharing hate speech on its site.[16] Although the judgment in the main proceedings is pending, the *BVerfG*'s reasoning appears to have tended towards the stance that the indirect effect of fundamental rights in the public area affects social media platforms similarly to how it affects private entities.[17]

On 29 July 2021, the *BGH* ruled against Facebook in a similar case in which it had deleted two users' posts and temporarily blocked their accounts for breaching the community standards in the terms and conditions by posting hate speech.[18] The *BGH* decided that, although Facebook could delete posts and block users' accounts for violating the community standards in some circumstances, in this case, it was not entitled to. Its terms and conditions put the platform's users at an unreasonable disadvantage because good faith requires, *inter alia*, a party unilaterally providing terms and conditions to not attempt to unfairly assert its own interests at the expense of its contractual partner without taking due consideration of the latter's interests from the outset and granting reasonable compensation.[19]

2. Fundamental rights in national social media jurisprudence

While they are sometimes embedded in the civil law framework, decisions regarding social media are predominantly framed as fundamental rights cases. The following subsections discuss how assessment of the nature of the parties involved determines the effect of fundamental rights in a dispute: first, how German courts qualify social media platform terms and conditions; then, the specific rights asserted by users and platforms; and finally, the outcome of compensation claims in social media cases.

2.1 *The nature of the parties involved*

In cases against Facebook, lower courts have had varying opinions on the extent to which, despite being a private entity, the social network should be held to the same standards of fundamental rights protection as a state entity because of its influence on public life. The consistent position of German courts is that, in disputes between private persons, the parties cannot directly invoke fundamental rights against each other. Instead, both parties are beneficiaries of fundamental rights that directly bind only persons and bodies exercising state power.[20] Fundamental rights in private disputes therefore exercise a so-called "indirect effect". For German courts, this means that "*fundamental rights must be mutually reconciled . . . . To this end, the conflicting fundamental rights positions must be recorded in their interaction and balanced in accordance with the principle of practical equal importance [*praktische Konkordanz*] in such a way that they are as effective as possible for all parties involved*".[21] In other words, fundamental rights must be "*developed in the balance of equal freedom*".[22]

To respect the principle of *praktische Konkordanz* – the practical equal importance of different fundamental rights – restriction of one right must be proportional to reach the aim of the "*greatest possible development and effectiveness*" of a conflicting right. To this end, the courts determine if a restriction appears suitable and necessary.[23] For instance, the Higher Regional Court of Nuremberg ruled that, in order to enjoy freedom of expression, platform users can be expected to express themselves "*sufficiently clearly and unambiguously*"[24] and that the platform can instruct the user to not take advantage of full-scale freedom of expression as is provided for in the citizen-state relationship.[25] In any event, parties' conflicting legal positions only need to be balanced against each other if the user's claim is not in violation of any laws that restrict free speech within the limits allowed in the GG to protect certain interests, such as the protection of minors.[26]

In the user-public entity relationship, fundamental rights enjoy direct effect. A nuanced issue arose in a dispute between a user whose comments were deleted from the corporate Facebook page of Mitteldeutscher Rundfunk (MDR). MDR is a public broadcasting institution with legal capacity subject to indirect state administration. It is therefore directly bound by fundamental rights in its relationships with third parties. At the same time, MDR enjoys freedom to broadcast in its special manifestation of freedom of programming under Article 5 GG – the same article that guarantees platform users freedom of expression.[27] MDR's public mandate led the user whose off-topic comments were deleted to argue that MDR had to tolerate them as long as they fell within freedom of expression as guaranteed by the GG, rather than relying on MDR's terms of use. The user additionally argued that the terms of use contradicted German constitutional and European Union (EU) law in certain points; for example that they violated Article 18 of the Treaty on the Functioning of the European Union (TFEU) prohibiting discrimination on grounds of nationality by stipulating that posts in foreign languages were undesirable.[28]

The Leipzig Administrative Court found that MDR exercised a virtual domiciliary right (*virtuelles Hausrecht*) when it deleted off-topic comments on its Facebook page. As the Cologne Administrative Court clarified, *[t]he public law domiciliary right entails the right to decide who is allowed to be on the premises of a public institution in order to safeguard the purpose of that institution and, in particular, to prevent interference with its daily operations.*

For virtual services, a corresponding "virtual domiciliary right" is enforced by blocking the user, be it manually or by technical means, such as by programming the software to no longer allow certain users access to services.[29] A right to remove off-topic comments is set out in MDR's terms of use, thus permissibly restricting users' freedom of expression under Article 5 GG and substantiating participation rights[30] that derive from Article 3 GG.[31]

Facebook's role in public life has been considered differently by German courts. The Bamberg Regional Court contended that "*fundamental rights do not have a direct effect, but only a radiating effect*" in disputes between private parties.[32] However, regarding Facebook, it stated that the platform enjoys a quasi-monopoly position among social networks in its influence on public life and therefore "*fundamental rights can claim almost direct validity*".[33] According to the Bamberg Regional Court, Facebook exercises a state-like telecommunication service function and therefore its terms and conditions must be interpreted narrowly in favour of users' freedom of expression.[34] This reasoning does not find support in judgments by a number of other German courts that consider Facebook's importance in the market, leading to it being "*inescapable*" for users, and treating this as an additional factor in weighing rather than a starting point.[35] These courts have concluded that Facebook's market position merely means that the platform must comply with legal equality requirements and it cannot treat users differently; if it avoids this, there is no abuse of market power.[36] Even when a dispute concerned blocking a political party's account ahead of the 2019 European elections,[37] it still resulted in the conclusion that, for providers like Facebook, there is a high intensity of fundamental rights obligations, yet they do not have direct effect.[38]

2.2 *Terms and conditions*

To balance rights, German courts read fundamental rights in "*general clauses and other terms that are open to interpretation and require interpretation*".[39] In their reasoning, German courts rely principally on contractual agreements between users and social media platforms. These agreements are "*decisive*" in determining if a disputed post can be deleted, although they are "*partially overridden by the provisions of constitutional and ordinary law*".[40] Courts rely on provisions in the Terms of Use and Community Standards and analyse whether they are transparent and the measures they provide are not unexpected and are proportional.[41] Furthermore, the courts interpret platforms' terms of use in the light of the values in the GG and the CFR.[42]

A prominent issue in case law has been whether or not social media platforms can reserve the right to delete content or block user accounts because of violations of community standards, even if the content itself is not illegal. The recent BGH decision mentioned in the introduction constitutes such a case. It established the right of platforms to implement their terms of service but also provided minimum procedural standards regarding how these terms of service are implemented.[43]

In its terms and conditions, which the users in question had agreed to, Facebook reserved the right to delete so-called "hate speech" as a breach of community standards. The question arose whether this clause put users at an unfair disadvantage contrary to the principle of good faith and was therefore invalid under §307(1) German Civil Code (BGB). The reasonableness test in §307(1) BGB requires a comprehensive assessment and weighing of conflicting interests: freedom of expression on the side of the user (Article 5(1) GG) and freedom of professional activity on the part of the social media platform (Article 12(1) GG). As neither of the parties' fundamental rights take precedence, the conflict is resolved by applying the methodological principle of practical equal importance described previously. The BGH concluded that, under certain circumstances, Facebook could delete content because of a breach of its community standards. However, to provide a reasonable balance of conflicting interests, the terms and conditions must oblige Facebook to inform the users concerned (at least, *post factum*) that their content has been blocked, and to notify them in advance in the case of blocking an account.[44]

The position of the BGH differs from the earlier reasoning of lower courts. For a while, there appeared to be consensus that the principle of practical equal importance implied that companies like Facebook can shape the rights of their users through general terms and conditions[45] and that a post may be considered *prima facie* in breach of platform standards and removed when in doubt – e.g. if "*one of several interpretations fulfils the characteristics of 'hate speech'*".[46] The rationale for this was that companies like social network operators and owners of the hardware used in their operations have an interest in generating income, so they need to attract as many users as possible.[47] Platforms compete for users, for whom they strive to set certain standards of quality and conduct, and they balance the risk of losing some users if they tolerate expressions that might repel them against that of losing users if they restrict freedom of expression too much.[48] In such cases, German courts concluded that platforms have the right to make a business decision about how to balance these risks and to reflect them in their terms and conditions.[49] Additionally, platforms "*may, to a certain extent, show consideration of the fundamental rights and positions worthy of protection of third parties whose personal rights could be endangered by unnecessarily rude communications*".[50] The underlying logic is not to protect users from encountering dissent but to regulate the manner in which opinions are expressed.[51]

As intermediaries, platforms additionally face the risk of liability for illegal content spread by users.[52] The courts acknowledged concerns about the constitutionality of the NetzDG[53] imposing additional liability on platforms.[54] However, even if the NetzDG is invalid, platform accountability can arise from a breach of the duty of care (Section 1004 BGB) and negative liability for not remedying infringements on the basis of Article 14(3) of the E-Commerce Directive 2000/31/EC.[55] Setting stricter requirements for users than in the NetzDG has been justified by the fact that the latter only produces minimum standards.[56]

2.3 Specific rights invoked by parties

2.3.1 User rights

FREEDOM OF EXPRESSION

When it comes to specific fundamental rights that are relevant in balancing, the courts note that users enjoy freedom of expression as is guaranteed by Article 5(1) GG.[57] Freedom of expression encompasses sharp, polemical, exaggerated expressions and expressions that generalise, point out possible consequences, and maybe even hurt others.[58] In this sense, right-wing extremist opinions are also protected.[59] One of the reasons for such a generous reading is that "*citizens are not legally required to personally share the values of the constitution*" and "*it is not possible for every user to express himself at the highest level of argumentation*".[60] German courts reason that social media platforms provide users with a "*public marketplace*" for information and the exchange of opinions. Therefore, permissible expressions of opinion – which are a manifestation of the concept of democratic opinion-forming in the constitutional state – may not be removed from them.[61]

The upper limit of permissible freedom of expression is reached when it is used not to further a dispute on merits but to disparage a person or a group and particularly to incite hatred, which is criminalised under German law.[62] For instance, "*undifferentiated disparagement of migrants*" was found in a case in which a user linked an internet article entitled "*M. regime wants to expropriate land from citizens in order to build houses for illegals*" to his Facebook page. The Munich Higher Regional Court found that the content of the article constituted hate speech, and although the user had not added any content of his own, making the post on the linked page accessible to the public implied attribution to the user and Facebook had the right to block the account.[63] At the same time, German courts are careful not to push back the limits of freedom of expression. When an offensive comment concerned a public official, the Stuttgart Higher Regional Court underlined that weighing the common right of personality and the right to freedom of expression must take into account the specific content of the statement, its form, the circumstances of dissemination along with its effects, its contribution to public opinion and the public official status of the person addressed in the comment, which widened the boundary of permissible expressions.[64]

When it comes to interpretation of disputed content (a post or comment, etc.), the decisive factor for German courts is the "*objective meaning from the perspective of an unbiased and reasonable audience*" rather than the subjective ideas of the parties.[65] To this end, German courts analyse the wording of a statement in its context[66] and determine if it is unambiguous and can be used as a basis for further examination or ambiguous in the sense that a significant part of the audience understand the content differently.[67] It is users that have the burden of presenting and proving that sanctions imposed on them were unjustified, meaning that uncertainty over the classification of a user's contribution due to a lack of information about its context is to the user's detriment.[68] In the case of value judgments expressed by users, weighing also involves consideration of whether or not the expressed opinion is based on true, factual assertions. Incorrect information is not *a priori* excluded from protected freedom of expression, but when weighed against other conflicting interests, it does not enjoy priority.[69]

Context-sensitive interpretation implies that "*[i]n the case of short contributions on the internet . . . the court must base its assessment on the average reader who reads the contributions in passing*".[70] At the same time, the user posting the statement has more time to consider the choice of words online (than in in-person interaction). Therefore, higher standards of care are applied.[71] In another example of context-dependent interpretation, the Nurnberg Higher Regional Court reasoned that use of the term "gold pieces" (*Goldstücke*) in a derogatory manner regarding refugees is not a formal insult or defamatory criticism, as the word itself usually has a positive connotation and therefore context was required to detect the derogatory nature of the statement.[72]

In German court jurisprudence, recognisable irony and satire belong to protected freedom of expression.[73] For instance, the Munich Higher Regional Court stated that, in itself, a comparison of migrants to "*us stupid Germans*" is ironic.[74] Sharing a photo depicting Hitler sitting on a sofa apparently playing a Game Boy with the headline "*Terrible suspicion: Was Hitler a gamer?*"[75] was interpreted by the Frankenthal Regional Court as an act of trivialisation that lacked critical examination or an obviously ridiculous depiction.[76]

THE RIGHT TO INFORMATION

An incidental right argued for in a number of social media cases in German courts is users' right to information; namely, information about whether their profile was blocked or deactivated by a third company commissioned by the defendant, and if so, by which company.[77] German courts have consistently denied enjoyment of this right due to "no apparent basis for this claim" – either in the License Agreement, the General Terms and Conditions or in the good faith principle, noting at least on one occasion that such assertions might amount to an abuse of rights.[78] The apparent concerns of users in relevant cases were that the platform "*had complied with unlawful directives of the federal government regarding the deletions and blockings in dispute*".[79] The German courts sided with Facebook. They interpreted these allegations as conspiracy theories[80] and underlined that, in any event, platforms alone were responsible vis-à-vis users, and found that there was no basis for a lawsuit against the German Federal Government under the NetzDG.[81] Even if third parties block users' profiles on behalf of Facebook, it would not constitute a violation of the users' rights of personality and freedom of expression, since enjoyment of these rights on the Facebook platform is only available to users on the basis of user agreements. As enjoyment of rights in such a context is not absolute, it also provides no basis for claims of third-party violations.[82]

2.3.2 Platform rights

The rights of social media platforms are on another weighing scale. For instance, in addition to freedom of profession, which was discussed previously in relation to platform terms and conditions, the Koblenz Regional Court ruled that Facebook has a "*virtual domiciliary right – which can be traced back to Article 14 GG [the right to property], but also to Article 2 GG [free development of personality]*".[83] In the MDR case mentioned previously, the German court referred to freedom of programming as a core of the freedom to broadcast guaranteed under Article 5 GG.[84]

Regarding the free development of personality, the Nurnberg Higher Regional Court pointed out that Facebook enjoys an ordinary right to terminate a contractual relation, which exists to prevent situations in which exercise of the freedom of development of personality would be undermined.[85] The question remains whether platforms like Facebook can also rely on media freedoms like freedom of the press and freedom to report. The Nuremberg Higher Regional Court has expressed doubts, since such platforms do not disseminate their own content.[86] However, this court also drew a parallel between the position of platforms and press/broadcasters when concluding that Article 5(1) GG does not give rise to a user's right to performance – i.e., the right to demand dissemination of a user's statements.[87]

2.4 *Compensation claims*

Claims for monetary compensation of users have been based on alleged violations of the general right to personality, which is protected in Articles 2(1) and 1(1) GG.[88] For German courts, the general right to personality encompasses, *inter alia*, "*the right to dispose of one's own person, the right to one's own word, the right to informational self-determination and the right to guarantee the confidentiality and integrity of information technology systems*".[89] According to German courts, using Facebook is not essential for personal development.[90] The right to personality "*protects the narrower personal sphere of life and the development of its basic conditions*", monetary compensation for infringement of which is only available if an encroachment is serious and impairment cannot be compensated in another way.[91] In the case of temporarily blocking a social media profile, there is no serious restriction on personal development, since possibilities to express oneself in other ways are available.[92] For German courts, an abstract loss of communication possibilities "*cannot be considered a damage for a person not engaged in business*".[93] Moreover, the Nurnberg Higher Regional Court disagreed with a user that conceivable loss of reputation occurred because of blocking, since no evidence had been provided that other users knew that the partial blocking was based on an accusation of violating community guidelines.[94]

German courts have also denied users' claims for damages based on a "fictitious license fee". This concept has been linked to compensation for social media platforms continuing to employ a user's data for advertising purposes during the period when the user's account is blocked and the user is therefore unable to take advantage of the platform's services.[95] As German courts have noted, by agreeing to the platform's terms of services without any reservations, users consent to the use of their data even while their accounts may be temporarily blocked.[96]

Similar claims for damages based on Article 82 of the General Data Protection Regulation (GDPR)[97] have been equally unsuccessful. German courts have rejected users' assertions that platforms processed their data without their authorisation.[98] In addition, although users whose accounts are temporarily blocked lose control over their data for that timespan[99] and are concurrently temporarily prevented from disseminating their opinions on the specific platform, German courts do not assume that this necessarily causes any material or immaterial harm.[100] The Dresden Higher Regional Court conceded that "*data protection law per se protects a subjective right that has a strong connection to the personal feelings of the individual*", but breach of GDPR requirements cannot be found for "*every individually perceived inconvenience or in the case of petty infringements without serious damage to a person's self-image or reputation*".[101] A user's right to informational self-determination, as German courts have noted, protects against third parties taking possession of the user's data without the user's authorisation but not against deletion of contributions.[102]

3. Judicial dialogue

In disputes between private parties in German courts, fundamental rights are developed by balancing them. This largely corresponds to the understanding of balancing by the ECtHR, even though the German approach to the application of fundamental rights between private parties, the notable doctrine of *Drittwirkung*, is more nuanced.[103] German courts underline Facebook's quasi-monopoly position among social networks in its influence on public life and its importance for the exercise of freedom of expression. Although no direct reference to ECtHR case law is made in this regard, the reasoning of German courts reminds one of the "unique position of the Internet" for the exercise of freedom of expression, as is emphasised in Strasbourg case law.[104]

Similar to the *Handyside* dictum that freedom of expression is applicable to "[ideas and information] that offend, shock or disturb",[105] German courts underline that freedom of expression includes sharp, polemical, exaggerated expressions that may even hurt others. At the same time, German courts stress the importance of allowing platforms to moderate according to their own standards. They also accept that irony and satire are protected under freedom of expression.[106]

When German courts balance conflicting rights to achieve practical equal importance, they assess whether restriction of one right is legal, legitimate, with a view of a legitimacy goal, and necessary and proportional with regard to that goal and in the light of the "*greatest possible effectiveness*" of a conflicting right. In ECtHR case law, a similar three-part test is developed to assess the legality of interference with, *inter alia*, freedom of expression: the interference must be provided for by law; it must pursue a legitimate aim; and it must be necessary in a democratic society.[107]

Particularly regarding value judgments, German courts sometimes rely on ECtHR case law in their reasoning, which requires a sufficient factual basis in value judgments for an opinion to be protected under freedom of expression.[108] They further interpret disputed content on the basis of its "*objective meaning from the perspective of an unbiased and reasonable audience*" rather than the parties' subjective ideas.

Despite similarities in approach and reasoning, German courts do not often explicitly refer to ECtHR case law in this area. As the *BVerfG* stated in its *Görgülü* judgment, national courts are obliged to take ECtHR case law into account when deciding a case.[109] In practice, however, it does not often play a large role in judicial reasoning (with the exception, to a certain extent, of criminal law and family law), especially in lower courts – be it due to a lack of awareness of and significance attributed to international jurisprudence in general, time constraints or even language barriers.[110]

Turning to the rights of platforms, German courts have found different legal bases for their recognition, including European provisions. The Munich Higher Regional Court has reasoned that Facebook, as a foreign legal entity under private law, "*cannot directly invoke the fundamental rights of the GG pursuant to Article 19 (3) of the GG. However, it does have 'property-like' rights to the platform it provides. In addition, . . . the European Charter of Fundamental Rights must be taken into account, which also protects legal persons and Art. 16 of which explicitly recognises entrepreneurial freedom under Union law and national laws and practices*".[111] This differs from the position expressed by the Nuremberg Higher Regional Court that Facebook, "*notwithstanding its capacity as a foreign legal person, can invoke the protection of fundamental rights*"; namely, freedom of profession, enjoyed by companies, and their right to the free development of personality,[112] guaranteed in Articles 12(1) and 2(1) GG respectively.[113] The Hamm Higher Regional Court has also stated that Facebook can invoke fundamental rights like a domestic company and further added that the extension of the fundamental right entitlement to legal entities from EU Member States is based on Articles 26(2) and 18 TFEU, which respectively protect fundamental freedoms in the internal market and prohibit discrimination on grounds of nationality.[114]

4. Conclusions

Social media platforms give people access to information and allow opinions to be formed and voiced at an unprecedented level. They have become the communication engines of our modern societies and have opened up significant new spaces for interaction.

As the social media case law discussed here shows, where people communicate, rules are needed. In small groups, these rules can emerge in a decentralised manner and be enforced socially. In larger social communication spaces, however, decentralised enforcement is no longer possible. For this reason, social media companies have created so-called community guidelines – "house rules" that define what is and is not permissible on their platforms. These house rules are sometimes in conflict with national laws and courts are often called on to navigate these conflicts. This is an important task because weighing private and public speech rules is essential to ensure a free communication space, which, by itself, is essential for free democratic processes. States are obliged to counterfactually ensure the existence of this free communication space and courts are responsible for navigating conflicts. Incidentally, one of the key normative developments within the Digital Services Act lies in defining what differing obligations platforms have with regard to illegal and non-illegal content.

In October 2021, the Higher Administrative Court of Saxony ruled that posters of the far-right party "Der III. Weg" with the text "Hang the Greens" had to be taken down (6 B 360/21). The reasoning stated that the posters were "*capable of heating up the psychological climate, increasing the potential for aggression in the social fabric and poisoning the political climate by generating hatred*". It was "*a matter of creating a danger to political and social peace*". "*Human dignity*" was "*not capable of being weighed in relation to freedom of expression*". This happened offline, but very similar cases have happened online. Balancing different rights is a key task for the judiciary.

(Regulated) self-regulatory models play an important role in practice in protecting against illegal and problematic content. The forthcoming European Digital Services Act (DSA) obliges platforms to regularly review what risks to the community their services might pose. Restoration rights for incorrectly deleted content are intended to put a stop to over-blocking; explanatory rights for algorithmic decisions are intended to make automatic deletion mechanisms transparent.

Negotiating and clarifying the rights of the major platforms in court will continue to serve as the best tool for taking action against and removing non-illegal, but – especially in the aggregate – problematic content that leads to a decrease in social cohesion or supports a culture that violates rights. However, their terms and conditions and community standards must meet the content- and process-related thresholds introduced by Germany's courts, including its highest courts.

Germany is a country with a globally influential approach to social media regulation. Its Network Enforcement Act and social media jurisprudence have impacted social media law and practice globally. Judicial dialogue is still in its infancy, but some promising conceptual exchanges are visible. A promising German contribution to social media jurisprudence that is echoed in the approach of the Digital Services Act is the procedural approach as a "*way out to bolster rule of law online without imposing stricter rules on free speech itself*".[115]

Notes

1 Medienstaatsvertrag (MStV) 23 April 2020 (GVBl. p 450, 451, BayRS 02–33-S).
2 Netzwerkdurchsuchungsgesetz (NetzDG) (BGBL 2017 I p. 3352), last amended by Art 1 G zur Änd. des NetzwerkdurchsetzungsG 3.6.2021 (BGBl I S 1436).
3 The NetzDG defines social media networks as "telemedia service providers which, for profit-making purposes, operate internet platforms which are designed to enable users to share any content with other users or to make such content available to the public" (Art 1(1) NetzDG). Note that this and the following translations from the German original are by the authors.
4 On 1 February 2022, the last two clauses relating to access by researchers to platform data and a database containing specific types of deleted content at the Federal Criminal Office entered into force.
5 NetzDG, para 3b.

6 Telemediengesetz (TMG) 26.2.2007 (BGBl I 179), last amended by Art. 3 zur Änd. des Strafgesetzbuches – Strafbarkeit des Betreibens krimineller Handelsplattformen im Internet 12 August 2021 (BGBl I S 3544).

7 Directive (EU) 2018/1808 of the European Parliament and of the Council of 14 November 2018 amending Directive 2010/13/EU on the coordination of certain provisions laid down by law, regulation or administrative action in Member States concerning the provision of audio-visual media services (Audiovisual Media Services Directive) in view of changing market realities [2018] OJ L 303/69. On video-sharing platforms coming within the scope of Directive 2018/1808, see Chapter 1 by Evangelia Psychogiopoulou and Federica Casarosa in this volume.

8 (JuSchG) 23.7.2002 (BGBl I S 2730), last amended by Zweites G zur Änd des JugendschutzG 9.4.2021 (BGBl I S 742).

9 Grundgesetz für die Bundesrepublik Deutschland (GG) 23rd May 1949 /BGBl S 1, last amended by Art 1 G 29 September 2020 (BGBl I S 2048).

10 *cf* BVerfG, 15.12.1983–1 BvR 209/83 [Volkszählung].

11 Art 59 section 2 GG.

12 *cf* BVerfG, 14.10.2004–2 BvR 1481/04; BVerfG, 4.5.2011–2BvR 2333/08; BVerfG, 12.6.2018–2 BvR 1738/12.

13 Christian Calliess, *Staatsrecht III – Bezüge zum Völker- und Europarecht* (3rd edn., Beck Verlag 2020) 48.

14 Article 93 s 1 No. 4a and 4b GG [Jurisdiction of the Federal Constitutional Court].

15 *cf* BVerfG, 6.11.2019–1 BvR 16/13 [*Recht auf Vergessen I*]; BVerfG, 6.11.2019–1 BvR 276/17 [*Recht auf Vergessen II*].

16 BVerfG, 22.5.2019–1 BvQ 42/19.

17 Erik Tuchtfeld, 'Marktplätze, soziale Netzwerke und die BVerfG-Entscheidung zum "III. Weg"' (*Verfassungsblog*, 26 May 2019) <www.verfassungsblog.de/marktplaetze-soziale-netzwerke-und-die-bverfg-entscheidung-zum-iii-weg> accessed 3 October 2022.

18 Bundesgerichtshof, judgments of 29 July 2001, III ZR 179/20 und III ZR 192/20 (not yet published). See the press release on the judgment, <www.bundesgerichtshof.de/SharedDocs/Pressemitteilungen/DE/2021/2021149.html?nn=10690868> accessed 3 October 2022.

19 Ibid.

20 OLG Nürnberg, 4.8.2020–3 U 3641/19 [84]. In OLG München, 18.2.2020–18 U 3465/19 Pre [79]-[80]; OLG Düsseldorf, 4.12.2020–7 U 131/19 [46]; OLG München, 17.9.2018–18 W 1383/18 [21]-[22]; LG Koblenz, 21.4.2020–9 O 239/18 [164]. *Cf* BVerfG 22.2.2011–1 BvR 699/06 [47]. See Benjamin Raue, 'Meinungsfreiheit in sozialen Netzwerken: Ansprüche von Nutzern sozialer Netzwerke gegen die Löschung ihrer Beiträge' (2018) 73 *JuristenZeitung* 961, 964–965.

21 OLG Nürnberg, 4.8.2020 [87], [106]; OLG Düsseldorf, 4.12.2020 [46]; VG Leipzig, 11.9.2019 [89].

22 OLG München, 17.9.2018 [22].

23 VG Leipzig, 11.9.2019–1 K 1642/18 [90]-[95]. *Cf* BVerfG 22.2.2011 [102].

24 OLG Nürnberg, 4.8.2020 [138]. Read in conjunction with [131]: 'Since the Community Standards have the character of general terms and conditions, ambiguities in this respect generally benefit the user. Likewise, due to the indirect third-party effect of Article 5(1) GG, the user's right of expression must be given priority in cases of doubt.' Cf. LG Bamberg, 18.10.2018 [116]: 'An ambiguity with regard to the interpretation of a statement subject to freedom of expression always has an effect in favour of the interpretation that is more favourable to the user, if only for reasons of protection of fundamental rights.'

25 OLG Nürnberg, 4.8.2020 [138].

26 Cf. OLG München, 18.2.2020 [85].

27 VG Leipzig, 11.9.2019 [88].
28 Ibid [32].
29 VG Köln 18 8.6.2021 – K 717 [42].
30 The rights to participate in political and in public life are indispensable for the elimination of discrimination. They are inextricably linked to the rights to peaceful assembly and association, freedom of opinion and expression. See, e.g. *OHCHR*, Guidelines for States on the effective implementation of the right to participate in public affairs [2018] A/HRC/39/28, [1], [14]-[18].
31 VG Leipzig, 11.9.2019 [85]-[87].
32 LG Bamberg, 18.10.2018–2 O 248/18 [79].
33 LG Bamberg, 18.10.2018 [83].
34 Ibid [82]-[84].
35 OLG Nürnberg, 4.8.2020 [73], [89], [105]. *See* also the user's arguments in OLG Düsseldorf, 4.12.2020–7 U 131/19 [8]; LG Koblenz, 21.4.2020–9 O 239/18 [166]; LG Offenburg, 26.9.2018–2 O 310/18[57]. Cf. the interim injunction decision of the German Constitutional Court in case BVerfG, 22.5.2019 [15], [19], which underlines the importance of Facebook for the dissemination of political messages and notes that the question of the effect of the platform's market position in weighting rights "has, however, neither been conclusively clarified in the case law of the civil courts nor in the case law of the Federal Constitutional Court. The constitutional legal relationships are still unresolved in this respect". Cf. BVerfG 22.02.2011 [49], [60], [113], [115], [123]. Generally, in the view of OLG Nürnberg, 4.8.2020 [67] the nature of these contractual agreements between users and Facebook are sui generis service contracts with elements of rental, work and service contracts.
36 OLG Nürnberg, 4.8.2020 [113]-[114]; LG Koblenz, 21.4.2020 [168].
37 BVerfG, 22.5.2019.
38 OLG Nürnberg, 4.8.2020 [85].
39 OLG Nürnberg, 4.8.2020 [88]; OLG München, 18.2.2020 [80]; OLG München, 17.9.2018 [23]; KG Berlin, 22.3.2019–10 W 172/1 [19].
40 OLG Nürnberg, 4.8.2020 [67].
41 OLG Nürnberg, 4.8.2020 [3]-[18], [116]-[128]; OLG Düsseldorf, 4.12.2020–7 U 131/19 [24] for Facebook's position; OLG München, 17.9.2018–18 W 1383/18 [25]-[36]; LG Koblenz, 21.4.2020–9 O 239/18 [160]-[162]; OLG Karlsruhe, 25.6.2018–15 W 86/18 [21]; LG Heidelberg, 28.8.2018 – 1 O 71/18 [28]-[32]; VG Leipzig, 11.9.2019–1 K 1642/18 [86]; OLG Stuttgart, 6.9.2018–4 W 63/18 [77]; OLG Hamm, 15.9.2020–29 U 6/20 [72], [82], [85], [147]-[149].
42 OLG Nürnberg, 4.8.2020 [83]. *See* also BVerfG, 22.5.2019 [21].
43 Bundesgerichtshof, judgments of 29 July 2021, III ZR 179/20 und III ZR 192/20 (not yet published). See the press release on the judgment: <www.bundesgerichtshof.de/SharedDocs/Pressemitteilungen/DE/2021/2021149.html?nn=10690868> accessed 3 October 2022.
44 Ibid.
45 OLG Nürnberg, 4.8.2020 [95]; VG Leipzig, 11.9.2019 [89].
46 OLG Nürnberg, 4.8.2020 [135]-[136]; OLG Düsseldorf, 4.12.2020 [24] for Facebook's position; LG Frankenthal, 8.9.2020–6 O 23/20 [71]. In case OLG Nürnberg, 4.8.2020 [211] the court reasoned that although the first two sentences of the disputed post were consistent with Facebook's Community Standards, Facebook was allowed to delete the whole post to prevent distortion of the user's statement – by analogy with the principle of counterstatement in the press.
47 LG Koblenz, 21.4.2020 [165].
48 OLG Nürnberg, 4.8.2020 [96].

49 OLG Nürnberg, 4.8.2020 [97], [110]; OLG München, 18.2.2020 [82]; LG Koblenz, 21.4.2020 [165]; LG Heidelberg, 28.8.2018–1 O 71/18 [38]; OLG Dresden, 16.6.2020–4 U 2890/19 [33].
50 OLG Nürnberg, 4.8.2020 [49], [97]. *See* also OLG Düsseldorf, 4.12.2020 [47].
51 OLG Nürnberg, 4.8.2020 [100]. *Cf.* OLG München, 17.9.2018 [10].
52 OLG Nürnberg, 4.8.2020 [101]; Cf. BVerfG, 22.5.2019 [5]; Oreste Pollicino and Oleg Soldatov, 'Judicial Balancing of Human Rights Online', in Mart Susi (ed), *Human Rights, Digital Society and the Law: A Research Companion* (Routledge 2019) 142; Matthias C. Kettemann and Wolfgang Benedek, 'Freedom of Expression Online', in Mart Susi (ed), *Human Rights, Digital Society and the Law: A Research Companion* (Routledge 2019) 68, 71–73; Amélie Heldt and Stephan Dreyer, 'Competent Third Parties and Content Moderation on Platforms: Potentials of Independent Decision-Making Bodies From A Governance Structure Perspective' (2021) 11 *Journal of Information Policy* 266, 268–272; Bernd Holznagel and Lorna Woods, 'Rechtsgüterschutz im Internet – Regulierung durch Sorgfaltspflichten in England und Deutschland' (2021) 76 *JuristenZeitung* 276, 277.
53 On the NetzDG see Demaske [2021] 28–30; Kettemann and Benedek [2019] 70; Holznagel and Woods (n 52) 276–277, 280–285; Raue (n 20) 962; Brown and Sinclair [2020] 447; Vijay K Bhatia, '"Fake News" as Interdiscursive Illusion', in Vijay K Bhatia and Girolamo Tessuto (eds), *Social Media in Legal Practice* (Routledge 2021) 225.
54 OLG Nürnberg, 4.8.2020 [102]. Cf. OLG Stuttgart, 6.9.2018–4 W 63/18 [76].
55 Ibid. *See* also Gerhard Wagner, 'Haftung von Plattformen für Rechtsverletzungen (Teil 1)' (2020) 4 GRUR 329–338.
56 OLG Nürnberg, 4.8.2020 [108].
57 OLG Nürnberg, 4.8.2020 [91]; OLG Düsseldorf, 4.12.2020 [73].
58 OLG Nürnberg, 4.8.2020 [92]; OLG München, 17.9.2018 [49]. For an example of a German court finding a comment 'unnecessary sharp, polemical and aggressive,' see LG Heidelberg, 28.8.2018 [40]. See also OLG Stuttgart, 6.9.2018 [75]. Cf. LG Offenbach, 26.9.2018–2 O 310/18 [46].
59 OLG München, 17.9.2018 [49]. *Cf* Viera Pejchal, *Hate Speech and Human Rights in Eastern Europe: Legislating for Divergent Values* (Routledge 2020) 137.
60 OLG Nürnberg, 4.8.2020 [93]; OLG München, 17.9.2018 [49].
61 OLG München, 17.9.2018 [21]; LG Heidelberg, 28.8.2018 [38].
62 OLG Nürnberg, 4.8.2020 [94]; OLG München, 17.9.2018 [49]. At the same time, since in public matters a presumption in favour of free speech is applicable, the threshold for interpreting a statement as inciting hatred should be regarded to be high. On this, see OLG München, 17.9.2018 [49].
63 OLG München, 17.9.2018 [1], [38]-[47]. *Cf.* LG Frankenthal, 8.9.2020–6 O 23/20 [72]. Cf. OLG Dresden, 1.6.2018–4 U 217/18 [15]. This court stated that contrary to the 'like' function, mere 'sharing' on a Facebook page is not sufficient for an attribution and should not be given any weight beyond the dissemination of the post.
64 OLG Stuttgart, 8.9.2020–4 W 54/20 [18]. Cf. Jacob Rowbottom, 'Careful What You Wish For: Press Criticism of the Legal Protection of Human Rights', in Michelle Farrell, Eleanor Drywood and Edel Hughes (eds), *Human Rights in the Media: Fear and Fetish* (Routledge 2019) 213.
65 See e.g. OLG Düsseldorf 4.12.2020 [51]. *Cf.* OLG Dresden, 9.4.2018–1 OLG 21 Ss 772/17 [7]-[8].
66 OLG Nürnberg, 4.8.2020 [132]; OLG München, 18.2.2020 [86]; OLG Düsseldorf, 4.12.2020 [51]; OLG München, 17.9.2018 [41]; OLG Köln, 9.5.201–15 W 70/18 [4]; KG Berlin, 22.3.2019 [23]. *Cf.* Pejchal (n 59) 136–137.
67 OLG München, 17.9.2018 [41].

68 OLG München, 18.2.2020 [77], [89], *cf.* [6]; OLG Köln, 18.10.2018–15 W 57/18 [6].
69 Ibid [160]-[162]; OLG Köln, 9.5.2019 [1].
70 OLG Nürnberg, 4.8.2020–3 U 3641/19 [134]; OLG Düsseldorf, 4.12.2020 [51], [24] for Facebook's position.
71 OLG Nürnberg, 4.8.2020 [139].
72 OLG Nürnberg, 4.8.2020 [150].
73 Ibid [177].
74 OLG München, 18.2.2020 [5], [29], [87]. The ruling further reads: 'Because of the recognisable reference to "ethnicity" or "national origin" of the persons with whom the contribution deals, it is not remote or even impossible that it could be assessed in a conceivable context as a "hate message" . . .'. For other examples of ironic and satirical comments, see OLG Düsseldorf, 4.12.2020 [52]-[53], [64]; OLG Dresden, 7.4.2020–4 U 2805/19 [15].
75 LG Frankenthal, 8.9.2020 [18].
76 Ibid, 73. For the context of German history of the Nazi regime for the legal regime of hate speech, see Brown and Sinclair [2020] 81–85.
77 OLG München, 18.2.2020 [9]; OLG Nürnberg, 4.8.2020 [183].
78 OLG Nürnberg, 4.8.2020 [187]; OLG Dresden, 11.6.2019–4 U 2890/19 [3],[6]; OLG München, 18.2.2020 [65]-[68] – See also [17], where Facebook argued that such requests come "out of the blue."
79 OLG Nürnberg, 4.8.2020 [189].
80 OLG Dresden, 11.6.2019 [6]; OLG München, 18.2.2020 [49] for Facebook's position.
81 OLG Nürnberg, 4.8.2020 [189]; OLG München, 18.2.2020 [17], [43], [70].
82 OLG München, 18.2.2020 [71]. See also OLG Düsseldorf, 04.12.2020 [85].
83 LG Koblenz, 21.4.2020 [165]. Cf. LG Bamberg, 18.10.2018–2 O 248/18 [79] weighing users' freedom of expression with a platform's general freedom of action, freedom to exercise one's profession and the right to an established and practised business (referring to Arts 2, 12, 14 GG). On the virtual domiciliary right, cf. also LG Bamberg, 18.10.2018 [86]; KG Berlin, 22.3.2019 [19]; LG Offenburg, 26.9.2018 [49]-[52], [56]; OLG Köln, 09.5.2019–15 W 70/18 [4]; BVerfG 22.2.2011 [56], [86]-[89].
84 VG Leipzig, 11.9.2019 [89]. Additionally, when the Facebook page of a political party was blocked, Article 21(1) GG was invoked: "Parties participate in the formation of the political will of the people". – see BVerfG, 22.5.2019 [9].
85 OLG Nürnberg, 4.8.2020 [77].
86 Ibid [98].
87 Ibid [103].
88 Ibid [193]; OLG Düsseldorf, 4.12.2020 [80].
89 OLG Düsseldorf, 04.12.2020 [81]
90 OLG München, 18.2.2020 [11].
91 OLG Nürnberg, 4.8.2020 [111], [194]; OLG München, 18.2.2020 [50], [100]; OLG Düsseldorf, 4.12.2020 [82], OLG Dresden, 11.6.2019–4 U 760/19 [8].
92 OLG Nürnberg, 4.8.2020 [195]; OLG Düsseldorf, 4.12.2020 [86]; OLG Frankfurt a.M., 7.9.2018–16 W 38/18 [25]; *Cf.* BVerfG, 22.5.2019 [6].
93 OLG München, 18.2.2020 [11].
94 OLG Nürnberg, 4.8.2020 [197].
95 OLG Nürnberg, 4.8.2020 [199]-[200]; OLG München, 18.2.2020 [44].
96 OLG München, 18.2.2020 [105]-[106]; OLG Dresden, 11.6.2019 [9].
97 Datenschutz-Grundverordnung (DSGVO) (ABl. L 119 vom 4. Mai 2016).
98 OLG Nürnberg, 4.8.2020 [202]; OLG München, 18.2.2020 [107], OLG Dresden, 11.6.2019 [12]-[13].

99 In OLG München, 18.2.2020 [104].
100 OLG Nürnberg, 4.8.2020 [199]-[202]; OLG München, 18.2.2020 [44], [107]. *Cf* Case OLG Dresden, 11.6.2019 [11]-[13].
101 OLG Dresden, 11.6.2019 [13].
102 OLG Düsseldorf, 4.12.2020 [83]. See also OLG Dresden, 11.6.2019 [13].
103 See e.g. Peacock, [2019] 84; Gemmo Bautista Fernandez, 'Free Marketplace of Ideas: Applying the Approach of the UN Human Rights Committee and the European Court of Human Rights in Philippine Internet Hate Speech Cases', in Myungkoo Kang, Marie-Orange Rivé Lasan, Wooja Kim and Philippa Hall (eds), *Hate Speech in Asia and Europe: Beyond Hate and Fear* (Routledge 2020) 136, 140; Rowbottom (n 64) 211; Pejchal (n 59) 142–143, 148, 162; Kettemann and Benedek (n 52) 64; Pollicino and Soldatov (n 52) 132–141; Jukka Viljanen, 'Combating Hate Speech Online', in Mart Susi (ed), *Human Rights, Digital Society and the Law: A Research Companion* (Routledge 2019) 232.
104 See, e.g. ECtHR, *Yildirim v. Turkey* App. no. 3111/10 (18 December 2012) [48], [54]; ECtHR, *Cengiz v. Turkey*, Apps. Nos. 48226/10 and 14027/11 (1 December 2015) [49],[52]; ECtHR, *Editorial Board v. Ukraine,* App. no. 33014/05 (5 May 2011) [30], [63]. See Peacock (n 103) 78–80; Kettemann and Benedek (n 52) 58; Pollicino and Soldatov (n 52) 135.
105 ECtHR, *Handyside v United Kingdom*, Application no. 5493/72 (7 December 1976), [49]. See Kučs and Viljanen [2018] 192; Andrei G Richter, 'Threats to Freedom of the Press', in Mahmood Monshipouri (ed), *Why Human Rights Still Matter in Contemporary Global Affairs* (Routlege 2020) 267–271.
106 For satire in the ECHR regime, see Richter (n 105) 277; Pejchal (n 59) 147, 226–227; Kettemann and Benedek (n 52) 66.
107 See e.g. ECtHR, *Müller v Switzerland*, App. no. 10737/84 (24 May 1988) [19]. See Richter (n 106) 269.
108 OLG Nürnberg, 4.8.2020 [163] referring to ECtHR, *Pedersen v Denmark* App. no. 49017/99 (17 December 2004); ECtHR, *Annen v Germany* App. no. 3690/10 (26 November 2015). See Richter (n 106) 277–229.
109 BVerfG, 2 BvR 1481/04, Görgülü (2004).
110 Christiane Schmaltz, 'Das Verhältnis zwischen europäischer und nationaler Rechtsprechung – Beobachtungen einer an den Europäischen Gerichtshof für Menschenrechte abgeordneten Amtsrichterin', in Armin Höland (ed), *Wirkungen der Rechtsprechung des Europäischen Gerichtshofs für Menschenrechte im deutschen Recht* (BWV 2012); Barbara Seeling, 'Ein Rückschritt im Dialog der Gerichte: der BGH übergeht den EGMR' (*Verfassungsblog* 27th May 2019) <https://verfassungsblog.de/ein-rueckschritt-im-dialog-der-gerichte-der-bgh-uebergeht-den-egmr> accessed 3 October 2022.
111 OLG München, 18.2.2020 [81].
112 Although the right to the development of personality is generally only enjoyed by natural persons, legal entities are afforded protection of their free development according to Art. 2 section 1 GG in connection with Art. 19 section 3 GG, albeit it to a lesser extent.
113 OLG Nürnberg, 4.8.2020 [91], [95].
114 OLG Hamm, 15.9.2020–29 U 6/20 [164].
115 Cf. Matthias C. Kettemann and Torben Klausa, 'Regulating Online Speech: Ze German Way', 20 September 2021 <www.lawfareblog.com/regulating-online-speech-ze-german-way> accessed 1 October 2022.

8 Social media before higher courts in Hungary

A focus on online comments

Zsuzsa Detrekoi

1. Introduction

Hungary has a civil law system. Social media sites are regulated by general laws, such as the Fundamental Law of Hungary,[1] the Civil Code[2] and the Criminal Code.[3] They are also obliged to pay advertising tax, according to the Hungarian Advertisement Tax Act.[4] The *Freedom and Responsibility* section of the Fundamental Law and the *Rights relating to personality* in part three of the Civil Code include fundamental rights which are also relevant to social media, and the Criminal Code determines criminal offences and the possible penalties to impose.[5]

The liability of social media platforms for user-generated content is established in the e-Commerce Law,[6] which implemented the EU e-Commerce Directive.[7] Social media platforms qualify as intermediaries – more precisely, as hosting service providers – according to the e-Commerce Law. They are therefore exempt from liability for information they host, as long as they take down content deemed to be illegal following the notice and take-down procedure laid down in the e-Commerce Law (and the e-Commerce Directive). This immunity (or "safe harbour") of social media platforms has been questioned by Hungarian courts on several occasions.[8] At the same time, the EU has also recently challenged this limitation of liability in the case of video sharing sites by adopting two directives.[9] The 2019 amendment of the Copyright Directive[10] explicitly denies safe harbour for video-sharing platforms and states that they perform an act of communication to the public and therefore they are responsible for the published content, including user-generated content.[11] For this reason, video-sharing sites have to obtain a license from rightsholders before users upload videos to the platform. The 2018 revised Audiovisual Media Services Directive (AVMSD)[12] prohibits *ex ante* control and upload filtering of user-generated content but requires social media platforms to remove certain objectionable user-generated content without further notice.[13] Both directives have been implemented in the Hungarian legal system: the AVMSD in 2019 and 2020 with amendment of Act CLXXXV of 2010 on media services and mass media[14] and the e-Commerce Law;[15] and the Copyright Directive with

DOI: 10.4324/9781003207085-10

the 2021 revised copyright law.[16] Both implementations basically introduced the same provisions as EU directives.

The parliament passed a new package of regulations affecting fundamental rights in June 2021, despite widespread national and international protests. The so-called "paedophile" law introduces a four-level content prevention/banning system addressing "pornography, content that is dominated by sexuality and content regarding transition from one's biological sex, change of gender and homosexuality with minors". The right to self-identity is narrowed to biological sex by amendments to the law. The amendments impacted the Family Protection Act of 2011,[17] the Child Protection Law of 1997,[18] the Advertising Act of 2008[19] and the Media Law. The amendment of the Media Law qualifies the content described previously as "not recommended for viewing by audiences under the age of eighteen", putting it in the same category as content dominated by graphic scenes of violence and/or sexuality. Whereas linear media services (i.e. broadcasters) may air such programs between 10 p.m. and 5 a.m. using the proper rating, on-demand media service providers should use an effective technical solution to prevent minors from accessing such content. Implementation of these provisions is supervised by the National Media and Info-communications Authority (NMHH), Hungary's media regulator, which is also responsible for supervising video-sharing sites. However, the amendments are recent, and the first procedures to fine allegedly infringing advertisements on social media sites were issued by the consumer protection authorities, which are responsible for enforcing the Advertising Act. Besides the improper, discriminative nature of the amendments and their political purpose, they also leave uncertainty over who should apply them.

Having said this, regulations protecting fundamental rights in Hungary are basically at three levels. Two major international treaties have been incorporated in the Hungarian legal system: the United Nations Universal Declaration of Human Rights[20] in 1976 and the European Convention on Human Rights (ECHR)[21] in 1993. These two treaties constitute the first level of protection. The second level is the new Fundamental Law adopted by the Hungarian parliament in 2011. Both these levels safeguard the umbrella right of freedom of expression, which makes the operation of social media sites possible and which is often in collision with other fundamental rights. Decisions by the Constitutional Court of Hungary based on the previous Constitution and the recent Fundamental Law are also key sources for the protection of fundamental rights, including freedom of expression. At the third level, mention can be made of general laws such as the Civil Code and the Criminal Code. The Civil Code sets out the limits to freedom of expression to protect human dignity, including reputation and privacy, and civil law sanctions for the violation of such rights. The Criminal Code specifies the criminal offences which may infringe personality rights, including defamation and slander, and the penalties to impose.

In the case of media content providers (newspapers and linear and non-linear audio-visual media services), mention should also be made of Act CIV of 2010 on the freedom of the press and the fundamental rules on media content,[22] and of Act CLXXXV of 2010 on media services and mass media.[23] The latter includes NMHH's administrative duties concerning video-sharing sites.

Turning to the Hungarian judicial system, it has a four-tier hierarchy: district courts; administrative and labour courts; regional courts; regional courts of appeal; and the Curia. Currently there are 158 courts in the judicial organisation. The different court levels are closely interconnected, but there is no subordination between them. Judges are independent and do not obey any instructions concerning their adjudication activities, thus rendering their decisions pursuant to the applicable laws and their own beliefs. The main judicial body is the Curia. Final and binding judgments can be reviewed by the Curia on request by a party invoking violation of law having an impact on the merits of a case or divergence concerning a question of law from a published Curia decision.[24]

Although, unlike traditional case law systems, the Hungarian legal system does not recognise precedents, the Curia also renders uniformity decisions in cases raising issues of theoretical importance in order to ensure the uniform application of law by the Hungarian judiciary. Such decisions are binding on all Hungarian courts.[25]

The Constitutional Court is a special court and it is situated outside the judicial system described previously. It has its own budget and its judges are elected by the Parliament. The Constitutional Court serves as the main body for the protection of the Constitution, its tasks being review of the constitutionality of statutes and protection of constitutional order and fundamental rights guaranteed by the Constitution. The Constitutional Court is responsible for judicial review of parliamentary acts. It is also responsible for examining constitutional complaints.[26] Constitutional complaints may be submitted to the Constitutional Court by a person or an organisation when the petitioner's right guaranteed by the Fundamental Law is alleged to be violated by a judicial decision. Exceptionally, the constitutional complaint procedure may also be initiated when, due to application of a law that is contrary to the Fundamental Law or when such a legal provision becomes effective, rights are directly violated without a judicial decision. The constitutional complaint is therefore not a claim for judicial review and the Constitutional Court is not a forum for obtaining legal remedy in concrete cases. There is no right of appeal on the decisions of the Constitutional Court.

Despite the attention that social media platforms have recently received, few social media cases have reached higher courts. No uniformity decision has been issued by the Curia, and only four cases have arrived at the Constitutional Court.[27] Of these four cases, one was then referred to the European Court of Human Rights (ECtHR).[28] The four decisions by the Constitutional Court were issued between 2014 and 2016. Given the rarity of cases, no increase has been noticeable in recent years. It is true that lower courts and appeal courts have dealt with cases where the fact leading to the lawsuit happened on a social media site, but looking at the factual circumstances of the cases, it emerges that social media were only used as a means to convey content to the public as would have happened with newspapers or other legacy media publications. The courts thus seem able to resolve cases on the basis of previous free speech cases without acknowledging any differences between the types of media selected by the posters.

2. Fundamental rights in national jurisprudence

The four cases of constitutional complaints that have arrived at the Constitutional Court have all naturally been framed as fundamental rights cases. Three of these cases focus on limited protection of the reputation and honour of public figures and its relation with freedom of expression. They therefore involve fundamental rights reasoning. So does the fourth case – *Association of Hungarian Content Providers* (*Magyarországi Tartalomszolgáltatók Egyesülete* – MTE), which also involves freedom of expression. Two of these cases began with a criminal proceeding and the other two, with a civil proceeding.

Only in one of the four cases – namely, the MTE case – did the social media service provider (MTE) participate as a party in the case, being the provider of a comment service.[29] In this case, the main question revolved around the liability of the provider for comments made by users on its site. In the other three cases, social media providers did not participate in the judicial proceeding; they only served as a surface enabling the publication of allegedly infringing information. These three cases were discussed before the court as conflicts between free speech and reputation and human dignity. In all of them, the victims – according to the defence – allegedly qualified as public figures: a notary in a small town accused of discrimination and racism,[30] an attorney who represented the wife of the defendant in a divorce case and was accused by the defendant on his social media profile of stealing and cheating;[31] and two celebrities who continually disputed with each other publicly in the media and on social media. In the latter case, one of the celebrities filed several lawsuits against the other. A defamation case ensued because the respondent called the plaintiff a psychopath and accused him of entering into improperly concluded contracts with the publicly funded national television. The case eventually ended up at the Constitutional Court.[32]

In 1994, the Constitutional Court laid down the fundamental principles for distinguishing between the personality rights of public figures and those of ordinary citizens.[33] The Court identified two outstanding interests: the possibility to criticise the activities of bodies and persons fulfilling state and local government tasks in public; and the ability of citizens to participate in political and social processes without uncertainty, compromise or fear. As such, the Constitutional Court drew a very narrow limit to protect the reputation of persons exercising state powers in comparison to private persons:

> *An expression of a value judgement capable of offending the honour of an authority, an official or a politician acting in public, and expressed with*

> *regard to his or her public capacity is not punishable under the Constitution; and an expression directly referring to such a fact is only punishable if the person who states a fact or spreads a rumour capable of offending honour, or uses an expression directly referring to such a fact, knew the essence of his or her statement to be false, did not know of its falsehood because of his or her failure to pay attention or exercise the caution reasonably expected of him/her pursuant to the rules applicable to his or her profession or occupation, taking the subject matter, the medium and the addressee of the expression in question into account.*[34]

In 2018, the Constitutional Court specified criteria to qualify public figures due to developments in telecommunications. According to the Constitutional Court, to decide the limits of the reputation of a person in a public debate, it should be examined whether the expression was a fact or an opinion, if it was made as a standpoint in a debate of general interest, if it was related to public affairs and if it violated the dignity or reputation of the person concerned.[35] As a general rule, the lower courts have discretion to decide if a poster has passed the limits of free speech. The Constitutional Court has the power to review whether a lower court has properly weighted the constitutional aspects of a case. In the case of the notary, the petitioner – a resident from Mezőcsát – had made a short post on her Facebook account titled "Clan of Mezőcsát", declaring that racism and discrimination exist in Mezőcsát and asking for the power of the city council and the notary to be reduced. The petitioner had also stated on her Facebook page that the notary discriminated against Roma people and in a public hearing had accused the notary of perjury. The first-degree court convicted the petitioner for defamation and slander, and the second degree court upheld the ruling. Although the Curia noticed the free speech aspects of the case and held that the petitioner's posts were opinions in public debate, at the same time, it qualified the posts as going beyond necessary criticisms and therefore as slanderous. The Constitutional Court found that the lower courts had failed to properly consider the constitutional aspects of the case; namely, that criticism of a notary – who has executive power local affairs in cases – comes within the scope of freedom to discuss public affairs. Therefore, the Constitutional Court found the decision of the Curia unconstitutional and annulled it.

In the case of the attorney, the defendant named the attorney in the personal details-related "domestic animal" rubric on a former Hungarian social network (former known as iwiw[36]) and called her a stealing-cheating-lying dog. While the first degree court condemned the defendant for slander, the second degree court acquitted the defendant due to lack of evidence. The Municipal Court of Appeal agreed with the acquittal but based its reasoning on a different legal argumentation. It qualified the attorney as a public figure, given that she represented the wife of the defendant in a lawsuit. According to the court, those listed as an attorney at the Bar automatically become public figures when they practise.

The Constitutional Court annulled the exculpatory judgment issued by the lower court on the grounds that the court had not used its discretion to properly examine whether the activity of the attorney was in relation to public affairs. According to the reasoning of the Constitutional Court, attorneys do not qualify as officials exercising executive power or as politicians acting in public, and therefore, are not obliged to tolerate more offensive statements. The Constitutional Court required the lower court to properly examine the issue in a renewed proceeding. As for the case concerning the celebrities, the plaintiff had alleged that the lower courts had failed to duly consider the guidelines in the Constitutional Court's case law regarding balancing the rights of free speech and reputation in its decisions. According to the complaint, the plaintiff did not qualify as a public figure and, accordingly, his tolerance level was limited. The Constitutional Court tested the expressions used by both the defendant and the plaintiff. It found that the plaintiff had willingly participated in the media and therefore qualified as an exceptional public figure. It also found that the expressions used by the defendant were basically in relation to the plaintiff's public activity. As a result, the Constitutional Court rejected the complaint.

The three cases discussed so far show that balancing freedom of expression and the reputation of public figures takes place on a case-by-case basis. There is no predominance of any set of rights. Additionally, the category of public figures changes depending on the context. In the case of the attorney, for instance, the Constitutional Court overruled the qualification of the lower court and classified the attorney as an ordinary citizen during his practice. In the case about the celebrities, due to the development of telecommunications and the Internet and the extension of the limits of tolerance based on voluntary participation in public debates – e.g. on social media sites – the Constitutional Court re-evaluated the criteria to qualify people as public figures.

The most important case from the social media perspective is *MTE and Index v Hungary*, in which the liability of social media sites for user-generated content was at stake.[37] MTE is an association of Hungarian content providers, a self-regulatory body providing a code of conduct and monitoring its implementation. Sometimes it also publishes opinions on relevant Internet-related ethical or legal issues. Index is a major Internet news portal in Hungary. At the time of the events, both had sites with a comment function which allowed users to comment on articles published. Registered users could upload comments which were not edited or moderated before appearing on the sites. A notice and take-down system ensured that any comments infringing personality rights would be deleted on request.[38] Comments on Index were partially moderated and removed, if necessary.[39] Both sites forbade the uploading of infringing comments.

The dispute arose with the online publication of an MTE opinion about the conduct of two real estate management websites with the same owner. The two websites provided their users with a thirty-day advertising package free of charge. At the end of this period, the service became subject to a fee without further notification. The terms and conditions of the two sites prescribed a fee after the 30-day period, and users accepted it by registering. Obsolete advertisements and personal data were removed from the sites when any overdue charges were paid. Many users became victims of this. MTE shared an opinion titled "Another unethical commercial conduct on the net", concluding that the conduct of the service providers was unethical and misleading. The Index consumer protection column also wrote about the opinion with the title "Content providers condemn [one of the incriminated property websites]" and published the full text of the opinion. The opinion attracted offensive comments from users with pseudonyms on both the MTE and Index sites. Without requesting removal of the comments according to the notice and take-down procedure, the company operating the two sites filed a lawsuit against MTE and Index (and a third website that had also published the MTE opinion) for defamation. According to the plaintiff, the content of the opinion was false and offensive and the subsequent comments had infringed its right to good reputation. Because of the suit, MTE and Index removed the impugned comments.

The first-degree court found the comments offensive, insulting and humiliating, and found that they exceeded the limits of freedom of expression. Regardless of the limitation of liability in e-Commerce legislation, the court rejected the applicants' argument that they were only intermediaries and that their obligation was to remove comments following a complaint. It found that the comments constituted edited content and could be qualified as "readers' letters". The respondents were therefore liable for enabling their publication, despite the fact that both had removed the comments when they had knowledge of the complaint.

The Court of Appeal changed the reasoning in the decision but upheld the liability of the applicants. According to the second-degree court, the safe harbour based on the e-Commerce Law did not apply to the applicants' case because the applicants did not operate commercial electronic services. The Court of Appeal circumscribed the scope of application of the e-Commerce Law by interpreting the definition of commercial electronic services in a narrow way, only including services the purpose of which was selling, purchasing or exchanging tangible and moveable property. Moreover, according to the Court of Appeal, the immunity provided in the law did not extend to expressions made by persons acting outside the spheres of economic or professional activities or public duties, even if posted in connection with a purchase on the Internet. For the Court of Appeal, the comments at issue were private utterances and therefore did not fall within the scope of the e-Commerce Law. Therefore, there was no reason to assess the meaning of the terms "hosting service providers" and "intermediaries" under the e-Commerce Law. Given the injurious quality of the comments, the court found the applicants liable for the publication of the comments, irrespectively of their subsequent removal.

The applicants filed a petition for review with the Curia. The Curia upheld the previous judgments, emphasising that, by enabling readers to make comments on their websites, the applicants had assumed objective liability for any injurious or unlawful comments made by readers. The Curia rejected the safe harbour for the applicants and held that they did not qualify as intermediaries according to the e-Commerce Law.

The applicant turned to the Constitutional Court with a constitutional complaint, arguing in essence that the courts' rulings holding them responsible for the contents of the comments amounted to an unjustified restriction of freedom of expression. While the Constitutional Court held the complaint admissible, with its decision, it finally dismissed it.[40] In its analysis of the proportionality of the interference, the Constitutional Court explained the absence of unconstitutionality in the case as follows:

> *[43] In the case concerned, in the Curia's judgment the operator of the webpage [both MTE and Index] did not moderate the comments. The identities of those primarily responsible, unless figuring nominatively, are unknown; and for that reason, the liability lies with the operator of the webpage.*
>
> *[44] In the present case, the aggrieved fundamental right is not the right to freedom of expression as such, but one of its particular elements, the right to freedom of the press.*
>
> . . .
>
> *[50] It is without doubt that blogs and comments constitute expressions and as such attract the protection of Chapter IX of the Fundamental Law.*
>
> . . .
>
> *[59] The liability incumbent on the operator of the webpage obviously restricts freedom of the press – which includes, without doubt, communication on the Internet.*
>
> . . .
>
> *[63] The legislation [civil code e.g.] pursues a constitutionally justified aim. It is also suitable for that purpose in that, without the liability of the operator of the webpage, the person concerned could hardly receive compensation for the grievance. However, the proportionality of the restriction is open to doubt from two perspectives: is it proportionate to hold the operator of the webpage liable for the expression which proved to be unlawful; and moreover, is the extent of the liability (that is, the amount of compensation) proportionate?*
>
> . . .
>
> *[65] If the liability for the publication of comments is based on the very fact of the publication itself, it is not justifiable to distinguish between moderated and non-moderated comments in regard to the proportionality of the restriction on the fundamental right in question. . . . The Constitutional Court has already held that the liability of press organs – not of the author – as applied in order to protect personality rights is constitutional.*

Given the anonymity of the users posting the comments, the Constitutional Court put contributory liability for the comments on the website operators (MTE and Index) and found this restriction proportionate in order to protect personality rights. Relying on Article 10 ECHR on freedom of expression, the applicants complained to the ECtHR about the Hungarian courts' rulings against them, which had effectively obliged them to moderate the contents of comments made by readers on their websites. They argued that this had gone against the essence of free expression on the Internet.

The ECtHR found that the Hungarian courts, when deciding on the notion of liability in the applicants' case, had not carried out a proper balancing exercise between the competing rights involved; namely, between the applicants' right to freedom of expression and the real estate companies' right to respect for their commercial reputation. Notably, the Hungarian authorities had accepted without further investigation that the comments in question were unlawful for being injurious to the reputation of the real estate management websites. In the case of third-party comments taking the form of hate speech and direct threats to the physical integrity of individuals, the rights and interests of others and of society as a whole could entitle ECHR contracting states – such as Hungary – to impose liability on internet news portals if they had failed to take measures to remove clearly unlawful comments without delay, even without notice from the alleged victim or from third parties. For these reasons in particular, in a previous case, *Delfi AS v Estonia*,[41] the ECtHR had held that in view of the "duties and responsibilities" of a large, professionally managed Internet news portal the finding of liability of such a portal for the comments made by users – identified or anonymous – who engage in clearly unlawful speech infringing the personality rights of others and amounting to hate speech and incitement to violence against them, was not contrary to the ECHR. The applicants' case was, however, devoid of the pivotal elements of hate speech and incitement to violence. The ECtHR found that, although offensive and vulgar, the comments at issue had not constituted clearly unlawful speech. Moreover, while Index was the owner of a large media outlet which should be regarded as having economic interests, MTE was a non-profit, self-regulatory association of Internet service providers, with no known such interests. The ECtHR applied the criteria developed in its established case law for the assessment of the proportionality of interference in situations not involving hate speech or calls for violence. On this basis, it held unanimously that there had been a violation of Article 10 ECHR.

3. Judicial dialogue with the CJEU and the ECtHR

Some of the cases reviewed refer to the ECHR, but mention of the ECHR provisions is not made alone. Despite the fact that the litigants and the lower courts relied on ECtHR cases in their argumentation, only in the case of the celebrities did the Constitutional Court discuss ECtHR case law in the main ruling. No case from the CJEU was referred to by the Constitutional Court, and only one concurring opinion in the case of the attorney mentioned a CJEU case. The Constitutional Court mainly uses its own previous decisions as references to balance fundamental rights.

Given the lack of broad reference to ECtHR case law, the only case that has been referred to by the Constitutional Court is *Bladet Tromso and Stensaas v Norway*.[42] This was mentioned in the case of the celebrities with reference to whether or not the allegedly infringing expressions were made on a matter of public interest. In *Bladet Tromso*, the ECtHR found the conviction for defamation of a publisher and editor to be unjustified. Their journal had published a report based on an inspection of seal hunting revealing cruelty by seal hunters. According to the ECtHR, the publisher and the editor had acted in good faith in discharging their public watchdog function by reporting on a matter of public interest. Public interest was emphasised by the Hungarian Constitutional Court as a reason for the protection of free political speech. In addition, the Constitutional Court used the example of the seal hunters to make the point that, although they did not want to act in public voluntarily or find themselves at the centre of a public debate, their right to reputation could be limited in the public debate about seal hunting. Otherwise, ECtHR case law was used to support the reasoning of the Constitutional Court, which was founded on its own previous decisions, and the ECtHR ruling referred to was not discussed or analysed in detail.

Regarding CJEU case law, the only CJEU ruling that appears in the case of the attorney in the concurring opinion of a judge is an old case, *Jean Reyners v the Belgian State*.[43] Here too, the national judge referred to it to strengthen domestic reasoning. In *Reyners*, the CJEU had found that the legal profession of *avocat* is not an exception to free movement under Article 51 of the Treaty on the Functioning of the European Union, since it cannot be considered to be connected with the exercise of official authority. Based on that case, the national judge held that not only the Constitutional Court but also the CJEU had found that, in the case of attorneys, a higher tolerance level for public figures is not justified. However, the reference to *Reyners* to support the argument that attorneys do not have such a higher tolerance level arguably shows a distorted understanding of the CJEU ruling.

Overall, for the Constitutional Court, the cases – in particular, concerning social media as only a forum to publish views and opinions – were not considered to be different from cases concerning online newspapers. Therefore, the Constitutional Court regarded such cases as traditional media cases dealing with conflicts between freedom of expression and the right to reputation – including the right to reputation of public figures – using its former jurisprudence to guide and support its reasoning.

4. Conclusion

To summarise, very few social media cases have reached the higher courts in Hungary, possibly due to the short time since the launch of platforms. Most cases adjudicated by the Hungarian Constitutional Court engaged in balancing reputation and free expression related to a limited tolerance level for public figures. From these cases, the conclusion can be drawn that Hungarian courts essentially treat social media platforms as traditional media.

Together with lower court rulings,[44] the *MTE* case points to an inability of domestic courts to interpret the immunity framework for intermediaries, which is a Hungarian particularity. Both lower and higher courts, such as the Curia and the Constitutional Court, have been unable to understand the limitation of liability based on the e-Commerce Law. Lower courts have tended to qualify user comments as "readers' letters". These courts circumscribed the scope of the e-Commerce Law and thus denied immunity for users' comments. The Curia supported objective liability for user-generated content, while the Constitutional Court did not distinguish between moderated and non-moderated content. However, the *MTE* judgment of the ECtHR had some impact: Hungarian lower courts tend to follow the ruling and they have started to qualify comment service providers as hosting service providers, thus providing them with immunity.

In other cases, ECtHR case law has not substantively influenced judicial decision-making. Hungarian courts, including the Constitutional Court, for the most part use principles established by the Constitutional Court in cases concerning newspapers and other media and regard social media as a new media platform which is not distinct from traditional media. The purpose of references to ECtHR case law (if any) is only to strengthen domestic judicial reasoning.

Notes

1 Fundamental Law of Hungary <http://hunconcourt.hu/uploads/sites/3/2021/01/thefundamentallawofhungary_20201223_fin.pdf> accessed 5 January 2022.
2 Act V of 2013 on the Civil Code, <www.ilo.org/dyn/natlex/natlex4.detail?p_lang=en&p_isn=96512&p_country=HUN&p_count=937&p_classification=01.03&p_classcount=4> accessed 5 January 2022.
3 Act C of 2012 on the Criminal Code https://thb.kormany.hu/download/a/46/11000/Btk_EN.pdf accessed 5 January 2022.
4 Hungarian Advertisement Tax Act no. XXII of 2014 <https://net.jogtar.hu/jogszabaly?docid=a1400022.tv> (only in Hungarian) accessed 5 January 2022.
5 On the implications of social media from different legal perspectives, see David Mangan and Lorna E Gillies, *The Legal Challenges of Social Media* (Edward Elgar Publishing 2017).
6 Act CVIII of 2001 on Electronic Commerce and on Information Society Services <https://english.nmhh.hu/document/213838/act_cviii_of_2001.pdf> accessed 5 January 2022.
7 Directive 2000/31/EC of the European Parliament and of the Council of 8 June 2000 on certain legal aspects of information society services – in particular, electronic commerce – in the Internal Market ('Directive on electronic commerce') [2000] OJ L 178/1.
8 See Fővárosi Bíróság judgment no. 19.P. 26.575/2008/3, 13 January 2009; Fővárosi Ítélőtábla judgment no. 8.Pf.21.129/2011/4, 27 October 2011; Debreceni Ítélőtábla judgment no. Pf.II.20.673/2008/5, 20 January 2009; Fővárosi Bíróság judgment no. 24.K.32.268/2009/11, 25 May 2010; Kúria judgment no.

Pfv.IV.20.217/2012/5, 13 June 2012; A Kaposvári Törvényszék judgment no. 23.P. 21.238/2015/19, 27 April 2016.

9 On this see Andrej Savin, 'Regulating Internet Platforms in the EU – The Emergence of the "Level Playing Field"' (2018) 34(6) *Computer Law & Security Review* 1215; Giancarlo F Frosio, 'Reforming Intermediary Liability in the Platform Economy: A European Digital Single Market Strategy' (2017) 112 *Northwestern University Law Review Online* 18; and Giovanni De Gregorio, 'Expressions on Platforms: Freedom of Expression and ISP Liability in the European Digital Single Market' (2018) 2(3) *European Competition and Regulatory Law Review* 203.

10 Directive (EU) 2019/790 of the European Parliament and of the Council of 17 April 2019 on copyright and related rights in the Digital Single Market and amending Directives 96/9/EC and 2001/29/EC [2019] OJ L130/92 (hereinafter the Copyright Directive).

11 Ibid, Art 17.

12 Directive (EU) 2018/1808 of the European Parliament and of the Council of 14 November 2018 amending Directive 2010/13/EU on the coordination of certain provisions laid down by law, regulation or administrative action in Member States concerning the provision of audio-visual media services (Audiovisual Media Services Directive) in view of changing market realities [2018] OJ L303/69.

13 Ibid, Art 28b of the AVMSD. On this see Maria Lilla Montagnani, 'A New Liability Regime for Illegal Content in the Digital Single Market Strategy' (2019) *Bocconi Legal Studies Research Paper Series* No 477007, June 2019 <https://papers.ssrn.com/sol3/papers.cfm?abstract_id=3398160> accessed 26 November 2021; and Frosio (n 9).

14 Act on Media Services and on the Mass Media (Media Law) <http://english.nmhh.hu/document/106487/act_clxxx_on_media_services_and_mass_media.pdf> accessed 5 January 2022.

15 Specific provisions relating to video-sharing platform services were implemented in Section 15/C-15W of the Act on Electronic Commerce and on Information Society Services <http://nmhh.hu/document/213838/act_cviii_of_2001.pdf> accessed 5 January 2022. On this see Zsuzsa Detrekoi, 'Practical Problems of Implementing the New AVMSD Provisions on Video-Sharing Platforms' (2021) 26 *Bloomsbury Communications Law* 149.

16 Act LXXVI of 1999 on copyright <www.hipo.gov.hu/sites/default/files/szjt_lxxvi_1999_en_rev_1.pdf> (this is a previous version consolidated in 2018) accessed 5 January 2022. On this see Zsuzsa Detrekoi, 'EU Copyright Directive: Sounding the Death Knell for Domestic Video-Sharing Platforms' (2020) 25 *Bloomsbury Communications Law* 231.

17 Family Protection Act (2011. évi CCXI. törvény a családok védelméről) <https://net.jogtar.hu/jogszabaly?docid=a1100211.tv> accessed 5 January 2022.

18 Child Protection Law (1997. évi XXXI. törvény a gyermekek védelméről és a gyámügyi igazgatásról) <https://net.jogtar.hu/jogszabaly?docid=99700031.tv> accessed 5 January 2022.

19 Advertising Act (2008. évi XLVIII. törvény a gazdasági reklámtevékenység alapvető feltételeiről és egyes korlátairól) <https://net.jogtar.hu/jogszabaly?docid=a0800048.tv> accessed 5 January 2022.

20 Universal Declaration of Human Rights <www.un.org/en/about-us/universal-declaration-of-human-rights> accessed 5 January 2022.

21 European Convention on Human Rights <www.echr.coe.int/documents/convention_eng.pdf> accessed 5 January 2022.

22 Act CIV of 2010 on the Freedom of the Press and the Fundamental Rules of Media Content <https://nmhh.hu/dokumentum/162262/smtv_110803_en_final.pdf> accessed 5 January 2022.

23 See Media Law (n 14).

24 Section 406 of Act CXXX of 2016 on the Code of Civil Procedure <https://njt.hu/translation/J2016T0130P_20200401_FIN.pdf> accessed 5 January 2022.

25 On the uniformity decisions of the Curia, see <https://kuria-birosag.hu/en/uniformity-decisions> accessed 5 January 2022.

26 Information on Constitutional complaints can be found at: <http://hunconcourt.hu/general-information> accessed 5 January 2022.

27 See Decision IV/03391/2015 of the Constitutional Court http://public.mkab.hu/dev/dontesek.nsf/0/4CF02CF91345CA89C1257F4F005DD2F4?OpenDocument accessed 5 January 2022; decision 1/2015 of the Constitutional Court http://public.mkab.hu/dev/dontesek.nsf/0/910bb47e5042c7d5c1257c910021bb4e/$FILE/0001_2015_hat%C3%A1rozat.pdf accessed 5 January 2022; decision IV/1628/2016 of the Constitutional Court <http://public.mkab.hu/dev/dontesek.nsf/0/99C984B5B36D2380C125804F0058956D?OpenDocument> accessed 5 January 2022; Decision 19/2014 (V.30.) AB <http://public.mkab.hu/dev/dontesek.nsf/0/4E4D071867671629C1257B0C00212E7F?OpenDocument> accessed 5 January 2022.

28 *Magyar Tartalomszolgáltatók Egyesülete and Index.hu Zrt v Hungary* App no. 22947/13 (ECtHR, 2 February 2016).

29 Fővárosi Bíróság judgment no. 19.P. 21.022/2010/7 of 31 March 2011; Fővárosi Ítélőtábla judgment no. 8.Pf.21.129/2011/4 of 27 October 2011; and Kúria judgment no. Pfv.IV.20.217/2012/5.szám of 13 June 2012.

30 See Decision IV/03391/2015 of the Constitutional Court (n 27).

31 See Decision 1/2015 of the Constitutional Court (n 27).

32 See Decision IV/1628/2016 of the Constitutional Court (n 27).

33 See Decision 36/1994 (VI. 24.) AB of the Constitutional Court <http://public.mkab.hu/dev/dontesek.nsf/0/E2AF731C9711A97FC1257ADA0052A5D3?OpenDocument> accessed 5 January 2022. See also Andras Koltay, 'The Freedom to Discuss Public Affairs and the Protection of Personality Rights in the Hungarian Legal System' (2019) 2019(1) *Elte Law Journal* <https://eltelawjournal.hu/the-freedom-to-discuss-public-affairs-and-the-protection-of-personality-rights-in-the-hungarian-legal-system/> accessed 5 January 2022.

34 See Decision 36/1994 (VI. 24.) AB of the Constitutional Court (n 33).

35 Pontosította a közszereplői minőség megállapításának szempontrendszerét az Alkotmánybíróság <https://alkotmanybirosag.hu/kozlemeny/pontositotta-a-kozszereploi-minoseg-megallapitasanak-szempontrendszeret-az-alkotmanybirosag> accessed 5 January 2022.

36 Note that the social media platform was shut down in 2014 for economic reasons.

37 See endnotes 27 and 28. See also Janos Tamas Papp 'Liability for Third-Party Comments before the European Court of Human Rights – Comparing the Estonian Delfi and the Hungarian Index-MTE Decisions' (2016) 2016 *Hungarian Yearbook of International Law and European Law* 315; Gabor Polyak, 'Media Economics as Factor of the Media Politics Development' (2018) 2018(1) *Studium Jura: A Pecsi Tudomanyegyetem Allam- es Jogtudomanyi Karanak tudomanyos lapja* 109.

38 The website adopted a notice and take-down system allowing deletion of comments infringing the terms of conduct of the platform (see *MTE v Hungary* (n 28), para 10). However, given that the limitation of liability for the platform was only applicable in the case of deletion of contested comments, the platform was keen to delete following any request without specific analysis of compliance with the terms of conduct.

39 Usually, the journalists checked their articles, but it was not mandatory.

40 See Constitutional Court (n 27).
41 *Delfi AS v Estonia* App no. 64569/09 (ECtHR, 10 October 2013. On this ECtHR ruling see also Chapter 3 in this volume.
42 *Bladet Tromso and Stensaas v Norway* App. no. 21980 (ECtHR, 21 May 1997).
43 Case 2–74 *Jean Reyners v Belgian State* [1974] ECLI:EU:C:1974:68.
44 See (n 8).

9 Social media, fundamental rights and courts

An Irish perspective

Elizabeth Farries

1. Introduction

Social media are understood to be underregulated in Ireland.[1] However, domestic legislative efforts are underway to address this concern,[2] and recent case outcomes in Higher Courts have set precedents, particularly in areas of data protection and defamation. These efforts can be connected closely to the work of the Law Reform Commission of Ireland – in particular, their 2016 report *Harmful Communications and Digital Safety*.[3] This report identified gaps in online regulation that require reform – including harmful communications – and then made recommendations for legal reform. Following its publication, together with public sympathy for prominent cases of online harassment in Ireland,[4] several pieces of legislation have been tabled. First, the Harassment, Harmful Communications and Related Offences Act 2020 entered into force in early 2021. While this technology-neutral legislation does not specifically address social media, its key provisions address behaviour in social media spaces. The legislation has been welcomed by the Irish public, given the well-communicated importance of the dignity and privacy of those impacted by image-based sexual abuse online.[5]

Second, while not yet entered into force, the General Scheme of the Online Safety and Media Regulation Bill (OSMRB) currently is moving through Irish Parliament (the Oireachtas).[6] The OSMRB seeks to underpin a system for the regulation of "harmful online content", including video-sharing platform services and on-demand audio-visual media services, and intends, in part, to transpose the EU Audiovisual Media Services Directive (AVMSD)[7] into Irish law. The AVMSD responds to numerous ways in which harmful content manifests online content. It imposes on European Union (EU) Member States obligations to ensure that video-sharing platform services deploy methods to protect children from content which may harm their mental, physical or moral development.[8] It also requires measures to protect the public from content inciting violence, hatred or illegal material under EU law.[9] While the AVMSD is technology neutral in so far as it does not address the specificities of social media by platform services which organise audio-visual content for sharing but which do not have editorial responsibility for that content, it arguably

DOI: 10.4324/9781003207085-11

captures services, including YouTube, Facebook, Twitter, Instagram and Tiktok. Experts have raised concerns that sections of the Irish OSMRB have gone beyond the AVMSD to create a national regime for content moderation that is not just for audio-visual content but rather for "a wide range of typed and spoken material on a wide range of platforms, private and public".[10]

Other Irish legislation which is technology neutral but nonetheless applicable to social media include:

- The Defamation Act 2009. Defamation is a civil law matter with a large body of legal precedent and a distinct relationship with Article 40.3.2°of *Bunreacht na hÉireann*, which requires the state to protect citizens against unjust attack and to vindicate the life, person, good name, and property rights of every citizen when attack is experienced; it has applications to defamatory speech uttered on social media. The Department of Justice and Equality is currently undertaking a review of the Defamation Act 2009.
- The Data Protection Act 2018. This Act affords individuals control of their personal data as outlines responsibilities on those holding and processing such data, including data processed on social media platforms. It establishes the Data Protection Commission and gives further effect to the EU General Data Protection Regulation 2016/679 (GDPR) in discrete areas.
- The Non-Fatal Offences Against the Person Act 1997. S 10 covers harassment by any means, not just online, and has application to social media harassment that occurs under the Act's narrowly defined provisions.
- The Criminal Justice (Public Order) Act 1994. S 6 can apply to social media and makes it an offence to use or engage in any threatening, abusive or insulting words or behaviour with intent to provoke a breach of the peace or being reckless as to whether a breach of the peace may be occasioned.
- The Criminal Damage Act 1991. This Act can be applied to social media, where an individual's social media account or email is targeted by unauthorised access or hacking to send harmful messages or post harmful material.
- The Criminal Law (Sexual Offences) Act 2017. S 8 contains an indictable offence for those who use information and communication technology (like social media) to facilitate sexual exploitation of children.

In addition to legislation, key sources of fundamental rights protection in Ireland's national order come from domestic legislation, *Bunreacht na hÉireann*, European law, and regional and international treaty body instruments. These include the Universal Declaration of Human Rights (UDHR),[11] the International Covenant on Civil and Political Rights (ICCPR),[12] the European Convention on Human Rights (ECHR)[13] and the Charter of Fundamental Rights of the European Union (EU Charter).[14] Ireland has ratified these core human rights treaties and therefore must comply with the obligations derived therein.[15] As with all EU treaties, the EU Charter has taken effect in Irish law under Article 29 of *Bunreacht na hÉireann* and by virtue of the European Communities Act 1972. Fundamental rights protections are also available in the GDPR, which regulates data protection and privacy for all individuals within the EU. As an EU Regulation, the GDPR has direct effect and does not generally require transposition into Irish law – though aspects are reflected in Ireland's Data Protection Act 2018.

Specific, non-exhaustive fundamental rights of note in this chapter include expression, privacy and data protection. The right to freedom of expression is protected in Ireland by Article 19 UDHR, Article 19 ICCPR, Article 10 ECHR and Article 11 EU Charter. The right applies to all forms of electronic and Internet-based modes of expression.[16] Article 40.6.1. of *Bunreacht na hÉireann* protects "The right of the citizens to express freely their convictions and opinions". The Irish Courts have adopted the proportionality doctrine,[17] which guides via the three-part test and measures the validity of limiting expression rights in specific instances. The right to privacy is protected by Article 12 UDHR, Article 17 ICCPR, Article 8 ECHR and Article 7 EU Charter. *Bunreacht na hÉireann* guarantees privacy as an unenumerated right under Article 40.3, which states the "State guarantees in its laws to respect, and, as far as practicable, by its laws to defend and vindicate the personal rights of the citizen". The EU Charter contains Article 8, an explicit right to the protection of personal data, stating that everyone has the right to the protection of personal data concerning him or her and that such data must be processed fairly for specified purposes and on a legitimate basis laid down by law. The GDPR also regulates data protection for all individuals within the European Union. Under Article 1, Member States shall protect the fundamental rights and freedoms – in particular, rights to privacy and personal data.

The structure of the domestic judicial system in Ireland is relevant to how rights protections are applied in Ireland. Under the terms of Article 34, *Bunreacht na hÉireann* established the three higher courts: the High Court, the Court of Appeal and the Supreme Court. Provision is also made for courts of local and limited jurisdiction, including District and Circuit Courts. Article 6 recognises and establishes a separation of powers between the legislature, executive and judiciary; however, this is not rigidly maintained. The High Court, Court of Appeal and Supreme Court step over this separation to invalidate legislation if it is found to be unconstitutional.[18] The High Court has full jurisdiction in and power to determine all matters and questions whether of law or fact, civil or criminal. Its jurisdiction also extends to the question of the validity of any law having regard to the Constitution. The High Court acts as an appeal court from the Circuit Court in civil matters. It has power to review the decisions of certain tribunals. It may also give rulings on questions of law submitted by the District Court. The Supreme Court is the highest court in Ireland and the court of final appeals. It is composed of the Chief Justice of Ireland and nine ordinary judges. A peculiarity of Irish law is that certain cases can "leapfrog" from the High Court directly to the Supreme Court, thereby passing the Court of Appeal.

Cases addressing social media in Ireland are growing. A search of higher courts on the (1) British and Irish Legal Information Institute and (2)

Westlaw databases between 1/1/2009–31/12/2020 reveals an upper limit of approximately 162 cases referencing the term "social media". Through a second search of higher courts of notable "big tech" social media platforms under examination, Facebook returned the highest number of results at 138, followed by Google (75), YouTube (16), Yahoo (8) and Instagram (4). Such numbers may refer to the fact that big tech companies have their main European seat in Ireland rather than in other EU countries. From this discrete group, significantly fewer cases related to social media and fundamental rights. Most search returns only mentioned social media tangentially and in reference to matters that were irrelevant to the subject matter under examination here. Some cases, for example, mentioned social media activities in reference to family law disputes and child custody matters,[19] debt collection[20] or contempt of court without considering fundamental rights concerns. The small group of social media cases reported in relation to higher courts that contained a fundamental rights dimension rested primarily with the High Court of Ireland. The sample size here was too small to describe a statistically significant upward trend in relation to fundamental rights and social media for cases between 2009 and 2020. However, anecdotally, an upward trend became more apparent following 2016.

The central set of cases in which there is judicial dialogue in Ireland through reference to the ECtHR and CJEU case law relate to the complaint filed by Max Schrems to the Data Protection Commissioner in relation to the processing of his personal data by Facebook. Schrems asserted that, in the light of Edward Snowden's disclosure of American state intelligence sharing practices, the transfer of Schrems' personal data by Facebook to its US parent, Facebook Inc., for processing was unlawful both under national and EU law. These cases show that there is some judicial dialogue through references to primarily CJEU case law. They demonstrate a willingness by the Irish courts to acknowledge the parameters the European courts' place around the essence of rights. This will be detailed further in the discussion that follows. These examples aside, and the small sample of cases described in this chapter notwithstanding, a peculiarity in Ireland regarding the development of social media case law appears to be a concerted focus on defamatory issues online.

The remainder of this chapter will go on to examine fundamental rights in national jurisprudence (section 2) and judicial dialogue with the CJEU and ECtHR (section 3) before providing some concluding remarks (section 4).

2. Fundamental rights in national jurisprudence

While social media cases are not frequently framed as fundamental rights cases in Ireland, a review of available reported cases in higher courts suggests that references to fundamental rights are increasingly occurring. The contribution of litigants and plaintiffs appears to trigger the incorporation of a fundamental rights dimension in social media case law; however, the Irish courts also engage fundamental rights reasoning of their own volition. In reference to discrete samples of case law, this section considers the fundamental rights dimension in judicial reasoning focusing primarily on free expression, privacy and protection of personal data. It reviews the contributions of litigants in this area and considers how Irish courts engage in an analysis of fundamental rights.

2.1 *Fundamental rights dimensions in judicial reasoning about social media defamation*

In the 2016 case of *Muwema v Facebook Ireland*,[21] the High Court of Ireland took notice of the defendant Facebook's arguments that reliefs sought for alleged defamatory content on its platform would amount to an interference with freedom of expression as guaranteed by Article 40.6.1 of *Bunreacht na hEireann* and Article 10 ECHR. A Ugandan lawyer, in relation to alleged defamatory posts about him by an anonymous Facebook user, sought orders, pursuant to the Defamation Act 2009, that Facebook take down content posted by a third-party user and prevent others from posting the same content. The High Court did not issue these orders, reasoning that there was a "reasonable likelihood" that Facebook as a platform host would succeed with a defence of "innocent publication" as provided for under s 27(2) of the Defamation Act 2009, which would absolve Facebook from being considered an author, editor or publisher of the posted material. An injunction would also not serve any practical purpose, as similar comments were being discussed by the plaintiff himself on other online media forums. Persuasive in this decision was the defendant's argument that granting reliefs sought for specific accounts would seriously impinge the fundamental rights of those affected amounting to censorship, an invasion of privacy and an interference with freedom of expression pursuant to Article 40.6.1 of *Bunreacht na hEireann* and Article 10 ECHR. The Defendant further submitted that such orders would also interfere with Articles 7, 8, 11 and 16 under the EU Charter.[22] However, while the domestic court acknowledged these arguments, it did not engage with them.

In another case regarding defamation, Ireland's High Court observed an argument from the defendant that granting an injunction against allegedly defamatory speech would curtail the defendant's expression rights under *Bunreacht ah Eireann*. In *Gilroy & anor v O'Leary*, the plaintiffs alleged that a video published on YouTube by the defendant – an autism rights campaigner – defamed them.[23] In the plaintiff's application for an interlocutory injunction requiring the defendant to remove the video from social media pursuant to s 33 of the Defamation Act 2009, Mr Justice Allen accepted case law from the defendant, including *Philpott v Irish Examiner* [2016] IEHC 62. This case said that, before granting an injunction against statements which would curtail a defendant's constitutional right to freedom of expression, a court must be "forcefully of the opinion" that the statements are defamatory and that the defendant has no defence. Mr Justice Allen in *Gilroy* thus concluded that "it could not conceive that the court would permanently interfere with free speech or the free expression of opinion unless in a case where it was satisfied and/or had made a finding that the statement was defamatory of the plaintiff and that the defendant had no defence".[24]

Similarly, in the High Court case *Board of Management of Salesian Secondary College (Limerick) v Facebook Ireland Limited*[25], Mr Justice Garrett Simons noted that the disclosure application requested pursuant to s 33 the Defamation Act 2009 presented significant legal issues in respect of privacy, data protection and freedom of expression. The applicant was a secondary school board of management seeking to identify those responsible for the publication of material which ridiculed school staff members by describing their personal appearances and which complained about school administration issues. The applicants sought an order against Facebook to discipline those responsible for the postings – who were suspected to be students or staff. Mr Justice Simons proposed to refer questions to the CJEU under the preliminary reference procedure facilitated by Article 267 of the Treaty on the Functioning of the European Union (TFEU) on the interpretation and validity of EU law. He proposed a reference to the CJEU to determine whether there was an implied right in Articles 7, 8 and 11 of the EU Charter to post material anonymously on the Internet. This would be subject always to any countervailing objective of public interest and as to the threshold to be met under the GDPR and/or the EU Charter before the provider of a social media platform could be compelled to disclose information which would tend to identify an otherwise anonymous account user. Mr Justice Simons also proposed referring to a question to the CJEU as to whether it was necessary for a national court to attempt to put the potentially affected person on notice of the application and to provide them an opportunity to make submissions anonymously to the court as to whether the order sought should be made. These were interesting jurisprudential questions which were ultimately not answered, as the domestic application was withdrawn.

We see in these samples of cases a focus on defamation alleged on social media platforms with a fundamental rights dimension in judicial reasoning. Privacy, expression, data protection and anonymity are balanced against the right to the public interest in the prosecution of criminal offences, which, in Ireland, is still a possibility in relation to defamatory material that is blasphemous. There is balance to be found in data protection matters in EU law; the nature of this balance was set out by Mr Justice Simons at para 54:

> The rights afforded to privacy, data protection and freedom of expression under EU law present a potential obstacle to the extension of the domestic law jurisdiction to grant disclosure orders.

The main social media issue identified by Simons J was stated at para 78:

> whether the user of a social media platform, who has chosen to remain anonymous, is entitled to an expectation that that choice will be respected absent some countervailing public interest in disclosure.

Mr Justice Simons opined that, when the balance tilts away from fundamental rights in favour of prosecuting criminal offences and defending reputational interests:

> Any expectation of anonymity must, of course, yield to the public interest in the prosecution of criminal offences, especially in respect of child abuse. Similarly, any expectation of anonymity must yield to the public interest in vindicating an individual's right to their reputation by way of proceedings for defamation.

This analysis of Simons J. was neatly laid out in a subsequent 2021 case of *Portakabin Limited and Portakabin (Ireland) Limited v Google Ireland Limited*.[26]

2.2 *Inconsistent fundamental rights reasoning in Irish courts*

Despite these examples of fundamental rights reasoning undertaken by the courts in Ireland, the way Irish courts balance distinct rights and interests in social media cases does not appear to be consistent. Rather, analysis takes place on a case-by-case basis. Indeed, the level to which the courts will acknowledge fundamental rights discussions varies. See another defamation example, where Mr Justice Allen at the High Court in *Parcel Connect v Twitter International Company*[27] acknowledged that the defendant, Twitter, espoused freedom of expression and privacy rights. However, discussion stopped at acknowledgment; the judge did not engage these arguments further in his written decisions, ultimately making an order requiring Twitter to email plaintiffs any details it held on the identity of a person managing a defamatory account. More engaged analysis comes from the case of *Muwema v Facebook Ireland Ltd*,[28] which was introduced earlier in this chapter. The court, in refusing certain orders sought by the Ugandan lawyer against an anonymous Facebook provider in a defamation action, stated that take-down orders would impinge seriously on the fundamental rights of those affected and amount to censorship and an interference with freedom of expression as guaranteed by Article 40.6.1 of *Bunreacht na hEireann* and Article 10 ECHR; and providing identities would be an invasion of privacy, contrary to Ireland's unenumerated constitutional right to privacy. The court commented on the "importance attached by the courts and society at large to freedom of expression".[29] Indeed, the jurisprudence emerging from the higher courts in Ireland appears to reveal a preference for freedom of expression and the reluctance to issue orders which might limit this constitutional and treaty body right.

These increasing references to European fundamental rights in the context of national jurisprudence appear to indicate that the national courts are nudging towards relying on the EU Charter and the ECHR, typically in combination with domestic constitutional provisions. This may follow legislative trends which reflect the same tendencies. As Bobek and Prassl describe in relation to the application of the EU Charter in Members States, EU case law reveals that, in Ireland, as elsewhere in the EU, any legislation that breaches the EU Charter is to be annulled or declared invalid and Irish law implementing EU law that contravenes the fundamental rights enshrined therein must be set aside.[30] However, De Burca notes an early reluctance to incorporate the ECHR into Irish law and the scepticism of the executive branch about "the prospect of incorporation of the ECHR into Irish law on the grounds of Irish constitutional sovereignty".[31] De Burca observed that Irish courts, in turn, demonstrated a pattern of engagement of early resistance to human rights law in favour of Irish sovereignty. However, following the incorporation of the European Convention on Human Rights Act 2003, case law invoking and using the ECHR has increased. The European Convention on Human Rights Act 2003 incorporates the standards set out in the ECHR and jurisprudence in Irish law, allowing them to be considered before the Irish courts. Courts have taken its provisions reasonably seriously in interpreting legislation and in imposing obligations on public bodies. For example, the Supreme Court made clear that domestic legal provisions must be compatible with Ireland's obligations under the ECHR. In the 2007 case of *Mahon v Post Publications*, Mr Justice Fennelly said that the Article 10 ECHR right to freedom of expression must be prescribed by law and be necessary in a democratic society.[32]

2.3 *Acknowledging how social media shapes fundamental rights in our digital age*

In following this tentative trend of upholding Ireland's obligations under the EU Charter and ECHR, courts in Ireland have also addressed the ways social media have shaped the exercise of distinct fundamental rights in our digital age. They have described how social media changes traditional understandings, including what distinguishes the traditional profession of journalists from lay people observing phenomena in online worlds. Consideration of the protection of journalist sources was given, for example, in *Cornec v Morrice*,[33] where Mr Justice Hogan stated in the High Court of Ireland that, while an individual posting online

> is not a journalist in the strict sense of the term, it is clear that his activities involve the chronicling of the activities. . . . Part of the problem here is that the traditional distinction between journalists and laypeople has broken down in recent decades, not least with the rise of social media. It is probably not necessary here to discuss questions such as whether the casual participant on an internet discussion site could invoke Goodwin v United Kingdom (App No. 17488/90 (1996) 22 E.H.R.R. 123 style privileges, although the issue may not be altogether far removed from the facts of this case.[34]

The courts of Ireland have also described risks posed by social media very broadly as a call to legislative redress and provision. Sitting in the High Court of Ireland, Mr Justice Peart said in *Tansey v Gill*:

> The internet has facilitated an inexpensive, easy, and instantaneous means whereby unscrupulous persons or ill motivated malcontents may give vent to their anger and their perceived grievances against any person, where the allegations are patently untrue, or where no right thinking person would consider them to be reasonable or justified. By such means, anything can be said publicly about any person, and about any aspect of their life whether private or public, with relative impunity, and anonymously, whereby reputations can be instantly and permanently damaged, and where serious distress and damage may be caused to both the target, children and adults alike, leading in extreme cases to suicide. So serious is the mischief so easily achieved that in my view the Oireachtas should be asked to consider the creation of an appropriate offence under criminal law, with a penalty upon conviction sufficient to act as a real deterrent to the perpetrator. The civil remedies currently available have been recently demonstrated to be an inadequate means of prevention and redress.[35]

This analysis seems to move away from defending the defence of distinct fundamental rights in favour of protecting against reputational risks. However, as shall be seen in the discussion that follows, Irish courts are reluctant to permanently interfere with free speech or the free expression of opinion,[36] though they have, as described previously, with seemingly negative connotation, labelled fundamental rights as an "obstacle" to the extension of domestic law jurisdiction.[37]

3. Judicial dialogue with the CJEU and ECtHR

There is some evidence of judicial dialogue with the CJEU and ECtHR, though this area is underdeveloped, particularly with respect to the ECtHR.

3.1 The CJEU

As outlined previously, national courts in Ireland have sometimes referred to and drawn on the jurisprudence of the CJEU when adjudicating social media cases. As a further example of comparative reasoning, the High Court's consideration of jurisprudence at the CJEU occurred in *Muwema v Facebook Ireland Ltd*,[38] where the High Court considered the cases of C-70/10 *Scarlet v SABAM* ECLI:EU:C:2011:771 and C-360/10 *SABAM v Netlog NV* ECLI:EU:C:2012:85. In those cases, the CJEU had to consider whether or not the ISP defendants, who were used by third parties to access copyright-protected music and media, were obliged to monitor their customers in order to prevent copyright infringement in compliance with the e-commerce directive.[39] If they were obliged, they would have had to install customer monitoring and filtering technology. The CJEU weighed intellectual property rights of creators against freedom to conduct a business, the right to protection of personal data and the freedom to receive or impart information. The CJEU considered that monitoring and filtering technology would technically require indiscriminate and unlimited application to all ISP customers to prevent copyright-infringing downloads. It found that such a measure would be disproportionate and contrary to the e-commerce directive. The High Court only addressed the impact of the e-commerce directive in this comparative reasoning. However, they also acknowledged the "reluctance of the courts here and in other jurisdictions to grant prior restraint orders reflects the importance attached by the courts and society at large to freedom of expression".[40]

Judicial dialogue with the CJEU in Ireland also sometimes rests on the preliminary reference procedure (Article 267 TFEU) on the interpretation and validity of EU law.[41] However, the most prominent example of judicial dialogue with the CJEU is through use of the preliminary reference procedure in relation to Schrems I and Schrems II. In June 2013, following Edward Snowden's revelations of US intelligence agency spying, then law student Max Schrems made a formal complaint to the DPC about the processing of his personal data by Facebook Ireland. He said that Facebook Ireland's transfer of his personal data overseas to Facebook Inc. in the US for processing breached national and EU law based on the use of data by US intelligence agencies. The DPC declined to investigate Mr Schrems' complaint, deeming it to be frivolous and unsustainable in law by reason of a European Commission Decision (the so-called Safe Harbour Decision) finding under the then Data Protection Directive[42] (now superseded by the GDPR) that the US ensured adequate protection for personal data from authorities' surveillance activities.[43]

Mr Schrems was not deterred by this initial rejection of his complaint by the DPC. In October 2013, he brought judicial review proceedings challenging the DPC's refusal in the Irish High Court. In *Schrems v Data Protection Commissioner*, Mr Justice Hogan of the High Court referred questions to the CJEU under Article 267 TFEU on issues concerning the interpretation and validity of the Safe Harbour Decision in light of Articles 7, 8 and 47[44] of the EU Charter.[45] The CJEU, in Case C-362/14 *Maximilian Schrems v Data Protection Commissioner* (Schrems I),[46] gave its judgment to that reference on 6 October 2015 that the Safe Harbour Decision was invalid; US intelligence agencies circumvented the Safe Harbour Scheme, accessing communications data and content and breached Article 7 and 47 of the EU Charter because the US legislation did not provide people in the EU with sufficient guarantees and remedies to exercise their rights. Following this decision, the Privacy Shield was adopted in July 2016 to replace Safe Harbour. While both the Safe Harbour and Privacy Shield are mechanisms for allowing companies to provide protection for personal data transfers from the EU and the US, the Privacy

Shield as a result of Schrems' litigation provides further clarification on the rules around data retention, bulk collection of data and Standard Contractual Clauses (SCCs) for third party data transfers.

Returning to the matter of preliminary reference procedure, following the judgment in Schrems I, Mr Justice Hogan issued a High Court order on 20 October 2015. The order quashed the DPC's decision to refuse to investigate Schrems' complaint and then remitted Schrems' complaint to the DPC. The DPC, in response, made an application on 4 July 4 2016 to the High Court for a further reference to the CJEU for a ruling on the validity of transfers by Facebook to the US facilitated by SCCs having regards to Articles 7, 8 and 47 of the EU Charter. In the 2017 decision of *Data Protection Commissioner v Facebook Ireland Ltd & anor*, Mr Justice Costello delivered a judgment in indicating that the High Court intended to make an order for reference for a preliminary ruling pursuant to Article 267 TFEU.[47] On 12 April 2018, in *Data Protection Commissioner v Facebook Ireland Ltd & anor*, the High Court delivered that order for reference while also declining Facebook's application for a stay so that Facebook could appeal the order for reference.[48] In 2020, the CJEU in Case C-311/18 *Data Protection Commissioner v Facebook Ireland and Maximillian Schrems* (Schrems II) invalidated the Privacy Shield.[49] However, the CJEU held that SCCs were still valid as a transfer mechanism in principle, while raising doubts as to whether they might be legitimised by the European Commission's standard for personal data transfers to the US and globally.

The significance of this judgment then followed in the 2021 High Court decision *Facebook Ireland Ltd v Data Protection Commission*, where Facebook Ireland challenged the DPC investigation into Facebook's international transfers of personal data in reference to Article 20 of the EU Charter, the principle of equality, Article 40.1 of *Bunreacht na hÉireann* and Article 14 ECHR on protection from discrimination.[50] Facebook also alleged that the DPC's inquiry into Facebook but not social media platforms was disproportionate, *ultra vires* and a misuse by the DPC of its discretion. In dismissing Facebook Ireland's request for judicial review, the High court noted the significance of the Schrems II reference and its transformative impacts:

> The judgment of the CJEU in Schrems II was undoubtedly a very significant one. All parties were agreed on that. In correspondence with Mr Schrems' solicitors, Ahern Rudden Quigley ("ARQ"), after the judgment, the DPC's solicitors, Philip Lee, described the judgment as being "transformative of the law as it relates to EU/US data transfers" (letter from Philip Lee to ARQ dated 24th July, 2020). That description was repeated in the DPC's letter to ARQ dated 10th September, 2020.[51]

The CJEU ruling was transformative for Irish court consideration of CJEU jurisprudence and judicial dialogue with the CJEU resting on the preliminary reference procedure. When Mr Justice Barniville with the High Court dismissed Facebook's application, he stated in relation to Facebook's claims:

> I do not accept that principles of equality or of consistency or good administration . . . required the DPC to explain why it had decided to commence an inquiry in respect of [Facebook] and not in respect of other entities. The DPC was entitled to do so and provided that it explained why it had decided to commence an inquiry in respect of [Facebook], it did not have to provide an explanation as to why it was not commencing inquiries into other entities.[52]

In acknowledging the impact of Schrems' litigation interventions into EU-US data transfer processes in defence of fundamental freedoms, of particular relevance for this chapter was when, in the 2014 High Court decision in *Schrems v Data Protection Commissioner*,[53] Mr Justice Hogan referred to the CJEU decision in *Digital Rights Ireland and Others*[54] to note that the CJEU had described how the content of one's data constitutes the essence of privacy. Mr Justice Hogan referred to the CJEU decision in *Digital Rights Ireland and Others* to note that the CJEU had described how the content of one's data constitutes the essence of privacy, with Article 7 and 8 protections being triggered by the interception of private online communications by State authorities, though not always in manners that are unlawful.

3.2 *The ECtHR*

The use by national courts in Ireland of the jurisprudence of the ECtHR when adjudicating social media cases in underdeveloped. The Schrems cases, however, indicate some engagement. In 2017, when the High Court again sent a reference to the CJEU in the *Data Protection Commissioner v Facebook Ireland Ltd & anor*,[55] in doing so, the Court considered the meaning of an effective remedy in the context of national security within the meaning of the ECtHR jurisprudence presented by defendant Facebook. However, this discussion was solely in relation to effective remedies. The court considered *Klass v Germany*[56] and *Silver v The United Kingdom*[57] to argue that effective remedy cannot carry the same meaning in the context of secret, intrusive measures because the efficacy of such measures depends upon their remaining secret.

Apart from Schrems decisions, in this sample of retrieved cases, very limited judicial dialogue exists through reference to the ECtHR. One case in this sample set exists where Ireland's High Court considered the right to privacy of the infant plaintiff and the right to freedom of expression on the part of the defendant newspaper. See *X (an infant) -v- Sunday Newspapers Ltd (trading as 'The Sunday World')*, [2014] IEHC 696. In that case, a notorious gangland figure fathered two children while behind bars, and an investigation was initiated after his partner recently announced publicly on a social media site that she was pregnant again and was openly congratulated by her caged lover's family. The minor's mother, becoming aware that the defendant newspaper proposed to publish an article involving her minor child, sought *ex parte* relief from the Court. The Court considered the issue of prior restraint by referring to the jurisprudence of the ECtHR in *The Observer and the Guardian v United Kingdom* (1992) 14 EHRR 153.[58]

Apart from these sparse examples, there appears to be very limited judicial dialogue through reference to the ECtHR.

4. Conclusion

In an unreported criminal law case in Ireland, a man avoided a prison sentence for criminal damage to his ex-girlfriend's Facebook page in contravention of the Criminal Damage Act 1991. The Act carries a maximum penalty of ten years in prison and a €10,000 fine. Mr Justice Sheehan asked Counsel for the Director of Public Prosecutions how he could assess damages under the Act if, by damaging Facebook, nothing was *physically* broken. Counsel replied that the damage was reputational rather than financial – an offence which was more comparable to harassment than criminal damage in the traditional sense. The judge noted there was no relevant precedence to guide him in sentencing and imposed a €2,000 fine.[59]

This case and this chapter's discussion illustrate the rapid development of case law – domestic and EU legislation – in response to social media activities. Case law is growing for discrete platforms, but for newcomers like Tiktok, there are very few precedents. With the rapid evolution of the shape and character of social media progressing, it is hard to predict the future role of Irish courts shaping the development of legal and fundamental rights standards for social media in Ireland. Thus far, the body of social media and fundamental rights jurisprudence in the higher Irish courts appears to have been dedicated primarily to fundamental rights reasoning in relation to defamation actions. Through these cases, there is, nonetheless, a growing body of jurisprudence with implications for enshrined rights including privacy, freedom of expression, data protection and anonymity. Schrems I and II are also ground-breaking and transformative, leading perhaps to significant changes for enforcement by Ireland's data protection authority, the Data Protection Commission. For example, following Schrems I, officers for the Data Protection Commission have commenced numerous inquiries under their statutory authority in relation to cross-border personal data processing: The DPC commenced 83 inquiries under s. 110 of the Data Protection Act 2018 in the period from 25 May 2018 and 27 January 2021, which involve cross-border processing.[60]

Similarly, new legislation is now in force in Ireland, including the Harassment, Harmful Communications and Related Offences Act 2020, which entered into force in early 2021. Bills like the OSMRB are also seeing significant progression through the Oireachtas. In particular, the proposed OSMRB brings together several significant initiatives, including the transposition of the revised AVMSD and certain actions from the Action Plan for Online Safety 2018–2019.[61] The proposed Bill would also establish a Media Commission; establish a framework for the regulation of online safety to address the proliferation of harmful online content, encompassing the regulation of video-sharing platform services, to be administered by the Media Commission; provide the Media Commission with appropriate compliance powers, including the power to issue information requests, initiate authorised, officer-led investigations and to audit the complaint or issues handling mechanisms operated by online services; and, provide the Media Commission with appropriate sanction powers, subject to court oversight, including administrative financial sanctions, the power to compel compliance and the power to block online services.[62]

The OSMRB appears to be moving forward, despite concerns raised by Irish experts as detailed at the beginning of this chapter, creating a regime for content "that is essentially unprecedented in Irish or European law".[63] Similarly, the Bill is noteworthy for the forms of online content it omits to address, including hate crime. Currently, OSMRB defines categories of harmful content to include criminal offences and three further categories, including cyberbullying, the promotion of suicide and self-harm, and the promotion of eating disorders. Gaps in Irish legislation therefore continue to exist in managing certain forms of content, including hateful content. While Ireland does not have laws against hate crime, the *Prohibition of Incitement to Hatred Act 1989* provides for limited criminal offences addressing incitement to hate speech against those who can be identified as sharing one or more protected characteristics. This legislation is limited in scope and outdated for the purposes of addressing hate crimes in online spaces. In August 2020, Amnesty International Ireland called on Ireland to create hate crime laws following the high-profile media stories of people being abused based on intersecting factors of race and gender.[64] The Irish government announced plans for hate speech legislation in 2020.[65]

What this new suite of legislation, investigations and judicial findings means for Irish court trends towards upholding Ireland's fundamental rights obligations under *Bunreacht na hÉireann*, domestic legislation, the EU Charter and the ECHR is uncertain. However, judicial dialogue with the CJEU appears to be developing specifically in relation to defamation and Ireland's Article 8 and 11 EU Charter obligations. Further input into this unfolding space comes from Recommendation CM/Rec(2016)4 of the Council of Europe's Committee of Ministers on the protection of journalism and safety of journalists and other media actors.[66] The Committee of Ministers requires that Member States review relevant domestic laws and practice and revise them, as necessary, to ensure their conformity with States' obligations under the ECHR. Ireland has been responsive to this recommendation; per the Department of Justice, defamation laws "fall squarely within the scope of these reviews" and they will be reviewing the Defamation Act 2009 in accordance with the ECHR and the principle of proportionality, as developed in the relevant judgments of the European Court of Human Rights.[67] However, these promises were made by the Department of Justice in 2016. Subsequent failure to reform Irish defamation law, despite "long-standing promises" by successive Irish governments, are warned to present "significant threats" to the state's press freedoms.[68]

Notes

1 Colm Keena, 'Minister Urged to Set Up Committee to Examine Social Media Regulation', (*Irish Times*, 4 July 2020) <www.irishtimes.com/news/crime-and-law/minister-urged-to-set-up-committee-to-examine-social-media-regulation-1.4295595> accessed 2 August 2021.

2 Sarah Burns, 'Online Safety Body "Needs Teeth" for Complaints Against Social Media Platforms' (Irish Times, 13 July 2021) <www.irishtimes.com/news/social-affairs/online-safety-body-needs-teeth-for-complaints-against-social-media-platforms-1.4619263> accessed 2 August 2021.

3 Law Reform Commission, 'Report on Harmful Communications and Digital Safety' (2016), para 2 <www.lawreform.ie/_fileupload/Reports/Full%20Colour%20Cover%20Report%20on%20Harmful%20Communications%20and%20Digital%20Safety.pdf> accessed 2 August 2021.

4 Elizabeth Farries, 'What Happened to Dara Quigley Should Never Happen to Anyone Else' Dublin Inquirer (23 October 2019) <www.dublininquirer.com/2019/10/23/elizabeth-what-happened-to-dara-quigley-should-never-happen-to-anyone-else> accessed 23 October 2019.

5 Kerry OShea, 'More than 40k Sign Petition to Make Revenge Porn a Crime Ireland' (*Irish Central*, 20 November 2020) <www.irishcentral.com/news/revenge-porn-ireland> accessed 2 August 2021.

6 Department of Tourism, Culture, Arts, Gaeltacht, Sport and Media, *General Scheme of the Online Safety and Media Regulation Bill* (2020 January)<www.gov.ie/en/publication/d8e4c-online-safety-and-media-regulation-bill/#general-scheme-of-the-online-safety-media-regulation-bill> accessed 2 August 2021.

7 Directive 2018/1808 of the European Parliament and of the Council of 14 November 2018 amending Directive 2010/13/EU on the coordination of certain provisions laid down by law, regulation or administrative action in Member States concerning the provision of audio-visual media services (Audiovisual Media Services Directive) in view of changing market realities; OJ L 303/69.

8 Directive 2018/1808 OJ L 303/69 art 19.

9 Directive 2018/1808 OJ L 303/69 art 47.

10 See Dr TJ McIntyre's testimony, Houses of the Oireachtas, Joint Committee on Tourism, Culture, Arts, Sport and Media debate – Wednesday, 26 May 2021 General Scheme of the Online Safety and Media Regulation Bill 2020: Discussion (Resumed) <www.oireachtas.ie/en/debates/debate/joint_committee_on_tourism_culture_arts_sport_and_media/2021-05-26/3/> accessed 2 August 2020.

11 Universal Declaration of Human Rights (adopted 10 December 1948) UNGA Res 217.

12 International Covenant on Civil and Political Rights (adopted 16 December 1966, entered into force 23 March 1976) 999 UNTS 171.

13 Convention for the Protection of Human Rights and Fundamental Freedoms (adopted 4 November 1950, entered into force 3 September 1953) 213 United Nations Treaty Series 22.

14 Charter of Fundamental Rights of the European Union 2000 OJ (C 364) 1.

15 Department of Foreign Affairs, 'Human Rights in Ireland' (n.d.) <www.dfa.ie/our-role-policies/international-priorities/human-rights/human-rights-in-ireland/> accessed 2 August 2022.

16 United Nations Human Rights Committee, General Comment No.34 on Article 19: Freedoms of opinion and Expression (2011) CCPR/C/GC/34 <https://www2.ohchr.org/english/bodies/hrc/docs/gc34.pdf> accessed 2 August 2021.
17 Constitution Review Group, *Report of the Constitution Review Group* (1996) <http://archive.constitution.ie/reports/crg.pdf> accessed 2 August 2021.
18 Catherine Allen and Rachel Hanly, 'Mason Hayes & Curran LLP', *Legal Systems in Ireland: Overview* (*Thomson Reuters* 2021) <https://uk.practicallaw.thomsonreuters.com/w-009-0803> accessed 2 August 2021.
19 For example, a man's upset about posts his wife had made on social media. See DK v PIK [2021] IEHC 516.
20 The People [At the Suit of the Director of Public Prosecutions] v Kevin Molloy [2020] IECA 254.
21 *Muwema v Facebook Ireland* [2016] IEHC 519.
22 *Muwema v Facebook Ireland* [2016] IEHC 519 at para 45.
23 *Gilroy & anor v O'Leary* [2019] IEHC 52
24 *Philpott v Irish Examiner* [2016] IEHC 62 para 53.
25 *Salesian Secondary College (Limerick) v Facebook Ireland Limited* [2021] IEHC 287 para 2.
26 *Portakabin Limited and Portakabin (Ireland) Limited v Google Ireland Limited* [2021] IEHC 446, para 12.
27 *Parcel Connect v Twitter International Company* [2020] IEHC 279.
28 *Muwema v Facebook Ireland Ltd* [2016] IEHC 519.
29 *Muwema v Facebook Ireland Ltd* [2016] IEHC 519 at para 65.
30 Michal Bobek and Jeremias Prassl, *The EU Charter of Fundamental Rights in the Member States* (Bloomsbury 2020).
31 Gráinne De Búrca, 'The Domestic Impact of the EU Charter of Fundamental Rights' (2013) 49 *Irish Jurist* 49 at 58.
32 *Mahon v Post Publications* [2007] 3 IR 338, at 59.
33 *Cornec v Morrice* [2012] 1 IR 804 at para 65.
34 Goodwin privileges refer to the right of journalists to protection their sources. See CEARTA.IE, 'The Limits of the ECHR's Protection of Journalists' Sources' (4 May 2009) <www.cearta.ie/2009/05/the-limits-of-the-echrs-protection-of-journalists-sources/> accessed 8 March 2022.
35 *Tansey v Gill* [2012] IEHC 42.
36 *Gilroy & anor v O'Leary* [2019] IEHC 52.
37 *Salesian Secondary School v Facebook Ireland (Identity disclosure application)* [2021] IEHC 287.
38 *Muwema v Facebook Ireland Ltd* [2016] IEHC 519.
39 Directive 2000/31/EC of the European Parliament and of the Council of 8 June 2000 on certain legal aspects of information society services, in particular electronic commerce, in the Internal Market (e-commerce Directive).
40 *Muwema v Facebook Ireland Ltd* [2016] IEHC 519 at para 65.
41 This is discussed earlier in this chapter in reference to the High Court case *Board of Management of Salesian Secondary College (Limerick) v Facebook Ireland Limited* [2021] IEHC 287, where Mr Justice Simons also proposed referring to a question as to whether it was necessary for a national court to attempt to put a potentially affected person on notice of a defamation application and to provide them an opportunity to make submissions anonymously to the court as to whether the order sought should be made.
42 Directive 95/46/EC of the European Parliament and of the Council of 24 October 1995 on the protection of individuals with regard to the processing of personal data and on the free movement of such data.
43 European Commission, Decision 2000/520/EC (Safe Harbour Decision).

44 Article 47 of the Charter provides that everyone whose rights and freedoms guaranteed by the law of the Union are violated has the right to an effective remedy before a tribunal in compliance with the conditions laid down by Article 47. These include a fair and public hearing within a reasonable time by an independent and impartial tribunal previously established by law.
45 *Schrems v Data Protection Commissioner* [2014] IEHC 310.
46 C-362/14 *Schrems v Data Protection Commissioner*, EU:C:2015:650.
47 *Data Protection Commissioner v Facebook Ireland Ltd & anor* [2017] IEHC 545, para 340.
48 *Data Protection Commissioner v Facebook Ireland Ltd & anor* [2018] IEHC 236.
49 C-311/18 *Data Protection Commissioner v Facebook Ireland Limited and Maximillian Schrems*, EU:C:2020:559.
50 *Facebook Ireland Ltd v Data Protection Commission* [2021] IEHC 336.
51 Ibid, para 29.
52 Ibid, para 38.
53 *Schrems v Data Protection Commissioner* [2014] IEHC 310.
54 Cases C-293/12 and C-594/12 *Digital Rights Ireland Ltd v Minister for Communications, Marine and Natural Resources and Others and Kärntner Landesregierung and Others* EU:C:2014:238
55 *Data Protection Commissioner v Facebook Ireland Ltd & anor* [2017] IEHC 545; [2017] IEHC 545.
56 *Klass v Germany* (App. No. 5029/71) [1978] 2 EHRR 214.
57 *Silver v The United Kingdom* (1983) 5 EHRR 347.
58 *X (an infant) -v- Sunday Newspapers Ltd (trading as 'The Sunday World')*, [2014] IEHC 696 at para 33. The ECtHR held that Article 10 ECHR does not, in terms, prohibit the imposition of prior restraints on publication; however, the dangers inherent in prior restraints are such that they call for the most careful scrutiny. The High Court, in granting interlocutory relief, stated that the right to freedom of expression is not an unqualified right, as is the minor's right of privacy, and any discussion which calls into question his parentage in a national newspaper interferes with and is a breach of his right to privacy.
59 Irish Times 'Man Avoids Jail for 'Criminal Damage to Facebook Page' (*Irish Times*, 30 June 2014). <www.irishtimes.com/news/crime-and-law/courts/man-avoids-jail-for-criminal-damage-to-facebook-page-1.1850417> accessed 2 August 2021.
60 *Facebook Ireland Ltd v Data Protection Commission* [2021] IEHC 336 at para 203.
61 Department of Tourism, Culture, Arts, Gaeltacht, Sport and Media, 'Action Plan for Online Safety 2018–2019' (17 April 2019) <Action Plan for Online Safety 2018–2019> accessed 8 March 2022.
62 See full list of policy obligations at Government of Ireland, Regulatory Impact Assessment Online Safety and Media Regulation Bill (November 2020).
63 See Dr TJ McIntyre's testimony, Houses of the Oireachtas, Joint Committee on Tourism, Culture, Arts, Sport and Media debate – Wednesday, 26 May 2021 General Scheme of the Online Safety and Media Regulation Bill 2020: Discussion (Resumed). <www.oireachtas.ie/en/debates/debate/joint_committee_on_tourism_culture_arts_sport_and_media/2021-05-26/3/> accessed 2 August 2020.
64 Patsy McGarry, 'Human Rights Group Calls for Hate Crime Legislation in Ireland to be Updated' (*The Irish Times*, 16 August 2020) <www.irishtimes.com/news/social-affairs/human-rights-groups-call-for-hate-crime-legislation-in-ireland-to-be-updated-1.4331517> accessed 2 August 2021.
65 Conor Gallagher, 'Planned Hate Speech Laws Will Contain Higher Bar for Prosecution' (*Irish Times*, 17 December 2020) <www.irishtimes.com/news/crime-and-law/planned-hate-speech-laws-will-contain-higher-bar-for-prosecution-1.4438867> accessed 2 August 2021.

66 Recommendation CM/Rec(2016)4 of the Committee of Ministers to member States on the protection of journalism and safety of journalists and other media actors, 13 April 2016.

67 Tarlach McGonagle, Review of the Defamation Act 2009 – Public consultation 2016 Organised by: the Department of Justice and Equality Individual submission (rev.) by: Dr Tarlach McGonagle <www.justice.ie/en/JELR/Dr_Tarlach_McGonagle.pdf/Files/Dr_Tarlach_McGonagle.pdf> accessed 2 August 2021.

68 Cantilon, 'How Long Will "Prohibitive" Irish Defamation Law Remain Unreformed?' (*Irish Times*, 20 April 2021) <www.irishtimes.com/business/media-and-marketing/how-long-will-prohibitive-irish-defamation-law-remain-unreformed-1.4541817> accessed 2 August 2021.

10 Social media before higher courts in Italy

A thorough adaptation of existing rules and protection of constitutional rights online

Federica Casarosa[1] *and Maria Concetta Causarano*

1. Introduction

Social media are not subject to specific legislation in Italy. No provision clearly defines the concept either *per se* or within a selected area. However, this does not mean that social media and their impact on citizens have been disregarded by the Italian legislator and consequently by courts. Many legal provisions addressing civil, criminal and administrative law sectors have been drafted taking into account the technological developments that have occurred in the last two decades. Alternatively, where this forward-looking approach has not been adopted, national judges have been able to interpret existing provisions so as to identify whether and how they can be applied to the social media environment.[2]

One of the most relevant points of reference for courts is the Italian Constitution. This was drafted in the aftermath of the Second World War, so clearly before the development of the Internet and web 2.0. Nonetheless, the articles in the Constitution have been progressively interpreted in an evolutionary way. For instance, data protection, which plays a relevant role for social media, has no place in the Constitution, although it has been qualified as a third-generation right encompassed by Article 2 Const.[3] In particular, this article provides:

> *The Republic recognises and guarantees the inviolable rights of the person, both as an individual and in the social groups where human personality is expressed. The Republic expects that the fundamental duties of political, economic and social solidarity be fulfilled.*

Since the landmark decision in *Soraya*,[4] the Court of Cassation has affirmed that privacy is a right that is not limited to confidentiality but extends to the expression of those aspects of life the intimate character of which stems from the fact that they take place in an ideal home. Accordingly, the Court of

DOI: 10.4324/9781003207085-12

Cassation acknowledged in subsequent jurisprudence that the rights to privacy and, most importantly, the protection of personal data are not limited to the specific cases expressly provided for in secondary law, but rather they should be framed in a more general perspective as they are fundamental rights that fall within the individual rights protected by Article 2 Const.

Other constitutional rights applicable to social media include freedom and confidentiality of communication (Article 15 Const.) and freedom of expression (Article 21 Const.). Article 15(1) Const. provides that "*Freedom and confidentiality of correspondence and of every other form of communication shall be inviolable*". This freedom entails both the fact that communications should reach the receivers without any obstacle and also the secrecy of communication – i.e. no other individual shall access the content of the communication.[5] It is clear that communication via Internet cannot guarantee the full secrecy of communication due to the needs of the technical infrastructure. However, there are a set of criteria for confidentiality that allow verification of whether Article 15 Const. is complied with. These include the actual intention (*animus*) of the sender and, subordinately, of the recipient of the communication; the number of recipients of the communication; the substitutability of the addressee(s);[6] and the suitability of the means to keep the content of the communication secret according to objectively reasonable expectations.[7] As a result, courts are able to verify, for instance, whether a communication to a mailing list in a social network chat or in a newsgroup can be deemed confidential and therefore safeguarded by the constitutional guarantees.[8]

Article 21 Const. on freedom of expression is also applicable to social media as outlets where individuals can express their views and opinions. However, the application of this constitutional provision to social media has raised lively judicial debate, as its paragraph (3) provides that "*The press may not be subjected to any authorisation or censorship*". The Court of Cassation has faced a set of cases aimed at identifying the boundaries of the constitutional guarantees. It has, in particular, assessed whether or not the prohibition of seizure is applicable to both the traditional press and social media. After a number of decisions lacking uniform criteria, a Plenary Chamber decision of the Court of Cassation in 2015 provided lower courts with guidelines affirming that the constitutional guarantees are applicable to the printed press and that they can be extended to the "online press", insofar as the latter has the same structure and characteristics as the printed press. Hence, according to the court, blogs, mailing lists, chats, newsletters, e-mails, newsgroups, etc. do not fall within the concept of the press.[9]

Along with the constitutional articles, there are several secondary law provisions applicable to social media, such as the criminal provisions addressing defamation (Article 595 Crim. Code). Domestic jurisprudence confirms that the offence of defamation can also be committed when the defamatory content is disseminated through social networks, internet sites, blogs and other electronic means. Social media communication may also qualify as an aggravating circumstance increasing the sanction applicable under Article 595(3) Crim. Code. For the Court of Cassation, dissemination of defamatory content on Facebook falls under Article 595(3) Crim. Code – i.e. dissemination "*via other means of publicity*", as such conduct is potentially capable of reaching an indeterminate or quantitatively appreciable number of persons.[10]

Other criminal law provisions apply when social media are the means used to perpetrate a crime. For instance, in the case of child pornography, Article 600-ter Crim. Code includes "electronic means" among the forms of dissemination of child pornography without distinguishing between them (audiovisual media, social media, peer-to-peer networks, etc.).[11] Similarly, Article 414 Crim. Code on the crime of incitement to commit a crime has been applied to communication via social networks.[12] The Court of Cassation has affirmed that the crime is committed when an individual includes on his social network profile communications containing references to terrorism and terrorist organisations, thus enhancing the dissemination of such content and encouraging users to contribute economically to the cause.[13] Moreover, the Court of Cassation has interpreted Article 494 Crim. Code on impersonation (i.e. illegitimate substitution of oneself for another person in order to obtain benefits or cause damage) as also applying to the creation of a false social network profile.[14] Regarding stalking under Article 612-bis Crim. Code, the jurisprudence shows increasing attention to the technological means in order to evaluate conduct. The publication of merely mocking and derisive posts on a Facebook page that is accessible to anyone does not constitute a prosecutable act. According to the Court, stalking requires that "private" messages should be perceived as invasive by the receiver.[15] The same should apply to messages that are publicly available, such as posts on social networks, in order for such conduct to constitute an offence.[16]

Regarding the structure of the Italian judicial system, it is regulated by the national Constitution and legislative acts. These acts set out the competences, responsibilities and operational principles of the judicial bodies concerned. They also lay down rules for the distribution of cases. Domestic constitutional provisions safeguard the independence of the judiciary. Judges are independent in their decision-making and are bound only by the law. The Constitution prohibits the creation of special courts with the exception of administrative courts and martial courts. Administrative courts have two functions: the protection of "*interessi legittimi*"; that is, the protection of individual interests directly connected with public interests and protected only for that reason; and supervision and control of public funds.

The Court of Cassation and the Council of State are the highest judicial authorities. They respectively have jurisdiction in civil, criminal and labour law cases and administrative cases. Supreme courts generally rule on legal remedies that challenge decisions made by lower courts on points of law.[17] They ensure uniform application of the law and they are commonly entrusted with interpretative responsibilities in cases of conflicting case law. Through their rulings, they play an important role in guaranteeing the unity of jurisprudence.

Moreover, in Italy, a specific procedure is available for this purpose: any section of the Court of Cassation when deciding on a dispute can raise a question to the Grand Chamber of the Court of Cassation to receive clarification on a certain point of law and in the case of pre-existing conflicting interpretations of the law between the Court's chambers to solve such conflict. The decision of the Grand Chamber acts as an authoritative precedent to be followed not only by the requesting court but by all courts.

The Italian Constitutional Court is the institution of judicial power that engages in constitutional review. It rules on: a) controversies relating to the constitutional legitimacy of laws and enactments with the force of law by the state and the regions; b) jurisdictional disputes between the powers of the state, between the state and the regions and between the regions; c) accusations made against the President of the Republic in accordance with the Constitution (pursuant to Article 90). In fulfilling their functions, an important dimension of the jurisprudence of constitutional courts concerns ensuring respect for fundamental rights and freedoms safeguarded by the Constitution, domestic bills of rights and international human rights instruments.

Particularly regarding fundamental rights, recent developments in the jurisprudence of the Constitutional Court could have an important impact on potential dialogue among Italian courts, the Court of Justice of the EU (CJEU) and the Constitutional Court itself. In its decision no. 269/2017, the Constitutional Court affirmed (in an *obiter dictum*) that courts may choose, or rather should choose, to present a referral to the Constitutional Court when a national provision is allegedly in conflict with fundamental rights principles enshrined not only in the Italian Constitution but also in the EU Charter of Fundamental Rights (CFR). Then, the Constitutional Court can perform its review "*in the light of internal parameters and, potentially, European ones as well . . . in the order that is appropriate to the specific case*".[18] This strong position was then nuanced in subsequent decisions of the Constitutional Court which affirmed that national courts are free to pursue both paths before the CJEU and the Constitutional Court and that they are in charge of applying the principle of direct effect of EU law (implying disapplication of national provisions that are not in contrast with EU law) even after the constitutional review.[19] Accordingly, when addressing fundamental rights, the choice to present a preliminary ruling request to the CJEU or a referral to the Constitutional Court constitutes an important step in the dialogue between Italian and European jurisprudence.

The case law of the Italian Supreme Court concerning social media in the period 2009–2021 addresses a great variety of issues ranging from perpetration of criminal offences online to monitoring the conduct of employees, assimilation of social media to legacy media and reviewing online statements made by politicians or judges. However, analysis shows that relevant cases are not generally framed as fundamental rights cases. Specifically, the majority of the cases under review concern violations of criminal law or labour law provisions, and the fundamental rights dimension often emerges because applicants bring it up in their pleadings. There are also a small number of cases which address the protection of selected fundamental rights, such as freedom of expression or dignity and reputation, with direct constitutional relevance either concerning a specific provision (e.g. Article 21 Const.) or concerning interpretation on the basis of the umbrella clause in Article 2 Const.

When different fundamental rights are at stake, as typically happens in cases of defamation, Italian judges tend to balance the relevant rights relying heavily on the relevant Constitutional provisions rather than European sources of law. The impacts of the CFR and of the European Convention on Human Rights (ECHR) are still limited in the argumentative structure of Italian judgments concerning social media, even if their relevance is slowly increasing. In some recent judgments, for instance, greater sensitivity can be observed on the part of lower courts to giving adequate attention to the European and international regulatory framework on fundamental rights.[20] One possible reason for the limited attention to CFR and ECHR may be that most legal proceedings concerning social media are not constructed as constitutional cases in which the focus is on identifying the limits of individual fundamental freedoms. Leaving aside the jurisprudence of the Constitutional Court, such operations often remain implicit and focus on assessment of violations of specific sectoral rules (e.g. in the field of criminal law).

Our identification of social media cases in the Italian constitutional and supreme courts reviewed has drawn on the online databases available.[21] These provide access to all cases delivered. The judgments were identified using a set of generic keywords or tags.[22] The cases collected were reviewed to ensure that they were indeed about or related to social media. Analysis of a total of 152 decisions, of which 128 are in the field of criminal law (see the following table), shows that the majority of the judgments by supreme courts were

Year	*Total number of decisions*	*Court of Cassation – criminal law section*	*Court of Cassation – civil law section (incl. labour law)*	*High Administrative Court*	*Constitutional Court*
2009	2	2	-	-	-
2010	1	1	-	-	-
2011	3	2	1	-	-
2012	2	1	1	-	-
2013	10	9	-	-	1
2014	13	12	-	1	-
2015	11	9	1	1	-
2016	10	8	2	-	-
2017	20	15	4	1	-
2018	26	22	4	-	-
2019	29	25	3	1	-
2020	25	22	1	-	2
Total	152	128	16	4	3

issued in the period 2018–2020, while social media-related decisions were scarce in the early years of the decade considered.

2. Fundamental rights in national jurisprudence

Social media and similar user-generated content platforms are generally considered public fora enabling users to express themselves in flat, open, neutral spaces with the possibility of reaching a vast audience.[23] However, the exercise of freedom of expression online and the actual identification of its limits, as opposed to those related to legacy media, have been debated by Italian judges for quite some time. At the heart of the legal discussion has been differentiation between the legal treatment of social networking platforms and that of the traditional press; namely, whether and in what terms the existing rules on the press apply to the publication of content online. The lack of *ad hoc* regulation identifying and circumscribing the responsibility for texts divulged on the web in recent decades has led to constant questioning on the discipline applicable to the freedom of expression on Internet and specifically on the possibility of extending the regime related to the press. In this regard, there is a discrete corpus of decisions by the Court of Cassation concerning defamatory, degrading and insulting content published online which deal with the application of specific provisions of criminal law (e.g. Art. 595(3) Crim. Code), the special guarantee of prohibition of seizure of the press provided for in Article 21 Const. and provisions on the relevant liability of newspaper editors. All these issues presuppose as a preliminary step the legal qualification of social media and other online channels of expression, calling for an evolutionary and constitutionally oriented interpretation of the term "the press" by national judges.

In decision no. 31022/2015 mentioned previously, the Plenary Chamber of the Court of Cassation held that the constitutional principles and guarantees applicable to the printed press can be extended to the "online press" if it has the same structure and characteristics as the traditional press. In addition, the Court of Cassation reiterated its non-assimilation of social media to the press in evaluation of the case of aggravated defamation under Article 595(3) Crim. Code.

Consistently with this jurisprudence, in another decision,[24] the Court of Cassation excluded the applicability of the special regime of criminal liability for failure to control defamatory content published by the administrator of an Internet website under Article 57 Crim. Code,[25] as this rule is only applicable to newspapers but not to the various digital means of expression (forums, blogs, newsletters, newsgroups, mailing lists, Facebook, etc.).[26] By contrast, after initial uncertainty on the application of this special liability regime to directors of online journals – mostly due to the prohibition of analogy in *malam partem* under criminal law – the Court of Cassation built its *revirement* on a "figurative" notion of "the press", which corresponds to professional journalistic information, whether disseminated in print or on the web. The Italian Court of Cassation confirmed[27] the application to online journals not only of the constitutional guarantees in Article 21 Const. but also of provisions aimed at preventing the perpetration of crimes through the press, among which the provision in Article 57 Crim. Code is particularly important.

In addition to this "distinguishing" operation carried out by Italian judges for the application of the existing legal framework on the press to social media platforms, the case law on defamatory content online offers interesting insights into the blurred boundary between the exercise of freedom of expression and the publication of illicit content in digital environments. In this respect, the Italian case law on social media contains many examples which share the common element of laudable attempts to balance the relevant fundamental rights and individual interests involved.

For instance, the Court of Cassation in several cases has dealt with the question of whether or not making offensive statements about one's employer in a social media context can justify dismissal in accordance with domestic labour law. In decision 10280/2018, the Court of Cassation held that contested statements made on an employee's social media profile were defamatory, breached the trust relationship between the employee and the employer and therefore constituted "justified grounds" for dismissal.[28] By contrast, in decision 2499/2017, the Court of Cassation found that the publication of a denigrating image of the employer's trademark published by an employee in a Facebook chat did not amount to defamatory speech but to satire, and therefore, it did not justify dismissal.[29]

A similar outcome was reached in another case in which an employee was dismissed for "justified reasons" on the basis of information gathered through anonymous sources about offensive statements he had made about the company he worked for in a Facebook group chat.[30] However, the Labour Chamber of the Court of Cassation did not focus its reasoning on freedom of expression but on the protection of private communication under Article 15 Const. In particular, the Court noted that communication via Facebook groups was aimed at a closed group of people (in the case at hand, the members of a trade union) and was not intended to be open to the public. In addition, the judges observed that application of the constitutional guarantee regarding secrecy of communication precluded participants implicitly accepting dissemination of the content of a conversation to third parties.

On the contrary, there is another important decision in which the balance between the employee's right to confidentiality was sacrificed to protection of the company's assets. In a judgment of 27 May 2015, no. 10995, the Court of Cassation affirmed the legality of secret defensive controls carried out by an employer through the creation of a fake Facebook profile by staff members if they are aimed at ascertaining unlawful conduct other than a mere failure to perform work in quantitative and qualitative terms.[31] According to the judges, this form of control falls outside the scope of application of Article 4 of Law no. 300/1970 (the Italian workers' rights statute), which prohibits the use of remote monitoring equipment by employers, making its installation conditional on agreement with the relevant trade unions only when such equipment is made necessary by organisational and production requirements. By dwelling on the relevant jurisprudential precedents,[32] the Court of Cassation confirmed the legality of this type of hidden remote control, provided that it is not aimed at verifying mere failures to perform work and it is carried out in a non-invasive manner that respects the constitutional guarantees of freedom and dignity of workers. Hence, assessment of the proportionality of measures adopted to monitor employees should be conducted on a case-by-case basis, and it should take into account all the relevant interests involved.

Finally, with regard to social media, it is also worth mentioning a group of decisions concerning the exercise of freedom of expression by specific professional figures belonging to the state apparatus – e.g. parliamentarians and judges. Decision no. 313/2013 of the Italian Constitutional Court focused on a conflict of competences between the judiciary and parliament regarding the exemption of parliamentarians from liability for defamatory speech in the case of political speech. In particular, the case revolved around an allegedly defamatory speech by a member of the Italian Senate on the President of the Italian Republic, which can be punished under Article 278 Crim. Code.

Pursuant to Article 68(1) Const., the free speech of parliamentarians is subject to wider protection than the freedom of speech of other individuals if certain criteria are met. This constitutional provision provides that, before initiating any criminal proceedings against a member of parliament, the parliament should decide whether the impugned statements were functional to presenting (even aggressively) the political views of the parliamentarian. If such a "*functional nexus*" between the statements and political activity exists, the parliamentarian is immune from liability.

According to the Board for the Election and Immunities of the Parliament – the body in charge of authorising the start of criminal proceedings against a member of parliament – the statements in the case at issue should be interpreted as being related to the political activity of the parliamentarian concerned. They were accordingly covered by Article 68(1) Const. and liability for them was excluded. The Tribunal of Rome contested this decision. It held that the Board had overcome the limits of its competence because any analysis concerning the substance of the statements, and thus, whether they could qualify as political statements or not, could only be made by the judiciary. According to the tribunal, the Board was responsible for verifying the existence of a clear and direct connection between political activity and the statements made, whereas the courts were competent to assess the content of the statements.

As a result of the conflicting interpretations by the two institutions concerned, the Tribunal of Rome presented a plea to the Constitutional Court to solve the conflict of competence. The Constitutional Court interpreted the constitutional provision of Article 68(1) in the light of the evolution of the communication and technological context. The Constitutional Court acknowledged, in particular, that new means of communication, such as blogs and social networks, allowed immediate contact by politicians with the public.

However, it would be unreasonable to confirm the existence of a "functional nexus" between parliamentarians' statements and their political activity in all instances that they reached citizens, given the current trend towards a continual flow of communication by politicians on any subject via social media.[33] Such an interpretation would be too vague and could collide with the constitutional guarantee provided in Article 68 Const. on political speech. The case shows that the Constitutional Court has been eager to engage in an *evolutionary* interpretation of constitutional provisions in line with technological developments, opting for an "up-to-date" interpretation of the criterion of *functional nexus* that considers the new forms of political communication on social media.

In a later case, the Court of Cassation dealt with a case concerning defamatory statements made by a judge when participating in heated debate in the discussion forum of a blog.[34] The intervention by the judge was aimed at defending the work of the judiciary with strongly negative statements about the lawyers' bar association. The local council of the lawyers' bar association had condemned the use of such statements and its president had complained, in a letter, of an unjustified attack on the members of the association. The Disciplinary Section of the Judicial Council had subsequently found the judge responsible for damage to the reputation of the magistracy and for seriously incorrect conduct in the exercise of judicial functions under Article 2(1)(d) and Article 4(1)(d) of Legislative Decree 109/2006. The judge appealed against the decision before the Court of Cassation.

The Court of Cassation held that exercise of free speech by the judiciary did not qualify as exercise of judicial activity, even in relation to matters concerning the administration of justice. The Court of Cassation took the position that the role of judges in the administration of justice should not imply an excessive limitation on their ability to participate in public debate. This would amount to disproportionate limitation of their freedom of expression. Only when exercising judicial functions could a judge's free speech be limited, but again, under strict conditions.

3. Judicial interactions between Italian and European courts

The phenomenon of judicial interactions between courts at the European and national levels has been discussed by academics since the early 1990s, with an initial focus on the comparative jurisprudence method and different types and patterns of dialogue,[35] and then on the efforts of the judicial community to engage in mutual interactions, thanks to direct exchanges, training participation and networking activities with the aim of enhancing mutual trust, and consequently, opportunities for judicial dialogue.[36]

The Italian supreme and constitutional courts have participated in judicial dialogue on several occasions,[37] either by triggering dialogue – e.g. by presenting a preliminary ruling to the CJEU – or by contributing to the development of judicial discourse at the national level – e.g. by interpreting national provisions in the light of the jurisprudence of the CJEU or of the European Court of Human Rights (ECtHR). However, in the case law on social media, national judges have not exploited opportunities for judicial dialogue to the full potential. In only a few cases have higher courts discussed in detail the impact of European courts' decisions. In addition, among other arguments, references to European judgments have often presented a supporting argument for the final decision. However, there are some exceptions, and it is interesting that the relevant cases address sensitive issues that show the impact of social media, as opposed to legacy media, on the means of expressing individual opinions, particularly from the perspective of the freedom of expression of politicians and journalists.

Regarding the former, decision no. 313/2013 of the Constitutional Court – on parliamentarians' exemption from liability for defamatory speech in the case of political speech mentioned previously – supported part of its reasoning on two judgments by the ECtHR. In particular, the Constitutional Court referred to the ECtHR rulings in *Cordova v. Italy* and *CGIL and Cofferati v. Italy* to confirm that parliamentary immunity cannot include activities which are not related to the performance of parliamentary functions. In *Cordova v. Italy*, the ECtHR had accepted that states can afford immunity to members of parliament, noting that parliamentary immunity should not "*in principle be regarded as imposing a disproportionate restriction on the right of access to a court*" embodied in Article 6 ECHR on the right to a fair trial. However, parliamentary immunity should not be granted for statements that appear to have been made in the context of a personal quarrel. In fact, arguing otherwise would amount to a violation of Article 6(1) ECHR, restricting the right of individuals to have access to a court whenever allegedly defamatory statements are made by a parliamentarian. Similar conclusions were reached in *CGIL and Cofferati v. Italy.* Against this background, the Italian Constitutional Court affirmed that statements by a politician expressed with no connection to the exercise of parliamentary duties should be subject to judicial review in order to safeguard the right of access to justice.[38]

Regarding the distinction between social media and legacy media, another relevant distinction lies in the issue of journalists' free speech. On this point, it is important to stress that the Italian legal system is one of the few in European context where the qualification of journalist is subject to registration in a specific association (the so-called *ordine dei giornalisti*).[39] The legal qualification of journalists is based on the activity carried out, regardless of the means of communication used, be it a traditional medium or social media. The Court of Cassation affirmed this principle in its decision no. 21764/2021. The Court examined if the activity carried out in the press office of a public administration could be qualified as journalistic activity and consequently required registration with the *Istituto Nazionale di Previdenza dei Giornalisti Italiani* (INPGI). Although the case addressed the activity of a press office, the Court analysed the issue in more general terms, taking into account activities carried out both on legacy media and social media. In particular, the court referred to

CJEU and ECtHR jurisprudence in order to justify the need to evaluate the activity in a substantial manner rather than limiting its interpretation to formal criteria; namely, the fact that the individuals working in a press office are subject to the trade agreement applicable to professional journalists in public administration. In particular, the Court of Cassation referred to CJEU case C-73/07, *Satakun Markkinaporssi*, acknowledging that the CJEU equated the traditional press to the online press, considering irrelevant the medium used for publication and having regard only to the purpose of dissemination to the public of information, opinions or ideas. Then it mentioned the ECtHR decision in *Delfi As v. Estonia*,[40] in which the ECtHR recognised that websites greatly contribute to improving public access to current affairs and generally facilitate the communication of information.[41] Relying on this European case law, the Court of Cassation concluded that the activity carried out by the press office staff was characterised by creativity and originality like that of journalists, rather than being mere transfer of data and news concerning the public administration to the outside world.[42]

If the distinction between professional journalists and journalistic activity carried out on different types of media, including social media, has been interpreted in an extensive manner by the CJEU and the ECtHR, thanks to the supporting case law, the distinction between legacy and social media is still present in Italian jurisprudence. On this topic, the Italian supreme courts have also engaged with the jurisprudence of the ECtHR, although the level of detail of the analysis varies.

As was mentioned previously, on several occasions the Italian Court of Cassation has had the opportunity to address the qualification of social media vis-à-vis the definition of legacy media for the purpose of considering the legitimacy of an injunction to seize the online press, given the prohibition of seizure that applies to the printed press. Decision 31022/2015 of the Italian Court of Cassation was a landmark decision, and it provides clear guidelines in this area. By referring to ECtHR jurisprudence, the Court of Cassation affirmed that the principles and guarantees applicable to the printed press can only be extended to the "online press" if it has the same structure and characteristics as the printed press.[43] However, references to relevant ECtHR decisions, including *Fressoz and Roire v. France*, *Vogt v. Germany*, *Observer and Guardian v. United Kingdom* and *Wegrzynowski and Smolczewsky v. Poland*,[44] were not accompanied by specific analysis of their content but they were used by the Court of Cassation to support its argument on the role of the press as a watchdog for democracy.

National case law on defamation also offers useful insights into the dialogue between Italian courts and the ECtHR. In this regard, decisions by the Court of Cassation nos. 13993/2021 and 24579/2021 focused on the application of Article 595(3) Crim. Code, which provides the possibility of imposing detention in cases of defamation of "exceptional severity" in which the alleged defamatory content has been published on social media.[45] Decision of the Court of Cassation no. 13993/2021 addressed a claim of defamation against an individual who published some posts on Facebook attacking the activity of the deputy mayor of a municipality. The Court of Cassation provided a rich and detailed analysis of the compatibility of the Italian legal framework with Article 10 ECHR and with the jurisprudence of the ECtHR. First, the Italian judges referred to the leading case, *Cumpana and Mazare v. Romania*,[46] and recalled how the case law of the ECtHR requires proportionality of restrictive measures, with particular reference to criminal sanctions. In the case of a custodial sentence for a media-related offence, even if it is suspended, it can only be compatible with journalists' freedom of expression guaranteed in Article 10 ECHR in exceptional circumstances – in particular, when other fundamental rights have been seriously infringed, as, for example, in the case of hate speech and incitement to violence. The Court of Cassation applied the standard regarding exceptional circumstances to the case at stake and affirmed that the publication of false information could not qualify as "exceptional circumstances", as was also confirmed by the ECtHR decision in *Sallusti v. Italy*.[47]

Interestingly, the Court of Cassation focused on interpretation of the notion of "exceptional gravity" applied to defamation committed via means other than the traditional press; namely, social media communication. Relying on ECtHR jurisprudence, the Supreme Court judges held that application of a proportionality test is not limited to journalistic activity but that it also applies in other cases where the sanction may have a dissuasive ("chilling") effect. In particular, the Court of Cassation analysed in detail the decisions in *Morice v. France*[48] and *L.P. and Carvalho v. Portugal*,[49] in which the ECtHR stressed the potential impact of a sentence of detention on legal professionals.

The Court of Cassation linked this interpretation to a need to rethink the criteria for balancing freedom of expression and reputation by taking into account "*the rapid evolution of technology and the means of communication that has occurred in recent decades*" and the "*effects of rapid and lasting amplification of defamatory charges determined by social networks and internet search engines*".[50] On this basis, the Court concluded that detention could only be imposed in cases of exceptional gravity when journalistic activity is carried out on social media. Accordingly, the Court of Cassation quashed the appeal decision with regard to the sentence applied.[51]

Notably, the dialogue did not end there, as the Constitutional Court was called on to rule on the question of the constitutionality of Article 595 (3) Crim. Code on defamation for violation of freedom of expression enshrined in Article 21 Const. and Article 10 ECHR. With its decision no. 150/2021, the Court declared that Article 595 (3) of the criminal code complies with the constitutional principle of freedom of expression. In particular, the Constitutional Court argued that, when balancing freedom of expression and the right to dignity, one should consider that unlawful attacks disseminated via other means of publicity (including radio, television, online newspapers, other websites, social media and so on) might have a major impact on the private, family, social, professional and political life of victims. Accordingly, the legal system should provide suitable, necessary and proportionate instruments able to sanction relevant illegal conducts.

For this purpose, the Constitutional Court relied extensively on ECtHR jurisprudence.[52] Based on this, the Court of Cassation listed cases in which detention was deemed compatible with Article 10 ECHR. It is interesting to note that the Court pointed not only to the well-known case of hate speech and incitement to hatred, but it also mentioned the case of disinformation campaigns conducted through the press, internet or social media, in which the information disseminated may seriously damage the victim's reputation and the authors consciously falsify information. The Constitutional Court concluded that the standard provided in ECtHR jurisprudence may apply to Article 595(3) Crim. Code, and it recalled as a "correct" example the previously mentioned decision of the Court of Cassation no. 13993/2021.

4. Conclusion

Social media have had a strong impact on the jurisprudence of the highest courts in Italy. Not only have many cases had social media as a factual circumstance, but social media has also been included in judicial reasoning as a means with which a crime has been committed (e.g. in cases of stalking and harassment, incitement to commit a crime and terrorism) and, most importantly, as triggering a new or better-extended interpretation of constitutional and other legal provisions. Italian judges have solved the majority of social media cases by applying existing provisions in the national legal framework, even when they were not drafted taking into account the specificities emerging from the development of technology. Although the provisions were adopted before the diffusion of social media, judges have extended their scope of application through the lens of technological neutrality.

Although the majority of the social media cases identified have no fundamental rights dimension, those that do span across different fundamental rights: freedom of speech, press freedom, dignity and reputation, workers' liberty and copyright. The interplay between legacy media and social media, instead, has resulted in a cluster of cases addressing freedom of expression and balancing it with the right to dignity and reputation. These cases required the Court of Cassation to rethink the interpretation of Article 21 Const., and in particular, the extent to which the constitutional guarantees for the press may extend to social media. The Court of Cassation acknowledged that freedom of expression was enhanced by the use of social media, although the constitutional protection against seizure provided in Article 21(3) was not to be interpreted as applicable regardless of the means of communication – in fact, excluding social media from the scope of application of the constitutional provision. The Court of Cassation has provided guidelines to distinguish the press (either traditional or online) from other forms of communication that cannot qualify for the same constitutional guarantees (and which, at the same time, are not subject to the same obligations, such as liability for published content, editorial control, etc.).

The difference between legacy media and social media, instead, is no more relevant to protection of the right to dignity and reputation in the case of defamation. The internal dialogue among the Constitutional Court and the Court of Cassation as regards interpretation of Article 595(3) Crim. Code acknowledged that defamation can be qualified as aggravated when the press or any other means of publication is used. Therefore, activities of professional journalists (including freelance journalists) and defamation cases not related to the press come within the scope of application of the relevant criminal law provision. Moreover, the case law in this field provides clear examples of judicial interaction between Italian and European courts: decisions by the Constitutional Court and the Court of Cassation have analysed in detail the jurisprudence of the ECtHR, assessing whether and how Italian legislation complies with the "exceptional circumstances" standard of the ECtHR regarding cases in which detention can be imposed for defamation.

Concerning judicial interactions, analysis of Italian cases shows that reference to the jurisprudence of European courts is still limited, and where available, it leans more towards the jurisprudence of the ECtHR. The rulings cited have been used as supporting arguments strengthening domestic judicial reasoning by showing its consistency with interpretations by the ECtHR. On the other hand, use of the preliminary ruling procedure by national courts could enhance the possibility of receiving guidance from the CJEU on social media issues. This path has not been followed by Italian courts so far.

Notes

1 The research by Federica Casarosa in this article was supported by the ERDF project "CyberSecurity, CyberCrime and Critical Information Infrastructures Center of Excellence" (No. CZ.02.1.01/0.0/0.0/16_019/0000822).
2 Federica Casarosa, 'Technology-Neutral Legislation: Are Judges Able to Keep Pace With Technological Innovation?' <https://ssrn.com/abstract=4391702> accessed 17 March 2023.
3 Court of Cassation, decision no. 5658/1998.
4 Court of Cassation, decision no. 2129/1975.
5 Note that Art. 15(2) Cost. provides some limitations and allows the possibility to access communications, but only in the cases provided by law and on a decision by judicial authorities.
6 This criterion addresses the case of communication with multiple receivers (e.g. on a mailing list). It is important to verify if the sender has precisely identified a person or if it was irrelevant for the sender which person among a selected group would receive the message.
7 See Corrado Caruso, 'La libertà e la segretezza delle comunicazioni nell'ordinamento costituzionale' (2013) 10 *Forum di Quaderni Costituzionali Rassegna* 1 <www.forumcostituzionale.it/wordpress/images/stories/pdf/documenti_forum/paper/0427_caruso.pdf> accessed 3 October 2022.
8 See section 2 of this chapter and, in particular, Court of Cassation, decision no. 21965/2018.
9 See Italian Supreme Court, decision no. 31022/2015. More detailed analysis on this follows in section 2 of this chapter.
10 Court of Cassation, decision no. 24431/2015.
11 Article 600-ter Crim. Code reads: "[. . .] Anyone who [. . .], *by any means, including electronic ones*, distributes, discloses, disseminates or advertises pornographic

material [. . .], or distributes or discloses news or information aimed at soliciting or sexually exploiting children under the age of eighteen years, is liable to imprisonment for a period of between one and five years and a fine of between 2,582 and 51,645 euros". [*emphasis added*].

In this case, the decisions of the Italian Supreme Court have interpreted the provision in a teleological way, affirming that also a *threat* to distribute pornographic material through social networks could qualify as the crime defined in Article 600-ter Criminal Code. See decision 19112/2016 of 10 March 2016 and see more in Evangelia Psychogiopoulou, Federica Casarosa and Anna Kandyla, *Report on National Courts, Social Media and Convergence*, Deliverable of Compact project, 2019 <https://compact-media.eu/wp-content/uploads/2021/02/D2.2.pdf> accessed 3 October 2022.

12 Article 414 Crim. Code reads: "*(1) Anyone who publicly instigates to commit one or more offences shall be punished, for the sole fact of the instigation . . .*

(4) Apart from the cases referred to in Article 302, if the incitement referred to in the previous paragraphs concerns terrorist offences or crimes against humanity, the penalty is increased by half. The penalty is increased by up to two thirds if the act is committed by means of computer or telematic tools."

13 Court of Cassation, decision no. 22163/2019.

14 Court of Cassation, decision no. 22049/2020; Court of Cassation, decision no. 12062/2021.

15 Court of Cassation, decision no. 34512/2020.

16 Court of Cassation, decision no. 45141/2019.

17 And any *other cases, as specified by law*.

18 If the scrutiny leads to a finding of unconstitutionality, the national legislation will be eliminated with *erga omnes* effects. See Nicole Lazzerini, 'Dual Preliminarity Within the Scope of the EU Charter of Fundamental Rights in the Light of Order 182/2020 of the Italian Constitutional Court' (2020) *European Papers* 1463–1476. See more generally, Giuseppe Martinico and Giorgio Repetto, 'Fundamental Rights and Constitutional Duels in Europe: An Italian Perspective on Case 269/2017 of the Italian Constitutional Court and its Aftermath' (2019) 15 *European Constitutional Law Review* 731–751; Daniele Gallo, 'Challenging EU Constitutional Law: The Italian Constitutional Court's New Stance on Direct Effect and the Preliminary Reference Procedure' (2019) 25 *European Law Journal* 434; Antonio Ruggeri, 'Svolta della Consulta sulle questioni di diritto eurounitario assiologicamente pregnanti, attratte nell'orbita del sindacato accentrato di costituzionalità, pur se riguardanti norme dell'Unione self-executing (a margine di Corte cost. no. 269 del 2017)' (2017) 1 *Rivista di diritti comparati* 234.

19 See Diletta Tega, 'Il seguito in Cassazione della pronuncia della Corte costituzionale no. 269/2017: prove pratiche di applicazione' (*Questione giustizia*, 12 March 2018).

20 Notably, two recent decisions by the Tribunal of Rome concerning the legitimacy of the suspension by Facebook of the relevant pages and posts belonging to the right-wing Casapound party are noteworthy for their qualification of the social network and the application of constitutional freedoms under European and national law. In particular, because of the allegedly illegal content published by Casapound, the social media platform had promptly blocked access to them because they violated the platform's content policies and conditions. The defendants argued that these actions were not legitimate, as they restricted the freedoms of expression and of political speech. However, the Tribunal of Rome held that, due to the special position of Facebook in the political debate and social relationships, the platform-users' relationship was not confined to a merely private dimension. Instead, respect for constitutional and legal principles constituted both a condition and a limit for

Facebook in its relationship with users requesting access to its service. Therefore, besides amounting to a violation of contractual agreements, the content published by Casapound was also unlawful according to the entire fundamental rights system both at the European and national levels. As a result, Facebook was not only entitled to terminate the relevant contracts for violation of the specific contractual clauses accepted at the time of their conclusion, but it also had a legal duty to remove the contested content once it became aware of them, otherwise facing a risk of incurring liability in accordance with the European case law on intermediary liability.

21 These are Iusexplorer.it (Giuffrè) and Leggi d'Italia.it (Cedam).

22 The keywords used include the following: social media, social networks, online comment, online media, blogs, web forum, chat rooms, the internet, internet service provider, intermediary and the names of leading social media (e.g. Facebook, Twitter, etc.).

23 The jurisprudence of the Italian Court of Cassation is quite telling in this respect. Due to the criteria included in some criminal provisions (e.g. Article 660 Crim. Code on harassment and Article 612-bis Crim. Code on stalking), judges had to evaluate whether Facebook qualifies as a public space. Based on an extensive interpretation of the law, the Court of Cassation affirmed that Facebook is to be considered a place open to the public as it constitutes a "virtual" place open to access by anyone using the network (see Court of Cassation, decision no. 37596/2014.). For the same reason, in another case, the Court of Cassation held that the publication of merely mocking and derisive posts on a Facebook page freely accessible by anyone lacks the requirement of inevitable invasiveness connected with the sending of private messages (SMS, WhatsApp) and telephone calls, which is relevant to the perpetration of acts of stalking (see Court of Cassation, decision no. 34512/2020.)

24 Court of Cassation, decision no. 1275/2018.

25 Article 57 Crim. Code reads as follow: "*Without prejudice to the liability of the author of the publication and except for cases of complicity, the editor or the deputy editor in charge who fails to exercise control over the content of the periodical directed by him to prevent crimes being committed by means of the publication shall be punished for negligence*".

26 However, recently in decision no. 7220/2021 the Court of Cassation held that the manager of an internet site is not responsible for the crime of failure to control as under Article 57 Crim. Code. However, if there are elements that indicate co-participation in the offensive conduct carried out by a third party, the manager can be held responsible as an accomplice in the crime of aggravated defamation.

27 Court of Cassation, decision no. 13398/2017.

28 Court of Cassation, decision no. 10280/2018.

29 Court of Cassation, decision no. 2499/2017.

30 Court of Cassation, decision no. 21965/2018.

31 Court of Cassation, decision no. 10955/2015.

32 Court of Cassation, decision no. 2722/2012; Court of Cassation, decision no. 2117/2011.

33 In this regard, a judgment by the Italian Council of State (decision no. 769/2015) ruled that a tweet posted by a Minister does not have any legal value under public law as it does not meet the legally relevant requirement of being an "administrative act" under the existing legal framework, from which a legal change in external reality can be inferred. Specifically, the Italian judges stressed that a tweet qualifies as a form of informal communication *"even, and even more so, in the current age of mass communications, messages, twitterings, followings and so on, due to new technologies and the new and pervasive ways of communicating political activity"*.

34 Court of Cassation, decision no. 6965/17.

35 Cfr. Claire L'Heureux-Dubè, 'The Importance of Dialogue: Globalization and the International impact of the Rehnquist Court' (1998) *Tulsa Law Journal* 15; Jörge Polakiewicz and Valerie Jacob-Foltzer, 'The European Human Rights Convention in Domestic Law: The Impact of the Strasbourg Case Law in States Where Direct Effect is Given to the Convention' (1991) *Human Rights Law Journal* 125; Marie-Ann Slaughter, 'A Global Community of Courts' (2003) 44 *Harvard International Law Journal* 1, 191; Marie-Ann Slaughter, 'A Typology of Transjudicial Communication' (1994) *University of Richmond Law Review* 99.

36 The term "judicial dialogue" is the commonest term. However, it may be misleading as the reciprocity that characterises dialogue is not always present among judicial actors. In fact, except for the case of preliminary rulings, where a national court directly asks the CJEU questions and later applies the principles and guidelines received in the subsequent decision, communication among courts is implicit and can be better qualified as monologue. For an analysis of the wider discourse on judicial interactions, see Federica Casarosa and Madalina Moraru, 'Introduction', in Federica Casarosa and Madalina Moraru (eds), *The Practice of Judicial Interaction in the Field of Fundamental Rights. The Added Value of the Charter of Fundamental Rights of the EU* (Edward Elgar 2022) 3.

37 See the well-known Taricco saga, CJEU C-105/14, *Taricco and Others*, Judgment of the Court (Grand Chamber) of 8 September 2015, ECLI:EU:C:2015:555; and the subsequent C-42/17, *M.A.S. and M.B.*, Judgment of the Court (Grand Chamber) of 5 December 2017, ECLI:EU:C:2017:936.

38 See the more detailed analysis in Evangelia Psychogiopoulou and Federica Casarosa, 'Social Media Before Domestic Courts in Europe: An Analysis of Free Speech Cases' (2020) 27(6) *Maastricht Journal of European and Comparative Law* 791.

39 Law 69/1963 provides that a professional journalist should exclusively exercise the journalistic profession, and in order to get access to the *Ordine dei giornalisti*, the person should hold a university degree and attend a two-year university. After the academic activity, the aspiring journalist should do an internship and sit a state exam to be registered as a professional. Alternatively, the journalist can be qualified as a freelance. In this case, there is no compulsory academic activity nor exclusivity clause, as a freelancer can exercise the profession as a secondary activity. Some requirements still apply; namely, the yearly publication of a number of articles and proof of economic collaboration with an editorial publication.

40 ECtHR, *Delfi As v. Estonia*, App. No. 64569/09 (16 June 2015), para 133.

41 As supporting cases, but not discussed in detail, the Supreme court also mentioned the ECtHR decisions in *Ahmet Yildirim v. Turkey*, (appl. no.3111/10),18 December 2012, para 48, and *Times Newspapers ltd. v. the United Kingdom*, (appls. nos. 3002/03 and 23676/03), 10 March 2009, para 27.

42 The court expressly mentioned that the individuals "did not limit themselves to reporting the text of statements made by the various company representatives, but introduced and commented on the news, putting it within a more organic structure similar to an article in a common newspaper, using language and style typical of journalism".

43 Subsequently, the Italian Supreme Court took the same position in other cases focusing on defamatory speech published on social networks and blogs, citing Decision no. 31022/2015 as a basis for its reasoning (see decisions nos. 4873/2016, 12536/2016, 322/2017 and 16751/2018 of the Italian Supreme Court).

44 ECtHR, *Fressoz and Roire v. France* (appl. no. 29183/95), 21 January 1999; *Vogt v. Germany* (appl. no.17851/91) 26 September 1995; *Observer and Guardian v. United Kingdom* (appl. no. 13585/88), 26 November 1991; and *Węgrzynowski and Smolczewsky v. Poland* (appl. no. 33846/07) 16 July 2013.

45 Court of Cassation, decision no. 13993/2021 and Court of Cassation, decision no.24579/2021.
46 ECtHR, *Cumpănă and Mazăre v Romania*, (appl. no. 33348/96), 17 December 2004.
47 ECtHR, *Sallusti v Italy* (appl. no. 22350/2013), 7 March 2019.
48 ECtHR, *Morice v France* (appl. no. 29369/2010) 23 April 2015.
49 ECtHR, *Ramos Nunes de Carvalho e Sà v Portugal*, (Appls nos 55391/13, 57728/13, 74041/13) 6 November 2018.
50 This need for a reframing had already been pointed out by the Constitutional court in its decision no. 131/2020.
51 The Supreme Court also stated that any different treatment would be contrary to constitutional principles. Excluding detention only in the case of defamation committed in the exercise of journalistic activity would risk compromising the principle of equality (Art. 3(1) Const.) with respect to all citizens (in particular, those who commit such an act not in the exercise of journalistic activity) and the principle of reasonableness (Art. 3(2) Const.), by providing unfavourable sentencing treatment (imprisonment) for acts usually characterised by less serious diffusion, and therefore overall offensiveness, compared to those committed in the exercise of journalistic activity.
52 The Constitutional court – briefly – mentioned several decisions, including *Cumpănă and Mazăre v Romania*, (n.46), *Balaskas v. Greece* (Appl. no. 73087/2017, 5 November 2020), *Atamanchuk v. Russia* (Appl. no.4493/2011, 11 February 2020), *Sallusti v. Italy* (n 47), *Belpietro v. Italy* (appl. no. 43612/2010, 24 September 2013), and *Katrami v. Greece* (Appl. no. 19331/2013, 6 December 2007).

11 Social media before higher courts in Slovenia

Judicial caution in imposing restrictions

Tanja Kerševan

1. Introduction

Scholarly research has demonstrated that social media have become a powerful factor in spreading disinformation, systematic distortion of facts and populism,[1] contributing to political polarisation and fragmentation[2] and normalising hate speech.[3] Despite the increasingly central role of social media in individuals' lives and in political communication and the economy, in Slovenia, as in many European Union (EU) countries, there is no law specifically regulating social media. Regulation applying to social media is fragmented over distinct legal areas and shares basic principles with relevant EU legislation. Until the Digital Services Act (DSA)[4] package is implemented, the most relevant legal acts in Slovenia with provisions (also) applying to social media are the law transposing the current EU acquis on electronic commerce and sectoral laws on electronic communications and on audio-visual media services, together with the criminal and obligation codes.

The Electronic Commerce Market Act (ZEPT)[5] defines the scope of the liability of providers of information society services. The Code of Obligations (OZ)[6] contains basic tort principles, according to which social media and other digital intermediaries may be held liable for illegal internet content. The electronic communications legislation[7] has long remained unharmonised with EU law, since the government failed to transpose the 2018 European Electronic Communication Code (EECC)[8] in time and the European Commission initiated legal action against Slovenia in September 2021. The Audiovisual Media Services Act (ZAVMS)[9] contains provisions on video-sharing platforms (VSP) which may also apply to social media. It faithfully follows the amended Audiovisual Media Services Directive[10] with no significant national specifics. While the national regulatory authority, AKOS, is responsible for supervision, VSP providers are expected to take measures to protect children from harmful content and to prevent the spread of incitement to hatred and terrorism.

If a social media provider does not take action on its own in line with its moderating standards and practice, a court may order it to block or remove illegal content. Among the most common grounds for interfering with the right to expression on social media are breaches of privacy and protection of

DOI: 10.4324/9781003207085-13

personal information, unauthorised distribution of copyright-protected material, defamation and sexual abuse of children. The 2011 Directive on combating sexual abuse and sexual exploitation of children and child pornography[11] was transposed by amendments to the Criminal Code (KZ).[12] Decisions on blocking child-abuse content remain within the realm of the judicial branch. Other international standards related to illegal Internet content, including ones referring to sexual exploitation and sexual abuse of children, have been transposed into national law via laws ratifying Council of Europe conventions.

The Slovenian judiciary is one of the three branches of power in the country. It is entrusted with protecting rights and freedoms stipulated in the Constitution of the Republic of Slovenia, EU law, general principles of international law, international treaties and Slovenian law. According to the Constitution, the highest court in Slovenia is the Supreme Court of the Republic of Slovenia, except in the fields of protection of constitutionality, legality, human rights and fundamental freedoms, in which, in accordance with the constitutional order, the Constitutional Court of the Republic of Slovenia is the highest court. With an important precedential role, the remit of the Supreme Court includes decisions on regular and extraordinary legal remedies, and decisions in disputes over jurisdiction between lower courts and on the transfer of jurisdiction between courts. The Supreme Court is also responsible for managing the national case law database.

Despite an increase in the number of cases specifically related to social media in the last few years, Slovenian social media case law is still somewhat limited, especially at the level of the two highest courts; namely, the Supreme Court and the Constitutional Court. More lawsuits are pending in lower and higher courts, with some, especially high-profile criminal lawsuits involving prominent public figures and politicians, taking longer and sometimes ending without a verdict because of the statute of limitations. Most lawsuits in which social media do not appear only as evidence (e.g. due to the content posted on them) are related to defamation in the broad sense of the word. This can partly be attributed to an increased use of Twitter by politicians. Several Slovenian politicians, including the most powerful ones, such as Janez Janša,[13] who posted over 100,000 tweets on his personal Twitter account from early 2011 to mid-2020,[14] and some other highly visible political figures, are using Twitter and other digital platforms for online harassment and smear campaigns against journalists, public service media and other established media.[15] Despite being one of the few countries in the region in which defamation is criminalised and being criticised for this by international organisations advocating freedom of expression and media freedom,[16] the case law shows that Slovenian courts normally take into consideration freedom of expression and give it priority when deciding on defamation cases.

Constitutional reasoning in Slovenia accepts that free individuals capable of rational decision-making are the cornerstone of a democratically organised political system. An indispensable component of such a system is open public debate on matters of general interest. Freedom of expression protects the dissemination of not only opinions that are approved by the public but also critical and harsh statements. In accordance with the third paragraph of Article 15 of the Constitution of the Republic of Slovenia,[17] the constitutionally guaranteed right to freedom of expression (Article 39 Const.) is limited by the right to protection of personal dignity (Article 34 Const.) and protection of personal rights (Article 35 Const.), including the right to protection of honour and reputation. Constitutional case law further shows that, in a conflict between the right to protection of honour and reputation and the right to freedom of expression, very harsh and reckless statements may not be ruled illegal if the reader or listener is still able to understand them as criticism or opinions and not as attacks on personality, humiliation, contempt or ridicule. Fear of punishment for certain value judgments, sharpness, rudeness and exaggeration can cripple public debate and restrain its role in a democratic society. Due to the important contribution by political parties and political figures to political debate in a free democratic society, their right to freedom of expression enjoys a high level of protection.[18]

The same is true for privacy- and personal data-related issues, which, in Slovenia as elsewhere in the EU, are regulated by the General Data Protection Regulation (GDPR)[19] and also enjoy constitutional protection (Art. 35 Const.). While the GDPR sets common EU rules, some substantive and procedural issues may be specifically regulated by the Member States. In Slovenia, some specific areas are expected to be addressed by the revised Personal Data Protection Act (i.e. ZVOP-2), which is still in the legislative process. The right to protection of personal data is not an absolute right. In accordance with the principle of proportionality, this right must be interpreted in the light of its role in society and is to be balanced with other fundamental rights, especially freedom of expression and information, freedom of thought, conscience and religion, freedom of economic initiative, the right to an effective remedy and an impartial tribunal, and cultural, religious and linguistic diversity. In issues related to the protection of personal data on the Internet, Slovenian legislation and case law were impacted by the decision of the European Court of Human Rights (ECtHR) in the *Benedik v Slovenia* case.[20] In a subsequent, similar case that was brought before the Constitutional Court, the court took due account of this judgment and ruled that, in the case of a plaintiff convicted of defamation under the Criminal Code for an anonymous comment on a web portal, her dynamic IP address should be subject to the protection of communication privacy. The lower courts' finding that the plaintiff had not been justified in expecting privacy was therefore recognised as a violation of the right to communication privacy under the first paragraph of Article 37 of the Constitution.[21]

This chapter examines Slovenian case law on social media and similar Internet services. The focus is first on the treatment of fundamental rights in the national jurisprudence. An overview of the case law of Slovenian higher courts, including the Supreme Court and Constitutional Court, is provided in the following key areas: (i) criminal offences against honour and reputation;

(ii) discriminatory speech; and (iii) privacy online. In the second section of the chapter, interaction of Slovenian courts with the ECtHR and CJEU jurisprudence is discussed. The chapter concludes by highlighting the main findings.

2. Fundamental rights in national jurisprudence

Our discussion of the case law of Slovenian courts related to social media and Internet services with similar characteristics focuses on cases from three prominent areas selected based on the number of cases; the importance of the cases in shaping Slovenian social media regulation; and the level of public attention they stimulated between 1 January 2010 and 1 March 2022. Due to the small number of cases resolved by the Supreme Court and the Constitutional Court, the analysis also covers cases before higher courts. Relevant cases were identified by searching[22] the database managed by the Supreme Court, which also includes cases before higher courts of general jurisdiction and two courts with higher court status,[23] and the one managed by the Constitutional Court of the Republic of Slovenia, which offers access to the decisions of the Constitutional Court. Second, we selected a sample for closer analysis using the following criteria: (a) they constitute precedents; (b) they have legal importance; and, due to the potential to impact ongoing considerations of the future regulatory framework, also (c) the public resonance of the cases.

2.1 Defamation: freedom of expression vs. the right to honour and reputation

In Slovenia, the criminal offences against the honour and reputation of an individual that are punishable with a fine or imprisonment are listed in the 18th chapter of the Criminal Code (KZ-1). They are the following: insult, slander, defamation, calumny and malicious false accusation of crime. In contrast to Anglo-Saxon law, where a distinction is made between slander (oral insult) and libel (written insult or in another medium), Slovenian criminal law and case law distinguish between encroachments on honour and reputation in the media and in other less publicly exposed forms. Pursuant to Article 27 of KZ-1, all the listed criminal offences qualify as such only if committed intentionally, but they all also have in common a qualified form defining the circumstances when the perpetrator of an individual criminal offence is punished more severely. Normally, if these offences are committed via the media or similar public platforms, they are punished with a larger fine or imprisonment.

Insult (Art. 158), which is normally punishable with a fine or imprisonment of up to three months, is punishable with a larger fine or imprisonment of up to six months if committed via the media or similar public platforms. When the offender knows a statement capable of causing damage to the honour or reputation of another person to be false, defamation (Art. 159) is punished with a fine or imprisonment of up to six months. If committed via media or similar public platforms, it is punished with a higher fine or imprisonment of up to a year. If it had "grave consequences" for the offended party, the maximum penalty increases to two years in prison. Offensive accusation (Art. 160) is punished with a fine or imprisonment of up to three months, and if committed via the media or similar public platforms, with a higher fine or imprisonment of up to six months. If it had "grave consequences" for the offended party, the maximum penalty increases to a year in prison. The same is true for calumny (Art. 161), which is defined as asserting or circulating any information concerning the personal or family affairs of another person that could injure that person's honour and reputation. It is punished with a fine or imprisonment of up to three months. If committed via the media or similar public platforms, it is punished with a fine or imprisonment of up to six months. If, by its nature, the act of calumny may result in "grave consequences", the maximum penalty increases to a year in prison. Malicious false accusation of a crime (Art. 162) is an act of calumny in which the assertion consists of falsely accusing someone of a crime "with the intention of exposing that person to contempt". The penalty is a fine or imprisonment of up to three months. If committed via the media or similar public platforms, it is punished with a fine or imprisonment of up to six months.

In 2010, the Criminal Law Department of the Ljubljana Higher Court decided that, if an offence of defamation is committed via electronic publication, it represents a qualified form of the offence, for which, according to the provisions in the Law on Courts (ZS)[24] and the Law on Criminal Procedure (ZKP),[25] the district court has material jurisdiction.[26] In one of its subsequent decisions adopted in 2014, the same court (again its criminal law department) recognised online blogs as forms of public communication and highlighted that the mere fact of committing a fundamental crime through the media or on websites is sufficient for it to be legally defined as a qualified form of crime against honour and reputation.[27] The court deemed it irrelevant that the Ministry of Culture does not register blogs as media in the so-called Media Registry. For the court, it was crucial that the blog published online was a means of communication or electronic publication accessible to the widest possible global public. Among the important features of blogs in favour of their qualification as media activity in the broadest sense, the court listed the following elements: "the author's work in the field of mass communication is intended for any interested reader", "information potential", "possible consequences and influence", and "accessibility".

Similarly, in a case related not to defamation but to determining the liability of a hosting service provider, the Commercial Law Department of the Ljubljana Higher Court discussed the elements of online forums that can be treated as elements typical of media and concluded that the website under consideration was intended for the provision of information, comments and opinions which, according to the court, matched the definition of "programmes" in Article 2, paragraph 2 of the Mass Media Act (ZMed).[28] The court also compared the activity of forum moderators to that of editors:

> they exercise the right to pre-censor certain contributions. Likewise, editors in traditional media do not publish all the answers to certain messages. . . . Therefore, in the present case, this is not a 'chat room', as indicated by the complainant, but a service for the provision of certain information for the purpose of informing (satisfying educational and other needs of the public, and mass communication) in accordance with Article 2, paragraph 2, ZMed (3).[29]

In other words, in the chat room, the court recognised constitutive elements of media outlets. However, three years later in 2016, the same court (commercial law department) ruled in a defamation case that publication on a forum (web chat room), as part of a (specialised) website, was not comparable to publication in the media and that insults committed via forums are not that serious, also because:

> The forums are primarily intended for exchange of personal opinions of individuals, and the register of expression is usually lower, often polemic and often in a conversational language (as the complainant acknowledges), and which may have a deteriorating tone without the author having the purpose of slander or insult.[30]

With the passing of time, this interpretation has been solidified and was confirmed, for example, in a judgment of Ljubljana Higher Court's Civil Law Department in 2017.[31] According to the court, the standards for objectivity in online forums are lower, so the plaintiff's claim of damage to reputation was not justified. In addition, the court decided that the operator of an online forum is not obliged to verify the truth of all posts but is only obliged to respond to notices received and remove any offensive and illegal messages, which is in line with the notice-and-action approach supported in the E-Commerce Directive.[32]

Recently, in a highly debated case, two journalists, Evgenija Carl and Mojca Šetinc Pašek,[33] sued the leader of the largest opposition political party and Deputy (and for some time during the proceedings also Slovenian Prime Minister), Janez Janša, for insulting statements on Twitter. The Celje District Court first sentenced Janez Janša to three months of suspended imprisonment with a probation period of one year and ordered him to pay the costs of the court proceedings in connection with the offensive tweet to the expense of the journalists. Both journalists also sued Janša for damages.[34] In May 2020, the Higher Court in Celje upheld the judgment of the Velenje District Court of the amount of €6,000 in damages to Eugenija Carl and ordered Janša to reimburse the costs of the civil proceedings.[35] In separate proceedings, the Supreme Court then rejected Janša's request for a review of the proceedings in which the higher court upheld the judgment related to Evgenija Carl but approved his request for a review in the Mojca Šetinc Pašek case.[36] Following the ruling of the Supreme Court, Mojca Šetinc Pašek filed an appeal with the Constitutional Court.[37]

Thus, in its decision, the Supreme Court adopted a position that criticism can be greater for journalists than for private individuals, especially when the criticism relates to journalists' behaviour linked with their socially important position, and allowed the revision of the lower court judgment. The fact that the insulting statement was made on Twitter, with Janez Janša having almost 40,000 followers at the time of his tweet, was not at the forefront of the judicial review in this particular case. Nevertheless, the Supreme Court drew a few important conclusions to explain, on the one hand, why the tweets did not have the damaging effect claimed by the plaintiff, and on the other hand, why over-sanctioning political expression on Twitter could have chilling effects on Members of Parliament and detrimental consequences for freedom of expression, the development of a democratic society and pluralism. In doing so, the court referred to the specificity of Twitter as a social network and its "specific style and mode of expression".[38] According to the Supreme Court, in the light of their role and the associated institutional responsibility, journalists should accept a higher tolerance threshold, such as is expected of holders of important public positions. While acknowledging that the Supreme Court is obliged to protect the constitutional rights of individuals against abuses of freedom of expression while at the same time being careful not to jeopardise democratic debate, the prevailing view of the majority of the Supreme Court Chamber was that freedom of political expression should be given priority over the journalist's right to honour and reputation.

Nevertheless, just one day before the statute of limitations expired, the Higher Court upheld the conviction of the first instance court which sentenced Janez Janša to three months in prison with a probation period of one year. The court concluded that Janša's tweet was a rude, sexist and offensive statement, and an *ad personam* attack on the journalist. It ruled that the first instance court had properly struck a balance between the rights at stake.[39]

2.2 *Hate speech: freedom of expression and personal data protection vs. human dignity and protection from discrimination*

The issue of hate speech online has been very polarising in Slovenia and can be linked, on the one hand, with the rise of populism,[40] and on the other hand, with fear that mistakes from the past, when so-called "verbal delict"[41] was prosecuted in the former political regime in ex-Yugoslavia, would be repeated.[42] Since Slovenia's independence in 1991, the definition of illegal hate speech has been amended several times. In 2012, the applicability of Article 297 of the Criminal Code (KZ-1) was restricted to only punishing conduct which is "either carried out in a manner likely to disturb public order or which is threatening, abusive or insulting", as stipulated in Council Framework Decision 2008/913/JHA.[43] In 2013, the Supreme State Prosecutor's Office issued a position[44] on the prosecution of hate speech limiting the interpretation of Article 297 of the Criminal Code (KZ-1) to cases with elements of a clear and present threat to public order and thus ignoring hate speech that was merely threatening, abusive or insulting.[45] The opinion affected judicial practice and, while it protected freedom of speech to the maximum, it also prevented effective prosecution of hate speech. Following an escalation of public dispute over the perceived mounting presence of hate speech on social media, several legal theorists increasingly looked for ways to expand the field of crime in Article 297 of KZ-1.[46] They criticised the position of the Supreme State Prosecutor's Office as being unfounded, demonstrating that it significantly interfered with the text of the legal provision in Art. 297 of KZ-1. The then attorney at law Rok Čeferin (currently Vice President of the Constitutional Court) claimed that the hate speech problem in Slovenia did not originate in the law but in the practice of prosecutors who set excessively high standards for what constitutes the offence of hate speech and described this as embarrassing:

> If we advocate an absolute freedom of expression for fear of excessively limiting it, it means that we protect this right while at the same time trampling on what is on the other side of the scales: the right to personal dignity and the safety of de-privileged groups and individuals.[47]

According to Rok Čeferin, it is necessary to protect all human rights and strike a balance between them. Each of them should be limited to the extent that allows the same level of the exercise of another right to be obtained. Čeferin's analysis of the case law in the period 2004–2010[48] points to the important work of the Constitutional Court, which, in more than half the cases reviewed, adopted a different position to that of the lower courts, bringing domestic case law closer to the standards of ECtHR case law. His key finding is that the domestic courts are more restrictive of the right to freedom of expression and press freedom than the ECtHR and also that Slovenian ordinary courts are more restrictive than the Constitutional Court, which has adopted criteria and standards set in ECtHR case law.

On assuming office in 2017, General State Prosecutor Drago Šketa listed the prosecution of hate speech as a priority.[49] An Expanded Expert Committee of Supreme Prosecutors discussed a proposal to intensify the prosecution of hate speech in 2018 but it did not endorse stricter penalisation of hate speech. The legal position from 2013, which was not binding on prosecutors, was, in their opinion, still appropriate and valid in 2018. However, a year later, in 2019, an important overturn of the previous practice occurred. In a case of hostile and threatening comments against the Roma published in 2011 in the comment section of a local radio station website, the Supreme Court ruled that public incitement to hatred, violence or intolerance is a criminal offence both in cases that may actually threaten public order and peace and in cases of just expressed threats and insults.[50]

Despite a slight increase in hate speech being penalised following this change of interpretation,[51] the case law on online hate speech is still scarce. This can be partly attributed to the fact that civil proceedings against unknown persons cannot be instituted in Slovenia. Data on the perpetrator of damage can only be obtained in criminal proceedings. Due to the constitutional protection of the right to privacy and confidentiality of communication[52] and the lack of regulation of the rights of anonymous commentators and offended individuals,[53] Slovenian legislation does not allow easy identification of authors of online posts using the IP number or other information. In the case of anonymous hate speech on social media, identifying the defendant, which is a prerequisite for filing a civil lawsuit, is practically impossible or at least very difficult. In addition, in the current framework, the liability of social media providers and other digital intermediaries used by individuals to spread hate speech is not as clear as it is for the traditional media.[54]

2.3 *Private vs. public on social media: freedom of expression and privacy online*

A judge in the District Court in Ljubljana, Urška Klakočer Zupančič, engaged in a critical and sharp exchange over the government on her Facebook account in 2020. Her posts were re-published by Vinko Gorenak, then State Secretary in the Office of the Prime Minister of the Republic of Slovenia, on his blog.[55] The judge was consequently relieved of her duties as Head of the Condominium Department and disciplinary proceedings were instituted against her before the Ethics and Integrity Commission of the Judicial Council. The question of whether the judge had violated the Code of Judicial Ethics and the provisions of the Judicial Service Act, thus committing a disciplinary offense or perhaps even a civil tort, was addressed by weighing the judge's freedom of expression, which is guaranteed by Article 39 of the Constitution, against protection of the reputation, independence and impartiality of the judiciary. Article 2(1) of the Judicial Service Act (ZSS, last reviewed in 2013),[56] stipulates that a judge must always act in the exercise of his or her rights in such a way as to protect the impartiality and independence of the trial and the reputation of the judicial service. Based on the second paragraph of Article 53 of the Judicial Council Act (ZSSve, 2017),[57] judges are also obliged to respect the Code of Judicial Ethics (2017),[58] both when performing judicial service and outside it.

Faced with disciplinary procedures, Judge Klakočar left her job and filed a private criminal lawsuit against State Secretary Vinko Gorenak, accusing him of the crime of illegal publication of private writings. Her records had been published on a closed Facebook profile and were not available to the general public. The parties later reached a court settlement,[59] according to which the defendant undertook to withdraw the disputed publication from his blog and to request its withdrawal from media outlet website Nova24TV within three days. Accordingly, the private, criminal action was withdrawn and all the criminal claims waived. Moreover, the three-member senate of the Ethics and Integrity Commission did not find any violation of the Judicial Service Act[60] (Felc 2021). The disciplinary proceedings against Judge Urška Klakočar Zupančič ended with the judge being acquitted.[61]

In an earlier, similarly high-profile case, the Supreme Court upheld the plaintiff's claim in which she requested a blog post on her sex life to be removed from a website operated by the national telecommunications operator Telekom Slovenia. A regular blogger (first defendant) in a special section of an online news and entertainment portal, Miha Guštin, posted an offensive text on the female writer in which he referred to her alleged sexual conduct and relationships in very explicit terms. The plaintiff, Ana Jud, claimed her rights to privacy, reputation and honour were violated and wanted the website operator (second defendant) to remove the contested blog post. The courts of first and second instance (i.e. district and higher) did not adhere to these arguments and found that, since it was evident from the first defendant's text that it merely summarised the content of Jud's book as it had been presented at her press conference, the plaintiff's claims were not justified. The Supreme Court, on the other hand, found that, even if the Internet was to be taken as part of a modern open dialogue, the text of blogger was not intended to inform the public or seek the truth. Instead, it sought the personal disqualification of the plaintiff, reflected in the fabrication of facts and leading to harassment and embarrassment in the light of the social consensus that open and frequent sexual activity was not appropriate for a young woman (especially if it was intended for other purposes than reproduction). The Supreme Court upheld the plaintiff's request for the contested blog post to be removed.[62]

In another case, which had a final epilogue at the ECtHR, the plaintiff appealed to the Constitutional Court and claimed violation of his rights under Articles 37 and 38 of the Constitution, since the judgment of a district court against him – i.e. for the criminal offence of possession and distribution of child sexual abuse material – had been based on evidence obtained by violating his right to privacy of communication. The Constitutional Court concluded that the object of protection in Article 37 of the Constitution is exclusively communication in relation to which a person reasonably expects privacy. According to the Court, obtaining information on the plaintiff's dynamic IP address did not constitute interference in his right to privacy of communication, since the plaintiff himself had given up his privacy when he had revealed his IP address to the file-sharing programme, and therefore, he could not have a legitimate expectation of privacy.[63] In *Benedik v Slovenia*,[64] the ECtHR disagreed with the Constitutional Court and decided that there had been a violation of Article 8 of the European Convention on Human Rights (ECHR) on the right to respect for private and family life with regard to the failure of the Slovenian police to obtain a court order before accessing subscriber information associated with the plaintiff's dynamic IP address. According to the ECtHR, the legal provision used by the Slovenian police to access subscriber information associated with a dynamic IP address without first obtaining a court order did not meet the ECHR standard of being "in accordance with the law". The ECtHR also highlighted that there was no control over how the police applied the statutory provision. According to the ECtHR, the legal framework was not sufficiently clear, did not offer adequate protection against arbitrary interference, did not have any safeguard against potential abuse and did not provide for independent supervision of police powers. The ECtHR awarded the convict €3522 to reimburse court costs, but no damages. The legislation which the ECtHR found inadequate has since been corrected and a similar case that was brought before the Constitutional Court was ruled on taking into account the ECtHR decision.[65]

3. Judicial dialogue with the CJEU and the ECtHR

The evidence from the cases examined shows that judicial dialogue with the ECtHR has been more frequent than judicial dialogue with the CJEU. Overall, however, ECtHR/CJEU case law is rarely mentioned in the case law of the Slovenian higher courts analysed. References to relevant provisions in the ECHR and to EU law are more common. Judgments of the Supreme Court and the Constitutional Court contain more references to various ECtHR cases, and in some cases, to the jurisprudence of other EU and European countries. Comparison over time indicates that judicial dialogue is becoming increasingly present and substantive.

ECtHR jurisprudence was referred to in the reasoning of the Constitutional Court in five decisions related to social media and other internet services in the period between 1 January 2010 and 1 March 2022. In the case of the Supreme Court, this occurred in eight cases. The ECtHR cases referred to include *Lingens v Austria*, *Thorgeir Thorgeirson v Iceland*, *The Observer and Guardian v UK*, *Jacubowski v Germany*, *Von Hannover v Germany No. 2*, *Axel Springer AG v Germany*, *M. L. and W. W. v. Germany*, *Węgrzynowski and Smolczewski v Poland* and many others.[66] There have also been examples in which courts have mentioned the case law of other countries; for instance, in relation to the German doctrine on the liability of hosting providers, as in the so-called *Alone in the Dark* case of the German Federal Court of Justice (BGH).[67]

In a study conducted in 2004, it was found that references to the ECHR and to the jurisprudence of the European Commission of Human Rights and the ECtHR had been steadily increasing since the ratification of the ECHR in 1994:

> This led to a situation where there are practically no major decisions not resulting from an analysis of ECtHR decisions. In doing so, the Constitutional Court referred to the ECHR and ECtHR jurisprudence even in cases where the complainants did not mention them in their applications.[68]

Authors[69] agree that, especially when it comes to the collision between freedom of expression and the rights of others, the Slovenian Constitutional Court looks up to the ECtHR when balancing competing rights.[70] The judicial dialogue the courts engage in ranges from simple referencing to comparative reasoning. The courts at the highest level mention ECtHR and CJEU cases to substantiate their reasoning in cases where there is an absence of domestic case law; for example, regarding the right to be forgotten, or with the aim of strengthening and corroborating domestic judicial reasoning in cases of conflicting fundamental rights.

4. Conclusion

In the case law studied and the relevant literature, there is evidence supporting the conclusion that a main characteristic of Slovenian case law is a certain caution and reserve when it comes to the application of restrictions on communication on social media and digital forms of communication with similar features. In the absence of specific rules dealing with social media and other online communication services, judges follow a case-by-case approach with attention to the specific circumstances and context of each case. Therefore, on the one hand, there are cases in which digital platforms are recognised as regular media and treated accordingly, while, on the other hand, there are also cases in which judges acknowledge lower standards in online communication.

The cases analysed confirm that freedom of expression is highly valued in Slovenian jurisprudence. Normally, it is unlikely to be significantly limited by other rights, especially in the case of public figures, journalistic expression and political speech. In the event of a conflict between two human rights, the case law indicates that the Constitutional Court consistently engages in a substantive assessment of both rights, including benchmarking the significance of the rights involved and evaluating the severity of the intervention, all in the light of the specific circumstances of the case. Especially in cases related to journalistic reporting, weighing of conflicting human rights in decisions by the Constitutional Court and the Supreme Court has been repeatedly in favour of freedom of journalistic expression. Even in cases focused on online communication, the courts first examine whether such communication has any elements of journalism or a media outlet. However, in a case involving a conflict between political speech and journalistic honour, the Supreme Court gave priority to political speech, warning against possible chilling effects in the realm of politics instead of journalism.

The evolution of Slovenian regulation of the Internet has been quite dynamic, with a few slips towards restrictiveness, especially in administrative measures aimed at protecting the business interests of a highly regulated national gambling industry. So far, there have been no specific regulations or coherent public policies on social media, which may, however, change in the foreseeable future, as has been announced by the government as a result of the nascent EU framework on digital platforms. The absence of targeted regulation is reflected in the national case law on online communication, which is still somewhat limited, especially at the higher judiciary level. Most of the case law deals with the right to reputation and honour (of either legal or physical persons). Another area that appears more often is privacy. Both the legal framework and the case law indicate sensitivity to safeguarding freedom of expression online while also protecting personal rights in justified cases. The most contested issue remains the question of prosecution of hate speech, which, so far, is very rare but is receiving increasing attention from politicians, the judiciary and the general public.

While mentions of relevant provisions in the ECHR and in EU legislation are present in the jurisprudence analysed, references to ECtHR/CJEU case law are seldom made, especially in lower instances. Cases of the Supreme Court and particularly of the Constitutional Court contain significantly more references to various ECtHR cases and occasionally also to the national case law of other EU and European countries. These mentions are normally used to substantiate Slovenian courts' decisions in cases involving conflicting fundamental rights and in cases where there is no domestic case law available. This confirms the importance of European case law in the development of judicial reasoning in Slovenia when it comes to social media. Social media are no longer a new phenomenon but the case law in this area is still being established.

Notes

1 Yochai Benkler, Robert Faris and Hal Roberts, *Network Propaganda* (Oxford Scholarship Online 2018); Samantha Bradshaw and Philip N Howard, 'The Global Organization of Social Media Disinformation Campaigns' (2018) Journal of International Affairs 71(1).
2 Joshua A Tucker et al., 'Social Media, Political Polarization, and Political Disinformation' (2018) <http://dx.doi.org/10.2139/ssrn.3144139> accessed 2 February 2022.
3 Silvio Waisbord, 'Truth is What Happens to News' (2018) 19(13) *Journalism Studies.*
4 Proposal for a Regulation of the European Parliament and of the Council on a Single Market for Digital Services (Digital Services Act) and amending Directive 2000/31/EC COM/2020/825 final [2020].
5 Zakon o elektronskem poslovanju na trgu – ZEPT (Electronic Commerce Market Act) [2009] Official Gazette of the Republic of Slovenia, No. 61/2006, 96/09 – official consolidated text, 19/15 in 189/21 – ZDU-1M.
6 Obligacijski zakonik – OZ (Obligation Code OZ) [2007] Official Gazette RS, No. 97/07 – official consolidated text, 64/16 – odl. US in 20/18 – OROZ631.
7 Zakon o elektronskih komunikacijah – ZEKom-1 (Electronic Communications Act) [2017] Official Gazette RS, No. 109/12, 110/13, 40/14 – ZIN-B, 54/14 – odl. US, 81/15, 40/17 & 189/21 – ZDU-1M.
8 Directive (EU) 2018/1972 of the European Parliament and of the Council of 11 December 2018 establishing the European Electronic Communications Code (Recast) [2018] OJ L 321/18.
9 Zakon o avdiovizualnih medijskih storitvah – ZAVMS (Audiovisual Media Services Act) [2021] Official Gazette RS, No. 87/11, 84/15 in 204/21.
10 Directive (EU) 2018/1808 of the European Parliament and of the Council of 14 November 2018 amending Directive 2010/13/EU on the coordination of certain provisions laid down by law, regulation or administrative action in Member States

concerning the provision of audio-visual media services (Audiovisual Media Services Directive) in view of changing market realities [2018] OJ L 303/69.

11 Directive (EU) 2011/93 of the European Parliament and of the Council of 13 December 2011 on combating the sexual abuse and sexual exploitation of children and child pornography, and replacing Council Framework Decision 2004/68/JHA [2011] OJ L 335/1.

12 Kazenski zakonik – KZ-1 (Criminal Code) [2021] Official Gazette RS, No. 50/12 – official consolidated text, 6/16 – popr., 54/15, 38/16, 27/17, 23/20, 91/20, 95/21 & 186/21.

13 Janez Janša has been one of the leading figures in Slovenian politics for more than 30 years. He has led one of the strongest political parties, the Slovenian Democratic Party, since 1993 and served as Prime Minister of Slovenia three times, in 2004–2008, 2012–2013 and 2020–2022.

14 Jernej Amon Prodnik, 'Donald Trump: veliki komunikator? Se premier Janša zgleduje po njem? (Donald Trump: A great communicator? Is Prime Minister Janša inspired by him?) *Večer* (24 October 2020) 20, 21.

15 Blaž Petkovič, 'Ko se nasilje nad novinarji iz ust politikov prenese v fizični prostor: "In ne slepomišimo, to sovraštvo ima ime"' (When Violence against Journalists is Transferred from the Mouths of Politicians to Physical Space: "And Let's Not Go Blind, This Hatred Has a Name)" (2021) *Večer* < https://moj.vecer.com/slovenija/ko-se-nasilje-nad-novinarji-iz-ust-politikov-prenese-v-fizicni-prostor-in-ne-slepomisimo-to-sovrastvo-ima-ime-10251896> accessed 1 February 2022.

16 IPI, 'Slovenian Investigative News Outlet Necenzurirano Hit with 39 SLAPP Lawsuits' (2020) <https://ipi.media/slovenian-investigative-news-outlet-necenzurirano-hit-with-39-slapp-lawsuits/> accessed 3 February 2022; OSCE, 'Journalists in Slovenia Should Not Face Criminal Charges for Their Work, OSCE Representative Says', (2015) www.osce.org/fom/143006 accessed 3 February 2022.

17 Constitution of the Republic of Slovenia 1991 (and subsequent changes, the last in 2021).

18 For example, Up-515/14 [2017] Constitutional Court of the Republic of Slovenia (RS); VSRS Sodba II Ips 75/2019 [2020] Supreme Court of RS.

19 Regulation (EU) 2016/679 of the European Parliament and of the Council of 27 April 2016 on the protection of natural persons with regard to the processing of personal data and on the free movement of such data, and repealing Directive 95/46/EC (General Data Protection Regulation) (Text with EEA relevance) [2016] OJ L 119/1.

20 *Benedik v Slovenia* App. no. 62357/14 (ECtHR, 24 April 2018).

21 Cf. Up-540/11 [2014] Constitutional Court of RS; Up-153/17 [2021] Constitutional Court of RS.

22 Our search employed a set of generic keywords or tags – i.e. social media, social networks, social network/networking (sites), user-generated content, online comment, online media, news portals, blogs, web forum, website, Internet service provider, intermediary. Additionally, we searched for mentions of the most common brands of international and Slovenian social media and Internet services that share characteristics with social media – in particular, connective communication, user-generated content and interactivity.

23 I.e. the Higher Labour and Social Court and the Administrative Court of the Republic of Slovenia.

24 Zakon o sodiščih – ZS (Courts Act) [2020] Official Gazette of the Republic of Slovenia, No. 94/07 – official consolidated text, 45/08, 96/09, 86/10 – ZJNepS, 33/11, 75/12 – ZSPDSLS-A, 63/13, 17/ 15, 23/17 – ZSSve, 22/18 – ZSICT, 16/19 – ZNP-1, 104/20 and 203/20 – ZIUPOPDVE.

25 Zakon o kazenskem postopku – ZKP (Criminal Procedure Act) [2021] Official Gazette of the Republic of Slovenia, no. 176/21 – official consolidated text.

26 VSL Sklep V Kp 201/2010 [2010] Higher Court in Ljubljana.
27 VSL Sodba II Kp 13079/2012 [2014] Higher Court in Ljubljana.
28 Zakon o medijih – ZMed (Mass Media Act) [2016] Official Gazette of the Republic of Slovenia, No. 110/06 – official consolidated text, 36/08 – ZPOmK-1, 77/10 – ZSFCJA, 90/10 – odl. US, 87/11 – ZAvMS, 47/12, 47/15 – ZZSDT, 22/16, 39/16, 45/19 – dec. US, 67/19 – dec. US and 82/21).
29 VSL sklep I Cpg 862/2013 [2013] Higher Court in Ljubljana.
30 VSL Sodba I Cpg 1419/2015 VSL [2016] Higher Court in Ljubljana.
31 VSL sodba I Cp 3097/2016 [2017] Higher Court in Ljubljana.
32 Directive 2000/31/EC of the European Parliament and of the Council of 8 June 2000 on certain legal aspects of information society services – in particular, electronic commerce, in the Internal Market ('Directive on electronic commerce') [2000] OJ L 178/1. On Directive 2000/31 see Chapter 1 in this volume.
33 Mojca Šetinc Pašek decided to leave journalism, joined a newly formed political party, ran in the 2022 parliamentary elections and became an MP.
34 RT 'Janez Janša obsojen na pogojno zaporno kazen (Janez Janša sentenced to a suspended prison sentence)' (2021) *Vestnik* <https://vestnik.si/clanek/slovenija/padla-odlocitev-celjskega-sodisca-947259> accessed 1 February 2022.
35 VSC Sodba Cp 131/2019 [2020] Higher Court in Celje.
36 VSRS Sodba II Ips 75/2019 [2020] Supreme Court.
37 At the time of submitting this chapter, the Constitutional Court had not yet ruled on the matter.
38 VSRS Sodba II Ips 75/2019 [37] Supreme Court [37].
39 The limitation period was stopped by the pronouncement of the judgment and the judgment is final, but Janša's attorney announced an appeal to the Supreme Court. By the time of submission of this chapter, the case was not available in the jurisprudence public database. The details on the rulings were taken from news reports – e.g. Špela Kuralt, 'Janez Janša pravnomočno obsojen zaradi žaljivega tvita' (Janez Janša Sentenced in Final Judgment for Offensive Tweet) (2022) *Delo* <www.delo.si/novice/crna-kronika/janez-jansa-pravnomocno-obsojen-zaradi-zaljivega-tvita/> accessed 1 February 2022.
40 Andrej Motl and Veronika Bajt, 'Sovražni govor v Sloveniji: pregled stanja', in *Hate Speech in Slovenia: An Overview of the Situation* (Mirovni inštitut 2016).
41 In the former Yugoslavia, "verbal delict", such as singing certain (nationalist) songs or expressing hostile statements against the regime, was punishable as a crime of "hostile propaganda" as stipulated in Article 133 of the Criminal Code until 1990. During the 1970s and 1980s, approximately 500 lawsuits were filed against "verbal delinquents" every year. For more details, see <http://cultural-opposition.eu/registry/?uri=http://courage.btk.mta.hu/courage/individual/n222586> accessed 1 February 2022.
42 Centre for Human Rights and the Ombudsman of the Republic of Slovenia, 'Kazenskopravni pregon sovražnega govora v Sloveniji po 297. členu kazenskega zakonika (KZ-1): analiza tožilske prakse pregona kaznivega dejanja javnega spodbujanja sovraštva, nasilja in nestrpnosti v obdobju 2008–2018' (Criminal prosecution of hate speech in Slovenia under Article 297 of the Criminal Code (KZ-1): Analysis of prosecutorial practice regarding the criminal offence of public incitement to hatred, violence and intolerance in the period 2008–2018) [2021] <www.varuh-rs.si/fileadmin/user_upload/pdf/Razne_publikacije/Sovrazni_govor_knjizica2.pdf> accessed 2 February 2022.
43 Council Framework Decision 2008/913/JHA of 28 November 2008 on combatting certain forms and expressions of racism and xenophobia by means of criminal law [2008] OJ L 328/55.

44 Supreme State Prosecutor's Office, Pregon kaznivega dejanja Javnega spodbujanja sovraštva, nasilja ali nestrpnosti po 297. členu KZ-1 – pravno stališče, Ktr 2/13–6/HJ-TL/vg, 27. 2. 2013 (Prosecution of the criminal offence of Public Incitement to Hate, Violence and Intolerance under Article 297 KZ-1 – Legal Position, Ktr 2/13–6/HJ-TL/vg, 27 February 2013) [2013].

45 Aleš Završnik, 'Zakaj obsodb sovražnega govora v Sloveniji ni? od okov implementacije do rigidnosti razlage', in *Zagovor javnosti: med svobodo izražanja in sovražnim govorom (Why Are There no Condemnations of Hate Speech in Slovenia? From the Shackles of Implementation to the Rigidity of Interpretation)* (SAZU, Razprave – Dissertationes 33, 2017) 101.

46 Jan Stajnko, Sedin Kičin and Luka Martin Tomažič, 'Kriminalitetnopolitično razumevanje 297. člena KZ-: sovražni govor in dva koncepta svobode (Criminal-Political Understanding of Article 297 of Criminal Code (CC-1): Hate Speech and Two Concepts of Liberty)' (2020) 71(1) *Revija za kriminalistiko in kriminologijo*; R Čeferin, N Kogovšek Šalamon and D Korošec, 'Javno spodbujanje sovraštva, nasilja ali nestrpnosti: 297. člen (Public incitement to hatred, violence and intolerance: Article 297)', in Damjan Korošec, Katja Filipčič and Stojan Zdolšek (eds), *Veliki znanstveni komentar posebnega dela Kazenskega zakonika (KZ-1): Knjiga 3 (Scientific Commentary on a Special Part of the Criminal Code (KZ-1): Book 3)* (Uradni list Republike Slovenije, Pravna fakulteta 2019).

47 Sonja Merljak, 'Rok Čeferin: "Ugotovitev tožilstva se mi zdi popolnoma absurdna" (Rok Čeferin: "The Finding of the Prosecutors Seems Completely Absurd to Me")' (2016) *Delo* <www.delo.si/novice/slovenija/ugotovitev-tozilstva-se-mi-zdi-popolnoma-absurdna.html> accessed 2 February 2022.

48 Rok Čeferin, *Meje svobode tiska: analiza sodne prakse Ustavnega sodišča Republike Slovenije in Evropskega sodišča za človekove pravice (The Limits of Freedom of the Press: An Analysis of the Case Law of the Constitutional Court of the Republic of Slovenia and the European Court of Human Rights)* (GV založba 2013).

49 Peter Petrovčič, 'Intervju: Drago Šketa, generalni državni tožilec (Interview: Drago Šketa, Attorney General)' (*Mladina* 2018) <www.mladina.si/187326/drago-sketa-generalni-drzavni-tozilec/> accessed 1 February 2022.

50 Case VSRS Sodba I Ips 65803/2012 [2020] Supreme Court.

51 Vrhovno državno tožilstvo, 'Skupno poročilo o delu državnih tožilstev za leto 2020' (Joint Report on the Work of State Prosecutors for 2020) (2021) <www.dt-rs.si/files/documents/Letno%20poroc%CC%8Cilo%20DT%20za%20leto%202020.pdf> accessed 1 February 2022.

52 See, for example, the judgment of the Up-106/05 [2008] Constitutional Court.

53 Information Commissioner of the Republic of Slovenia, 'Opinion No. 0712–1/2012/1999 on Obtaining Identifying Information on the Commenter on the Forum' (2012) <www.ip-rs.si/mnenja-zvop/pridobitev-identifikacijskih-podatkov-o-komentatorju-na-forumu> accessed 1 February 2022.

54 Rok Čeferin and Špelca Mežnar, 'Online Hate-Speech and Anonymous Internet Comments: How to Fight the Legal Battle in Slovenia?' (2014) 24(3) *ANNALES*.

55 Vinko Gorenak, 'Neodvisna sodnica ali leva politična aktivistka – primer Urške Klakočar Zupančič [Independent Judge or Left-Wing Political Activist – the Case of Urška Klakočar Zupančič]' (*vinkogorenak.net*, 1 December 2020) <www.vinkogorenak.net/2020/12/01/neodvisna-sodnica-ali-leva-politicna-aktivistka-primer-urske-klakocar-zupancic/> accessed 3 February 2022.

56 Zakon o sodniški službi – ZSS (Judicial Service Act) [2017] Official Gazette of the Republic of Slovenia, No. 94/07 – uradno prečiščeno besedilo, 91/09, 33/11, 46/13, 63/13, 69/13 – popr., 95/14 – ZUPPJS15, 17/15, 23/17 – ZSSve in 36/19 – ZDT-1C.

57 Zakon o sodnem svetu – ZSSve (Judicial Council Act) [2017] Official Gazette of the Republic of Slovenia, No 23/17 and 178/21 – odl. US.
58 Code of Judicial Ethics [2017] <www.sodni-svet.si/#/kei/kodeks> accessed 4 February 2022.
59 Opr. št.: I K 8928/202 [2021].
60 Mitja Felc, 'Sodničin zapis ni bil neprimeren in nedostojen (The Judge's Post Was Not Improper and Indecent)' (2021) *Delo* <www.delo.si/novice/slovenija/sodnicin-zapis-ni-bil-neprimeren-in-nedostojen/> accessed 1 February 2022.
61 Similarly to another target of prominent politicians in the Slovenian Democratic Party (SDS), Mojca Šetinc Pašek, Urška Klakočer Zupančič also joined the newly formed political party Gibanje svoboda, ran in the 2022 parliamentary election and is now Speaker of the Slovenian Parliament.
62 VSRS sodba II Ips 307/2014 [2015] Supreme Court.
63 Up-540/11 [2014] Constitutional Court.
64 *Benedik v Slovenia* n 20.
65 Up-153/17 [2021] Constitutional Court.
66 *Lingens v Austria* App no 9815/82 [ECtHR, 8 July 1986]; *Thorgeir Thorgeirson v Iceland* App no. 13778/88 [ECtHR, 25 June 1992]; *The Observer and Guardian v UK* App no 13585/88 [ECtHR, 24 October 1991]; *Jacubowski v Germany* App no 15088/89 [ECtHR, 23 June 1994]; *Von Hannover v Germany* App no. 59320/00 (ECtHR, 24 June 2004) and *Von Hannover v Germany No. 2* App no 40660/08 and 60641/08 [ECtHR, 7 December 2012]; *Axel Springer AG v Germany* App no 39954/08 [ECtHR, 7 February 2012]; *M. L. and W. W. v Germany* App no 60798/10 and 65599/10 [28 June 2018]; *Węgrzynowski and Smolczewski v Poland* App no 33846/07 [ECtHR, 16 July 2013].
67 Atari Europe v Rapidshare BGH, [2012] I ZR 18/11.
68 Ciril Ribičič, 'Uveljavljanje evropskih standardov v praksi slovenskega ustavnega sodišča (Enforcement of European Standards in Jurisprudence of the Slovenian Constitutional Court)' (2014) *Revus – Journal for Constitutional Theory and Philosophy of Law* 3.
69 Kristina Čufar, 'Legal Aspects of Content Moderation on Social Networks in Slovenia', in *The Impact of Digital Platforms and Social Media on the Freedom of Expression and Pluralism* (Ferenc Mádl Institute of Comparative Law; Central European Academic Publishing 2021); Andraž Teršek, 'Človekove pravice in temeljne svoboščine/39. člen/Komentar: Opredelitev pravice in razmerje do drugih ustavnih pravic (Human Rights and Fundamental Freedoms/Article 39/Commentary: Definition of the Right and Relationship to Other Constitutional Rights)', in Matej Avbelj (ed) *Komentar ustave Republike Slovenije (Commentary on the Constitution of the Republic of Slovenia)* (Nova univerza, Evropska pravna fakulteta 2019).
70 E.g. decisions Up-614/15 and Up-407/14.

12 Social media before higher courts in Spain

Judicial dialogue on innovative and difficult cases and the resolution of disagreements between courts

Joan Solanes Mullor

1. Introduction

Spain has recognised the singularity of the phenomenon of social media by adapting part of its legislation. From the civil perspective, Organic Law 3/2018 of 5 December on data protection and digital guarantees incorporates all the measures adopted in the General Data Protection Regulation (GDPR), and therefore, it regulates processing of data and its connection with privacy. It also recognises so-called digital rights, with the Spanish legislator for the first time using this kind of terminology.[1] The Spanish Constitution (SC) does not use this language, and even though some constitutional fundamental rights may have a digital dimension, Organic Law 3/2018 offers a fresh look because it provides a new, detailed list of rights in the digital sphere. Some of these rights are specifically related to social media, such as the right to rectification on the Internet, with social media companies being required to create protocols to erase contents violating privacy rights, the right to be forgotten, which is specifically recognised in the context of social media, and recognition of the right of portability of personal information between different social media services (i.e. the right to transfer personal information between different social platforms). Law 34/2002 of 11 July on information society services and e-commerce,[2] when applied to social media, completes the specific adaptation of Spanish legislation to the social media phenomenon.

Beyond these changes, in the civil realm, old constitutional provisions and legislation remain applicable. Therefore, Articles 18 and 20 of the SC are the central provisions in the civil sphere involving possible conflicts in the context of social media. These articles recognise the right to freedom of expression and information, the rights to honour and personal and family privacy, the right to one's own image, the right to secrecy of communications and the right to personal data. At the legislative level, Organic Law 1/1982 of 5 May and Law 2/1984 of 26 March provide details on resolving conflicts between some of the previously mentioned constitutional rights. Finally, old legislation on consumer protection, intellectual property and advertising is also applicable to social media.[3]

DOI: 10.4324/9781003207085-14

From the criminal perspective, in 2015, substantive and procedural reforms were introduced addressing some specificities of social media. From the substantive point of view, the Criminal Code was amended to modify and introduce new crimes related to the Internet and social media.[4] *Inter alia*, the new legislation regulated cyberbullying, pornography and minors, the use of personal communications and data, the appropriation of IT resources and piracy on the Internet. In relation to freedom of expression and social media, hate speech was introduced as a specific crime and the diffusion of messages which may affect public order was criminalised. Moreover, all crimes related to terrorism were adapted to the new social media phenomenon, especially addressing terrorist and violent extremist propaganda on the Internet.[5] From the procedural point of view, the Code of Criminal Procedure was amended and a new framework was established for judicial authorisation of interceptions of communications, including on social media.[6] Lower courts challenged this procedural reform and sent a preliminary reference to the Court of Justice of the EU (CJEU), but the legislative reform was considered compatible with EU law.[7]

This legislation should be contextualised in a system in which fundamental rights are constitutionally protected because they are entrenched in the Spanish Constitution.[8] However, the level of protection differs among fundamental rights.[9] Those recognised in Articles 14 to 29 SC (and Article 30.2) have the maximum protection. These provisions include freedom of expression/information and privacy rights. These fundamental rights can only be amended through the most rigid constitutional amendment process; regulation of them at the infra-constitutional level is reserved to the legislator, not the government, through organic and ordinary legislation;[10] and finally, ordinary courts protect them through preferential and speedy processes and the Constitutional Court by means of individual constitutional complaints. The rights recognised in Articles 30 to 38 SC enjoy lower protection (*inter alia*, rights such as the right to property and freedom of enterprise); that is, they can be amended through a less rigid constitutional amendment process, there is not a reservation for organic law (only for ordinary law) and they are judicially protected through ordinary processes in which individual constitutional complaints before the Constitutional Court are not included. Finally, rights recognised in Chapter III of Title I of the SC (most of the economic, social and cultural rights) are protected through less rigid constitutional amendment, and they are only informative for public powers. In addition to judicial protection, a non-jurisdictional institution like the Ombudsman oversees fundamental rights in relations between citizens and public powers.[11]

The key source of fundamental rights protection, therefore, is the judiciary. Individuals may request protection in all the jurisdictions (civil, criminal, social/employment, contentious-administrative and military). The Supreme Court (SSC) is the last resort of ordinary courts and has cassational jurisdiction in all the branches of law.[12] The National High Court (NHC) is a special court, the decisions of which may be reviewed by the Supreme Court. It focuses on terrorism, serious crimes and other specific areas, such as judicial review of regulatory agencies (e.g. the Spanish Data Protection Agency).[13] This chapter also covers the National High Court, although it is not a higher court, because of its special relevance. The Constitutional Court (SCC) is the maximum interpreter of the Constitution, and therefore, it has the last word on all issues of constitutional relevance.[14] The individual constitutional complaint is a subsidiary mechanism that can be used by citizens to protect their fundamental rights (only those in Articles 14 to 29 and 30.2 SC) after they have exhausted all the ordinary court remedies, including the Supreme Court. Apart from this mechanism, specific, legitimised public bodies such as the President, parliamentary groups and autonomous community bodies can apply to the Constitutional Court and also for judicial review of legislation violating fundamental rights, using the unconstitutional challenge mechanism, which can be launched directly against passed legislation. Finally, ordinary courts can send preliminary constitutional questions to the Constitutional Court when they have doubts about the constitutionality of norms with the rank of law which are applicable to specific cases under their jurisdiction.

Against this backdrop, this analysis draws on a total of 8 Constitutional Court cases, 77 Supreme Court cases and 201 National High Court cases[15] in the period between 1 January 2009 and 31 December 2020. There is a clear increase in the number of cases over the years, especially after 2015.[16] Section 2 focuses on the types of cases that have been brought before domestic courts which clearly involve fundamental rights conflicts in the context of social media: five types of cases related to conflicts involving freedom of expression; freedom of information; privacy; personal data and secrecy of communications; due process; and political rights. As shall be seen, Spanish courts have confronted social media and they have recognised and applied fundamental rights in their approach to them. Section 3 addresses how the Spanish judiciary has engaged in judicial dialogue with the Court of Justice of the European Union (CJEU) and the European Court of Human Rights (ECtHR) on these cases. Section 4 provides some concluding remarks about the significant role of Spanish courts in addressing conflicts involving social media, the use of fundamental rights and the engagement of domestic courts in judicial dialogue with the CJEU and the ECtHR.

2. Fundamental rights in national jurisprudence

Social media are clearly linked to fundamental rights in the Spanish courts' case law. Five types of cases can be identified in which the dimension of fundamental rights on social media plays a role. The standard balancing test is applied in these cases with only some specificities which recognise the singularity of social media. References to the European Convention on Human Rights (ECHR) and the Charter of Fundamental Rights of the European Union (CFR) are used along with national provisions and the case law of the ECtHR and the CJEU, but never as the only source. In this regard, the position of Spanish courts is predominantly national, mostly based on national constitutional law. Any external references are made in support of national law or in the context of judicial dialogue with the two European courts.

2.1 Typology of cases

Freedom of expression cases concerning social media are predominant. This is above all because of the relevance in the national context of the phenomenon of terrorism. Spanish courts have confronted conflicts related to propaganda, incitement and glorification of terrorism through social media. On the one hand, jihadism and social media have gained momentum and both the Supreme Court and the National High Court have ruled on many cases in this regard.[17] These are mostly terrorism indoctrination cases involving publication of videos and messages on social media.[18] On the other hand, Spanish courts have dealt with cases related to national terrorism in which propaganda, incitement of ETA and GRAPO actions and humiliation of their victims have led to multiple judgments. Examples include songs published on social media and tweets glorifying terrorism,[19] sarcastic references to ETA terrorist attacks[20] and comments on social media denigrating victims of national terrorism.[21] Ordinary courts have analysed these cases considering freedom of expression but with a clear inclination to favour the application of criminal penalties.[22] The Constitutional Court has pointed out that freedom of expression, especially its institutional dimension (i.e. its special relevance for the proper functioning of the democratic system), should be more and better weighted, and therefore, ordinary courts must undertake more accurate analyses.[23] The Constitutional Court tried to reinforce freedom of expression in the well-known *Strawberry* case[24] and sent a clear message to ordinary courts.

Apart from the terrorism phenomenon, there have also been many cases on the relationship between freedom of expression and privacy rights in the context of social media. Clashes with the right to honour have been a constant, and some examples include cases on blogging, such as critiques of *Sociedad General de Autores y Editores* (SGAE) and *Air Berlin* and of individuals (politicians and actors).[25] Twitter has also been a protagonist in this context, with cases in which the right to honour has been invoked against an exchange of critiques between individuals or sharp attacks on homeopaths.[26] Related to the right to honour, in its collective variant and the criminalisation of hate speech, xenophobic and racist comments and ones against gender violence on Twitter have also led to some cases before Spanish courts.[27] Finally, Facebook has been relevant in the clash between freedom of expression and the right to one's own image, especially when users have used and discussed images of other users of the social network,[28] but also in cases regarding insults to a dead public person.[29]

Freedom of information constitutes another important source of cases in the context of social media. The most frequent cases confront this fundamental right with the right to one's own image. In particular, Spanish courts have addressed the problematic use of images extracted from social media in the context of the exercise of freedom of information. After several judgments issued by the Supreme Court debating whether it was necessary to obtain the consent of the owner to use images previously published on Facebook,[30] the Constitutional Court ended the debate and decided that, *per se*, the publication of an image on Facebook does not entail consent for it to be used outside the social network.[31] On the contrary, freedom of information prevails in the case of publication of images of police officers on social media when they are on duty, and therefore, the need for previous authorisation introduced by the legislator was declared unconstitutional.[32] Other cases involved freedom of information and the right to honour, such as critiques on social media about plagiarism and the quality of streaming broadcast on a soccer platform,[33] and the relationship between digitalisation of newspapers and the right to be forgotten.[34]

The right to be forgotten practically monopolises the cases involving social media, the right to personal data and secrecy of communications. After *Google Spain*, which originated in a preliminary reference sent by the Spanish National High Court,[35] both the National High Court and the Supreme Court have decided many cases related to the right to be forgotten in the context of social media.[36] Beyond this flow of cases, two relevant Constitutional Court cases should be highlighted regarding access by the police to the content of mobile phones, including social media, in which it was implied that social media should be understood as a form of personal communication and therefore protected by the right to secrecy of communications.[37] The Supreme Court followed up this interpretation and required judicial authorisation to obtain passwords to social networks and, in general, to access social media content in a police investigation.[38] In the employment sphere, the Supreme Court has stressed the need for consent of employees to access all personal data on their computers, and therefore, it has limited the surveillance powers of employers.[39] Other cases in this context include protection of Apple IDs and Apple services from intrusion by the partner and criminalisation of such conduct[40] and the nature of consent given to users of Tuenti regarding its surveillance power over illegal content in a case in which the platform decided to report private chats to the police when it detected corruption of minors.[41] Finally, the Constitutional Court declared unconstitutional a piece of legislation which allowed, without specifying the aim and procedural guarantees, indiscriminate collection of the political opinions of individuals – also on social media – by political parties.[42]

Recent cases also show a link between due process and social media.[43] The Supreme Court has validated evidence collected from social media as a sufficient burden of proof to satisfy the right to be presumed innocent.[44] In this case, it was sufficient for conviction for the testimonies of social media users to identify the Facebook account used by the accused to incite terrorism. Of particular note is a decision by the Supreme Court that juries will not be contaminated *per se* if they learn facts and details of cases from social media.[45]

However, the approach of the Spanish courts regarding the relationship between due process rights and social media is still fragmented and limited.[46]

The last type of cases reviewed involves social media and political rights. First, the Constitutional Court confirmed the constitutionality of denying a preventive detainee the possibility to increase his hours of Internet connection and to develop a political campaign on social media, declaring that the right to political participation was not violated (Article 23 SC).[47] This was a controversial case involving one of the Catalan independence leaders who was, at that time, in preventive detention and wished to participate in the Catalan election by means of social media. However, the Supreme Court found a violation of the right of association (Article 22 SC) of a political militant who created a dissenting social media platform against his party and, for this reason, was expelled.[48]

2.2 *The balancing test*

Judicial adjudication in Spain has recognised some specificities regarding the typology of social media cases analysed previously in this chapter. Because of its nature, the Constitutional Court is the court that has addressed most of these singularities. Few constitutional cases have only focused on social media, but despite this, relevant questions from the perspective of fundamental rights have been addressed. All these cases have involved social media and fundamental rights and the Spanish courts have debated on their relationship in detail. In general, these cases have been resolved by means of a standard proportionality/balancing test. Despite the new scenario that social media has introduced, Spanish courts have been traditional in their approach when fundamental rights are at stake. The clash of fundamental rights in the context of social media has been addressed on a case-by-case basis by applying a proportionality/balancing test. In essence, courts analyse the legitimate aim of conduct, its appropriateness, necessity and strict proportionality. For instance, in a case on the publication of images of police officers on social media, the Constitutional Court declared unconstitutional the need for previous authorisation, reinforcing the absolute prohibition of prior censorship in the context of freedom of information, but it subsequently declared that the proportionality principle should guide assessment of whether or not a specific image may be published.[49] The Supreme Court has similarly approached conflicts between freedom of expression and the right to honour in social media cases with a traditional proportionality/balancing test.[50] From this perspective, the social media context makes no difference in judicial adjudication.

Despite this traditional approach, Spanish courts have introduced some specificities to the previous structure of the proportionality/balancing test. The right to be forgotten brings new factors into the balancing, especially the "lapse of time", which is important when the right to be forgotten clashes with the right of freedom of expression/information. In this context, first *Google Spain* and, afterwards, the GDPR have enriched the proportionality/

balancing test in this field by adding new elements to consider for balancing purposes such as the "lapse of time" of the information/expression concerned and therefore its reduced interest for public debate. Spanish courts have dealt with many cases related to the right to be forgotten on social media and have applied this enriched proportionality/balancing test.[51] In addition, the nature of social media as a communication channel has also been considered in the application of the test. For instance, insults in a restricted Facebook forum did not have sufficient intensity to breach the right to honour because of their limited dissemination.[52] The Spanish courts are thus incorporating the impact of social media channels in the proportionality/balancing test. Finally, disagreement between Spanish courts on terrorism cases involving freedom of expression should be highlighted. Ordinary courts – the Supreme Court and the National High Court – have severely applied criminal sentences for incitement, indoctrination and glorification of terrorism. In the *Strawberry* case, the Constitutional Court upheld in principle the criminalisation of such conduct but called for case-by-case application of an intense proportionality/balancing test, which was not satisfied in *Strawberry*.[53]

2.3 *European fundamental rights*

European fundamental rights are integrated in the Spanish legal order in two different ways. Article 10.2 SC is the natural bridge between constitutional and European fundamental rights for consistent interpretation. That is, Spanish courts must interpret constitutional rights in accordance with the Universal Declaration of Human Rights and the international treaties on human rights ratified by Spain. This provision is fully applicable to the ECHR, and therefore, conventional rights and the case law of the ECtHR should guide consideration of national constitutional rights. In the case of the CFR and the case law of the CJEU, the avenue is different because of the principles of primacy and direct effect of EU law. In this regard, the CFR and the role of the CJEU are stronger, and beyond consistent interpretation, which is also applicable, a possible contradiction with national constitutional law may lead to disapplication of the latter. However, the limited scope of application of the CFR, which needs a substantive link with EU law to be invoked, reduces its impact. In any case, the combination of Article 10.2 SC and the primacy and direct effect of EU law ensures a deep *interiorisation* of European fundamental rights in the Spanish legal system.

Despite this interiorisation, the ECHR and the CFR have rarely been used alone, without reference to the case law of the ECtHR and the CJEU. Constitutional rights are the reference framework for Spanish courts and the ECHR and the CFR play roles in innovative and difficult cases or when there are disagreements between courts in which the case law of the ECtHR and the CJEU becomes either supportive or necessary for consistent interpretation. What is important to recall is that the starting point for Spanish courts, especially ordinary courts, is national constitutional law, which is the predominant conceptual framework for judges. European fundamental rights play a role in the context of judicial dialogue. They are not normally invoked outside it, and so what is relevant is the judicial interaction between Spanish courts, the ECtHR and the CJEU, an interaction that has also been significant in social media cases.

3. Judicial dialogue with the CJEU and the ECtHR

Spanish courts have been open to judicial dialogue on social media cases. A quick look at the case law shows that judicial interaction has occurred on innovative cases, "difficult" cases and disagreements between courts. Spanish courts have mostly used judicial dialogue to ensure consistent interpretation, to legitimise their own reasoning and, in cases of disagreements in adjudication, to reinforce their positions before other courts. This type of interaction is here called "soft" judicial dialogue because Spanish courts maintain a clear national stand, and judicial interaction only becomes instrumental to the national framework. In contrast, in the field of data protection, where EU law is determinant, Spanish courts have developed a more intense judicial dialogue. This has been central – especially because of the use of the preliminary reference – in the courts' reasoning.

3.1 Intense judicial dialogue: preliminary references and strong, consistent interpretation

The preliminary reference sent by the Spanish National High Court regarding *Google Spain* exemplifies the intense use of judicial dialogue in the field of data protection.[54] Despite not being directly related to social media, this landmark case has been referential for many subsequent cases in which the right to be forgotten has been invoked in the context of social media.[55] Therefore, the balancing test required in *Google Spain* has also been applied in social media cases in which the information/expressions to be supressed are found on social media platforms. In all these cases, the CJEU's analysis in *Google Spain*, and the GDPR after it was approved and implemented at the national level, have been pivotal in the resolution of disputes adjudicated by ordinary courts. Lower courts have also relied on the preliminary reference procedure and the CJEU to challenge Spanish legislation on interception of communications during investigations of serious crimes.[56]

The Supreme Court has not sent any preliminary reference to the CJEU in the field of data protection and social media, but in two cases related to data protection, judicial dialogue has been determinant. On the one hand, the Supreme Court has firmly declared that access by the police to data on social media needs specific judicial authorisation; a generic authorisation for access to the domicile is not enough.[57] This important decision was sustained with extensive reference to EU data protection law and the case law of the CJEU and the ECtHR.[58] The Supreme Court has brought protection into the so-called personal digital sphere, which comes within the scope of the right to personal data. Therefore, a specifically motivated judicial authorisation must be issued to access this sphere. Judicial dialogue was even more determinant in a case in which the Supreme Court debated access by an employer to personal data on an employee's computer, including social media.[59] In this case, the Supreme Court recognised the relevance of the *Barbulescu* test[60] and highlighted the relevance of the existence of a previous warning to the employee that the computer should only be used for professional purposes.[61] The *Barbulescu* test establishes a sort of reinforced proportionality test based on six checkpoints: notification of monitoring measures; the extent of monitoring and the degree of intrusion; the existence of legitimate reasons to justify monitoring; whether a less intrusive monitoring system would have been possible; the consequences of the monitoring for the employee; and whether the employee was provided with adequate safeguards. The Supreme Court expressly considered *Barbulescu* a landmark case and recognised its relevance to its decision in the case at hand by applying the *Barbulescu* test criteria.[62]

Neither has the Constitutional Court sent a preliminary reference to the CJEU regarding social media. This reflects the Constitutional Court's general attitude of reluctance to send preliminary references to the CJEU.[63] However, the intense Europeanisation of data protection has triggered intense judicial interaction between the Constitutional Court, the CJEU and the ECtHR, and this interaction has determined the outcome of some cases involving social media. For example, the Constitutional Court has declared unconstitutional a legislative provision which allowed political parties to indiscriminately collect citizens' political opinions, including those expressed on social media.[64] Reference to *Digital Rights Ireland* and the reasoning of the CJEU, which was directly adopted by the Constitutional Court, facilitated the declaration of unconstitutionality of a provision which lacked clarity, precision and guaranteed measures for accessing personal data.[65] Along the same lines, the Constitutional Court entrenched the right to be forgotten as a constitutional, fundamental right in a case concerning open, free access to the digital archives of a newspaper, the search engine of which allowed identification of the applicants regarding a noticeable and journalistically reported crime committed years ago.[66] The Constitutional Court included the right to be forgotten in the old-fashioned right to personal data, but it did so in a judgment in which *Google Spain* and the CFR, on the one hand, and the ECtHR case law, on the other, became essential factors in its own reasoning.[67] In this context, *Google Spain* has been used to build the constitutional nature of the right to be forgotten, whereas the ECtHR has been contacted to distinguish two different levels of protection of the freedom of information: the watchdog function of the press, which for the Constitutional Court deserves the maximum protection, and the creation of press archives for historical research, which deserves less protection.[68]

This close connection between European courts and the Constitutional Court in the field of data protection was also clear in one of the first cases in which the Constitutional Court dealt with the nature of data on a personal computer.[69] The Constitutional Court did not analyse social media in particular but highlighted that all content on a personal computer may qualify as personal data and therefore deserves protection, entailing that access by a third party needs the consent of the individual or appropriate judicial authorisation.[70] To clarify the nature of personal data on a personal computer, the Constitutional Court relied on European sources and engaged in judicial interaction with the CJEU and the ECtHR.[71] In the end, the Constitutional Court found permissible access to personal data with paedophile content by the police, whose action was triggered by a report by a computer technician repairing the applicant's computer.[72] Despite the result of the case, the theoretical construction of the protection of data on a computer was extensively based on European references. Engaging in similar analysis and interiorising the reasoning of this precedent, the Constitutional Court has also declared the same protection of personal data on a mobile phone.[73]

3.2 Soft judicial dialogue: seeking consistent interpretation

The intense Europeanisation of data protection has facilitated judicial interaction in Spain. The widespread presence of EU law in the field and the decisive intervention of the CJEU has made dialogue easy. However, the new scenario that social media and the phenomenon of terrorism have created in Spain is a different story.[74] In particular, propaganda and glorification of national terrorism on social media, a very sensitive question in the Spanish context, have led to disagreement between courts. In these difficult cases in which freedom of expression is limited by criminal law (in particular, Article 578 of the Criminal Code) to protect interests such as the honour of victims and the general prevention of terrorism, the national perspective becomes prevalent, and it seems that there is less room for judicial interaction between Spanish and European courts.

Disagreement between the Supreme Court and lower courts has been evident. A group of similar cases have produced different outcomes. The Supreme Court's decisions have differed, but mostly criminal convictions have been predominant, and therefore, ordinary courts have, overall, balanced the interests at stake in favour of limiting freedom of expression. To illustrate this, in the *Strawberry* case, the Supreme Court convicted César Strawberry for glorifying terrorism and humiliating its victims in tweets related to GRAPO and the former prison guard José Antonio Ortega Lara, who was kidnapped by ETA.[75] In a previous judicial instance, César Strawberry had been acquitted by the National High Court.[76] In the *Hasel* case, the Supreme Court convicted the singer Pablo Hasel for glorifying, among other crimes, terrorism in tweets and songs,[77] and in the *La Insurgencia* case, a rap group for glorifying GRAPO's actions in songs published on YouTube and other social media platforms.[78] In a similar case, the rapper Valtónyc was also convicted by the Supreme Court for glorifying terrorism, among other crimes, in his lyrics published on YouTube.[79] In contrast, in *Cassandra Vera*, the Supreme

Court acquitted a woman who authored sarcastic tweets regarding the former Spanish President Luis Carrero Blanco and the ETA terrorist attack on him.[80] Therefore, although the Supreme Court and the National High Court have mostly been aligned, they differed in *Strawberry* and *Cassandra Vera*. Despite this divergence, neither of these ordinary courts engaged in judicial dialogue with European courts.

Against this backdrop, the Constitutional Court has intervened, and in the *Strawberry* case, it sent a clear message to ordinary courts: freedom of expression should be more and better weighted and, in general, ordinary courts should be very accurate when applying the balancing/proportionality test in such cases.[81] The Constitutional Court stated that the institutional dimension of freedom of expression – i.e. its pivotal role in democracy – should be considered in the analysis. For the Constitutional Court, in *Strawberry*, the Supreme Court failed in that analysis.[82] This clear confrontation between the Constitutional Court and the Supreme Court appeared to create room for judicial dialogue with European courts. Indeed, the Constitutional Court introduced a section devoted to the case law of the ECtHR, in which it discussed the balancing criteria the ECtHR applied to cases of conflict between freedom of expression and glorification of terrorism.[83] Unlike ordinary courts, which did not engage in judicial dialogue, the Constitutional Court proved better prepared to deal with a difficult case and confronted ordinary courts with the support of the Strasbourg Court's case law. Judicial dialogue, even if secondary, became instrumental in reinforcing the Constitutional Court's own reasoning and its position against ordinary courts.

Judicial interaction by the Constitutional Court with the ECtHR can also be explained by the pressure created by recent convictions of Spain in freedom of expression cases. In a series of cases which were not related to social media, the ECtHR convicted Spain for inadequate balancing of conflicts between freedom of expression and prevention of terrorism and humiliation of victims or protection of the Crown.[84] Judicial interaction with the ECtHR may therefore have also sought to send a message to Strasbourg showing that the Constitutional Court was making an effort to adapt internal balancing to the ECtHR criteria. In *Strawberry*, the Constitutional Court discussed the Strasbourg Court's criteria, quashed the Supreme Court's judgment and indicated the direction for ordinary courts to follow in future cases. However, the Constitutional Court declared other individual constitutional complaints inadmissible, such as the ones filed by Valtónyc, members of the La Insurgencia group and Hasel. For the Constitutional Court, these complaints did not have special constitutional relevance. Only *Strawberry*, decided using the Supreme Court's criteria, has therefore been analysed on its merits by the Constitutional Court. Therefore, apart from *Strawberry*, it seems that the Supreme Court's criteria are predominant, which could lead to more convictions of Spain by the ECtHR.

Unlike the context of terrorism, two other cases show the willingness of the Constitutional Court to favour judicial interaction. First, the Constitutional

Court engaged in judicial dialogue with the ECtHR on a case concerning denying one of the Catalan independence leaders extension of the hours of Internet connection and access to social media for political campaigning.[85] In this case, the Constitutional Court quoted Article 3 of Protocol n° 1 to the ECHR on the right to free elections and several judgments in that field by the ECtHR and it devoted a section to the Strasbourg Court's criteria.[86] The Constitutional Court expressly stated that its own criteria to assess limitations of political rights were similar to those in the ECtHR's case law and that the Strasbourg Court's criteria were relevant, thanks to Article 10.2 SC, in interpretation of constitutional political rights (Article 23 SC).[87] It seems clear that, as in terrorism cases, the Constitutional Court wished to reinforce and legitimise its position, having in mind that the case could be analysed in the future by the ECtHR. Judicial interaction is a way of legitimation in difficult and controversial cases. Second, in an innovative case in which the Constitutional Court debated whether a user of a social platform had given his consent for images published on the social platform to be published outside it, the Constitutional Court made specific references to ECtHR case law to support its reasoning.[88] These references were sporadic and limited in scope, but the intent of judicial dialogue was clear. The innovative nature of the case opened the door to judicial interaction, and it served to reinforce the reasoning of the Constitutional Court.

4. Conclusion

Social media has only been recognised by the Spanish legislator in a fragmented way. Organic Law 3/2018 was a significant step because it incorporates the language of fundamental rights – digital rights – in the digital era, explicitly including social media. The legislative task, however, remains inconclusive, and it is expressed in principles and guidelines. There is room for judicial action, even with the approval of more pieces of legislation. The Spanish Constitution, enacted in 1978, does not refer to digital rights or the phenomenon of social media. Nevertheless, its bill of rights has demonstrated an ability to be adaptable to the new times, and thanks to judicial adjudication the old-fashioned rights of personal data, freedom of expression/information and secrecy of communications have gained a digital dimension.

Indeed, Spanish courts have been active in the context of social media. Analysis of their actions shows that the fundamental rights perspective has been considered. The Constitutional Court has discussed the right to one's own image vis-à-vis consent on Facebook, freedom of expression cases confronting terrorism, dissemination of images of police officers on social platforms and the collection of data, also from social media, by political parties. The Supreme Court and the National High Court have also addressed singular issues in the context of social media, such as access by employers to the social media data of employees, implementation of the right to be forgotten, conflicts between freedom of expression/information and privacy rights, and an incipient clash with due process. They have mostly faced these challenges using the old structure of the balancing/proportionality test, but there are some examples in which this test is starting to recognise the specificities of the digital sphere.

Judicial interaction with the European courts may help in this ongoing incorporation of the digital dimension of fundamental rights in the national arena. It is already playing a role. Two patterns of judicial interaction have emerged with reference to social media. On the one hand, strong judicial dialogue has appeared in the context of data protection because of the singularity of this field, in which EU law has conquered the space. Spanish courts have felt a need to interact with the CJEU, and even the National High Court has used the preliminary reference procedure. On the other hand, soft judicial dialogue is used in other fields where its role is more instrumental and secondary. In these cases, Spanish courts, and especially the Constitutional Court, seek to reinforce and legitimise their positions. This need arises because of three different factors: novelty of the case, difficulty of the case and disagreements between courts. For instance, the scope of consent given to Facebook and its clash with the right to one's own image was a fresh case. Denying a Catalan independence leader in preventive detention access to social media for political campaigning was a difficult case because of national sensitivities. Finally, conflict between freedom of expression and terrorist criminal law was a case of disagreement between higher courts (with the *Strawberry* case representing a peak). In all these situations, Spanish courts, and especially the Constitutional Court, needed judicial dialogue with the European courts to seek consistent interpretation and secure their positions.

Mention should be made, in particular, of judicial interaction in the *Strawberry* case, in which pressure from the ECtHR seems to have been a paramount factor to consider. Not only did the Constitutional Court use judicial dialogue internally – i.e. to secure its position against ordinary courts in a case of disagreement – but it was also eyeing the ECtHR, which, in non-social media-related cases involving freedom of expression and terrorism ramifications, had previously convicted Spain. Here, there is another motivation for judicial dialogue: the Constitutional Court seeking consistent interpretation in a context in which the ECtHR is finding repetitive violations of the ECHR by the country. Ordinary courts are not following the same path as the Constitutional Court, and they are not engaging in judicial dialogue with the ECtHR. At the same time, the Constitutional Court is only partially interacting with the ECtHR because it decided to review the *Strawberry* case only on its merits. Other cases were considered to be of no special constitutional relevance, and therefore, the individual constitutional complaints were declared inadmissible.

Social media cases show that judicial dialogue should improve in this field. The preliminary reference is still only used by ordinary courts, and it is used scarcely, whereas the Constitutional Court's position on EU law (i.e. conflicts between EU law and national law do not have constitutional relevance and therefore are left to ordinary courts) hinders the use of the preliminary reference. Strong judicial dialogue in data protection is an oasis full of singularities that is not reproduced in other areas. Soft judicial dialogue, seeking consistent interpretation, is predominant and is used mainly as a secondary and instrumental tool. There is room for improvement, especially at the level of ordinary courts. It is quite surprising that, in the middle of the ECtHR's convictions of Spain, ordinary courts, and even the courts that acquitted those investigated, did not engage in judicial dialogue, at least for fear of future convictions in Strasbourg. The national conceptual framework is also still there in the field of fundamental rights, and judicial dialogue and its role in enforcing European fundamental rights needs more attention.

Notes

1 Title X of Organic Law 3/2018, particularly Articles 85, 94, 95 and 87–91.
2 This law transposes Directive 2000/31/EC of the European Parliament and of the Council of 8 June 2000 on certain legal aspects of information society services, in particular electronic commerce, in the Internal Market ([2000] OJ L 178/1).
3 For an overview of the application of the old legislation, see Alberto Agustinoy Guilayn and Jorge Moclús Ruiz, *Aspectos legales de las redes sociales* (Bosch 2016).
4 The reform of the Criminal Code (Organic Law 10/1995 of 23 November) was introduced with Organic Law 1/2015 of 30 March. See Articles 172 ter, 183 ter, 186, 197, 197 bis, 270 and 510–559 of the amended Criminal Code.
5 The reform was introduced with Organic Law 2/2015 of 30 March. See the current Articles 571 to 580 bis of the Criminal Code.
6 See Organic Law 13/2015 of 5 October amending the Code of Criminal Procedure.
7 The case is not directly related to social media, but it is relevant in the digital era. The reform allowed access to a mobile phone SIM in all criminal investigations (current Articles 579.1 and 588 ter of the Code of Criminal Procedure). The Regional Court of Tarragona sent a preliminary reference to the CJEU, which found that simple access to a SIM without access to sensitive personal data does not need to be limited to serious crimes (Case C-207/16 *Ministerio Fiscal*, 2 October 2018, ECLI:EU:C:2018:788).
8 See Title I SC.
9 Articles 53, 81, 167 and 168 SC.
10 Ordinary laws are approved by a simple majority, whereas organic laws require a qualified majority in Parliament (Article 81 SC).
11 See Article 54 SC and Organic Law 3/1981 of 6 April.
12 Article 123 SC and Articles 53 to 61 sexies of Organic Law 6/1985 of 1 July on Judicial Power. There are a few exceptions to this all-inclusive cassational power related to some Autonomous Community laws which can only be reviewed by the Autonomous Community High Courts.
13 Articles 62 to 69 of Organic Law 6/1985 on Judicial Power.
14 Title IX SC and Organic Law 2/1979 of 3 October of the Constitutional Court.
15 The case law search was carried out using the public databases of the Constitutional Court (<https://hj.tribunalconstitucional.es/en>) and the Supreme and National High Courts: (<www.poderjudicial.es/portal/site/cgpj/menuitem.87fc234e64fd592b3305d5a7dc432ea0/?vgnextoid=8b5d93841e3eb210VgnVCM100000cb34e20aRCRD&vgnextlocale=en&vgnextfmt=default&lang_choosen=en>). Thanks to Mar Campos Vives for helping with this case research.

16 Between 2009 and 2015, there were only two cases before the Constitutional Court, nine cases before the Supreme Court and 41 cases before the National High Court. After 2015, there were six cases before the Constitutional Court, 68 cases before the Supreme Court (more than ten a year) and 160 cases before the National High Court (more than 20 a year).
17 In the period analysed, a total of 23 judgments by the Spanish Supreme Court and a total of 77 judgments by the National High Court were identified.
18 The cases mainly involved Articles 571 (members of terrorist organisations), 578 (incitement/glorification of terrorism) and 575 (indoctrination) of the Criminal Code. See, for instance, SSC nº 661/2017 of 10 October; 466/2019 of 14 October and 373/2020 of 3 July.
19 SSC nº 4/2017 of 18 January and SSC nº 79/2018 of 15 February; SSC nº 185/2019 of 2 April; SSC nº 135/2020 of 7 May.
20 SSC nº 95/2018 of 26 February.
21 SSC nº 623/2016 of 13 July; SSC nº 206/2017 of 28 March; SSC 334/2018 of 3 July.
22 Josep M Tamarit Sumalla, 'Los delitos de odio en las redes sociales' (2018) *Revista de Internet, Derecho y Política* 27, 23–27.
23 SCC nº 35/2020 of 25 February (paras. 4–5).
24 Ibid.
25 SSC nº 742/2012 of 4 December; SSC 811/2013 of 12 December; SSC nº 290/2020 of 11 June; SSC nº 438/2020 of 17 July.
26 SSC nº 75/2020 of 4 February; SSC nº 281/2020 of 10 June.
27 SSC nº 72/2018 of 9 February; SSC nº 675/2020 of 11 December.
28 SSC nº 746/2016 of 21 December; SSC nº 476/2018 of 20 July.
29 SSC nº 201/2019 of 3 April.
30 SSC nº 91/2017 of 15 February; SSC nº 426/2017 of 6 July; SSC nº 446/2017 of 13 July.
31 SCC nº 27/2020 of 24 February.
32 SCC nº 172/2020 of 19 November (para 7).
33 SSC nº 297/2020 of 12 June; SSC nº 485/2020 of 22 September.
34 SCC nº 58/2018 of 4 June.
35 CJEU, Case C-131/12 *Google Spain SL and Google Inc. v Agencia Española de Protección de Datos (AEPD) and Mario Costeja González* [2014] ECLI:EU:C:2014:317.
36 In the period analysed, a total of five judgments by the Spanish Supreme Court and a total of 65 judgments by the National High Court were identified.
37 SCC nº 173/2011 of 7 November; SCC 142/2012 of 2 July.
38 SSC nº 342/2013 of 17 April; SSC 97/2015 of 24 February; SSC 426/2016 of 19 May.
39 SSC nº 489/2018 of 23 October.
40 SSC nº 412/2020 of 20 July.
41 SSC nº 694/2020 of 15 December.
42 SCC nº 76/2019 of 22 May.
43 Vicente C Guzmán Fluja, 'Juicios paralelos en las redes sociales y proceso penal' (2018) *Revista de Internet, Derecho y Política* 27, 52–66.
44 SSC nº 380/2018 of 23 July.
45 SSC nº 93/2020 of 15 October.
46 Teresa Armenta Deu, 'Regulación legal y valoración probatoria de fuentes de prueba digital (correos electrónicos, WhatsApp, redes sociales): entre la insuficiencia y la incertidumbre' (2018) *Revista de Internet, Derecho y Política* 27, 67–78.
47 SCC nº 36/2020 of 25 February (para 6).
48 SSC nº 412/2020 of 7 July.
49 See (n 32).

50 See (n 25–29).
51 See (n 36).
52 SSC nº 281/2018 of 18 May.
53 See (n 23–24).
54 See (n 35).
55 See (n 36).
56 See (n 7).
57 SSC nº 426/2016 of 19 May (para 7).
58 Ibid. Considering its reasoning in case nº 173/2011 of 7 November, the SSC dealt in detail with the CJEU (discussing Case-275/06 *Productores de Música de España (Promusicae) v Tefelónica de España* [2008] ECLI:EU:C:2008:54) and the ECtHR (discussing *Amann v Switzerland* App. no. 27798/95, 16 February 2000; *Copland v the United Kingdom* App. no. 62617/00, 3 April 2007; *Iliya Stefanov v Bulgary* App. no. 65755/01, 22 May 2008).
59 SSC nº 489/2018 of 23 October.
60 ECtHR, *Barbulescu v Romania* App. no. 61496/08 (5 September 2017).
61 See (n 59), para 9.
62 Ibid, para 10.
63 *Melloni* so far remains the only case in which the Constitutional Court sent a preliminary reference to the CJEU. See Case C-399/11 *Stefano Melloni v Ministerio Fiscal* [2013] ECLI:EU:C:2013:107.
64 SCC nº 76/2019 of 22 May.
65 Ibid, para 5.
66 SCC nº 58/2018 of 4 June.
67 Ibid, para 7.
68 The Constitutional Court quoted *Times Newspaper Ltd (nos. 1 and 2) v The United Kingdom*, apps. nos. 3002/03 and 23676/03 (ECtHR, 10 March 2009).
69 SCC nº 173/2011 of 7 November.
70 Ibid, para 3.
71 Ibid, para 4. The SCC dealt in detail with the CJEU (discussing Case-275/06 *Productores de Música de España (Promusicae) v Tefelónica de España* [2008] ECLI:EU:C:2008:54) and the ECtHR (discussing *Amann v Switzerland* App. no. 27798/95, 16 February 2000; *Copland v the United Kingdom* App. no. 62617/00, 3 April 2007; *Iliya Stefanov v Bulgary* App. no. 65755/01, 22 May 2008).
72 Ibid, paras 5–7.
73 SCC nº 142/2012 of 2 July (para 3). This case, however, only addressed access by the police to the contact list on a mobile phone, even though access to the call history was not at stake. The Constitutional Court concluded that this kind of information was protected by the right to personal data but not by the right to secrecy of communications.
74 See section II.
75 SSC 4/2017 of 18 January.
76 NHC 20/2016 of 18 July.
77 SSC 135/2020 of 7 May.
78 SSC 291/2020 of 10 June.
79 SSC 79/2018 of 15 February.
80 SSC 95/2018 of 26 February. In the previous judicial instance, the National High Court convicted Cassandra Vera (NHC nº 9/2017 of 29 March).
81 SCC nº 35/2020 of 25 February.
82 Ibid, para 5.
83 Ibid, para 4. The SCC summarised the case law of the ECtHR and quoted the following cases: *Leroy v France* App. no. 36109/03, 2 October 2008; *Ozgur Gundem v Turkey* App. no. 23144/93, 16 March 2000; *Halis Dogan v Turkey* App.

no. 75946/01, 7 February 2006; *Hocaogullari v Turkey* App. no. 77109/01, 7 March 2006; *Oxturk v Turkey* App. no. 22479/93, 28 September 1999; *Bahceci and Turan v Turkey* App. no. 33340/03, 16 June 2009; *Gunduz v Turkey* App. no. 35071/97, 4 December 2003.

84 ECtHR, *Otegi Mondragon v Spain* App. no. 2034/07 (15 March 2011); ECtHR, *Stern Taulats and Roura Capellera v Spain* Apps. nos. 51168/15 and 51186/15 (13 March 2018); *Otegi Mondragon and Others v Spain* App. no. 4184/15 and 4 other applications (6 November 2018); ECtHR, *Erkizia Almandoz v Spain* App. no. 5869/17 (22 June 2021).

85 SCC n° 36/2020 of 25 February.

86 Ibid, para 4. The SCC quoted the following ECtHR cases: *Namat Aliyev v Azerbaijan* App. no. 18705/06, 8 April 2010; *Mathieu-Mohin and Clerfayt v Belgium* App. no. 9267/81, 2 March 1987; *Zdanoka v Latvia* App. no. 58278/00, 16 March 2006; *Etxeberria and others v Spain* Apps. nos. 35579/03, 35613/03, 35626/03, 35634/03, 30 June 2009; *Silay v Turkey* App. no. 8691/02, 5 April 2007; *Sobaci v Turkey* App. no. 26733/02, 29 November 2007; *Riza and others v Bulgaria* Apps. nos. 48555/10 and 48377/10, 13 October 2015; *Gitonas and others v Greece* Apps. nos. 18747/91, 19376/92 and 19379/92, 1 July 1997; *Abil v Azerbaijan* App. no. 16511/06, 21 February 2012; *Selim Sadak and others v Turkey* (n° 2) Apps. nos. 25144, 26149/95, 26154/95, 27100/95 and 27101/95, 11 June 2002; *Uspaskich v Lithuania* App. no. 1437/08, 20 December 2016; *Melnitchenko v Ukraine* App. no. 17707/02, 19 October 2004.

87 Ibid.

88 SCC n° 27/2020 of 24 February.

13 Social media, the European Court of Human Rights and apex courts in the United Kingdom

Contested competence at a time of constitutional change

Rachael Craufurd Smith

1. Introduction

Social media had 53 million active users in the United Kingdom (UK) in 2021.[1] The average user spent around 110 minutes a day on these services, with Facebook retaining a significant lead over its competitors.[2] Determining which laws and regulations apply in this context is complicated by the fact that the UK is fragmented into distinct nations and jurisdictions. There are four constituent nations – Northern Ireland, Scotland, England, and Wales – and three separate legal jurisdictions – those of Scotland, England and Wales (E&W), and Northern Ireland (NI). The law is developed through statute and the judge-made common law. The UK Parliament retains competence to legislate for Scotland, Northern Ireland and Wales in specific fields, including key areas relevant for the communications sector – notably, broadcasting, telecommunications, Internet services, electronic encryption, national security, competition and intellectual property.[3] The remaining areas are devolved.[4] There is no comparable devolution settlement for England. Scotland, NI, and Wales are specifically precluded from adopting legislation that conflicts with Convention rights,[5] a category established in the Human Rights Act 1998 (HRA 1998) that replicates the rights in the European Convention for the Protection of Human Rights and Fundamental Freedoms (ECHR).

The law relating to consumer protection, intellectual property, data protection, audio-visual media services, competition and online intermediaries has been heavily influenced by European Union (EU) law and is similar across the four nations. With the departure of the UK from the EU on the 31 January 2020, competence in these and other EU fields has been "repatriated", and, after a transition period, there is now scope to diverge from EU law in these "retained EU law" fields.[6]

In the three jurisdictions, the UK Supreme Court (UKSC) acts as the final court of appeal in civil matters and is the final court of appeal for criminal cases from E&W and NI. In Scotland, the High Court of Judiciary acts as the final criminal appeal court (HCJAC), with the exception of cases raising devolution

DOI: 10.4324/9781003207085-15

and "compatibility issues", which concern the compatibility of the actions of public authorities and acts of the Scottish Parliament with Convention rights.[7] An appeal to the UKSC is here possible, with permission from the HCJAC, or, failing that, the UKSC; and the UKSC, having determined the compatibility issue, then remits the matter to the HCJAC to conclude the case.[8] The UKSC replaced the Appellate Committee of the House of Lords (HL) in October 2009[9] and focuses on cases of key constitutional or public importance. It usually sits in a bench of five judges, though an enlarged bench can be empanelled where a case raises "an important point" relating to the ECHR.[10]

In both civil and criminal contexts, there is significant and increasing reliance on statute in the communications field.[11] Although the law is generally technology neutral, section 1 of the Malicious Communications Act 1988 (E&W) (MCA 1988) and section 127 of the Communications Act 2003 (CA 2003) establish specific offences relating to grossly offensive, threatening or knowingly false communications conveyed through electronic communications. In the aftermath of the 2016 murder of MP Jo Cox, the House of Commons Select Committee on Home Affairs carried out a rapid review of online hate crime and extremism, with a focus on social media.[12] It found that much of the criminal law predated "the era of mass social media" and called for review of the entire legislative framework.[13] The Law Commission (E&W) subsequently proposed a new suite of online communication offences and a recasting of the indeterminate MCA 1988 and CA 2003 offences to focus on serious harm and distress.[14] In addition, the UK government has proposed an overarching, regulatory framework for online communications in the form of the Online Safety Bill (OSB).[15] The Bill, as proposed, imposed a duty of care on online platforms to implement effective measures to protect users, particularly children, from illegal and most controversially, legal but harmful content, though significant changes are being made in review.

This chapter focuses on the three courts at the apex of the court hierarchy during the reference period: the HL in the early months of 2009, the UKSC thereafter, and the HCJAC. To date, these courts have decided only a handful of cases where social media communications have been directly in point. In relation to the HL, one case, *R v G*, concerned liability under the Terrorism Act 2000 for downloading materials from the Internet.[16] In relation to the UKSC, six decisions out of the 893 decided between the end of 2009 and 2020 were in scope: *Joseph v Spiller*,[17] *R v Gul (Mohammed)*,[18] *PJS v News Group Ltd*,[19] *Cartier International AG v British Telecommunications Plc*,[20] *Stocker v Stocker*,[21] and *Sutherland v HM Advocate*.[22] The number of cases rises to eight if we add *Attorney General v Crosland*[23] and *Google LLC v Lloyd*,[24] which reached the UKSC just outside the reference period in 2021, a year in which the UKSC decided a further 75 cases. Similarly, relatively few HCJAC cases raised significant points for social media, though *Murray (Craig) v HM Advocate*[25] and *Quinn John v HM Advocate*[26] are important. Although the final decision in *Murray* took place just outside the reference period, it is considered, as is *Crosland* and *Google*.

Areas covered by these cases include privacy and entrapment (*PJS, Quinn, Sutherland*); defamation (*Stocker, Joseph*); contempt of court (*Crosland, Murray*); terrorism (*G, Gul*); data protection (*Google*); and intermediary liability (*Cartier International*). In two cases, human rights were not raised for discussion (*G, Stocker*); while ECHR rights and jurisprudence were explored in *Gul, Joseph, Sutherland, PJS, Quinn, Murray, Crosland*, and *Google. Google* and *Cartier* considered the applicability of the EU principles of effectiveness and equivalence of remedies, while in *Google*, there was also reference to the Charter of Fundamental Rights of the EU (CFREU).

A further 17 UKSC decisions, primarily relating to mainstream media, are also potentially relevant for social media. These include a cluster of cases concerned with open justice and reporting restrictions;[27] responsibility for emotional distress caused by publication;[28] copyright;[29] privacy;[30] defamation;[31] access to justice/costs;[32] procedural rights to challenge reporting restrictions;[33] and access to information[34].

In carrying out this research, the online databases of the UKSC, British and Irish Legal Information Institute (Baillie) and Westlaw proved particularly useful. For European Court of Human Rights rulings and EU preliminary references, the Hudoc and Curia websites were employed.

2. Fundamental rights in national jurisprudence

2.1 General background

Within the UK, fundamental rights can be realised and protected through statute and the common law. The UK does not have a codified written constitution and, although the Human Rights Act 1998 (HRA 1998) could be considered a domestic bill of rights, its genesis, status as an ordinary statute and content – drawn directly from an international treaty, the ECHR – renders it distinct from most indigenous charters of rights.[35] These aspects have diminished public commitment to the act, facilitating current government proposals to curb significantly its operation, including the introduction of a permission stage, constraints on the operation of the proportionality principle, with an emphasis on deference to parliamentary intent, restrictions on interpreting Convention rights more expansively than the ECtHR and a limitation on the development of positive rights.[36] The proposals also require the courts to afford "great weight" to protecting freedom of expression.[37] Arguably, this would have little influence on how cases are decided, in that UK courts already recognise the individual and political importance of freedom of expression, but the proposals also include specific exceptions to this approach; for instance, in relation to "criminal proceedings", which could, paradoxically, lead to a weakening of protection in contexts where it is crucially important.[38]

The UK adopts a "dualist" approach to international law, so that treaties must be implemented in domestic law to create enforceable rights and obligations. The HRA 1998 does not make the ECHR directly binding in domestic law but instead recognises a set of "Convention rights" that replicate the rights established in articles 2–12 and 14 ECHR, article 1–3 of Protocol 1, and article 1 of Protocol 13, together with the flanking provisions in articles 16–18 ECHR.

Broadly speaking, these rights are implemented, firstly, by imposing an interpretative obligation on courts and tribunals to "read and give effect" to primary and secondary legislation "so far as . . . possible" compatibly with Convention rights.[39] Section 2 requires courts and tribunals, when determining a question relating to a Convention right, to "take into account" any "judgment, decision, declaration or advisory opinion of the European Court of Human Rights" (ECtHR), whenever made and "where the court considers this to be relevant". Secondly, section 6 HRA 1998 makes it unlawful for a "public authority", which includes courts and tribunals, to act contrary to a Convention right unless so required by primary legislation.[40] Section 12 HRA 1998 requires courts to consider the impact that any grant of relief could have on freedom of expression and to take all practical steps to inform those affected that such relief is being sought.

The HRA 1998 is not the only way in which fundamental rights are protected in domestic law. Prior to its adoption, certain HL judges suggested that the common law could adequately protect fundamental rights. Thus, Lord Goff stated, somewhat optimistically given subsequent Strasbourg case law,[41] that, in areas such as freedom of speech, there was "no inconsistency" between domestic law and the ECHR,[42] and that, wherever possible, domestic courts should interpret the law in line with the Crown's international obligations. In *Reynolds v Times Newspaper*, Lord Steyn went potentially further and stated that there was "a constitutional right to freedom of expression in England", imbued with a "higher normative force".[43] In fields such as privacy, the common law has indeed been the vehicle through which enhanced protection, influenced by Strasbourg case law, has been afforded individual rights.[44]

While an EU Member State, the UK was required to give effect to the CFREU in fields covered by EU law. In *Vidal-Hall v Google*, for example, the Court of Appeal (CA)(E&W) disapplied part of a domestic statute with reference to article 7 CFREU, which protects private and family life, and article 8 CFREU, which protects personal data.[45] The case underlined the different internal effect of the CFREU, which, prior to Brexit, could in certain situations have direct effect, and the ECHR, which could not, and cannot. By virtue of section 5(4) of the EU (Withdrawal) Act 2018 (EUWA 2018), the CFREU is, post 31 December 2020, no longer part of domestic law,[46] but section 5(5) keeps in play "fundamental rights or principles" existing in EU law "irrespective of the Charter".[47] Section 6 also provides that the validity, meaning and effect of retained EU law is to be determined with reference to both retained EU law and general principles, though the UKSC and HCJA, save in compatibility or devolution matters, are not bound by retained law.[48] CJEU decisions and principles made after 31 December 2020 have no binding force, and preliminary references can no longer be made to the Court of Justice.[49]

2.2 The influence of fundamental rights in social media cases

Over 20 years on from the adoption of the HRA 1998, litigants are well aware of the implications of a successful human rights claim. Communication cases frequently raise one or more Convention points, leading to detailed consideration of ECtHR jurisprudence, in line with section 2 HRA 1998. There has been, however, political and judicial criticism of over-reliance on the HRA 1998 where the common law or statute could offer independent protection.[50] In *Kennedy*, Lord Mance observed that Convention rights generally, though not always,

> find their homologue in the domestic common or statute law . . . [so that] the natural starting point in any dispute is to start with domestic law, and it is certainly not to focus exclusively on the Convention rights, without surveying the wider common law scene.[51]

This is not to exclude a final cross-check to ensure that the balance struck between competing values by the common law is in line with the approach adopted under the Convention rights.[52]

O v A illustrates how, even in cases that are recognised to raise clear free speech concerns, there may be little reference to Convention rights or the ECHR.[53] The UKSC was here required to consider an interim injunction prohibiting the appellant from making "generally available to the public by any means all or any part of the information referred to" in a confidential schedule. This information, included in an autobiographical book, covered graphic details of the sexual abuse endured by the appellant when a child. Publication was opposed on the basis of the English tort of wilfully causing harm without lawful excuse, it being argued that exposure to this content could cause severe emotional distress to the appellant's son. The UKSC concluded that, for the tort to be made out, there must be an intention to cause psychiatric harm or severe mental or emotional distress, leading to physical harm or recognised psychiatric illness. The father considered it unlikely the son would see the book or e-book variant until he was older,[54] but the required mental intention established by the UKSC suggests that, even were some of the information in the schedule to be posted on social media, this particular cause of action would not be applicable. In particular, the UKSC emphasised that "it is difficult to envisage any circumstances in which speech which is not deceptive, threatening or possibly abusive, could give rise to liability in tort for wilful infringement of another's right to personal safety. The right to report the truth is justification in itself".[55] Those free speech cases reviewed by the court were all domestic, and although Lord Neuberger briefly noted the relevance of Article 10 ECHR towards the end of his judgment, he concluded that the Strasbourg case law "did not take matters much further".[56]

The impact of the ECHR can also be obscured by incremental development of the common law. When balancing competing free speech and privacy interests, for example, judges frequently refer to a cluster of domestic cases that set out what is considered a well-established methodology,[57] even though Strasbourg cases have undoubtedly shaped that approach.[58] In some instances, judges consider that, in framing legislation, the legislator has already sought to balance fundamental rights, thereby obviating the need for further analysis.[59]

Articles 6 (right to a fair trial), 8 (right to respect for private and family life), and 10 (right to freedom of expression) ECHR are the main articles relied on in the cases reviewed, with occasional recourse to article 17 (abuse of law) ECHR,[60] and articles 2 (right to life) and 3 (freedom from torture and inhuman treatment) ECHR.[61] Domestic courts also seek guidance from a wide range of international treaties and standards, not just the ECHR,[62] and are willing to adopt a comparative approach when faced with complex issues, often with reference to common law jurisdictions.[63] In the context of the ECHR, UK courts sometimes review the approaches of other state parties in order to establish whether there is a broad consensus on a particular point.[64] In relation to EU law, articles 7 (respect for private and family life), 8 (protection of personal data), 11 (protection of freedom of expression) and 47 (right to an effective remedy) CFREU are the main Charter articles relied on in the cases reviewed, as well as the EU principles of equivalence and effectiveness.[65]

Although section 12 HRA 1998 emphasises the importance of freedom of expression, domestic courts have rejected, in line with Strasbourg case law,[66] that article 10 ECHR is to be afforded enhanced weight in relation to other competing rights.[67] In *NT1 and NT2 v Google LLC* (NT1), the High Court (E&W) held that the right to receive information was no less weighty than the right to impart it.[68]

The analytical approach developed by the Strasbourg court to balancing distinct rights, or rights and interests, has, as noted previously, influenced domestic law. In *R v McGreechan*, which considered the legitimacy of state restrictions on qualified rights, the Court of Appeal (NI) endorsed the previously expressed view of Baroness Hale that judges would be "well advised to adopt the same structured approach to an article 8 case as would be applied by the Strasbourg court".[69] In *PJS*, which concerned a conflict between article 10 and 8 rights, the UKSC confirmed that, even at an interim stage, it was necessary to engage in an "intense focus on the comparative importance of the rights . . . claimed"; "the justifications for interfering with or restricting each right"; as well as the proportionality of any restrictions.[70] Lord Mance noted that this process, which is in line with ECtHR guidance, was akin to an exercise of discretion and that, if undertaken on a correct basis, "would not readily attract appellate attention".[71] There is nothing to indicate this approach would differ depending on the medium, though the medium may affect circulation, audience and impact, thereby influencing the outcome of such a test. Indeed, where proceedings relate to "journalistic, literary or artistic material", section 12(4) HRA 1998 requires consideration of the extent to which the material is, or is about to be, made available to the public, the public interest in publication and any relevant privacy code. In *PJS*, the UKSC considered the fact there had been extensive coverage of the appellant's sexual conduct in websites and on social media was not a sufficient basis for lifting an interim injunction. The UKSC anticipated that such action would "add extensively and in a qualitatively different medium", notably through the printed press and newspaper websites, to the existing online invasions of privacy.[72]

One factor afforded considerable weight in the balancing process is child protection. In *PJS*, the interests of the children were not considered "trump cards", but they were highly influential in maintaining the interim injunction preventing media reporting.[73] Section 12(4)(b) HRA 1998 requires the courts to consider "any relevant privacy code", and the Independent Press Standards Organisation (IPSO) Editors' Code provides that "editors must demonstrate an exceptional public interest to over-ride the normally paramount interests [of children under 16]".[74] Similarly, although the open justice principle does not establish a presumptive *priority* in favour of publication, a convincing and cogent justification for any constraint on this principle must be established.[75]

2.3 *The impact of social media on the interpretation of fundamental rights*

What do the UK superior court cases tell us about the application of fundamental rights in the social media context? The general starting point, in line with the principle of liberty, is that the mass media do not enjoy a specially privileged position when it comes to freedom of expression over and above individual citizens.[76] In *Kennedy*, Lord Mance rejected the suggestion that an Article 10-based right to receive information could be sensibly restricted to the press and "social watchdogs", given that many other individuals could have perfectly legitimate interests in enforcing such a right.[77] On the other hand, courts and the legislature continue to recognise the democratic and social value of professional journalism,[78] and a number of privileges, such as access to court hearings closed to the public, as well as statutory protections and exemptions relating to "journalism" or "journalistic materials", have been established.[79]

If these statutory provisions are interpreted restrictively, then those using social media sites may be threatened with prosecution and/or deterred from exchanging information and points of view. In *NT 1*, the English High Court held that the "broad concept" of journalism in EU law extends "beyond . . . media undertakings" to encompass "other activities, the object of which is the disclosure to the public of information, opinions and ideas".[80] This approach, reflected in the Information Commissioner's Office guidance on the General Data Protection Regulation,[81] does not, however, encompass all online activities, the court in *NT1* concluding that the Google search service had been developed for commercial not journalism ends, even if journalistic material could be recovered through a search.[82]

In *Murray*, the HCJAC considered whether an online commentator could benefit from the principle, established in *Cumpănă v Romania*,[83] that only in exceptional circumstances, notably where other fundamental rights were seriously impaired, would it be compatible with article 10 ECHR to imprison a journalist.[84] Mr Murray was sentenced to eight months in prison for publishing, contrary to a court order, a series of online articles and a tweet, enabling the "jigsaw" identification of complainers in a sex offence trial. The HCJAC was not prepared to classify Mr Murray as a journalist, even though he attracted an online readership of around 77,000 and reported on legal and political matters of genuine public interest.[85] A journalist was defined as "a person who writes for or edits a newspaper or periodical", whether hard copy or online, and an individual could not become a journalist simply by publishing their thoughts online, "whether by operating a website, running a blog or tweeting".[86]

The existence of some form of internal or external check to ensure responsible and accurate reporting was considered relevant. The Court noted that Mr Murray was not subject to any editorial control, nor did he subscribe to any professional code of conduct.[87] Indeed, the HCJAC contrasted Mr Murray's deliberate evasion of the reporting restriction with the behaviour of the mainstream press, which refrained from publishing complainers' names without the need for a court order. But even if Mr Murray were considered a journalist, the Court considered the deliberate and unjustified incursion into the article 8 ECHR rights of the complainers brought him squarely within the *Cumpănă* exception. From a free speech perspective, this latter approach is preferable, given that social media reporters are unlikely to be able to establish the internal or external checks that the court considered necessary to be categorised as a journalist.

A related issue is whether it is legitimate to impose greater constraints on social media communications than comparable exchanges among individuals offline. In the *Chambers* case, Paul Chambers was convicted under section 127 CA 2003 for sending a tweet threatening to blow up an airport if not reopened in time for his flight.[88] His conviction was overturned on appeal on the basis that the tweet was evidently a joke, would have been so understood by those reading it and could not seriously be considered "menacing".[89] The case led the Crown Prosecution Service (E&W) to develop specific guidance on how human rights concerns should be incorporated into prosecution decisions regarding social media.[90] The guidance seeks to pre-empt, through structured consideration, human rights challenges further down the line.

Subsequent cases reflect the CA's emphasis in *Chambers* on the importance of taking into account the context and means of distribution when interpreting online communications.[91] In *Stocker*, the UKSC stated that, when determining the meaning of a statement, it was necessary to consider the ordinary reader of the communication service in question and that Facebook, like Twitter, was "a casual medium . . . in the nature of conversation rather than carefully chosen expression . . . one in which the reader reads and passes on".[92]

Despite existing guidance on the need to take into account the specific nature and context of social media communications, two cases that reached the CA illustrate continuing risks to freedom of expression online. *Scottow v Crown Prosecution Service* concerned a conviction for sending offensive tweets, contrary to section 127 CA 2003.[93] The Divisional Court found that there had been an insufficiently structured and rigorous application of article 10 ECHR and a failure to recognise "the well-established proposition that free speech encompasses the right to offend".[94] The judge, at first instance, had considered that online acts of unkindness could only be justified if they made a contribution to a "proper debate".[95] In *Miller*, Mr Miller's tweets expressing his gender-critical beliefs were reported to the police by a reader who found them transphobic and offensive, leading the police to record a "non-crime hate incident".[96] The AC considered that police recording of non-criminal expression was likely to have "a serious chilling effect on public debate", and although perception-based recording pursued a legitimate aim, there were insufficient safeguards built into the specific recording system to address the threat posed to legitimate expression.[97]

The difficulty of controlling the dissemination of information online can also lead to the removal of freedoms that the public would otherwise have enjoyed. In *Robinson*, the NICA concluded that court reporting restrictions would be insufficient to protect the appellant's article 8 ECHR interest in the confidentiality of medical information, given the ease with which details revealed at trial could be posted on the Internet.[98] The Court consequently ordered the proceedings to be closed to the public, thereby derogating from the open justice principle.

Fundamental rights have little value if actions cannot be brought to protect them, or a remedy obtained when infringed. A number of first instance and appeal court cases have considered the difficulty of obtaining a remedy where the author of the online content remains anonymous, is difficult to trace or is unlikely to respond to a court order.[99] Given these difficulties, the ability to pursue an action against the social media service provider, seeking effective removal of online content and/or payment of damages for ongoing publication, will often be crucial.[100] In the context of defamation actions, proceedings have been struck out where there has been minimal publication,[101] and the English Defamation Act 2013 now requires, as a threshold requirement, proof of serious harm. This can have knock-on effects, as in *Payam Tamiz v Google Inc*,[102] where an application to serve proceedings outside the jurisdiction on Google was set aside on the basis that the impact of any delay by Google in contacting the author of the defamatory posts was relatively trivial. Even where there is an important point of law at play, a case may thus never proceed to trial.[103]

In *Vidal-Hall*, the CA (E&W) relied on the CRFEU to disapply a section of a statute that prevented the award of damages for distress caused by data protection breaches;[104] and in *Gulati v MGN*,[105] it was prepared to award damages for "loss of control" over personal data in an action for misuse of private information involving celebrity phone hacking. In *Google*, however, the UKSC, reversing the decision of the CA, refused to allow a representative action to proceed that sought compensation for loss of control arising from data protection breaches, without the need to show material damage or distress.[106] In the UK, collective proceedings, which do not require proof of each class member's loss, are only available in competition cases, and group actions are not usually viable where there are many claims for relatively small amounts.[107] Representative actions can be brought where one or more person has the same interest in a claim, but the UKSC did not consider that the Data Protection Act 1998 could be interpreted to create the right to compensation claimed. Without the ability to bring collective proceedings, technology companies involved in wide-scale, low impact infringements, may be effectively immune from private suit, even where they have benefitted significantly from the wrongful conduct.

3. Judicial dialogue with the CJEU and ECtHR

It was apparent from the debates surrounding the passage of the HRA 1998 that section 2 was not intended to require domestic courts to follow Strasbourg case law, affording them scope to "give a lead to Europe as well as to be led".[108] In an influential opinion in 2004, however, Lord Bingham held that the duty of national courts was "to keep pace with Strasbourg jurisprudence as it evolves over time: no more, but certainly no less".[109] Although Lord Bingham left open the possibility of divergence where there were "special circumstances", subsequent case law indicated an unwillingness to depart from, or step ahead of, Strasbourg rulings.[110]

Seven years later, in *Manchester City Council v Pinnock*, Lord Neuberger MR held that it would be "impractical and sometimes inappropriate" for the UKSC to follow every ECtHR decision, even a decision of the Grand Chamber, as this "would destroy its ability to engage in constructive dialogue with the ECtHR".[111] Deviation could be appropriate where a consistent line of Strasbourg case law was inconsistent with a "fundamental substantive or procedural aspect" of UK law, or overlooked or misunderstood "some argument or point of principle".[112] *Pinnock* consequently outlined a more engaged role for domestic courts, evaluating the extent to which the Strasbourg jurisprudence "fits" with fundamental aspects of UK law.

There have subsequently been a number of cases where the UKSC has declined to follow a clear lead from the ECtHR, in some instances leading the ECtHR to then modify its own approach.[113] This two-way dialogue is illustrated by the *Animal Defenders* litigation, where the HLs refused to follow earlier ECtHR judgments that considered political advertising bans on broadcast television to be disproportionate restrictions on Article 10 ECHR, noting, in particular, that the restriction did not extend to other media.[114] On referral, the ECtHR accommodated the UK position on the basis that greater latitude should be afforded a "general measure" subject to extensive parliamentary scrutiny, particularly where there was no European consensus.[115]

Rather than reject outright a Strasbourg ruling, a domestic court may prefer to distinguish or contain it. In *Times Newspapers Ltd v Flood*,[116] the UKSC emphasised that it afforded considerable weight to an earlier Strasbourg judgment, *MGN Ltd v UK*, albeit this was an isolated Section decision reached without oral argument.[117] In *MGM*, the Strasbourg court had held that the inclusion of success fees and ATE premiums in cost orders against an unsuccessful defendant in libel and privacy actions would infringe the defendant's freedom of expression. Such actions will often involve the mainstream media but may also relate to publications on websites and social media. Although the ECtHR confirmed that the UK was pursuing a legitimate aim in assisting access to justice and enjoyed a wide margin of appreciation when implementing social and economic policies,[118] a number of factors led it to conclude that, exceptionally, the UK scheme constituted a disproportionate restriction on freedom of expression. Firstly, an extensive review of civil litigation costs in England and Wales by Lord Justice Jackson had highlighted fundamental problems with the operation of the cost provisions, and, secondly, the impact of the order in the instant case was to virtually double the costs that the defendant was required to reimburse.[119]

The UKSC in *Times Newspapers*, faced with challenges to the application of the same cost provisions at issue in *MGN*, contained direct conflict with the Strasbourg ruling by identifying specific grounds enabling it to carve out two exceptions to the ECtHR's own exceptional approach. Firstly, it refused to confirm the existence of a general rule that the imposition of success fees and insurance costs on an unsuccessful publisher would normally infringe article 10 ECHR, at least where [the publisher was] a newspaper or broadcaster.[120] This was because endorsing such a rule would make it more difficult for the UK government to re-open and challenge the reasoning in *MGN*.[121] Secondly, in relation to the actions commenced before *MGN*, the UKSC considered that the respondents had not only a legitimate expectation that their additional costs would be reimbursed but also a property right under article 1 of protocol 1 ECHR.[122] In reaching this conclusion, it drew on Strasbourg case law on legitimate expectations, an issue not addressed in *MGN*, to tip the balance of interests in favour of the respondents. Finally, in relation to the action commenced after *MGN* had been decided and having noted that Strasbourg judgments are not directly effective, the UKSC held that the illegal phone-hacking carried out by the newspaper reduced the weight to be afforded its article 10 ECHR interests, again tipping the balance in favour of recoupment of the success fees.[123]

In other instances, the ECtHR has not provided a definitive answer to the point at issue,[124] leading, in ***Sutherland***, to a restricted interpretation of the scope of article 8 ECHR.[125] More often, domestic courts are faced not with a "problematic" but clear ruling, or no ruling at all, but rather a wide range of potentially relevant cases and principles, leading to detailed, sometimes conflicting, analyses by domestic judges. In *Kennedy*, Lord Mance found the Strasbourg jurisprudence on the right to receive information "neither clear nor easy to reconcile".[126] Faced with divergent Grand Chamber and Section decisions, he considered that the responsibility of the domestic court was to do its best to "understand underlying principles".[127] Since the various Sections had not clearly explained why they diverged from the principles established by the Grand Chamber, he indicated that, if a decisive issue, he would have followed the Grand Chamber rulings, in part to avoid the creation of a general and unspecific European freedom of information law.[128]

In *JR38*, a newspaper case of potential relevance for social media, Lord Kerr, supported by Lord Wilson, after reviewing key ECtHR decisions such as *Sciacca v Italy*,[129] concluded that it was not necessary for there to be a reasonable expectation of privacy for article 8 ECHR to be engaged.[130] In particular, Lord Kerr drew on international law when interpreting article 8 ECHR, which led him to consider a different principle: the best interests of the child. The risk that publication of the child's criminal activity could affect his or her development led him to conclude that article 8 ECHR was in play.[131] The majority did not accept that there could be a reasonable expectation of privacy in relation to behaviour such as rioting and concluded that article 8 ECHR was not engaged. They either distinguished the Strasbourg cases addressed by Lord Kerr or disagreed with his interpretation. Statements by the ECtHR that a reasonable expectation of privacy might not be conclusive for the application of article 8 ECHR were regarded as "intriguing but obscure".[132]

In *Sutherland v HM Advocate*, the question was whether an adult, as opposed to a child, could rely on article 8 ECHR to prevent, firstly, the disclosure to the police of sexually explicit online messages sent via a WhatsApp messaging service to a decoy "paedophile hunter", and, secondly, reliance on that material as evidence in a criminal prosecution.[133] In this instance, the UKSC was unanimous in holding that the reprehensible nature of the communications meant that article 8 ECHR was not engaged, a view bolstered by reference to article 17 ECHR and the fact that the ECtHR had left open their response to this question in *KU v Finland*.[134] The decoy did not have a reasonable expectation that potentially criminal online messages would not be passed to the police.

Moreover, the online messages were between private individuals, so that, if article 8 ECHR were to be engaged, it would operate to impose a *positive* duty on the state to intervene to protect children from harm by others, not to protect the potential abuser. The UKSC considered the decision to use the messages as evidence in court fell within the broad margin of appreciation afforded states when implementing positive obligations.[135] In *Quinn*, a Scottish case that led to the appeal in *Sutherland*, the HCJAC held that although, "at a general level, a person's internet chats [might fall] . . . within the broad ambit of art.8(1)", where there was no longstanding pre-existing relationship between the appellants and the decoys, the appellants could have no reasonable expectation their online communications would remain confidential.[136]

If we consider "dialogue" from the Strasbourg side, not only has the overall number of UK applications fallen dramatically, down from 1,542 in 2011 to 301 in 2021,[137] but the proportion of "dynamic" decisions – those identifying a violation of the ECHR and thus requiring a change in the law or judicial approach, to "static" decisions, those where no violation is found and which thus endorse the domestic status quo – has also been falling.[138] Amos found this shift most noticeable during 2015–2017, which may reflect more effective human rights protection within the domestic system but could also indicate that the ECtHR has responded to trenchant political and media criticism within the UK through wider application of the margin of appreciation.[139]

Of those cases with direct or potential relevance for social media communications, static and dynamic cases were fairly evenly divided. The static cases identified were *MGN*,[140] regarding the substantive law of privacy, *Tamiz*,[141] *Dallas*[142] and *Mosley*.[143] In *Tamiz*, the ECtHR held that,

> given the important role that information society service providers . . . performed in facilitating access to information and debate on a wide range of political, social and cultural topics, the respondent state's margin of appreciation . . . was necessarily a wide one.[144]

It was thus legitimate to refuse service outside the jurisdiction on Google Inc., where the claim was relatively trivial. In *Mosley*, the ECtHR was not prepared to impose on the UK a pre-publication notification requirement in privacy cases where there was no evidence that other state parties endorsed such an approach.[145]

Dynamic cases included *Financial Times v UK*,[146] regarding the protection of journalists' sources; *Big Brother Watch v UK*, where the Grand Chamber found there to be insufficient protection of journalists' communications under the UK's bulk interception surveillance regime;[147] *MGN*, in relation to costs;[148] and *Mackay v UK*,[149] on the right to challenge court reporting restrictions. The UK publishes annual reports on those ECHR cases brought against it and the steps taken to respond to negative rulings,[150] enabling developments to be tracked over time.

As the *MGN* case illustrates, domestic judges may not be in a position to satisfactorily respond to ECtHR decisions, necessitating legislative intervention to address policy implications.[151] In *MGN*, the Government ultimately excluded recovery of lawyers' success fees from the losing party, which, together with changes introduced in the Defamation Act 2013, were considered to adequately address the article 10 ECHR concerns.[152] In relation to *Big Brother Watch*,[153] legislative changes in the form of the Investigatory Powers Act 2016 did not address the concerns relating to bulk interception and journalists' materials, necessitating further action by the UK.[154] In other contexts, judges can adequately respond to a "dynamic ruling" through development of the common law or their interpretation of statutory provisions. The principles relating to the protection of journalists' sources, identified in *Financial Times*, and the earlier case of *Goodwin v UK*,[155] have, for example, gradually gained judicial traction, particularly in the context of private disputes. Thus, the English High Court in *Arcadia Group Ltd Topshop/Topman Ltd, Sir Philip Green v Telegraph Media Group Ltd* set out a number of guidelines derived directly from *Goodwin*, which it considered to be both "clearly established" and "not controversial".[156] But journalists' materials may still be compromised by the exercise of police or surveillance powers provided for in a range of statutory provisions,[157] as the *Big Brother Watch* case illustrated.[158] Domestic courts may also take into account the broader implications of a "dynamic" ECtHR decision, beyond the specific legal context of that decision. Thus, in *A v BBC*,[159] the UKSC drew on *Mackay v UK*, which concerned reporting restrictions under section 4(2) of the Contempt of Court Act 1981, in a case involving an anonymity order under section 11 of the same act. The UKSC recognised that it would often be impractical for those potentially affected by an anonymity order, including "bloggers, social media users and internet-based organisations",[160] to be given an opportunity to be heard prior to an order being made. The protection of their article 10 interests could, however, be preserved by allowing them to seek a speedy hearing at which the recall of the order could be considered.[161]

A number of cases reviewed considered the relationship between EU law and Convention rights. In *R(National Council for Civil Liberties) v Secretary of State for the Home Department*, the Divisional Court (E&W) declined to interpret the CFREU in line with the 2021 Grand Chamber *Big Brother Watch* ruling, on the basis that this would give direct, domestic force to the Strasbourg judgment via EU law, which it would not otherwise have had.[162] The Court observed that the CJEU did not regard itself bound by judgments of the ECtHR and "jealously guards its own independence in matters of EU law".[163] In *Google*, the UKSC was not prepared to accept that because data protection rights and the right to prevent misuse of private information both aimed, at a general level, to protect article 8 ECHR, similar remedies should be available in both contexts. The scope and nature of the interests at play were different. In particular, the UKSC noted the latitude afforded states not only by the ECtHR where positive ECHR obligations were in play but also by the CJEU when determining whether a state had provided an effective remedy for a breach of EU law.[164]

4. Conclusion

Both the ECHR and EU law have been decisive in strengthening, if not establishing, important rights and protections relevant for the communications sector in the UK. With the departure of the UK from the EU, the HRA 1998, with its bridge to Strasbourg case law, offers ongoing protection for human rights at a time of political and economic change. The dwindling number of applications from the UK to the Strasbourg court suggests that human rights concerns are being more systematically and appropriately addressed within the domestic judicial system – a view supported by the greater proportion of "static" to "dynamic" ECtHR judgments. But the exchange is not all one way, and there continue to be cases involving "robust and effective dialogue between the UK Courts and the ECtHR", enabling each to "learn from and influence the other".[165] Moreover, the substance of the "dynamic" communications cases discussed previously in this chapter – undue costs, confidentiality of sources, secret surveillance, open justice – underline the ongoing importance of the ECtHR in supporting accountable, democratic processes in the UK.[166]

To date, relatively few social media cases have found their way to the UKSC. Why is this? Firstly, the UKSC focuses on cases raising significant points of law, while many social media cases turn on the outcome of balancing competing rights or interests, a fact-dependent exercise that is difficult to challenge.[167] Secondly, certain first instance and appeal court judges have considerable expertise in the field, and their decisions may not be readily appealable.[168] Thirdly, threshold requirements and potential costs will, in many instances, prevent or deter first instance or appeal proceedings, save for the odd celebrity, businessperson or politician.[169] Fourthly, given the difficulties in raising representative, collective or group actions, it may not be economically viable to seek redress where there are multiple but low-value claims.[170] Finally, technology companies may prefer to settle individual actions, without admission of fault, to avoid risking a negative precedent.[171] Key issues may thus never be finally resolved in court. Given these factors, the number of social media cases reaching the UKSC seems destined to remain low; but this is just the small tip of a larger, more diverse and, arguably, impactful iceberg of lower court decisions floating just below the surface.

Notes

1 Jovana Zivkovic, 'UK Media Statistics and Facts [2022]' (31 March 2022) <https://cybercrew.uk/blog/social-media-statistics-uk/> accessed 30 July 2022.
2 Ibid.
3 Scotland Act 1998, schedule 5; Government of Wales Act 2006, schedule 7A, as amended by the Wales Act 2017; Northern Ireland Act 1998, schedules 2 and 3.
4 Scotland Act 1998; Government of Wales Act 2006, as amended by the Wales Act 2017; Northern Ireland Act 1998.
5 Scotland Act 1998, section 29(2)(d), Government of Wales Act 2006, section 108A(2)(e); Northern Ireland Act 1998, section 6(2)(c).
6 European Union (Withdrawal) Act 2018, as amended by the European Union (Withdrawal Agreement) Act 2020. Discussion of the various implications for the devolved nations is out with the scope of this chapter.
7 See Part 1, Schedule 6, Scotland Act 2012.
8 UKSC, The Jurisdiction of the Supreme Court of the United Kingdom in Scottish Appeals: Human Rights, the Scotland Act 2012 and the Courts Reform (Scotland) Act 2014 <www.supremecourt.uk/about/role-of-the-supreme-court.html> accessed 12 August 2022.
9 Constitutional Reform Act 2005.
10 James Lee, 'Against All Odds: Numbers Sitting in the UK Supreme Court and Really, Really Important Cases' in James Daly (ed), *Apex Courts and the Common Law* (University of Toronto Press 2019) 94.
11 Consider, for example, the Defamation Act 2013 (E&W) and Defamation and Malicious Publications (Scotland) Act 2021.

12 House of Commons Home Affairs Select Committee, Hate Crime: Abuse, Hate and Extremism Online, Fourteenth Report of Session 2016–17, HC609. Mrs. Cox's murder at a time of heightened tensions in the run up to the EU membership referendum highlighted the vulnerability of MPs to extremist attack and the level of disturbing online threats to which MPs, particularly female, are exposed, see Report paras. 2 and 17.
13 Ibid, 56.
14 Law Commission, Modernising Communication Offences, A Final Report, Law Com No 399, 21 July 2021.
15 UK Government, Draft Online Safety Bill, CP 405, 12 May 2021. Although the Bill responds to similar concerns and shares some of the regulatory approaches in the EU Digital Services Act (for instance, staggered responsibilities dependent on scale, distinction between illegal and harmful content), it is very much a domestic proposal, following a distinct post-Brexit trajectory. The Bill has been significantly amended during parliamentary review and changes can be tracked at <https://bills.parliament.uk/bills/3137/publications> accessed 30 September 2022.
16 [2009] UKHL 13, [2010] 1 AC 43.
17 [2010] UKSC 53, [2011] 1 AC 852.
18 [2013] UKSC 64, [2014] AC 1260.
19 [2016] UKSC 26, [2016] AC 1081.
20 [2018] UKSC 28, [2018] 1 WLR 3258.
21 [2019] UKSC 17, [2020] AC 593.
22 [2020] UKSC 32, [2020] 3 WLR 327.
23 [2021] UKSC 58, [2022] 1 WLR 367.
24 [2021] UKSC 50, [2021] 3 WLR 1268.
25 [2022] HCJAC 14, 2022 SLT 647, leave to appeal to the UKSC having been refused.
26 [2019] HCJAC 61, 2022 SLT 541, with appeal to the USKC in *Sutherland* (n 22).
27 For instance, *Guardian News and Media Ltd, Re* [2010] UKSC 1, [2010] 2 AC 697; *A v BBC* [2014] UKSC 25, [2015] AC 588 and *Khuja v Times Newspaper* [2017] UKSC 49, [2019] AC 161.
28 *O v A* [2015] UKSC 32, [2016] AC 219.
29 *Public Relations Consultants Association Limited (Appellant) v The Newspaper Licensing Agency Limited and Others* [2013] UKSC 18, [2013] 2 All E.R. 852.
30 *JR 38's Application for Judicial Review, Re* [2015] UKSC 42, [2016] AC 1131.
31 For instance, *Flood v Times* Newspapers Ltd [2012] UKSC 11, [2012] 2 AC 273, *Lachaux v Independent Print Ltd* [2019] UKSC 27, [2020] AC 612.
32 *Times Newspapers Ltd v Flood* [2017] UKSC 33, [2017] 1 WLR 1415.
33 *R (on the application of British Sky Broadcasting Limited) (Respondent) v The Commissioner of Police of the Metropolis (Appellant)* [2014] UKSC 17, [2014] AC 885.
34 *BBC v Sugar* [2012] UKSC 4, [2012] 1 WLR 439; *Kennedy v The Charity Commission* [2014] UKSC 20, [2015] AC 455.
35 Rene Wolfsteller, 'Out of Sync: The Failed Translation of International Human Rights in the Creation of the UK Human Rights Act' (2020) 19 *Journal of Human Rights* 325.
36 Ministry of Justice, Human Rights Act Reform: A Modern Bill of Rights, December 2021, CP588, see further the follow-up Bill of Rights Bill 117, 2022–2023 <https://publications.parliament.uk/pa/bills/cbill/58-03/0117/220117.pdf> accessed 30 September 2022 The Bill proposes a permission stage for actions brought against a public authority for infringement of a Convention right, with a requirement that the person affected must have suffered, or would suffer, a 'significant disadvantage', though this criterion may be disregarded where there are 'wholly exceptional public interest' reasons (section 15).

37 Bill of Rights Bill 117, 2022–2023 (n 36), section 4.
38 See Jacob Rowbottom, 'Will the Bill of Rights Enhance the Protection of Freedom of Speech?' (Inforrm's Blog, 29 June 2022) <https://inforrm.org/> accessed 1 October 2022.
39 Section 3 HRA 1998.
40 Section 6 HRA 1998.
41 See cases detailed at (n 146)-(n 149).
42 *Attorney General v Guardian Newspapers Ltd [No.2]* [1990] 1 AC 109, Lord Goff [283]-[284].
43 *Reynolds v Times Newspapers* [2001] 2 AC 127, [1999] 3 WLR 1010, Lord Steyn [207]. On the shift from residual liberties to presumed rights see Dan Meagher, 'Is There a Common Law "Right" to Freedom of Speech' (2020) 43 *Melbourne University Law Review* 269.
44 The leading case being *Campbell v Mirror Group Newspapers* [2004] UKHL 22, [2004] 2 AC 457. For discussion of judicial attitudes to engaging with Convention rights see Michael Blackwell, 'Indeterminacy, Disagreement and the Human Rights Act: An Empirical Study of Litigation in the UK House of Lords and Supreme Court 1997–2017' (2020) 83 *Modern Law Review* 285.
45 *Vidal-Hall* [2015] EWCA Civ 311, [2016] QB 1003.
46 C Barnard, 'Farewell, Auf Wiedersehen, Adieu: Brexit and the Charter of Fundamental Rights' (2019) 82 *Modern Law Review* 350.
47 The general principles extend to rights recognised in the ECHR: see article 6(3), Treaty on European Union, 2016 consolidated version, OJ C 202, 7 June 2016, 13.
48 Though further complication by schedule 1(3), discussed by E Frantziou, 'The Horizontal Effect of Human Rights After Brexit: A Matter of Renewed Constitutional Significance' (2021) 4 *European Human Rights Law Review* 365.
49 Section 6.
50 For an overview of case law, see Gross, Davis, O'Loan, Laws, Mullen, Cahill, Giovannetti, Bates, The Independent Human Rights Act Review, December 2021, CP 586, 61–63, and, for academic discussion, Conor Gearty, *On Fantasy Island: Britain, Europe, and Human Rights* (OUP 2016), chapter 9.
51 *Kennedy* (n 34) 46.
52 *A v BBC* (n 27) 57.
53 *O v A* (n 28).
54 Ibid, 75.
55 Ibid, 77.
56 Ibid, 120.
57 *PJS* (n 19), Lord Neuberger [59]-[60].
58 For instance, *Axel-Springer AG v Germany* [2012] 55 EHRR 6.
59 *Riley v Murray* [2021] EWHC 3437 (QB), Nicklin J [129].
60 *Sutherland* (n 22).
61 *A v BBC* (n 27).
62 For example, in *JR38* (n 30) 49–53, where Lord Kerr relied, inter alia, on the UN Convention on the Rights of the Child (adopted 20 November 1989, entered into force 2 September 1990) 1577 UNTS 3.
63 See *Google* (n 24) 59–66.
64 *Guardian News* (n 27) 53–57.
65 *Google* (n 24) 119–137.
66 *Axel-Springer* (n 58)[87].
67 *PJS* (n 19) 19; *Khuja* (n 27) 23.
68 *NT1* [2018] EWHC 799 (QB), [2019] QB 344 [134].
69 *McGreechan* [2014] NICA 5 [28].

70 *PJS* (n 19) 20.
71 Ibid.
72 PJS (n 19) 1, see Jacob Rowbottom, 'Holding Back the Tide: Privacy Injunctions and the Digital Media' (2017) 133 *Law Quarterly Review* 177.
73 *PJS* (n 19) 72.
74 IPSO, 'Editors' Code' (January 2021) <www.ipso.co.uk> accessed 30 July 2022.
75 *R (on application of Rai) v Winchester Crown Court* [2021] EWHC 339, see also *Guardian News and Media Ltd.* (n 27) 35–36.
76 *Reynolds* (n 43) Lord Steyn.
77 *Kennedy* (n 34) 93.
78 See *McCartan Turkington Breen v Times Newspapers* [2001] 2 AC 277 [290].
79 See, for example, section 12 HRA; Police and Criminal Evidence Act 1984, sections 9, 11, 13, 14 and schedule 1; General Data Protection Act 2018, schedule 2, part 5; and note the negative appraisal of the protection for journalists under previous provisions in the Regulation of Investigatory Powers Act 2000, in *Big Brother Watch v UK* (2022) 74 EHRR 17 [456]-[457].
80 *NT1* (n 68) 95–102.
81 See ICO, 'Draft Journalism Code of Practice' (13 October 2021) <https://ico.org.uk/media/about-the-ico/documents/4018647/journalism-code-draft-202110.pdf> accessed 30 July 2022 and *Sugar* (n 34) 39.
82 *NT1* (n 68).
83 *Cumpănă v Romania* (2005) 41 EHRR 14 [113]-[115].
84 *Murray* (n 25).
85 Ibid, 40.
86 *Murray* (n 25) 77.
87 Ibid, 78.
88 *Chambers v DPP* [2012] EWHC 2157 (Admin), [2013] 1 WLR 1833.
89 Ibid, 29–34.
90 Crown Prosecution Service, *Guidelines on Prosecuting Cases Involving Communications Sent Over Social Media*, revised 21 August 2018, in particular paras 23–25, 28 <www.cps.gov.uk/legal-guidance/social-media-guidelines-prosecuting-cases-involving-communications-sent-social-media> accessed 30 July 2022.
91 See, for instance, on linked posts, *Wildcat Haven Enterprises CIC v Wightman* [2020] CSOH 30; 2020 SLT 473.
92 *Stocker* (n 21) 43.
93 *Scottow* [2020] EWHC 3421, [2021] 1 WLR 1828.
94 Ibid, 43.
95 Ibid.
96 *R.(On the application of Miller) v College of Policing* [2021]EWCA 1926, [2021] 12 WLUK 253.
97 Ibid, 108–122.
98 *Robinson v Sunday Newspapers Ltd* [2011] NICA 13 (25 May 2011) [24].
99 *Blackledge v Persons Unknown* [2021] EWHC 1994 (QB), [2021] 7 WLUK 179.
100 *AY v Facebook (Ireland) Ltd* [2016] NIQB 76, [2016] 9 WLUK 153; *NT1* (n 64).
101 *Jameel (Yousef) v Dow Jones & Co Inc* [2005] EWCA Civ 75, [2005] QB 946.
102 *Tamiz v Google Inc* [2013] EWCA Civ 68; [2013] 1 WLR 2151.
103 Freddy Mayhew, 'Higher Threshold of Harm Has Seen Number of UK Defamation Cases Drop as Celebs Look to Privacy Actions to Fight Libel' (*Press Gazette*, 23 April 2018) <News Archives – Press Gazette> accessed 28 July 2022.
104 *Vidal-Hall* (n 45).
105 *Gulati* [2015] EWCA Civ 1291, [2017] QB 149 [45].
106 *Google* (n 24).

107 Ibid, 25.
108 See Independent HRA Review (n 50) at 35, with reference to comments by the then Lord Chancellor, Lord Irvine.
109 *R (Ullah) v Special Adjudicator* [2004] UKHL 26; [2004] 3 WLR 23 [20].
110 See *Secretary of State for the Home Department v AF* [2009] UKHL 28; [2010] 2 AC 269. It is clear from *Kennedy* (n 34) that there remains a reluctance to move ahead of Strasbourg case law, though judicial openness varies, on which see Lord Wilson, *Sugar* (n 34) 59, and detailed case law analysis by the Independent HRA Review (n 50) 55–60.
111 *Pinnock* [2010] UKSC 45, [2011] 2 AC 104.
112 Ibid, 48.
113 Independent HRA Review (n 50) 139–145.
114 *Animal Defenders International v Secretary of State for Culture, Media and Sport* [2008] UKHL 15; [2008] 1 AC 1312 [32].
115 *Animal Defenders International v UK* (2013) 57 EHRR 21 [110]-[124].
116 *Times Newspapers* (n 32) 31–32.
117 *MGN* (2011) 53 EHRR 5.
118 Ibid, 200.
119 *MGN* (n 117) 217–218.
120 *Times Newspapers* (n 32) 27, 29. The presumptive exclusion of newspapers and broadcasters from liability to pay enhanced costs was presumably on the basis that these media perform a democratic function. But other publishers, such as citizen journalists and those communicating via social media, may similarly be deterred from publishing valuable commentary and opinions.
121 *Times Newspapers* (n 32) 29.
122 Ibid, 42–56.
123 Ibid, 57–63.
124 As in *Joseph* (n 17) 74, *Sutherland* (n 22) 40.
125 *Sutherland* (n 22) discussed further later.
126 *Kennedy* (n 34) 59.
127 Ibid, 60.
128 *Kennedy* (n 34) 94.
129 (2006) 43 EHRR 400.
130 *JR38* (n 30).
131 Ibid, 67–81.
132 *JR38* (n 30) 100–194, with reference to *PG v UK* (2001) 46 EHRR 1272 [57].
133 *Sutherland* (n 22).
134 Ibid, 40.
135 *Lopez Ribalda v Spain* (2020) 71 EHRR 7.
136 *Quinn* (n 26) 49.
137 Ministry of Justice, Responding to Human Rights Judgments, Report to the Joint Committee on Human Rights on the Government's response to human rights judgments 2020–2021 <https://assets.publishing.service.gov.uk/government/uploads/system/uploads/attachment_data/file/1038220/human-rights-judgments-response-2021.pdf> accessed 2 October 2022.
138 Merris Amos, 'From Dynamic to Static: The Evolution of the Relationship Between the UK and the European Court of Human Right' (2018) 42 *Teoria y Realidad Constitucional* 161.
139 Ibid, note also 2015 adoption of Protocol 15 ECHR, in force August 2021.
140 *MGN* (n 117).
141 *Tamiz v UK* [2017] 10 WLUK 270, [2018] EMLR 6.
142 *Dallas v UK* (2016) 63 EHRR 13, regarding the clarity of jury directions re internet searches.

143 *Mosley v UK* (2011) 53 EHRR 30.
144 *Tamiz* (n 141) 90.
145 *Mosley* (n 143).
146 *Financial Times v UK* (2010) 50 EHRR 46.
147 *Big Brother Watch* (n 79) (just outside the reference period).
148 *MGN* (n 117).
149 *Mackay v UK* (2011) 53 EHRR 19.
150 See Government website with links to the various reports at <www.gov.uk/government/collections/human-rights-the-governments-response-to-human-rights-judgments> accessed 2 October 2022.
151 See text accompanying n 120.
152 Ministry of Justice, Responding to Human Rights Judgments, Report to the Joint Committee on Human Rights on the Government's response to human rights judgments 2018–2019, p. 31 <https://assets.publishing.service.gov.uk/government/uploads/system/uploads/attachment_data/file/842553/responding-human-rights-judgments-2019.pdf> accessed 2 October 2022.
153 N 74.
154 Ministry of Justice 2020–2021 (n 137) 14, accessed 2 October 2022.
155 *Goodwin v UK* (1996) 22 EHRR 123.
156 [2019] EWHC 96 (QB), 2019 WL 00295144 [15].
157 See *R(on the application of Miranda) v Sec. of State for the Home Department* [2016] EWCA Civ 6, [2016] 1 WLR 1505, where powers under the Terrorism Act 2000 to stop and search someone at a border point were held incompatible with Article 10 ECHR in that they did not include adequate protection for journalistic material.
158 Judith Townend and Richard Danbury, 'Protecting Sources and Whistleblowers in a Digital Age' (22 February 2017) <https://papers.ssrn.com/sol3/papers.cfm?abstract_id=2961911> accessed 2 October 2022.
159 N 27.
160 Ibid, 67.
161 Ibid.
162 *NCCL* [2022] EWHC 1630 (Admin), [2022] 6 WLUK 286 [150]-[155].
163 Ibid, though consider relevance of article 52.3 CFREU.
164 *Google* (n 24) 124.
165 Independent HRA Review (n 50) 141.
166 Potentially significantly constrained by government proposals in: Human Rights Act Reform (n 36).
167 *PJS* (n 19) 20.
168 Ibid, 60.
169 *Tamiz* (n 102).
170 *Google* (n 24).
171 Consider *AY v Facebook (Ireland) Ltd* (n 100), which settled prior to determining whether Facebook should have used PhotoDNA, once notified, to prevent further posting of a sexualised image of a child; and *Vidal-Hall* (n 45), which settled before Google filed a defence, noted at *Google* (n 24) 2.

14 Courts, rights and powers in the digital age

Giovanni De Gregorio and Oreste Pollicino

1. The amplification of the role of courts in the digital age

The challenges raised by the digital environment, and particularly by social media, have underlined how courts play a critical role as engines of adaptation and reaction. This judicial momentum has led to an emerging imbalance between judicial and political actors in facing the new challenges associated with the protection of fundamental rights online.[1]

The amplification of this imbalance is part of the general increase of the judiciary role over politics from the nineteenth century, through the consolidation of the Welfare State, to the present post-modern globalised governance.[2] In the twentieth century, the executive branch replaced Parliament in taking the leading role within modern welfare societies. The Welfare State could no longer be based on the exercise of traditional, punitive functions or a limited role in the protection of negative freedoms. On the contrary, this new paradigm promised active and positive protection for citizens. Such an attitude involves, by definition, planning policies and actions for future developments, while formulating social aims and principles broadly, leaving the courts with the task of giving tangible meaning to these principles in context, as well as defining their extent and limits.

The limited role of lawmakers has encouraged judicial creativity and the amplification of judges' *marge de manoeuvre*.[3] The "road to juristocracy" is thus one of the main trends within post-modern constitutionalism in the era of judicial globalisation.[4] In other (more convincing) words, judicial power has moved from being the "weak ring" of the chain to becoming the strong one. Judge-made law seems to be better placed than legislative or administrative acts, both for its flexibility and its pragmatic approach, to face the challenges of legal systems as they become increasingly more interdependent, while subject to constant and unforeseen global transformations. To put it blandly, global governance seems to prefer the language of the "law in action" rather than the ink of the "law in the books".[5] And this trend has been confirmed by the role of courts in addressing the challenges raised by the digital environment.

This chapter primarily focuses on three main perspectives that underline the role of courts in the digital age, particularly with regard to the protection

DOI: 10.4324/9781003207085-16

of fundamental rights. By adopting a European perspective, first, this chapter addresses how courts rely on metaphors to address the transformation of the digital age, thus underlining the role of judicial imagination. Second, it examines how European judicial actors react to legislative inertia by expanding their role and the limit of interpretation to protect fundamental rights. Third, this chapter underlines that the expansion of the role of courts through imagination and reaction constitutes guidance for lawmakers and an opportunity for dialogue in the digital age.

2. Judicial imagination

The traditional gap between law and technology, where law lags behind technological advances, can be considered one of the substantive reasons for the amplification of judicial imagination. The burden of making up for this inevitable legislative inertia – at national and supranational level – falls heavily on the shoulders of the courts. In this context, political inertia (which is not always forced as sometimes power is delegated to courts with a view to avoiding difficult choices) has fostered judicial imagination within the digital era,[6] along with the resulting use of metaphors and frames to adapt legal systems to the peculiarities of the digital realm.[7]

Metaphorical language performs an irreplaceable role across different fields,[8] including the law. In fact, many legal categories and constructs have been developed through metaphorical processes. Within this ambit, metaphors perform a constitutive function of legal reality itself: consider, for instance, the categories of "legal person" or "sovereignty" in all of its manifestations (state, national, popular, etc.). As Blavin and Cohen write, "Courts and commentators employ metaphors as heuristics to generate hypotheses about the application of law to novel, unexplored domains. Metaphors structure the way lawyers conceptualize legal events, as they infiltrate, consciously and unconsciously, legal discourse".[9] These scholars have analysed three different ways of describing the Internet in metaphorical terms: "the information superhighway", "cyberspace", and the Internet as a "real space". They have shown how these conceptual metaphors influence the solution of legal problems involving the Internet.[10]

However, this aspect is not always fully appreciated and metaphorical language has not always been viewed favourably within arguments deployed by legal practitioners (above all, in those used by courts). Thus, for example, within the US debate, Posner has asserted that "analogies cannot resolve legal disputes intelligently. To say that something is in some respects like something else is to pose questions rather than answer them".[11] And before him, Cardozo argued – wearing his judge's hat – that "metaphors in law are to be narrowly watched, for starting as devices to liberate thought, they end often by enslaving it".[12] It is of singular significance that, in condemning metaphors Cardozo recourses to a dual metaphor; namely, the liberation of thought and its reduction to slavery. More generally, the creation of new fictions by the courts has been viewed with suspicion by various US scholars, as such activity is claimed to jeopardise the "judicial candor" that should – so the argument goes – characterise the decision-making processes of both judges and courts.[13]

Based on the conceptual and cognitive paradigm of the metaphor, it is also possible to infer a paradigm that is useful for studying some interesting issues arising in relation to judicial protection for fundamental rights in the digital environment: the frame. More specifically, particular attention must be dedicated to the interactive conception and the theory of conceptual metaphors. The interactive conception, which was developed from the 1950s onwards, above all by Black,[14] considers a metaphor to be the result of a process of semantic interaction, or more specifically, as the product of the combination of an expression used metaphorically (the "focus") and the enunciative structure within which the expression is framed (the "frame"). The conceptual and cognitive paradigm of the metaphor presupposes the fundamental concept of "frame". Within the specific context of legal argumentation, a "judicial frame" is the expressive structure and, more broadly, the reference context for the reasoning set out in the judgment.

Different balances are struck and diverging solutions are found, even in cases that are essentially similar or identical, depending upon the particular judicial frame chosen by a court. In other words, the notion of frame must be shifted from cognitive studies to the theory of interpretation and argumentation. As Sajó and Ryan point out, "translation of a technology and its consequences into the legal frame is not automatic".[15] This is where courts play an important role through the judicial process of translating something new into the language of past legal models by means of the judicial framing technique.

It is important to stress how this activity consisting of a "conceptual transfer" from the world of atoms to the world of bits is not neutral but is, rather, based on the frame of values on which it is founded. The use of a particular value frame is capable not only of influencing the argumentative structure of a decision and the balance struck by the courts, but also, consequently, of impinging upon the level of protection for the fundamental rights in play. This has been clear when considering the different judicial outcomes in the US and Europe. In the *Reno* judgment, the US Supreme Court held that:

> As a matter of constitutional tradition, in the absence of evidence to the contrary, we presume that governmental regulation of the content of speech is more likely to interfere with the free exchange of ideas than to encourage it. The interest in encouraging freedom of expression in a democratic society outweighs any theoretical but unproven benefit of censorship.[16]

The judicial frame adopted by the US Supreme Court not only enables protection for freedom of expression to be extended to the digital domain but also fosters its scope as a new channel for promoting the free marketplace of ideas.[17] This metaphor is in some ways deeply linked to a particular concept of liberal democracy, in which the role of the State is minimal.[18]

When comparing this passage to the findings reached in the decisions of the European Court of Human Rights (ECtHR) on the compatibility with Article 10 of the European Convention on Human Rights (ECHR), it is possible to identify a European judicial frame that seeks to re-moderate the expansive scope of freedom of expression in the digital domain. Perhaps the most complete manifestation of this cautious approach may be found in 2011, when the ECtHR in *Editorial Board of Pravoye Delo and Shtekel v Ukraine* case held that:

> The Internet is an information and communication tool particularly distinct from the printed media, especially as regards the capacity to store and transmit information. The electronic network, serving billions of users worldwide, is not and potentially will never be subject to the same regulations and control. The risk of harm posed by content and communications on the Internet to the exercise and enjoyment of human rights and freedoms, particularly the right to respect for private life, is certainly higher than that posed by the press. Therefore, the policies governing reproduction of material from the printed media and the Internet may differ. The latter undeniably have to be adjusted according to technology's specific features in order to secure the protection and promotion of the rights and freedoms concerned.[19]

It is evident that the ECtHR, without ever neglecting the added value of digital technology,[20] placed the emphasis less on the benefits of a further expansion in the exercise of freedom of expression online and more on the risks that such an expansion could have on the effective protection of the rights and freedoms that may come into conflict with it. In other words, the two courts seem to be working on the basis of opposite presumptions. Whilst the US Supreme Court presumes that content regulation does not give rise to greater benefits for freedom, the ECtHR, which is more suspicious, considers the digital environment as a threat to rights and freedoms, thus stressing the need for proportionate and necessary actions to limit the exercise of free speech. This approach has also been followed by national courts in Member States that have underlined the transformation driven by digital technologies as highlighted, for instance, in the case of Ireland.[21]

The *de facto* freedom enjoyed by the courts within the digital domain in choosing the metaphorical universe that is capable of offering the decisive parameters for resolving jurisdictional disputes that come before them has, for some time, triggered further debate in both North America and Europe concerning the institutional role of the courts.[22] These are familiar questions, which need not therefore be considered further here, and may be largely countered by an objection, which has been raised from various quarters concerning the supposed lack of democratic legitimacy for a decision-making body with such broad and fluid boundaries. It cannot be denied that the courts currently occupy a privileged position within their respective legal systems in identifying the risks of constitutionally relevant collisions between rights, both internally and externally.

The continuous and dizzying changes in the world of technology, coupled with the transnational nature of the web, considerably magnify the difficulties, which are already apparent in other areas that national (although also supranational) legislatures encounter in providing even minimum normative protection capable of addressing the most significant questions. It is evident that an immediate consequence of that inertia or inadequacy on the legislative side is the amplification of the creative, substitutive role of the courts in the digital age.

The rise and consolidation of social media is an example of how the European frame has led courts to expand their judicial imagination as a reaction to the challenges raised by the transformation of the digital age, including the exercise of quasi-public powers by social media and the privatisation of the protection of individual rights. While public enforcement has long since been the default option, based on the role of public authorities as monopolists within the context of fundamental rights protection, private enforcement has recently emerged as a new trend for protecting fundamental rights in the digital realm.

3. Judicial reactions

3.1 Judicial Activism

The consolidation of social media has triggered judicial reactions in Europe. Given the lack of any legislative review of either the e-Commerce Directive[23] or the Data Protection Directive[24] until recently, courts have played a primary role in highlighting the role of fundamental rights and democratic values that are hidden between the lines of the system of content. Apart from the reference to Article 10 ECHR,[25] there are no other points in the e-Commerce Directive expressing the relationship between online intermediaries and fundamental rights. This gap was evident in the case law of the Court of Justice of the European Union (CJEU) before the adoption of the Lisbon Treaty.

In *Google France*,[26] the CJEU underlined that, where an Internet-referencing service provider has not played an active role of such a kind as to give it knowledge of, or control over, the data stored, it cannot be held liable for the data that it has stored at the request of an advertiser, unless, having obtained knowledge of the unlawful nature of that data or of that advertiser's activities, it failed to act expeditiously to remove or to disable access to the data concerned. The CJEU made a step forward in *L'Oréal*.[27] In this case, the offering of assistance, including the optimisation, presentation or promotion of the offers for sale, was not considered a neutral activity performed by the provider.[28] It is worth observing how, firstly, the court did not recall the opinion of the Advocate General in *Google France*,[29] thus limiting the possibility for online platforms to rely on their economic interests in providing their services. Secondly, its decision acknowledged how automated technologies have led some providers to perform an active role, rather than the mere passive provision of digital products and services.

Still, both decisions are the results of a judicial frame based on the economic imprinting of the Union. The predominance of the economic narrative in the judicial reasoning of the CJEU was also the result of the lack of European constitutional parameters to assess the impact on fundamental rights and freedoms. It is not by chance that, after the adoption of the Lisbon Treaty, the CJEU changed its judicial approach, moving from a merely economic perspective to a fundamental rights-based approach.

Within this new constitutional framework, the CJEU has started to act as a quasi-constitutional court.[30] The Charter of Fundamental Rights of the EU (Charter) has become the parameter to assess the validity and interpret European legal instruments suffering the legislative inertia of the European lawmaker in relation to the challenges of the information society. This proactive approach has led to shifting from a formal dimension to a substantial application of fundamental rights, or constitutional law in action. Therefore, the Charter has arisen as a judicial tool to answer digital challenges in the lack of any approach from the political powers. As the next subsections show, the CJEU has adopted a teleological approach to ensure the effective protection of constitutional rights and freedoms in relation to the threats of digital technologies implemented by public actors and private businesses, such as online platforms.

The adoption of a constitutional, interpretative angle is clear when addressing two cases involving online intermediaries and, primarily, the extent of the ban on general monitoring. In *Scarlet* and *Netlog*,[31] the CJEU dealt with the complex topic of finding a balance between the need to tackle illegal content and users' fundamental rights – precisely, the right to privacy and freedom of expression, as well as the interests of the platforms not to be overwhelmed by monitoring systems. According to the CJEU, an injunction to install a general filtering system would not have respected the freedom to conduct business of online intermediaries.[32] Moreover, the contested measures could affect users' fundamental rights; namely, their right to the protection of their personal data and their freedom to receive or impart information.[33] Even more recently, the CJEU has interpreted the framework of the e-Commerce Directive in *Eva Glawischnig-Piesczek*, defining additional safeguards in the removal of identical and equivalent content.[34] Nonetheless, this reasoning has not been based on the protection of fundamental rights.[35]

Besides, the CJEU has not been the only European court to stress the relevance of fundamental rights in the field of content. The Strasbourg Court has also underlined how the activities of online intermediaries involve fundamental rights.[36] The ECtHR has repeatedly addressed national measures involving the responsibility of online intermediaries for hosting unlawful content, such as defamatory comments, as also underlined in the case of *Delfi v. Estonia*.[37]

Precisely, the ECtHR has highlighted the potential chilling effect on freedom of expression online resulting from holding platforms liable in relation to third-party conducts in the case *MTE v. Hungary*.[38]

The role of the European Courts in these cases provides some clues about the role of judicial activism in adjusting constitutional values to a different technological environment through legal tools, suffering the legislative inertia of the European lawmaker. In the field of data, the CJEU has not only focused on underlining the relevance of fundamental rights but also on consolidating and emancipating the right to data protection in the European framework.[39]

The primary role of European Courts can also be examined by looking at *Google Spain*.[40] Even if this case does not expressly deal with social media but search engines, it provides a landmark decision that underlines how the CJEU has provided an extensive constitutional interpretation of the rights to privacy and data protection to ensure their effective protection. The *Google Spain* ruling demonstrates a first judicial attempt to cope with the power of online platforms and answer to the legislative inertia of the Union.

The way in which the CJUE recognised that a search engine like Google falls under the category of "data controller" shows the predominant role of privacy and data protection as fundamental rights. When interpreting the scope of application of the Data Protection Directive, the ECJ observed that,

> [I]t would be contrary not only to the clear wording of that provision but also to its objective – which is to ensure . . . effective and complete protection of data subjects – to exclude the operator of a search engine from that definition on the ground that it does not exercise control over the personal data published on the web pages of third parties.[41]

In other words, considering Google as a mere data processor would not have ensured effective protection to the data subjects' rights.

This judicial approach has also led the CJEU to entrust search engines to delist online content connected with personal data of data subjects even without requiring the removal of the content at stake.[42] As a result, one can argue that this interpretation has just unveiled an existing legal basis in the Data Protection Directive to enforce this right against private actors. However, by framing this decision within the new constitutional framework, the CJEU has recognised a right to be forgotten online through the interpretation of the Data Protection Directive.

Such a constitutionally oriented interpretation can be considered the expression of a horizontal enforcement of the fundamental rights enshrined in the Charter. Despite this high level of protection of fundamental rights and the limitations on private actors' activities, at the same time, it is worth observing how the CJEU has delegated to search engines the task of balancing fundamental rights when assessing users' requests to delist, thus promoting the consolidation of private ordering.[43]

3.2 Horizontal Effect

These landmark decisions show the role of judicial activism in underlining the role of constitutional law in the digital environment as well as they underline a general trend of European courts expanding the boundaries of fundamental rights horizontally. The relevant historical, cultural and consequently constitutional milieu is clearly very different. The constitutional keyword is *Drittwirkung*, a legal concept originally developed in the '50s by the German Constitutional Court,[44] which presumes that an individual plaintiff can rely on a national bill of rights to sue another private individual alleging the violation of those rights. In other words, it can be defined as a form of horizontality in action or as a total constitution.[45] It is a legal concept that, as mentioned, has its roots in Germany and then subsequently migrated to many other constitutional jurisdictions, exerting a strong influence, even on the case law of the CJEU and ECtHR.[46] The CJEU had the opportunity to further develop the horizontal application of the Charter. More specifically, in four judgments from 2018 – *Egenberger*,[47] *IR v JQ*,[48] *Bauer*[49] and *Max Planck*[50] – the CJEU definitively clarified the horizontal scope of Articles 21, 31(2) and 47 of the Charter within disputes between private parties.[51]

Likewise, also the ECtHR has played a critical role in moving the perspective from a vertical to a horizontal approach. The European Court has strongly focused on developing the positive obligation doctrine that requires states to ensure the protection of human rights, also by regulating the private sector.[52] As the Council of Europe underlined, "As the ultimate guarantors of pluralism, States have a positive obligation to put in place an appropriate legislative and policy framework to that end. This implies adopting appropriate measures to ensure sufficient variety in the overall range of media types, bearing in mind differences in terms of their purposes, functions and geographical reach".[53] Therefore, the ECtHR has primarily relied on the positive obligation of States to protect human rights rather than enforcing the Convention to extend its boundaries to private actors such as social media.

This judicial landscape underlines why European courts play a reactive role, thus providing initial answers not only to legal gaps but also to the challenges raised by the expansion of (private) powers. However, this reactive approach does not exhaust the role of courts in the digital age. Judicial amplification also leads courts to guide lawmakers. As underlined in the case of social media, European courts have not only reacted to the challenges of private powers but also provided judicial paths for lawmakers to introduce regulatory instruments.

Nonetheless, national courts have adopted different approaches to the challenges for fundamental rights raised by social media. While some national courts have primarily dealt with the balancing among constitutional rights, as demonstrated by the chapters on Estonia, Finland, Hungary, Slovenia and the UK,[54] other national courts have also deeply reacted to the challenges raised by social media, as underlined by the approaches addressed in the chapters on Italy, Germany, France and Spain.[55] Particularly, some cases in Europe have underlined how courts have dealt with the horizontal extension of constitutional rights in private litigation with social media.[56] Although social media cannot be considered public actors per se, their role in moderating content has led courts to extend the boundaries of constitutional law. These examples underline how European courts have provided answers to the challenges raised by social media, also providing a guidance for lawmakers to address the role of these actors in the digital age.

4. Judicial guidance and dialogue

The changing landscape of the digital environment has led European courts to take the initiative, thus overcoming the inertia of political power. The CJEU's judicial activism has paved the way for a shift from the first approach based on digital liberalism to a new phase of digital constitutionalism characterised by the injection of democratic values into the digital environment.[57]

Within this framework, two primary drivers have characterised the rise of the democratic phase of European digital constitutionalism. Firstly, the Union has started to codify some of the CJEU's judicial lessons. Secondly, the Union introduced new limits to private powers by adopting legal instruments to increase the degree of transparency and accountability in content moderation and data processing. Both characteristics can be found in the Digital Single Market strategy.[58] According to the European Commission, online platforms should "protect core values" and increase "transparency and fairness for maintaining user trust and safeguarding innovation".[59] This is because the role of online platforms in the digital environment implies "wider responsibility".[60]

This political approach resulted in a new wave of soft-law and hard-law instruments whose objective is, *inter alia*, to regulate online platforms. Like other fields, such as net neutrality or the right to Internet access, the introduction of new safeguards constitutes the expression of key values of contemporary society.[61] Precisely, the Directive on Copyright in the Digital Single Market,[62] the amendments to the Audiovisual Media Services Directive,[63] the regulation to address online terrorist content,[64] or the adoption of the General Data Protection Regulation[65] are just some of the examples demonstrating how the Digital Single Market strategy has constituted a change of paradigm to avoid the consolidation of powers in the algorithmic society. The launch of the Digital Services Act[66] and the Digital Markets Act[67] can be seen as other two milestones on this path, also triggered by judicial activism in Europe.

Besides, judicial guidance is strictly connected to judicial dialogue,[68] which is not a substantive goal in itself but rather a procedural tool for improving the *status quo* that is not entirely satisfactory. In particular, the debate seems to show that, if there is something called European judicial dialogue,[69] it very often arises due to a (real or presumed) risk of constitutional collision between the domestic and European levels, especially as regards the standard of protection for fundamental rights.[70] It may also occur due to the willingness on the part of national courts to clarify what appears to be unclear in relation to the interpretation (or validity) of EU law by sending a reference to the CJEU, rather than aspiring to belong to different, but interacting, constitutional jurisdictions in order to build a judicial "*Harmonia Caelestis*".[71]

Therefore, the involvement of interconnecting jurisdictions in European judicial dialogue is, generally speaking, a reaction, and very rarely a spontaneous action, to either a lack of legal clarity regarding the interpretation and application within national law of EU law or the (risk of a) collision between EU law and Member States' constitutional systems. These considerations also extend to the horizontal dialogue between courts, particularly the CJEU and the ECtHR.[72] Despite some differences, judicial dialogue is not limited to the external relationship between powers – particularly lawmakers and judges – but also internal, as underlined by the reliance to approaches and interpretation of other judges. As explained in Chapter 2, in *Poland v Parliament and Council*,[73] the CJEU has relied on the ECHR to address the scope of freedom of expression in the Charter.

The need to maintain a symmetrical balance between the judicial and political powers in the digital era may not come from either hyper-activism on the part of the courts or inertia on the part of the legislator, but perhaps from the judicial ability to promptly react. Since judges appear to be best placed to identify the possible collision between fundamental rights online and, consequently, to be the bodies best equipped to provide an initial answer, the systemic answer (but not the final answer, as the last word is always left to the constitutional court) should come from the legislative branch by responding *lato sensu* and codifying the relevant case law, also coming from the requests of courts to intervene to protect fundamental rights. In other words, if it is the case, as it has been said, that the new round of judicial globalisation constitutes a response to a pre-existing problem involving a possible contrast between fundamental rights, a further response, after the initial judicial response, should come from the legislature.

This twofold response has been engaged, for instance, in relation to the European protection of fundamental rights in the digital age, such as within the GDPR, and it has worked quite well. Nonetheless, the challenges ahead raised by new technologies require us to reconsider the relationship between political and judicial power under the lens of digital constitutionalism, which, as it has been stressed,[74] tends to focus on the rise of private powers implementing algorithmic technologies, and, secondly, the constitutional remedies arising out of the mix between judicial and political instruments, respectively, in terms of the horizontal application of fundamental rights and the possible adoption of a new set of rights as a consolidation of existing charters and bills of rights.

5. Conclusions

Courts have demonstrated that they play a critical role in addressing the challenges of the digital age, including the consolidation of social media. These actors have raised constitutional questions, particularly for the protection of fundamental rights, that European courts have addressed by virtue of judicial imagination, reaction and guidance. The principal consequences of the enhanced role of the judiciary in the digital age is the ability for courts to enjoy broader room for manoeuvre, to react against the inertia of lawmakers and provide guidance to introduce regulatory instruments.

The use of metaphorical language and judicial frames has been a first step to underline the challenges of the digital age. The not-easy task of adapting "traditional" legal rules to new, technological paradigms implies greater judicial imagination. This approach has led courts, particularly the CJEU and the ECtHR, to develop metaphors that express their sensitivity about rights and freedoms in the digital environment.

Courts have also expanded their role due to the inertia of lawmakers. In this case, judicial imagination has also been a form of reaction. Judicial actors have played a critical role in providing answers to protect fundamental rights online. This form of judicial reaction has led courts, in some cases, to challenge the limit of adjudication and lead to extensive interpretations to protect fundamental rights. The expansion of judicial activism in Europe is an example of this trend, thus underlining the role of judicial reaction in filling legal gaps from a supranational and national perspective, even if national courts have been less reactive in some cases.

Imagination and reaction are also complemented by judicial guidance and dialogue. The role of courts as reactive actors in the digital age is also a system of guidance for the lawmaker. The development of the European digital policy is also the result of judicial lessons. In this case, courts contribute to underlining constitutional challenges that can then be addressed by introducing regulatory tools. In this case, European courts also provide a channel for horizontal and vertical dialogue that allows an exchange even of conflicting positions about the protection of fundamental rights in the digital age.

Notes

*Giovanni De Gregorio authored Sections 1, 3.2. Oreste Pollicino authored Sections 2, 3.1, 4, 5.

1 Oreste Pollicino, *Judicial Protection of Fundamental Rights Online. A Road Towards Digital Constitutionalism?* (Hart 2021).

2 As observed by Slaughter, this is a "process of judicial interaction across, above, and below borders, exchanging ideas and cooperating in cases involving national as much as international law". Anne-Marie Slaughter, 'Judicial Globalization' (2000) 40 *Virginia Journal of International Law* 1103, 1104.

3 It was not a coincidence that, at the beginning of twentieth century, in parallel with the previously mentioned change in the institutional balance between the State's constitutional powers, a cultural and juridical movement called "revolt against the formalism" was born to "fight" the excessive legalism of the post-codification era. According to this movement, deciding a case could not be limited to subjecting certain facts under the rule of law. In consonance with this view, the judgment itself will be added to the interpretation of the rule to be applied and may thus help to define its meaning. See François Gény, *Méthode d'interpretation et Sources en Droit Privé Positif* (LGDJ 1899).

4 Slaughter (n 2); Ran Hirschl, *Towards Juristocracy: The Origins and Consequences of the New Constitutionalism* (Harvard University Press 2004); C. Neale Tate and Torbjörn Vallinder (eds), *The Global Expansion of the Judicial Power* (New York University Press 1995).

5 The dichotomy between "law in action" and "law in the book" was originally underlined by Roscoe Pound, 'Law in Books and Law in Action' (1910) 44 *American Law Review* 12.
6 Lyndsey Stonebridge, *The Judicial Imagination: Writing After Nuremberg* (Edinburgh University Press 2011). See also Maksymilian Del Mar, *Artefacts of Legal Inquiry: The Value of Imagination in Adjudication* (Hart 2020).
7 Alessandro Morelli and Oreste Pollicino, 'Metaphors, Judicial Frames and Fundamental Rights in Cyberspace' (2020) 68(3) *American Journal of Comparative Law* 616.
8 George Lakoff and Mark Johnson, *Metaphors We Live By* (The University of Chicago Press 1980).
9 See Jonathan H. Blavin and I. Gleen Cohen, 'Gore, Gibson, and Goldsmith: The Evolution of Internet Metaphors in Law and Commentary' (2002) 16 *Harvard Journal of Law & Technology* 265, 266; Thomas W Joo, 'Contract, Property, and the Role of Metaphor in Corporations Law' (2001) 35 *U.C. Davis Law Review* 779. See also Dan Hunter, 'Cyberspace as Place and the Tragedy of the Digital Anticommons' (2003) 91 *California Law Review* 439.
10 The same idea is behind the book written by Larsson that uses conceptual metaphor theory "to strengthen the awareness of the strong metaphoricity in contemporary understandings of the Internet". Stefan Larsson, *Conceptions in the Code. How Metaphors Explain Legal Challenges in Digital Times* (OUP 2017).
11 Richard A. Posner, *How Judges Think* (Harvard University Press 2008) 181.
12 *Berkey v. Third Avenue Railway Co.* 244 N.Y. 84 (NY 1926) 95.
13 David L. Shapiro, 'In Defense of Judicial Candor' (1986–1987) 100 *Harvard Law Review* 731; Peter J. Smith, 'New Legal Fictions' (2006–2007) 95 *Georgetown Law Journal* 1484.
14 Max Black, *Models and Metaphors. Studies in Languages and Philosophy* (Cornell University Press 1962) 25; Max Black, 'Metaphor' (1954) 55 *Proceedings of the Aristotelian Society* 273; Ivor A. Richards, *The Philosophy of Rhetoric* (OUP 1936).
15 András Sajó and Clare Ryan, 'Judicial Reasoning and New Technologies: Framing, Newness, Fundamental Rights and the Internet' in Oreste Pollicino and Graziella Romeo (eds), *The Internet and Constitutional Law: The Protection of Fundamental Rights and Constitutional Adjudication in Europe* (Routledge 2016) 3, 7.
16 *Reno v American Civil Liberties Union* 521 U.S.844 (1997) 885.
17 On the metaphor of the "free marketplace of ideas", see Haig Bosmajian, *Metaphor and Reason in Judicial Opinions* (Southern Illinois University Press 1992).
18 *Abrams v United States* 250 U.S. 616 (1919).
19 *Editorial Board of Pravoye Delo and Shtekel v Ukraine* (ECtHR 2011) 63.
20 *Cengiz and others v Turkey* (ECtHR 2015) 49 and 52: "[T]he Internet has now become one of the principal means by which individuals exercise their right to freedom to receive and impart information and ideas, providing as it does essential tools for participation in activities and discussions concerning political issues and issues of general interest . . . Moreover, as to the importance of Internet sites in the exercise of freedom of expression, 'in the light of its accessibility and its capacity to store and communicate vast amounts of information, the Internet plays an important role in enhancing the public's access to news and facilitating the dissemination of information in general'. User-generated expressive activity on the Internet provides an unprecedented platform for the exercise of freedom of expression".
21 See Chapter 9 by Elizabeth Farries in this volume.
22 On this topic, see Allan Rosas, 'The European Court of Justice in Context: Forms and Patterns of Judicial Dialogue' (2007) 1 *European Journal of Legal Studies* 1; Hirschl (n 4); Julie Allard and Antoine Garapon, *Les juges dans le mondialisation. La nouvelle révolution du droit* (Seuil 2005).
23 Directive 2000/31/EC of the European Parliament and of the Council of 8 June 2000 on certain legal aspects of information society services, in particular

electronic commerce, in the Internal Market ('Directive on electronic commerce'), OJ L178/1.

24 Directive 95/46/EC of the European Parliament and of the Council of 24 October 1995 on the protection of individuals with regard to the processing of personal data and on the free movement of such data, OJ L281/31.

25 Convention for the Protection of Human Rights and Fundamental Freedoms (1950).

26 Joined Cases C-236/08, C-237/08 and C-238/08 *Google France v Louis Vuitton Malletier SA, Google France SARL v Viaticum SA and Luteciel SARL, and Google France SARL v Centre national de recherche en relations humaines (CNRRH) SARL and others* (2010) ECLI:EU:C:2010:159.

27 Case 324/09, *L'Oréal SA and Others v. eBay International AG and Others* (2011) ECLI:EU:C:2011:474.

28 Ibid, 116.

29 Joined Cases C-236/08, C-237/08 and C-238/08 (n 26), Opinion of the Advocate General (2009) ECLI:EU:C:2009:569.

30 Gráinne de Búrca, 'After the EU Charter of Fundamental Rights: The Court of Justice as a Human Rights Adjudicator?' (2013) 20(2) *Maastricht Journal of European and Comparative Law* 168.

31 Case C-70/10 *Scarlet Extended SA v Société belge des auteurs, compositeurs et éditeurs SCRL (SABAM)* (2011) ECLI:EU:C:2011:771; Case C-360/10 *Belgische Vereniging van Auteurs, Componisten en Uitgevers CVBA (SABAM) v Netlog NV* (2012) ECLI:EU:C:2012:85.

32 Case C-70/10 (n 31) 50.

33 Charter of Fundamental Rights of the European Union, Arts 8, 11.

34 Case C-18/18 *Eva Glawischnig-Piesczek v Facebook Ireland Limited* (2019) ECLI:EU:C:2019:821.

35 See Chapter 2 by Evangelia Psychogiopoulou in this volume.

36 See Chapter 3 by Lorna Woods in this volume.

37 See *Delfi AS v Estonia* (ECtHR 2015); *Magyar Tartalomszolgáltatók Egyesülete and Index.Hu Zrt v Hungary* (ECtHR 2016); *Rolf Anders Daniel Pihl v Sweden* (ECtHR 2017). On the Estonia case, see Chapter 4 by Meeli Kaur in this volume.

38 See Chapter 8 by Zsuzsa Detrekoi in this volume; and Robert Spano, 'Intermediary Liability for Online User Comments Under the European Convention on Human Rights' (2017) 17(4) *Human Rights Law Review* 665.

39 Orla Lynskey, *The Foundations of EU Data Protection Law* (OUP 2015); Paul De Hert and Serge Gutwirth, 'Data Protection in the Case Law of Strasbourg and Luxembourg: Constitutionalisation in Action', in Serge Gutwirth and others (eds), *Reinventing Data Protection* 3 (Springer 2009).

40 Case C-131/12 *Google Spain SL and Google Inc. v. Agencia Española de Protección de Datos (AEPD) and Mario Costeja González* (2014) ECLI:EU:C:2014:317.

41 Ibid, 34.

42 Ibid, 97.

43 Jean-Marie Chenou and Roxana Radu, 'The "Right to Be Forgotten": Negotiating Public and Private Ordering in the European Union' (2017) 58 *Business & Society* 74.

44 The Lüth case concerned a *querelle* about the distribution of the anti-Semitic movie *Jüd Jüss* in a private location. Following the conviction, Lüth appealed to the German Constitutional Court complaining of the violation of her freedom of expression. The German Constitutional Court, therefore, addressed a question relating to the extension of constitutional rights in a private relationship. In this case, for the first time, the German court argued that constitutional rights not only constitute individual claims against the state but also constitute a set of values that

apply in all areas of law by providing axiological indications to the legislative power, executive and judicial. In the present case, the protection of freedom of expression does not only develop vertically towards the state but also horizontally since civil law rules must be interpreted according to the spirit of the German Constitution. German Constitutional Court, judgment of 15 January 1958, BVerfGE 7, 198.

45 Mattias Kumm, 'Who Is Afraid of the Total Constitution? Constitutional Rights as Principles and the Constitutionalization of Private Law' (2006) 7(4) *German Law Journal* 341.

46 *X e Y v The Netherlands* App no 8978/80 (ECtHR 1985).

47 Case C-414/16 *Vera Egenberger v Evangelisches Werk für Diakonie und Entwicklung eV* (2018) ECLI:EU:C:2018:257.

48 Case C-68/17 *IR v JQ* (2018) ECLI:EU:C:2018:696.

49 Joined Cases C-569/16 and C-570/16 *Stadt Wuppertal v Maria Elisabeth Bauer and Volker Willmeroth v Martina Broßonn* (2018) ECLI:EU:C:2018:871.

50 Case C-684/16 *Max-Planck-Gesellschaft zur Förderung der Wissenschaften eV v Tetsuji Shimizu* (2018) ECLI:EU:C:2018:874.

51 Aurelia Colombi Ciacchi, 'The Direct Horizontal Effect of EU Fundamental Rights: ECJ 17 April 2018, Case C-414/16, Vera Egenberger v Evangelisches Werk für Diakonie und Entwicklung e.V. and ECJ 11 September 2018, Case C-68/17, IR v JQ' (2019) 15(2) *European Constitutional Law Review* 294; Eleni Frantziou, *The Horizontal Effect of Fundamental Rights in the European Union. A Constitutional Analysis* (OUP 2019); Sonya Walkila, *Horizontal Effect of Fundamental Rights in EU Law* (Europa Law Publishing 2016).

52 See, for example, *Von Hannover* v. *Germany* (2005) 40 EHRR 1; *Verein gegen Tierfabriken Schweiz (VgT)* v. *Switzerland* (2001) 34 EHRR 159. See Lech Garlicki, 'Relations Between Private Actors and the European Convention on Human Rights' in Andras Sajó and Renata Uitz (eds), *The Constitution in Private Relations: Expanding Constitutionalism* 129 (Eleven 2005).

53 Recommendation CM/Rec(2018)1 of the Committee of Ministers to member States on media pluralism and transparency of media ownership (7 March 2018).

54 See, respectively, Chapter 4 by Meeli Kaur, Chapter 5 by Marta Maroni, Tuomas Ojanen and Eveliina Ignatius, Chapter 8 by Zsuzsa Detrekoi, Chapter 11 by Tanja Kerševan and Chapter 13 by Rachel Craufurd Smith.

55 See, respectively, Chapter 6 by Sara Migliorini and Constance Bonzé, Chapter 7 by Federica Casarosa and Maria Concetta Causarano, Chapter 8 by Matthias C. Kettemann, Polina Kulish and Martha Routen and Chapter 12 by Joan Solanes Mullor.

56 See e.g., Court of Rome, CasaPound v Facebook (2019); German Federal Constitutional Court, Der Dritte Weg v. Facebook Ireland Ltd. (2019).

57 Giovanni De Gregorio, *Digital Constitutionalism in Europe. Reframing Rights and Powers in the Algorithmic Society* (Cambridge University Press 2022).

58 Communication from the Commission to the European Parliament, the Council, the European Economic and Social Committee and the Committee of the Regions, A Digital Single Market Strategy for Europe COM(2015) 192 final.

59 Communication from the Commission to the European Parliament, the Council, the European Economic and Social Committee and the Committee of the Regions, Online Platforms and the Digital Single Market Opportunities and Challenges for Europe COM(2016) 288 final.

60 Ibid.

61 Christoph B Graber, 'Bottom-Up Constitutionalism: The Case of Net Neutrality' (2017) 7 *Transnational Legal Theory* 524.

62 Directive (EU) 2019/790 of the European Parliament and of the Council of 17 April 2019 on copyright and related rights in the Digital Single Market and amending Directives 96/9/EC and 2001/29/EC (2019) OJ L 130/92

63 Directive (EU) 2018/1808 of the European Parliament and of the Council of 14 November 2018 amending Directive 2010/13/EU on the coordination of certain provisions laid down by law, regulation or administrative action in Member States concerning the provision of audio-visual media services (Audiovisual Media Services Directive) in view of changing market realities OJ L 303/69.

64 Regulation (EU) 2021/784 of the European Parliament and of the Council of 29 April 2021 on addressing the dissemination of terrorist content online OJ L 172/79.

65 Regulation (EU) 2016/679 of the European Parliament and of the Council of 27 April 2016 on the protection of natural persons with regard to the processing of personal data and on the free movement of such data and repealing Directive 95/46/EC (General Data Protection Regulation) OJ L119/1.

66 Proposal for a Regulation of the European Parliament and of the Council on a Single Market for Digital Services (Digital Services Act) and amending Directive 2000/31/EC, COM(2020) 825 final.

67 Regulation (EU) 2022/1925 of the European Parliament and of the Council of 14 September 2022on contestable and fair markets in the digital sector and amending Directives (EU) 2019/1937 and (EU) 2020/1828.

68 It is perhaps worth making clear that the term "judicial dialogue" is used here in a twofold way. Firstly, the reference is only to judicial relations between interconnected, "vertically" legal orders situated at different, not hierarchically based, levels (national, European and international); secondly the reference is only to the direct relationship between Courts and not to the broader situation of constitutional cross-fertilisation and judicial borrowing between legal systems where the judges generally conduct a form of dialogue through mutual citations. See Francis G Jacobs, 'Judicial Dialogue and the Cross Fertilization of Legal System: The European Court of Justice' (2003) 38(3) *Texas International Law Journal* 547; Allan Rosas, 'The European Court of Justice in the Context: Forms and Pattern of Judicial Dialogue' (2007) 1(2) *European Journal of Legal Studies* 1.

69 Martin Belov (ed), *Judicial Dialogue* (Eleven 2019); Amrei Müller (ed), *Judicial Dialogue and Human Rights* (Cambridge University Press 2017); Giuseppe Martinico and Oreste Pollicino, *The Interaction Between Europe's Legal Systems: Judicial Dialogue and the Creation of Supranational Laws* (Edward Elgar 2012).

70 Neil MacCormik, 'Risking Constitutional Collision in Europe?' (1998) 18(3) *Oxford Journal of Legal Studies* 517.

71 Péter Esterházy, *Harmonia Caelestis* (Feltrinelli 2003). Along the same lines, in a broader and philosophical based context, Jurgen Habermas and Jacques Derrida argue that 'the image of a peaceful cooperative Europe, open toward other cultures and capable of dialogue, floats like a mirage before all of us. See Jürgen Habermas and Jacques Derrida, 'February 15, or What Binds Europeans Together: A Plea for a Common Foreign Policy, Beginning in the Core of Europe' (2003) 10(3) *Constellations* 291, 293.

72 See Chapter 2 by Evangelia Psychogiopoulou and Chapter 3 by Lorna Woods in this volume.

73 Case C-401/19 *Republic of Poland v European Parliament, Council of the European Union* (2022) ECLI:EU:C:2022:297.

74 Giovanni De Gregorio, 'From Constitutional Freedoms to Power. Protecting Fundamental Rights Online in the Algorithmic Society' (2019) 11(2) *European Journal of Legal Studies* 65.

Index

For Product Safety Concerns and Information please contact our EU
representative GPSR@taylorandfrancis.com
Taylor & Francis Verlag GmbH, Kaufingerstraße 24, 80331 München, Germany

www.ingramcontent.com/pod-product-compliance
Lightning Source LLC
LaVergne TN
LVHW021121300926
849160LV00010B/813

* 9 7 8 1 0 3 2 0 7 4 6 9 6 *